COMPUTATIONAL SEMANTICS

Fundamental Studies in Computer Science

VOLUME 4

NORTH-HOLLAND PUBLISHING COMPANY
AMSTERDAM · NEW YORK · OXFORD

Computational Semantics

An Introduction to Artificial Intelligence and Natural Language Comprehension

Edited by:

EUGENE CHARNIAK
Institute for Semantic and Cognitive Studies, University of Geneva

and

YORICK WILKS
Department of Artificial Intelligence, University of Edinburgh

NORTH-HOLLAND PUBLISHING COMPANY
AMSTERDAM · NEW YORK · OXFORD

North-Holland ISBN for the Series: 0 7204 2500 X
North-Holland ISBN for this Volume: 0 7204 0469 X
1st edition 1976
2nd printing 1978
3rd printing 1981

Published by:

NORTH-HOLLAND PUBLISHING COMPANY
AMSTERDAM, NEW YORK, OXFORD

Distributors for the U.S.A. and Canada:

ELSEVIER/NORTH-HOLLAND INC.
52 VANDERBILT AVENUE
NEW YORK, N.Y. 10017

Library of Congress Cataloging in Publication Data

Main entry under title:

Computational semantics.

(Fundamental studies in computer science ; v. 4)
Bibliography: p.
Includes index.
1. Semantics--Data processing. 2. Artificial intelligence. I. Charniak, Eugene. II. Wilks, Yorick. III. Series.
P325.C56 412 76-10133
ISBN 0-444-11110-7 (American Elsevier)

PRINTED IN THE NETHERLANDS

ACKNOWLEDGMENTS

All of the authors would like to thank Signor Angelo Dalle Molle whose Foundation supported our work; Manfred Wettler, Director of the Institute for Semantic and Cognitive Studies, who brought us together and conceived the idea of the Tutorial Conference from which this enterprize grew; Barbara Méroz who daily defied entropy by extracting information from our seemingly random manuscripts; and Monique Lehnis who manned the fort throughout. The editors would like to thank Maggie King especially, who assumed many of the burdens that should have fallen on them.

EDITORS' PREFACE

Computational Semantics is not so much a new subject, as a new way of looking at old questions - those concerning meaning, language, and understanding. It is based on the assumption that a good way to explicate such difficult notions is to work toward the programming of an automaton, or digital computer, so that it could be said to understand language.

This goal, of course, can be justified on purely practical grounds. An understanding computer would be a useful thing to have. Not only would it allow more people to communicate with a class of machines, which is of ever increasing importance in our lives, but would also permit the automation of many tedious and unrewarding tasks: telephone operator, social security clerk, and conventional secretary, to name but a few. Yet the achievement of such goals must await considerable improvement in our understanding of the nature of language.

The questions can then be raised as to whether Computational Semantics will lead to such understanding, or, on the contrary, will the more traditional methods of philosophy, logic, linguistics and psychology uncover whatever there is to be known about the dark, though familiar, regions of meaning, language and understanding. The existence of this book makes clear that we do not see the latter as the case, but rather think that Computational Semantics is the best way we have of solving the difficult problem of language comprehension.

This explains one feature of this text book which might otherwise strike the reader as odd - this is a text with a strong point of view. So, although the rudiments of the more established disciplines listed above are introduced here, they are all presented from what might be called an "artificial intelligence point of view". This makes the presentation of other disciplines in the book non-standard, but we hope illuminating nontheless.

Within this overall point of view the readers will soon see that the authors hold a number of sub-views and consequently disagree with each other about quite fundamental issues. We believe that in a young subject like this one, such a method of presentation is essential if honesty is to be preserved, since there _is_ no consensus on many questions.

This brings us to a second way in which this text differs from standard introductory texts: it is a product of several hands rather than the normal one. The explanation lies in its origins as lecture notes for a course on Computational Semantics given at the Institute for Semantic and Cognitive Studies in Switzerland in 1975. The book thus springs from the actual task of teaching the rudiments of a new and complicated subject to people from diverse backgrounds. Moreover, since all the authors were then fellows of the Institute, the notes were subject to long and difficult committee sessions, so, although the writers are experts in different aspects of the field, their approaches were, with some effort, harmonized and inter-connected. The chapters in this volume, then, are not in any sense separate sequential contributions, for they constantly cross-refer to, and presume upon, each other, in a way we hope is clear and helpful.

Eugene Charniak
Yorick Wilks

CONTENTS

Robot drawings by Walter F. Bischof

E. Charniak and Y. Wilks (eds.), Computational Semantics

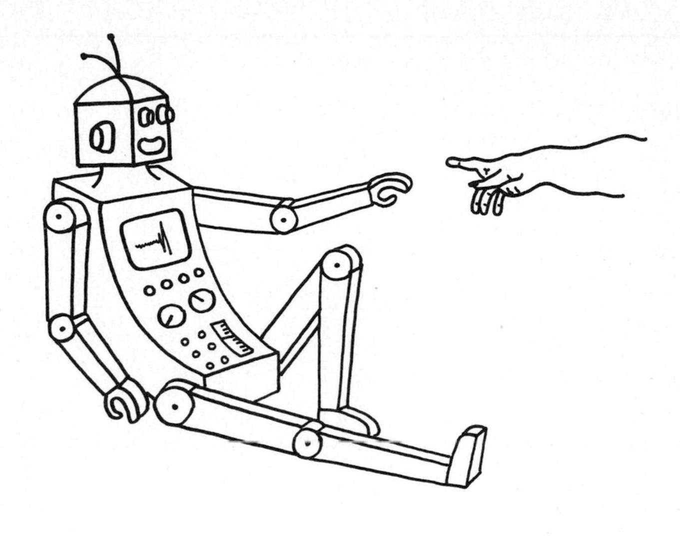

INFERENCE AND KNOWLEDGE PART 1

Eugene Charniak

Artificial Intelligence (AI) is concerned with the creation of computer programs capable of performing tasks normally considered to require intelligence - from chess playing to medical diagnosis. Many such tasks involve the use of natural language, and by this route Artificial Intelligence adds itself to the list of disciplines concerned with the problems of language comprehension. Computational Semantics, the name we have given here to the study of language based upon Artificial Intelligence methods, therefore approaches language by asking how language is used in translating languages, question answering based on language texts, etc. This approach assumes that "language is as language does", an idea not unknown to the older disciplines of linguistics, psychology, etc., but Computational Semantics is unique in making this idea the basis for the entire study of language. It is the contention of this approach that it is at best ill advised, and at worst meaningless, to talk of "understanding" without reference to some task in which language is being used, whether as narrow as sentence completion questions in an IQ test, or as vague as flirting at a party.

So one must begin the study of language by asking how it is used. However, this would seem to have the unfortunate implication that before we can even start we must broaden our study from simply "language" to include everything from IQ test construction to social behavior at parties. No discipline can hope to get very far with such a broad mandate. The solution to this problem is to isolate some features common to most uses of language and simply study them, usually in the context of one or two tasks which emphasize those features we see as important. Consider, for example, answering simple questions about a simple story. For example:

(1) One Saturday Jack decided he wanted some cereal for breakfast. However he had to go to the supermarket, where, after finding the shelf where the milk was, he payed for it and left. When he got home he found that the milk was sour. "Why do these things always happen to me," thought Jack.

Questions: Why did Jack go to the supermarket?

What did Jack pay for?

By the last line had Jack finished his cereal?

What was Jack complaining about?

Although the answers to the questions seem obvious to us, notice that the story does not explicitly answer any of them. Instead, we are only able to answer questions like these because we know such facts as:

Normally, cereal is eaten with milk.

Supermarkets primarily sell food.

Sour milk tastes bad.

Except under special circumstances one quickly stops eating bad tasting food.

But simply knowing such facts is not enough since one must also be able to select from everything one knows those facts which are relevant to the text, and secondly be able to combine the relevant facts with the information in the story in order to infer the answers to the questions.

These same abilities are needed in other language related tasks as well. For example, if we were to translate (1) into German, it would be necessary to infer that the "it" in line two refers to milk and not shelf, since the pronouns one would use in the two cases would be different in German. (Notice that one cannot rely on the fact that the last mentioned object in the story was "milk" since the story could equally well have been written "after finding the milk on the shelf".) To take another job involving language, that of summarizing a piece of text, we again need these abilities. To realize that one can safely do without "One Saturday" but not "cereal" in the story requires knowing the causal connections in the story and observing that "Saturday" plays no role whereas "cereal" gives the motivation for much of what follows. But the causal connections in (1) are left out and must hence be inferred by using one's general knowledge.

What is being suggested then is that one important feature common to most language use involves applying previously gained knowledge to a text or utterance in order to make inferences. So by studying these processes one is likely to help explicate a wide range of language behavior. This point is strengthened when one further notes that many of the processes which we typically call "linguistic" require inference making. Linguistics, for example, is concerned with the structure of sentences. But consider:

Waiter, I would like spaghetti with meat sauce and wine.

You would not expect to be served a bowl of spaghetti floating in meat sauce and wine. That is, you would expect the meal represented by structure (2) rather than that represented by (3).

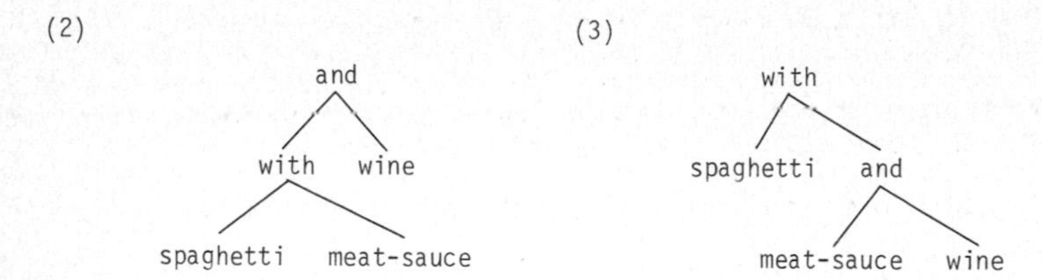

Note, however, that if you had asked for spaghetti with butter and garlic you would have wanted structure (3). We say that such sentences are "structurally ambiguous". So to get your order right the waiter must "disambiguate" the sentence by making an inference based on his knowledge of food.

A similar sort of problem arises due to the fact that words often have more than one meaning (or "sense"), as in:

The pen is in the next room.

Here "pen" might be either the writing implement or a baby pen. But now consider:

The baby picked up a pen.

Given knowledge of typical strength we may infer which sense of "pen" is intended.

Finally, the problem of determining the reference of a pronoun often requires making an inference. We have already seen this in example (1) where the "it" in "he payed for it" referred to the milk we assume Jack wanted to buy, and not, say, the shelf on which the milk was located.

Such examples merely serve to reinforce our decision to study how language is used by asking the narrower question of how knowledge is used to make inferences in the comprehension of language.

A complete solution to this problem would require answering the following five questions. The questions will only be stated briefly here as their precise meaning will be best understood by the repeated reference to them throughout this chapter as well as Chapter 8.

1. SEMANTIC REPRESENTATION. What concepts, and in what combination, are needed to represent a) the knowledge we bring to bear on language, and b) the semantic content of natural language expressions themselves. The problem of semantic representation will be covered extensively in later chapters, so little will be said about the issue here.

2. INFERENCE TRIGGERING. Under what circumstances, and for what reasons, do we make inferences? For example, when do we make an inference - when new information comes in, or when there is a specific need for the inference, as when a question is asked?

3. ORGANIZATION. Given we want to make an inference, how do we locate the needed information? The all purpose answer here is that we have "pointers" to the information. The question then becomes how do we organize these pointers? So we might, for example, imagine that certain pieces of information, like that about supermarkets, are "grouped" together. What "grouping"

might mean is that there is a pointer from some central topic to each piece of information.

4. INFERENCE MECHANISM. Once we have located a fact, how do we know how to use it? For example, in predicate logic, which we will be studying next, there are "rules of inference" which specify what inferences may be made from a set of facts.

5. CONTENT. What is the knowledge which we have of the world that enables us to understand language? Note that while the answers to the other questions would hopefully be culture independent (with the possible exception of (1)), the knowledge we have is clearly quite culture dependent, and even idiosyncratic.

FIRST ORDER PREDICATE CALCULUS

This chapter will be devoted to presenting two partial answers to the above questions, first order predicate calculus (FOPC), and the programming language PLANNER.

FOPC was developed in an attempt to understand exactly what it was that mathematicians were doing - mathematicians "prove" things, but what exactly is proof? FOPC was developed to help answer questions like this. Furthermore, FOPC can be very precisely defined so that it is possible to prove facts about FOPC itself. However, within AI FOPC was not used for either of these purposes. Rather it was hoped that a program based on FOPC could give the inference making capability we need to, say, understand language. Since we will not be proving theorems about FOPC we need not be precise in our definitions but will instead leave things at an intuitive level.

The Language of FOPC

Roughly speaking FOPC consists of a language for expressing facts and rules for deriving new facts from old. The language consists of

CONSTANTS. A constant is some "thing" which we can talk about like "FIDO". We will typically use the symbols "a", "b" and "c" for constants, but occasionally use proper names in capitals (FIDO, JOHN).

VARIABLES. A variable can stand for different things at different times. We will use "x", "y" and "z" as variables.

PREDICATES. If we say DOG(FIDO) we are simply saying that the predicate "DOG" is true of the constant "FIDO". Or to put this in more usual terms, "FIDO is a DOG". We say that a predicate takes one or more "arguments". In the case of DOG(FIDO), DOG takes one argument and in this case the argument is FIDO. GIVE(a, b, c) has three arguments which we would normally interpret as "a gave b to c". Predicates are true or false. That is, either FIDO is a dog or it isn't.

FUNCTIONS. A function is something which produces a value. So the function COUNTRY-OF-BIRTH(a) would presumably (given the name chosen) have as its value the name of the country where a was born. Functions also have arguments, and like predicates, a given function always takes the same number of arguments, but (again like predicates) there is no limit on what that number might be. Notice that a function may be an argument of a predicate, as in the case where we might want to say that DOG(COUNTRY-OF-BIRTH(a)) is always false (which is to say that a country cannot be a dog). But a predicate cannot be the argument of a function (or of another predicate). That is, it would not make any sense to say COUNTRY-OF-BIRTH(DOG(a)) since DOG(a) does not have a value in the same way a function does but rather is simply true or false.

LOGICAL CONNECTIVES. The usual logical connectives are

AND (often written "$\wedge$", as in $A \wedge B$). To say that GOD(a) AND MAN(a) is true is to say that both statements are true, i.e. that a is both a god and a man.

OR (often written "V"). To say GOD(a) OR MAN(a) is to say that a is either a god, or a man, or both. Notice that logical connectives are like predicates in that the thing we get by using one is either true or false. That is, it is either true or false that a is both a god and a man.

NOT (often written as "$\neg$" or "$\sim$", as in $\neg A$). To say NOT(GOD(a)) is to say that a is not a god.

IMPLIES (often written as "$\Rightarrow$"). To say that MAN(x) IMPLIES SINFUL(x) is to say that if x is a man then he is sinful. Note however that logical implication is defined such that if x is not a man we will say that the above statement is true whether or not x is sinful. So the only time an IMPLIES statement is false is when the second part is false while the first part is true, e.g., if x were a man but not sinful.

QUANTIFIERS. When we made the statement that MAN(x) IMPLIES SINFUL(x) we implicitly meant that this was true for any value of the variable x. That is we assumed the quantifier

FOR-ALL (often written "$\forall$"). So to be more accurate we should have written FOR-ALL(x) (MAN(x) IMPLIES SINFUL(x)).

There is another quantifier

EXISTS (often written "$\exists$"). To say "there exists a god" we would write EXISTS(x) (GOD(x)). That is, there is some value of the variable x such that GOD(x) is true. If we wanted to say "all men own dogs" we might write FOR-ALL(x) (EXISTS(y) (MAN(x) IMPLIES (DOG(y) AND OWN (x,y)))). Which is to say that for any man there exists a dog such that the man owns the dog.

When in the above we used the same variable name in different statements (such as the variable "x" appearing in both "all men owned dogs" as well as "God exists" it was assumed that the reader would not confuse the two and think that somehow God and dog owning men were the same. The reader, of course, used his intuition, but this confusion is avoided by formal means in FOPC. Each variable is said to have a "scope". Within its scope each occurrence of the same variable name indicates the same variable. However we may use the same name to represent different things in different statements provided the scopes do not overlap. We adopt the convention here that the scope of a variable is what is enclosed by the first pair of balanced parentheses following the quantifier which introduces the variable (ignoring parentheses in other quantifiers). So in FOR-ALL(x) FOR-ALL(y) (P(x) AND Q(y)) the scope of both x and y is (P(x) AND Q(y)).

Notice that many of these things could be defined in terms of each other. The reader should convince himself that the following correspond to the intuitive definitions we have just seen.

(4) A IMPLIES B is the same as NOT(A) OR B

(5) FOR-ALL(x) (P(x)) is the same as NOT(EXISTS(x) (NOT(P(x))))

(6) A AND B is the same as NOT(NOT(A) OR NOT(B))

Rules of Inference

Given just these intuitive definitions a person could make some inferences. So for example if we are told that A AND B is true we would be prepared to infer that A is true. But using a computer requires that everything must be done formally, since the computer does not have any intuition it can depend on. So we have formal rules of inference. Some examples are:

(7) We may infer A OR B from A

We may infer A from A OR A

We may infer (A OR B) OR C from A OR (B OR C)

We may infer B OR C from A OR B and NOT(A) OR C

These rules go most of the way to defining (formally) what we mean by OR and NOT. To complete the process we need the rule (this is really called a "<u>logical axiom</u>") NOT(A) OR A is always true. One rule of inference which is <u>useful in proving</u> things is that if by assuming A one can prove B then A IMPLIES B is true. So suppose we wanted to prove (X OR Y) IMPLIES (Y OR X). It would go like this:

1. (X OR Y) assumption
2. NOT(X) OR X logical axiom
3. (Y OR X) from 1 and 2 along with the fourth rule in (7)
4. (X OR Y) IMPLIES (Y OR X) by the rule we just mentioned

The third step was a confusing one, so let's look at it a bit more closely. The rule of inference says from A OR B and NOT(A) OR C infer B OR C
and we had X OR Y NOT(X) OR X
so by equating X with A and C, and Y with B we get Y OR X

Resolution Theorem Proving

But there are several problems with proving new facts from old using the system we just outlined. First, and most obviously, there is the problem of deciding which rule of inference to use. But even worse, the reader cannot have missed how tricky that last proof was. In step 2 we simply pulled NOT(X) OR X "out of thin air". There was no real reason given for doing so. It was simply a trick which made the proof work. But again, computers are not very good at pulling off tricks. What is needed is a system of doing proofs which is more mechanical. One response to this need is a system called resolution. In effect resolution has only one rule of inference, so there is never any question about which rule to use.

Resolution theorem proving was devised in the middle sixties, and at first it led many people to hope that the problem of inference was finally solved. By the late sixties there were many people working to apply this technique to problems like question answering, automatic program writing, and many others. (For a typical example of this approach, see (Green 1969).) However, for reasons that we will come to shortly, all these projects failed, and it is probably fair to say that few people in AI still believe that resolution theorem proving has solved, or will solve, the problem of inference.

The general idea of resolution is to put all statements into a special form, called "clause form". A clause is simply a list of predicates where it is understood that they are connected by OR's. Each predicate may or may not be preceded by a NOT. So the familiar inference that, from A IMPLIES B and A we may infer B becomes in resolution:

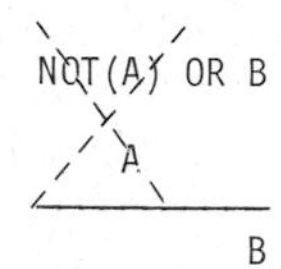

where we have, in effect, NOT(A) and A cancelling each other out. (Remember from (4) that A IMPLIES B may be rewritten NOT(A) OR B.)

Putting Statements in Clause Form. It can be proven that any FOPC statement can be put in clause form, but we will not do so here. Instead we will go through one simple example just to give an idea for how it is done. We will start with a statement which roughly corresponds to the statement that all men own dogs.

FOR-ALL(x) (EXISTS(y) (MAN(x) IMPLIES (DOG(y) AND OWN(x,y))))

The first step is the tricky one. This requires that we replace all EXISTS(y) with what are called "skolem" functions. To get the general idea of this, let us ask what the above statement is intended to mean. What we originally said was that it was meant to represent "All men own dogs". Now we could express this slightly differently as "For each man one can associate with him a dog that he owns". And we can now paraphrase this by "There is a function which given any man has as its value a dog that he owns". Let us call this function (which is a skolem function) "MAN'S-DOG". So if a is a man then MAN'S-DOG(a) has as its value the dog that a owns. With this in mind we now change our statement to:

FOR-ALL(x) (MAN(x) IMPLIES (DOG (MAN'S-DOG(x)) AND OWN (x, MAN'S-DOG(x))))

The statement is now in skolem form, and could be read as "if x is a man then the function MAN'S-DOG(x) has as its value a dog which the man owns."

The rest of the transformation into clause form is relatively straightforward. Notice that now all the variables (namely "x") have the FOR-ALL quantifier, since we have replaced all the EXISTS quantifiers with skolem functions. Hence we can just drop the FOR-ALL and have it simply understood. This gives us:

MAN(x) IMPLIES (DOG(MAN'S-DOG(x)) AND OWN(x, MAN'S-DOG(x)))

We now replace the IMPLIES with the transformation we used earlier. That is, we replace A IMPLIES B with NOT(A) OR B.

NOT(MAN(x)) OR (DOG(MAN'S-DOG(x)) AND OWN(x, MAN'S-DOG(x)))

At this point the general form is A OR (B AND C). We now change this into two separate statements A OR B along with A OR C. The reader should convince himself that we have not changed the meaning any by doing so. This finally gives us our two clauses:

(8) NOT (MAN(x)) OR DOG(MAN'S-DOG(x))

(9) NOT (MAN(x)) OR OWN(x, MAN'S-DOG(x))

Roughly speaking (8) says that if x is a man the function MAN'S-DOG(x) will have a dog as its value, while (9) says that furthermore this dog will be owned by the man. (8) and (9) are both in clause form.

Using Resolution. Now that we have our statement in clause form it is easy to show how to prove things. Say we know that John is a man.

(10) MAN(JOHN)

Now we ask the question, "Does John own anything?" That is

(11) EXISTS(y) (OWN(JOHN, y))

To answer this question using resolution we assume that the answer is no and then try to show that this will lead us into contradiction. We show that there is a contradiction by inferring the "null clause". That is, in resolution we are constantly cancelling things against one another. So if we were able to prove that A is true, and (NOT A) is also true we could cancel the two against each other and get ( ), i.e. the null clause. Here is how it works for proving (11).

The negation of (11) is simply:

NOT (EXISTS(y) (OWN(JOHN, y)))

but this is not in clause form, since, for example, there is an EXISTS in it. To put this in clause form we use a rule we saw earlier, (5), which says:

FOR-ALL(x) (P(x)) is the same as NOT(EXISTS(x) (NOT(P(x))))

Applying this rule gives us:

FOR-ALL(y) (NOT (OWN(JOHN, y)))

Suppressing the FOR-ALL gives us the clause in (12).

(12) NOT (OWN(JOHN, y))

Now we want to "resolve" (12) and (9). That is, try to cancel things out.

(9) NOT (MAN(x)) OR OWN(x, MAN'S-DOG(x))

(12) NOT (OWN(JOHN, y))

Now we can cancel the two OWN's providing we let x = JOHN and MAN'S-DOG(JOHN) = y. Doing this we get:

(13) NOT (MAN(JOHN))

That is, (13) is what is left of (9) after cancelling the OWN and replacing x by

JOHN. If we now resolve (13) against (10) we get the null clause.

(13) NOT (MAN(JOHN))

(10) MAN(JOHN)

( )

So we have shown that John owns something by showing that its negation cannot be true and that is really all there is to it.

Answering the Five Questions. Having now taken a look at FOPC, let us try to see what answers it provides to the five questions we posed at the start of the chapter.

SEMANTIC REPRESENTATION. Does FOPC tell us what predicates we need? Well, for the most part the answer must be no. We have seen that FOPC leaves us free to use whatever predicates we choose, with only a few restrictions. So it does not say if we should have a predicate TRADE (w, x, y, z) which means that w gave x to y for z, or if we should break TRADE up into more basic elements. One possibility based on the work of Schank (see Chapter 7) would be:

(14) TRANSFER (w, w, x, y) (w was the actor in transferring x from himself to y)

(15) TRANSFER (y, y, z, w) (y gave z to w)

CAUSE ((14), (15))
CAUSE ((15), (14)) ((14) and (15) mutually caused each other)

(Technically the two "CAUSE" statements are not legal FOPC statements as written, but there are well known ways to change things so that they are legal.) So the only answer FOPC gives to the question is that certain items like AND, OR and NOT are useful to use, but otherwise you can do much as you choose.

INFERENCE TRIGGERING. What does FOPC say about when and why we make inferences? Well, it is hard to be too firm about this, since one can always change things slightly, but the general idea behind FOPC is that one only makes inferences when one is asked a question. At the moment, this may not seem like much of a limitation but we will see that it is.

ORGANIZATION. How do we locate a needed fact in FOPC? Here there is no answer at all. In the proof that John owned something we never explained why we used certain clauses and not others. This was because FOPC in general, and resolution theorem proving in particular, says very little on the subject. Indeed, this is a very serious problem that we will come back to shortly.

INFERENCE MECHANISM. Given that we have located the facts we intend to use, does FOPC tell us what to do with them? Here the answer is an unequivocal "yes", especially when we are talking about resolution theorem proving. In resolution theorem proving, to produce a new fact from old there is only one thing you can do with the old facts - resolve them together. When you come right down to it, FOPC is primarily a theory of inference mechanism.

CONTENT. FOPC says nothing about what facts one needs to know about the world. It turns out that there are some facts which are difficult, if not impossible, to express in FOPC, but aside from that, FOPC makes no suggestions.

To summarize, FOPC says a lot about inference mechanism, and a little about semantic representation. As we see then, one problem with FOPC is that it does not provide answers to most of our questions.

The Combinatorial Explosion

As we noted in the last subsection, FOPC does not say how one is to locate the facts which are to be used to prove the desired result. In the case of resolution theorem proving this means that we are not told by FOPC which clauses to resolve against each other. Suppose for the sake of argument we simply tried all possible combinations. Let us assume, just to see what happens, that we have 10 clauses, and that we know that the shortest proof will take 10 resolutions. (That is, on the 10th resolution we derive the null clause). On the first try there are 10 possibilities for one of the resolvants (the clauses which are resolved against each other are called resolvants) and 10 for the other, or 100 ($=10^2$). Of course, resolving A against B gives the same result as resolving B against A, so really we only need do about half of these. (In fact, we need a bit more than half - 55 to be exact. But the arithmetic is easier with 50, and the numbers will get so large it hardly matters.) There will be another $\frac{100}{2}$ possibilities for the second resolution so we will have $\frac{100}{2} \times \frac{100}{2}$ ($= \frac{10^4}{4}$) possible combinations for the first two resolutions together. (Again we are rounding down as there will really be 11 possibilities for the second resolution. There will be the 10 original clauses plus the new clause created in the first resolution.) We can continue this way, so that by the tenth resolution there are $\frac{10^2}{2} \times \frac{10^2}{2} \; ..... \times \frac{10^2}{2} = \frac{10^{20}}{2^{10}}$ possible ways we could have made the ten resolutions. Now $2^{10} \approx 10^3$ which leaves us with about 10^{17}. It is of course possible that more than one of these paths will lead to the null clause, but we have already rounded down so much that it easily compensates. To give you some idea of how large this number is, the number of seconds in a century is less than 10^{10}.

Now people interested in FOPC have not ignored this problem, but answers they have come up with have been weak. For example there is one rule called "set of support". Roughly it goes as follows: we start out with the clause we are trying to prove and negate it. We now want to disprove this negated clause. To do this we can restrict ourselves to resolving things against the negated clause, or against results obtained by previously doing so. To put this slightly differently if we are trying to show that assuming NOT(P) leads to a contradiction, it is not necessary to resolve two completely unrelated clauses together in the course of the proof.

Now this has a rather dramatic effect on the number of proofs it is necessary to look at before one finds a correct one. Rather than 10^{17} we have only 10^{10} (again rounding down considerably). But even so, assuming we could do complete proofs at the rate of 10,000 a second, it would still take us about ten days to do the proof.

This sort of situation, where one starts out with a comparatively small number of possibilities, but can combine them in many ways and by doing so come up with a very large number of possibilities is called the "combinatorial explosion". It is a very serious problem, and not only for FOPC. Every inference system known has the same problem. However, most people in the field are beginning to believe that the problem is worse in FOPC. The reason is closely connected to one of the great advantages of FOPC. It is possible to show that every truth expressable in FOPC can be proved. This property is called "completeness", and naturally it is a desirable property to have, everything else being equal. But many people now believe, although nobody can prove it, that any complete system *must* suffer at the hands of the combinatorial explosion. That is, only in an incomplete system is there hope for solving the problem.

WHEN DO WE MAKE INFERENCES?

And there are still other problems with FOPC. To understand them however it will be necessary to take a close look at the circumstances under which we will want our inference systems to make inferences. In particular we want to answer the simple question, when do we make an inference?

Let us assume we are talking about a question-answering system which accepts information expressed in a natural language and will answer questions based on it. Then there are two obvious times when we might make an inference. The first is when a question is asked which requires the inference be made. The second is that point in the input when the system has been given enough information to make the inference. We will call these two possibilities "question time" and "read time", respectively.

There are obvious advantages to making inferences only at question time. Given a particular set of facts there are an incredible number of inferences which might be drawn (remember the combinatorial explosion). We clearly cannot make all possible inferences, so by waiting until a question is asked we guarantee that we will only be making those inferences which we must make in order to answer the system user's question. However, there are good reasons why this is a bad thing to do.

As a Psychological Question

If we wanted to build a model which simulated people reading a text, we could ask the purely empirical question, do people make inferences about the text while they read? In a typical psychological experiment on the question a subject will be given a piece of text to recall, only to have him "remember" facts which were not present in the text, but which were inferred from the text. This suggests that the inferences were made at read time, although the psychologists note that the inferences could have been made at recall time. There are however other experiments which seem to eliminate the latter possibility (see Chapter 10).

Is it Even Possible to Postpone all Inference?

But even if we were not interested in a psychological model, we have already seen reasons why our model could not postpone all inference making until question time. It is not possible to do word sense or structural disambiguation, or pronoun reference without making inferences. We saw several examples of this at the start of the chapter; let us look at one more here.

(16) Today was Jack's birthday. Janet and Penny went to the store. They had to get presents. "I will get a top," said Janet. "Don't do that," said Penny. "Jack has a top. He will make you take it back."

The problem here is that the "it" in the last sentence does not refer to the last mentioned inanimate object (Jack's top) but rather the second to last (the top Janet was thinking of getting). To get this reference correct one must make use of one's knowledge about exchanging things at stores.

Problem Occasioned Inference

Considerations like this have produced a consensus that some inference must be done at read time. The question now becomes how much and of what sort. A useful distinction in this regard is that between "problem occasioned" and "non-problem occasioned" inference. (See Chapter 9 for further discussion.) A problem occasioned inference is one which we perform in order to accomplish the translation into internal representation. It is called "problem occasioned" because we perform such inference only when we run into a problem like an ambiguous word, or a pronoun whose referent is in doubt. A typical example of a non-problem occasioned inference is exhibited by the story "Janet shook her piggy-bank. There was no sound". The inference that there is nothing in the piggy-bank is non-problem occasioned since no ambiguity in the story required this inference for its resolution.

Those who believe in non-problem occasioned inference at read time feel that certain inferences must be made before a person or machine can be said to have "understood". The idea behind problem occasioned inference is that by restricting read time inferences to those which clearly must be made, the number of such inferences can be kept low, presumably much lower than the "understanding" level demanded by those supporting non-problem occasioned read time inferences. In fact nobody really knows whether the necessary number of problem occasioned inferences would be low, but we will assume it is, as otherwise the entire debate becomes academic.

The position presented here is that non-problem occasioned inferences must be made, and in fact they are even necessary to perform the translation into internal representation. (For a different view, see Chapter 9.) Of course, the problem occasioned inference position says that any inference which must be made will be made, so more accurately we will be arguing that the number of required inferences is much higher than expected.

In particular, let us consider the problem of determining pronoun reference. To get some feel for the problems involved, the reader might try the following test. Pick up a mystery or novel you have not read, open to the center, and skim the page for pronoun references. If our experiences are similar you will find that in most cases one can figure out the reference on the basis of the last few lines. However, sometimes this is not possible, and it is interesting to look at this situation because here the reader is in roughly the position of a computer which is called on to determine a reference, but which has understood absolutely nothing of the earlier text. (Of course a reader who only makes problem occasioned inferences will have gained something from the prior text, so this is not a precise analogy, but we will return to this point later.) Let us consider one such pronoun reference situation.

> At four o'clock, after dishwashing and dozing, <u>we</u> started back toward Henley. (From <u>Blood Sport</u> by D. Francis, page 22 of the Pocket Book edition.)

Who "we" refers to cannot be determined from the sentence, and the two surrounding lines do not help.

> Before: I smiled and answered when I was spoken to and concentrated carefully on the taste and texture of what I was eating, and all that happened was that the fat black slug of depression flexed its muscles and swelled another notch.
>
> After: My refusal to go to America hadn't basically disturbed Teller or Keeble an ounce.

The reader might ask himself how he might try to figure this out.

This example was given to three people in a *very* informal experiment. The subjects (i.e. the people who took part in the experiment) were asked to determine the referent, and keep track of how they did it. All found it difficult, and two of the three reported roughly the same detailed behavior; upon deciding that the immediate surroundings gave no clue, these two subjects backed up to the preceding paragraph (half a page back) and read up to the sentence in question. This told them, among other things, that there were six people eating a picnic by a river. This suggests that "we" might be all six, since quite often everybody arrives and leaves a small picnic together, but there are clearly other reasonable possibilities. This led the subjects to go one and a half pages further back in the text to the beginning of the chapter and read the new one and a half pages. This gave no reason to suspect anybody would stay behind, and the general group behavior led to the feeling that there were no particular subgroups, so the subjects reported that "we" referred to all six, but felt slightly unsure. (The third subject went five pages back and gathered enough evidence to feel sure of this choice.)

The above illustrates that a program which made no attempt to "keep up" with the story would have a hard time determining the reference. But what of a program which had been making only problem occasioned inference? It is hard to be sure what such a program would have noticed, but for the sake of argument assume that it had picked up all of the above particulars. It is still true, however, that what finally decided the issue for the subjects was that they could not find any evidence against their hypothesis. But to determine this requires a careful reading of several pages, which presumably is not compatible with the low level of detail picked up by only problem occasioned inference.

Question Answering and Problem Occasioned Inference

Finally, it will probably be extraordinarily difficult to do question answering on complex stories unless the system performs non-problem occasioned inference. Consider the following story.

> Janet wanted to trade her colored pencils for Jack's paints.
> Jack was painting a picture of an airoplane. Janet said to
> him, "Those paints make your airoplane look bad."

Notice that a system which only makes problem occasioned inference would not note at read time that Janet's comment is less than unbiased truth. But suppose we asked such a system whether Janet believed what she said in this instance. How would the system decide to say no? Presumably the system would have a rule to the effect that we assume a person believes what he says unless we have reason to believe otherwise. But how would we show that Janet had reason to believe otherwise? The number of possible reasons why a person might lie seems too large to try to look for each one in the story. It would seem much more to the point to start with the facts in the story and infer that Janet has reason to lie (rather than vice-versa). But while the crucial lines in this story fragment occurred just prior to Janet's statement, in a real story the separation could be much larger, so it is again hard to imagine how the system could know where to look for the needed information if it had not been performing non-problem occasioned inferences.

Implications

Assuming then that our program will be making inferences as it reads, what does this say about the system we use to make inferences.

First, it cannot have only question driven inference. As we noted earlier, FOPC is a question driven system for making inferences. But we saw that not all inferences will be due to user questions, and even if we broaden our concept of question to include what we have called problem occasioned inference, it is likely that many of our inferences will still not be question driven. On the other hand, we could not make all possible inferences at read time, there are simply too many. (In theory FOPC allows an infinite number of inferences from any set of facts.) Hence our system must be able to distinguish between those inferences which are "important" and hence should be made immediately, and those which are not, and hence could be postponed until (and if) the need arises. For example, in story (16) it would seem reasonable to postpone the inference that Janet has lungs and a heart.

This is not to say however that these problems could not be overcome in a FOPC system. Perhaps it will be possible to come up with some set of all purpose questions like "Why was I told that" and "Why did that happen" such that a FOPC system could handle non-problem occasioned inference by stopping after every line and asking each of the questions. But one is entitled to be suspicious of a system when it is necessary to circumvent its natural properties. Besides, in stopping to ask questions like this one has already moved some distance from a pure FOPC system.

Secondly, whatever system one uses must tolerate contradiction. It is not hard to see that any system which is making inferences as the story comes in is bound to make a mistake now and then. For example, instead of story (16) where we assumed that Janet and Penny were going to the store in order to buy presents we could have had:

(17) Today was Jack's birthday. Janet and Penny went to the store. They had to get presents. They had decided to make the presents and needed glue from the store.

That is to say, after reading the first three lines, it is reasonable to assume that they are going to buy presents at the store, but it is not an absolute certainty. In (17) the new information must be seen as contradicting our inference, so that the inference must be withdrawn. Hence our system must be able to cope with seeming contradictions. However, this is another weakness of FOPC. In fact, it is a well known property of FOPC that anything can be proved from a contradiction. To see this in the resolution theorem prover we outlined all we have to do is note that if both A and NOT(A) are clauses, all we have to do is resolve them and we get the null clause, hence proving whatever we set out to prove. Again, one might come up with various ways to get around this problem, but it is once again the case that the inherent properties of FOPC do not seem well suited to the task at hand.

PLANNER

What then are the alternatives to FOPC? One possibility is just to use the natural properties of LISP or some other programming language to make inference. This is, in fact, what was done in some of the early question answering programs, for example Raphael's SIR-Semantic Information Retrieval (Raphael 1968).

Sir

To explain what Raphael did it is necessary to back up a minute and explain LISP property lists. In LISP every basic symbol ("atom") has something called a "property list". So, if we wanted to say that a nose is part of a person, one could represent this in LISP in the following way:

```
PERSON --property list--> (SUBPART(NOSE))
NOSE ---------------------> (SUPERPART(PERSON))
```

That is, the property list is just a list of pairs, where the first item is the property, and the second is the value of the property. If we wanted to add that a heart was also part of a person, and that girls were a subclass of people we would add on:

```
HEART --------------------> (SUPERPART(PERSON))
GIRL ---------------------> (SUPERSET(PERSON))
```

and we would change the property list of PERSON.

```
PERSON -------------------> (SUBSET(GIRL) SUBPART(HEART NOSE))
```

Raphael did exactly this. He had programs which translated a few kinds of sentences into such property list structures, and then he wrote programs which searched these structures in order to answer questions. So if we asked "Does a girl have a heart", the program for SUBPART would first look to see if there was a SUBPART property on GIRL, and failing this would note that GIRL was a SUBSET of PERSON so it would look to see if PERSON had a SUBPART property. This of course would succeed in the above case and the program would respond YES.

But LISP has problems as an inference system. Raphael at the end of (Raphael 1968) notes that SIR was becoming unmanageable, because when he wanted to add some new facility, it often required rewriting some of the old property list search routines. He then suggests that FOPC would be the solution to this problem. Indeed it would, but as we have already seen, at the cost of giving us many new problems.

An alternative is to make programming languages more suited to the needs of inference making. This is exactly what Hewitt did when he designed the programming language PLANNER. Now PLANNER has much in common with unicorns: we know quite a bit about it, but it never existed. That is, no language called PLANNER has yet been implemented. Nevertheless, the idea of PLANNER has been quite influential, and several subsets and variations of PLANNER have been implemented. One of the most well known is MICRO-PLANNER (Sussman et.al. 1971). What will be described here corresponds mostly to MICRO-PLANNER. (This description probably cannot be understood without a slight knowledge of LISP. The reader without this knowledge should read at least the first half of Chapter 12. On the other hand, nothing depends on knowing MICRO-PLANNER until Part 3, so both Chapter 12 and the remainder of this chapter can be postponed.)

Using PLANNER

To get some idea of what PLANNER is, we will present a simulated session where a person sits down at a computer console and uses MICRO-PLANNER. Note however that for the sake of simplicity many particulars of MICRO-PLANNER syntax have been changed, so nothing would really work as described.

```
(ASSERT (AT JOHN KITCHEN))
```

This has the effect of putting the "assertion" (AT JOHN KITCHEN) into the "data base". (A "data base" is simply where facts can be stored and retrieved.) Note that the only symbol here MICRO-PLANNER understands is ASSERT. None of the others like AT, mean anything to the program. If we had said (AT JOHN SINCERITY) MICRO-PLANNER would have been none the wiser. For the same reason it is not necessary to put the predicate first. We could have said (JOHN AT KITCHEN). However, in keeping with FOPC notation we will continue to put the predicate first.

```
(GOAL (AT JOHN ?))
* (AT JOHN KITCHEN)
```

To find things in the data base we use the GOAL statement. The "?" indicates that we do not know what is to go into this space and will accept anything. Hence we have the ability to pick up a complete assertion by knowing part of it. A "*" will indicate the computer's responses. Note that the program's ability to recognize (AT JOHN KITCHEN) as a match for (AT JOHN ?) indicates a rudimentary "pattern matching" facility. We could also have asked:

```
(GOAL (? JOHN KITCHEN))
* (AT JOHN KITCHEN)
```

That is to say we could have asked in effect, "What is the relation between JOHN and KITCHEN?"

```
(GOAL (AT JOHN HOUSE))
* ( )
```

The ( ) response indicates that it was not able to find a matching assertion. Naturally, the program knows nothing of the relation between kitchens and houses unless we tell it. To do so we need what are called "theorems", which correspond to "programs" in other programming languages.

```
(CONSE LOC-FINDER
     :LOC-FINDER is the name of the theorem. CONSE tells
     :MICRO-PLANNER that what follows is a "consequent theorem."
     :We will come back to this term later.
(OBJ LOC-A LOC-B)
     :This is just a list of local variables.
(AT ?OBJ ?LOC-A)
     :This is the "pattern" of the theorem. It tells the
     :program that if it is trying to show that some object
     :is at some location, this is a good theorem to use.
     :The "?" in ?OBJ shows that it is a variable.
(GOAL (AT ?OBJ ?LOC-B)
(GOAL (PART-OF ?LOC-B ?LOC-A)) )
     :These two goals say in effect that to show that OBJ
     :is at LOC-A, show it is at LOC-B which is part of LOC-A.
```

Naturally, the lines preceded by ":" are comments to the reader, and have no effect on the program. Now we try again.

```
(ASSERT (PART-OF KITCHEN HOUSE))
(GOAL (AT JOHN HOUSE) THEOREMS)
* (AT JOHN HOUSE)
```

We first put in the needed assertion that kitchens are part of houses, and we then repeated the goal we tried unsuccessfully earlier, only this time we added "THEOREMS" to indicate that if no appropriate assertion could be found in the data base, theorems should be tried also. It then tried LOC-FINDER because its pattern matched the goal pattern. In the process of matching the goal pattern and the theorem pattern it bound JOHN to ?OBJ and HOUSE to ?LOC-A. This ability to choose which theorems to use on the bases of their patterns is called "pattern directed invocation". MICRO-PLANNER then executed the two goals in LOC-FINDER, which in this case were (AT JOHN ?LOC-B) (which succeeded binding KITCHEN to ?LOC-B) and (PART-OF KITCHEN HOUSE) (which also succeeded).

```
(ASSERT (AT JOHN USA))
(GOAL (AT JOHN HOUSE) THEOREMS)
* (AT JOHN HOUSE)
```

It may not be surprising to the naive reader that after asserting that JOHN is in the USA we were still able to show that JOHN was in the HOUSE, but it took a lot of hidden processing to produce this result. Let us look in some detail at what happened when we did the GOAL.

Find that no assertion matches (AT JOHN HOUSE).

Look at theorems. Find that LOC-FINDER has a pattern which matches our goal of (AT JOHN HOUSE).

Start executing LOC-FINDER. First bind JOHN to ?OBJ and HOUSE to ?LOC-A.

Execute the goal (GOAL (AT ?OBJ ?LOC-B)). ?OBJ is bound to JOHN, so this will find not one, but two, assertions which match the pattern. Namely, (AT JOHN USA) and (AT JOHN KITCHEN). For reasons which do not concern us it will choose the first of these two, hence binding ?LOC-B to USA. However, it will remember that there was a second alternative.

Execute the goal (GOAL (PART-OF ?LOC-B ?LOC-A)) which in this case is (PART-OF USA HOUSE). Naturally this will not succeed so GOAL will report failure.

An alternate way of looking at this material is in terms of the following diagram:

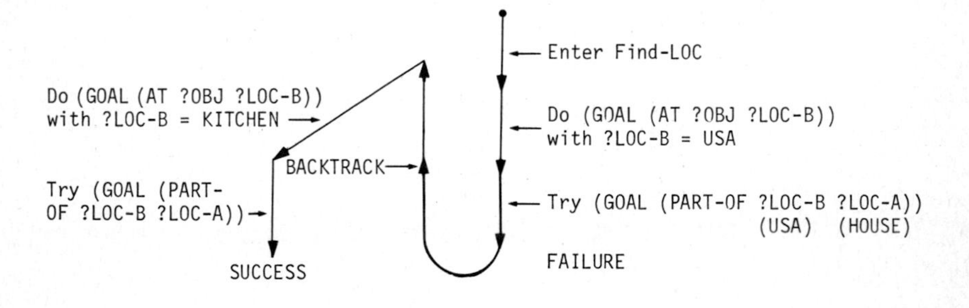

So far we have traced the operation down to FAILURE. Now here is where things get really interesting. The goal's reporting failure causes MICRO-PLANNER to start what is called "back up". In effect what back up does is see if the failure can be repaired in a simple way. To do this MICRO-PLANNER goes back through what was done to see if any earlier choices might be changed. In this case there was such a choice. The goal (GOAL (AT ?OBJ ?LOC-B)) used the assertion (AT JOHN USA) rather than the assertion (AT JOHN KITCHEN). So MICRO-PLANNER backed up to that goal and the other alternative is tried.

> Back up looking for a "choice point". Find that (GOAL (AT ?OBJ ?LOC-B)) could also have used (AT JOHN KITCHEN). Start over from this point using that assertion, so ?LOC-B is now bound to KITCHEN.
>
> Execute (GOAL (PART-OF KITCHEN HOUSE)). This succeeds hence the theorem succeeds.

This activity corresponds to the left-hand branch of the above diagram. Notice that if we had erased (PART-OF KITCHEN HOUSE) from the data base this second try would also have failed, and the entire theorem would have had to report failure.

```
(ASSERT (AT JOHN STORE))
(GOAL (AT JOHN KITCHEN))
* (AT JOHN KITCHEN)
```

This is another example to show that unless you tell it, MICRO-PLANNER does not know what it is talking about. In most applications we would want to remove (AT JOHN KITCHEN) when we learned that he was at the store, or at least mark it to indicate that it is not currently true. It is possible to do either in MICRO-PLANNER, but we will do the former since it is slightly easier to illustrate.

```
(ANTE LOC-CHANGE

     :ANTE indicates that this is an "antecedent" theorem.
     :More on this term later.

     (OBJ NEWLOC OLDLOC)

     (AT ?OBJ ?NEWLOC)

     :This is the pattern. It tells MICRO-PLANNER that this
     :theorem is designed to be invoked when an assertion
     :which matches the pattern is asserted.

     (GOAL (AT ?OBJ ?OLDLOC))

     (THNOT (EQUAL ?OLDLOC ?NEWLOC))

     (ERASE (AT ?OBJ ?OLDLOC))      )

     :These three lines say that if it is asserted that
     :?OBJ is at some location other than ?NEWLOC erase
     :the old assertion.
```

Now in one respect LOC-CHANGE is different from anything we have seen so far. It is designed to be executed not in order to prove something, but rather when new information enters the data base. That is why it is called an antecedent theorem (and hence is marked ANTE). The name comes from the traditional names for the parts of an IMPLIES statement in FOPC, namely,

An antecedent theorem is one where we are given the antecedent and we assert the consequent, while with a consequent theorem we are asked to prove the consequent, and we go looking to see if we can find the antecedent. So LOC-FINDER was a consequent theorem because it was designed to be used when asked to find (AT ?OBJ ?LOC-A) and it did so by looking to see if certain assertions were in the data base. We would say that it was "question driven". LOC-CHANGE on the other hand is an antecedent theorem because it is designed to be used when a new location is asserted. It is "data driven". To use this theorem we will first erase (AT JOHN STORE) and then assert it again.

```
(ERASE (AT JOHN STORE))
(ASSERT (AT JOHN STORE) THEOREMS)
```

As with GOAL, theorems will only be used if their use is called for.

```
(GOAL (AT JOHN HOUSE) THEOREMS)
* (AT JOHN HOUSE)
```

Something is wrong. We still have John at the house. To find out what might have gone wrong we look to see what location statements we now have about John.

```
(FIND ALL ?X (X) (GOAL (AT JOHN ?X)))
* (STORE KITCHEN)
```

This says to find all values of the variable X such that (AT JOHN ?X).

Looking back through our statements we find that (AT JOHN USA) is now missing from the data base. Looking again at LOC-CHANGE we can see what must have happened. We just asked it to find an old location for JOHN and erase it. It must have found (AT JOHN USA), erased it, and considered its job done. To correct this we must rewrite LOC-CHANGE.

```
(ANTE LOC-CHANGE
      (OBJ NEWLOC OLDLOC)
      (AT ?OBJ ?NEWLOC)
    A (THCOND ((THAND (GOAL  (AT ?OBJ ?←OLDLOC))
                      (THNOT (EQUAL ?OLDLOC ?NEWLOC))
                      (THNOT (GOAL (PART-OF ?OLDLOC ?NEWLOC))))
               (ERASE (AT ?OBJ ?OLDLOC))
               (THGO A))
              ((THRETURN)) ) )
```

THCOND, THNOT, THGO and THRETURN are roughly the MICRO-PLANNER versions of the LISP functions COND, NOT, GO and RETURN. (In real MICRO-PLANNER everything starts with a TH but they were dropped when there was no overlap with LISP function names.) They differ from LISP in that the MICRO-PLANNER functions can accommodate back up. The variable ?←OLDLOC signals that the old value of OLDLOC should be ignored, and a new value taken. To test your understanding, try to trace out what will happen in the following case.

```
(ERASE (AT JOHN STORE))
(ASSERT (AT JOHN USA))
     :Note that we did not ask for THEOREMS
     :hence LOC-CHANGE will not be called.
(ASSERT (PART-OF STORE USA))
(ASSERT (AT JOHN STORE) THEOREMS)
```

For a really tough question, try to figure out how THCOND must operate to prevent the entire theorem from failing when we run out of old locations to erase.

Planner vs. Lisp

What exactly does PLANNER offer over LISP as a language for making inferences?

Data Base Management. SIR illustrated a common way to construct a data base in LISP, but the functions ASSERT GOAL ERASE make it much easier to do it.

Pattern Matching. MICRO-PLANNER offers a primitive pattern matching facility, so we can pull things out of the data base by knowing part of the pattern. We can bind variables at the same time. PLANNER, if it is ever written, will have a much more sophisticated pattern matching facility.

Pattern Directed Invocation. Theorems could be called on the bases of their pattern. In effect this allows us to write a function which calls a second function without ever knowing the name of the second function, but rather what it is supposed to do (insofar as we can represent this in the pattern of the theorem).

Back Tracking. This is one of the controversial features of PLANNER, but there seems little doubt that used in moderation back tracking is a useful feature. For example, SHRDLU (a program to be discussed in detail in Chapter 6) uses back tracking when it wishes to locate a "big blue block". The general idea is to set up three goals, the first looking for a block, the second checking that it is blue, and the third checking for size. It makes sense in the case like this to use simple back tracking because there is no way to "guess" in advance which block B1, B2 or B3 say, is the one which will have all three properties. The criticism of back tracking is that it tends to encourage the construction of programs which depend too heavily on blind search. This in turn brings us back to the problem of combinatorial explosion. This criticism is well taken, and it was clearly a design mistake in MICRO-PLANNER that it is almost impossible to turn back tracking off. But there are cases where the search must be blind, and back tracking is a good thing to have in such cases.

Planner vs. FOPC

PLANNER does not suffer from the problems of FOPC. In particular:

Combinatorial Explosion. It is not hard to write programs in PLANNER which suffer from combinatorial explosion, but on the other hand the language offers at least the possibility to write inference systems which do not. The prime idea here is one which was not well illustrated in our MICRO-PLANNER examples, but which is crucial to the language. We saw that we could just ask for a search of the data base by saying (GOAL (AT CAT MAT)) and that if we want to use theorems we would say (GOAL (AT CAT MAT) THEOREMS). Even this already gives us some control over how much computation is done in search of an answer, but there are other options also, like "use the theorems named... first", "only use the theorem named...", "use any theorem with the following property first...", "use only theorems with the following property..." This in effect allows the user to include information which should help the system make the needed inferences without dying a horrible death by combinatorial explosion.

Coping with Contradiction. This is no problem in PLANNER. Since one writes one's own theorems, one would have explicitly to write a theorem which derived anything from a contradiction before that would happen. Furthermore, PLANNER is very well suited to one particular kind of semi-contradiction which comes up all the time. We would like to be able to say that all people have two legs, without worrying about the few rare cases where this is not true. On the other hand if Bill only has one leg we should be able to note the fact. In PLANNER this is done by making "Bill has one leg" an assertion, and "All people have two legs" a theorem. Since the data base is checked first when trying to establish a goal, the system will find that Bill has one leg before it attempts to use the general theorem to show that he has two legs.

Data vs. Question Driven Inference. While it was difficult to accommodate data driven inference in FOPC, there is no problem in PLANNER. Indeed, antecedent theorems exactly cover this situation.

Answer to the Five Questions

Finally what does PLANNER say in response to the five questions we asked at the start of the chapter.

1. SEMANTIC REPRESENTATION. Essentially nothing. There is nothing in PLANNER which in any way restricts what we can put in an assertion. Of course, some things will presumably be translated into theorems, and then PLANNER does say a little about the form of the theorem, namely that it is written in PLANNER, but that is hardly much of a restriction.

2. INFERENCE TRIGGERING. Again very little. As we have already noted, one of the benefits of PLANNER is that it does not make the restrictions that FOPC makes in this area.

3. ORGANIZATION. Here PLANNER does tell us something, but in a very qualified way. PLANNER offers several built-in organizational features. The primary one is pattern directed invocation. The secondary one is the means given to choose which theorems will be used to satisfy a goal, or react to a new piece of information. However, it should be remembered that PLANNER is a programming language, and it is certainly possible to program in other organizations. Nevertheless, it would seem fair to criticise PLANNER if the built-in organizational features it offered were not the ones we needed. As we will see later in Chapter 8, there is some reason to believe that this is the case.

4. INFERENCE MECHANISM. Like FOPC, PLANNER is primarily a theory of inference mechanism. Given a PLANNER theorem, there is no doubt about how to use it and run it as a program.

5. CONTENT. Again nothing.

E. Charniak and Y. Wilks (eds.), Computational Semantics

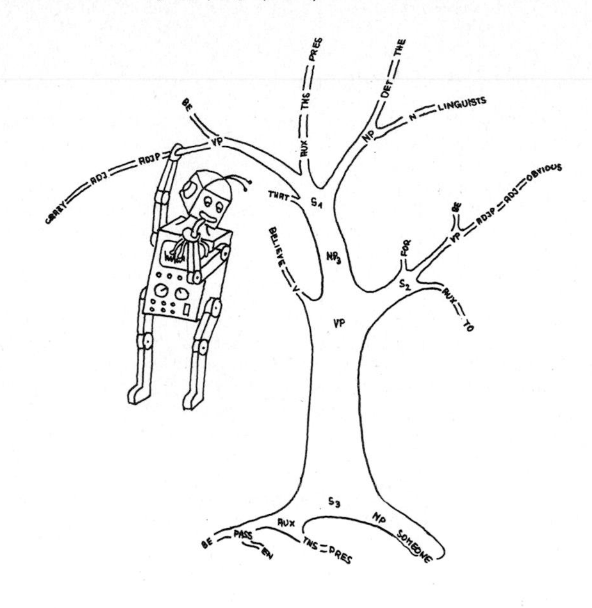

SYNTAX IN LINGUISTICS

Eugene Charniak

Much Artificial Intelligence work on language either rests on prior work in Linguistics, or stands in opposition to this work. As such it behoves us to have a passing familiarity with the field. It is, of course, impossible to cover an entire discipline in a single chapter so this brief introduction will first concentrate on syntax (and hence ignore the entire area of speech production and many other subtopics), and secondly we will only concern ourselves with syntax within the theory of transformational grammar. The reasons for this choice are fairly obvious. Originating in Chomsky's now classic book "Syntactic Structures" (Chomsky 1957), it was the pre-eminent grammatical theory in the United States by 1965, the date of Chomsky's equally famous "Aspects of a Theory of Syntax". All the semantic theories to be covered in the following three chapters were developed at this time (plus or minus two years) and were developed within the framework of transformational grammar. (Hence the version of transformational grammar to be presented here is roughly that of 1965.) But even with this topic restriction, this chapter will do little more than introduce some of the terminology, hopefully give a feel for the subject and its methods, and at the very end discuss the relation between transformational syntax and the artificial intelligence approach to language.

Before starting, the reader is warned that while the overall description of transformational grammar is, hopefully, accurate, all the particular grammatical rules presented will be matters of dispute (those that are not already discredited). No apology is made for presenting such unworthy rules, since at the current time transformational grammar has no other kind. Furthermore, to try to show the reader how the rules fail would only introduce impossible complexities into a beginner's course. Be forewarned.

I THE NATURE OF LINGUISTIC ARGUMENTS

The overall goal of transformational theory is to answer the question, what is it that speakers of English know that non-speakers do not? There is nothing special about English - we could ask the same about Russian, or Italian, except that the examples in this chapter will all be from English, so we will be concerned with what it is to know English. Well, one thing that English speakers know is that the following sentence is ungrammatical in modern English.

(1) *I washed me.

The star (*) before the sentence serves to indicate that the sentence is judged to be ungrammatical. The term "ungrammatical" is not being used in any technical sense. Presumably any native speaker of English would have an intuitive reaction to (1) that it is just not good English, and this feeling being similar for all languages there is no need to explain what "ungrammatical" means. Or to paraphrase a famous jazz musician explaining what Jazz was, if you have to be told you'll never know.

Naturally, (1) is not an isolated occurrence, and with a little thought we come up with the following paradigm.

(2) a) *I washed me b) I washed myself
c) You washed me d) *You washed myself
e) He washed me f) *He washed myself

(3) a) I washed you b) *I washed yourself
c) *You washed you d) You washed yourself
e) He washed you f) *He washed yourself

While we might not want to explain what ungrammatical means, if we are going to characterize what English speakers know we will have to come up with rules which account for the grammatical-ungrammatical distinction found in (2) and (3). Transformational syntax accounts for the above situation in the following way. Assume that initially we just had sentences without the reflexive pronouns (myself, yourself). That is, initially we just had the sentences on the left. We then assume the following rule.

(4) Reflexivization Rule: If subject and object refer to the same thing, the object is made into a reflexive pronoun.

This rule has the effect of transforming those ungrammatical sentences on the left into the corresponding grammatical ones on the right. So what we are left with are only grammatical sentences. More generally, in transformational syntax we account for the ability to distinguish grammatical from ungrammatical sentences by producing a set of rules which "generate" all grammatical sentences, and only grammatical sentences. Now the word "generate" should not be taken too literally here and we will come back much later to explain exactly what we mean by this term (which is being used technically), but for the moment it seems intuitively reasonable enough to see rule (4) as generating grammatical sentences like (3d) from ungrammatical ones like (3c).

Actually, rule (4) works in other cases also. For example, we can expand our paradigm to include "him".

(5) a) I washed him — b) *I washed himself

c) You washed him — d) *You washed himself

e) He washed him — f) He washed himself

At first (e) and (f) seem to contradict our rule, since both are grammatical, but notice that for (e) to be grammatical "he" and "him" must refer to different people, whereas in (f) "he" and "himself" refer to the same person. We can indicate this fact, and at the same time bring (5) into line with (2) and (3) by changing (5e) and (f) to read:

(5) e1) *He_i washed him_i — f1) He_i washed $himself_i$

e2) He_i washed him_j — f2) *He_i washed $himself_j$

Here the index indicates whether or not the pronouns are intended as referring to the same person.

Also notice that our rule accounts for our understanding of "Bill" and "himself" as the same person in:

(6) Bill washed himself.

However, there are cases it does not handle. For example:

(7) a) *$Jack_i$ painted a picture of him_i.

b) $Jack_i$ painted a picture of $himself_i$.

(8) a) *I locked the $chain_i$ to it_i.

b) I locked the $chain_i$ to $itself_i$.

The reason our rule does not cover these cases is because it is expressed in terms of subject and object, and in (7) and (8) the two references to the same object are not in the subject and object position. This suggests that we generalise our rule to:

(9) A pronoun is made into a reflexive if its referent is mentioned earlier in the same sentence.

However, (9) has problems because of sentences like:

(10) $Jack_i$ always sneezes when he_i is near flowers.

Here "Jack" and "he" refer to the same person and the sentence is grammatical. The difference between (10) and all the other examples we have seen is that in (10) we feel intuitively that we have combined two sentences into one, namely "Jack always sneezes" and "He is near flowers" whereas all the other sentences were only simple sentences. Intuitively then we need to change rule (9) so it calls for reflexivization only when the two mentions of the same referent are in the same simple sentence. In fact we will change this slightly so rule (9) now reads:

(11) A pronoun is made into a reflexive if its referent is mentioned earlier in the same simplex sentence.

For the moment the reader should ignore the word "simplex" and pretend instead that rule (11) calls for "simple" sentences. The difference will be explained later.

Now let us reflect a moment on what we have just done. We started out with a group of sentences (2) and (3) and proposed rule (4) to account for them. We saw however that there were other cases, (7) and (8) where intuitively the same thing happened, but because of the way we had formulated our initial rule it did not apply. To put this into terms typically used in transformational grammar we would say that rule (4) did not "capture the relevant generalization" where the relevant generalization was that (7a) was ungrammatical for the same reason that, say, (5el) was. To correct this we finally produced rule (11) which we hope does capture the relevant generalizations. This sort of argument is very common in transformational grammar, and it is how one goes about showing that one rule (in this case (11)) is better than another (namely (4)).

Before moving on to other examples we should note that while the formulation of rule (11) is in the transformational grammar style, the rule (and the generalizations it captures) could well have been formulated in other systems of grammar. The comparative advantages between these different systems is a complicated topic which we need not, and hence will not, discuss.

Let's now go through another example of how we gather evidence for a transformational rule. In this case we wish to find evidence to support:

(12) You-Deletion Rule: Delete second person subjects in imperative sentences.

This rule would take us from (13a) to (13b).

(13) a) You go to the store!

b) Go to the store!

Notice that (12) is a different kind of rule than the others we have seen. In particular, since for most people both (13a) and (13b) are grammatical, rule (12) is what is called an "optional" rule. That is, in the course of generating the sentences it may be applied or not.

One very strong piece of evidence for rule (12) are sentences like:

(14) a) Wash me! b) *Wash myself!

c) *Wash you! d) Wash yourself!

At first (d) seems to be an instance of a reflexive pronoun which is not accounted for by the reflexivization rule, (11), since there is no previous object with which it is co-referential. But notice that if we adopt the you-deletion rule, (12), then at some point in the generation of (14d) the sentence actually looked like:

(15) *You wash you!

If we assume that reflexivization applied at this point, then (15) would become:

(16) You wash yourself!

And this in turn has you-deletion applied to it to produce (14d). Again notice that we are really appealing here to the "capture the relevant generalization" argument. In this case we are saying that the reflexivization rule (11), should account for (14). If we needed a second rule we would be missing a generalization. But to use (11) to account for (14) we must assume the existence of something like the you-deletion rule.

Notice that in making this argument we are assuming that reflexivization applies before you-deletion does. That is, we first must have reflexivization transform (15) into (16) and then have you-deletion transform (16) into (14d). If the rules operated in the opposite order we would have

(17) a) You wash you!

b) *Wash you!

That is, after starting out with (17a) you-deletion would transform it into (17b) which would not be changed any further since it is not of the proper form to have the reflexivization rule apply to it. So we are assuming "rule ordering".

Nor are examples like (14) the only evidence for you-deletion. The reader should convince himself that (18) - (20) provide evidence for you-deletion.

(18) a) I am washing my own car

b) *I am washing your own car

c) *I am washing his own car

(19) a) *You are washing my own car

b) You are washing your own car

c) *You are washing his own car

(20) a) *Wash my own car!

b) Wash your own car!

c) *Wash his own car!

II SOME TYPICAL TRANSFORMATIONS

So far we have been acting as if sentences were simply strings of words which our rules manipulated. In fact, our intuition tells us that these strings really have an internal structure. So consider the sentence:

(21) The big boy laughs.

Intuitively we would divide this sentence into two parts, "The big boy" on one hand, and "laughs"on the other. A linguist might represent this structural division as follows:

(22)

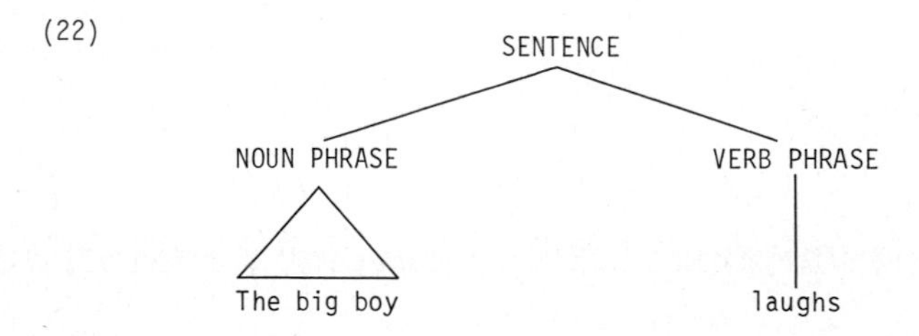

This structure is called a tree (because it sort of looks like an upside-down tree). In (22) there are two terms, "noun phrase" and "verb phrase" which refer to the parts of the sentence. You can think of noun phrases as referring to objects while verb phrases refer to actions, although really things are more complicated than this. At any rate, we could further divide sentence (21), in which case we would get something like this:

(23)

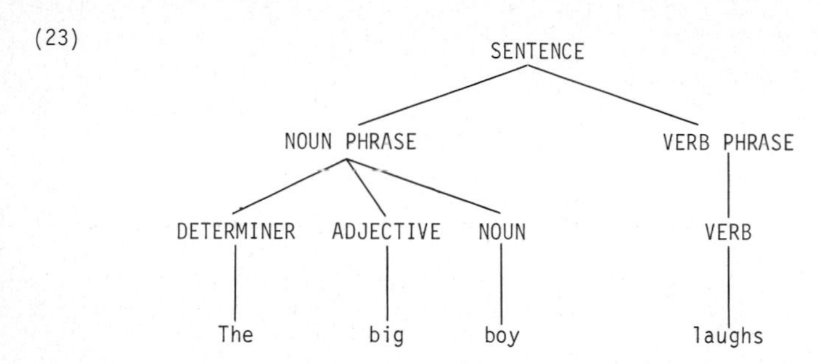

When we have completely divided and subdivided the parts of a sentence until we get down to individual words, as we did in (23), we have a diagram, the whole of which is called a "phrase marker", so called because it marks off the various subparts, or phrases, of a sentence. We will often call these subparts the "constituents" of the sentence. (We can also talk of the constituents of the noun phrase or any other part of the sentence.) The individual words are always at the bottom, or "terminal nodes", of the tree.

Besides corresponding to our intuitive feeling about the structure of sentences, phrase markers also make it easier (one might even say "make it possible") to write our transformational rules. Earlier we noted that the reflexivization rule, (11), needed the idea of simplex sentence. Given phrase markers we can define this concept precisely.

(24)

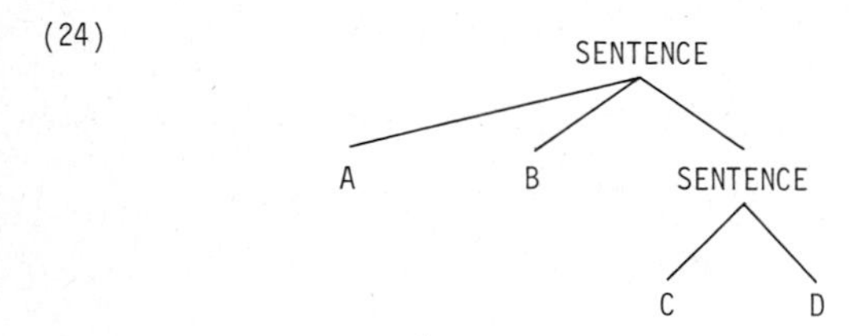

In (24) C and D are in the same simplex sentence, but B and C are not. Furthermore, A and B are in the same simplex sentence, although the sentence they are in is not "simple" since it contains a sub-sentence. (Hence the distinction between simple and simplex.) More formally, we say that two constituents are in the same simplex sentence if in the phrase marker the same SENTENCE node is immediately above both constituents.

A good example of a rule which really seems to depend on the use of phrase markers is the rule of "raising". This rule is designed to account for the relation between the following pairs of sentences, where, as we shall see, there is reason to believe that the subject of the lower sentence is raised into the upper sentence.

(25) a) Sue believes that he won the contest

b) Sue believes him to have won the contest

(26) a) Sue_i believes that she_i won the contest

b) Sue_i believes $herself_i$ to have won the contest

If you look at (26) for example it would seem in (26a) that "she" is in the lower sentence "she won the contest". We might give (26a) the following phrase marker:

(27)

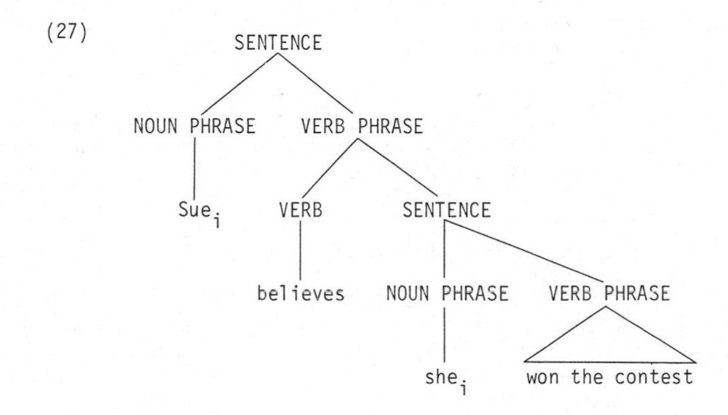

(A lot has been left out of (27) to keep it simple, and the reader should note that there are other ways to draw the phrase marker. For one alternative the reader is pointed to the chapter on case grammar.) But while "she" in (26a) seems to be in the lower sentence, the corresponding noun phrase in (26b) seemingly has moved up to the upper sentence. This is indicated in two ways. The most obvious is that "herself" is a reflexive and according to our reflexivization rule the two noun phrases have to be in the same simplex sentence. But "Sue" and "she" are not in the same simplex sentence in (27). Furthermore, notice that we said <u>her</u>self. In English "her" is the female pronoun which appears in the object position, while "she" is used for subjects. This difference suggests that while "she" is a subject in (26a), it is an object in (26b). This same distinction is even clearer in (25a) vs. (25b) only using "he" vs. "him". For both of these reasons we postulate that the phrase marker for (26b) is something like that in (28). The rule of raising in effect "raises" the "she" in the lower sentence of (27) so that it takes the place assigned to it in the upper sentence of (28).

(28)

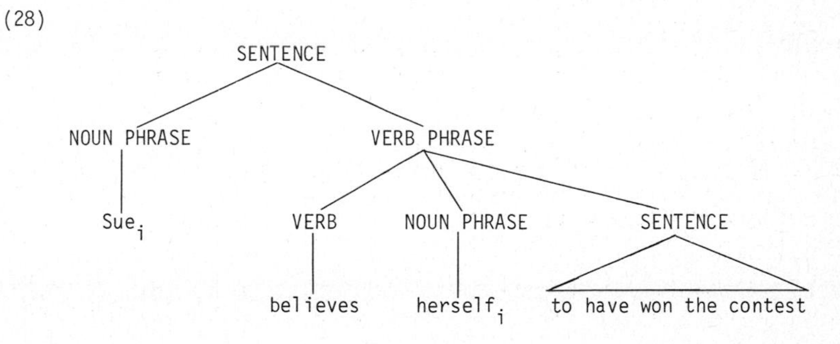

Another well-known transformational rule is that of "passivization". This rule is to account for the well-known correspondence of sentences like:

(29) a) Jack hit Bill b) Bill was hit by Jack

(29a) is called an active sentence, while (29b) is called a passive sentence. The passive rule transforms (29a) into (29b). (Actually, it would be more correct to say that the passive rule transforms the phrase marker underlying (29a) into the corresponding phrase marker for (29b) since, in fact, all transformational rules operate on phrase markers rather than sentences. However, it is easier to speak as if the rules applied to sentences since it gets tiresome to keep repeating the phrase "the phrase marker which underlies....".)

People often wonder why we should derive passive sentences from active ones, rather than vice versa. It is true that intuitively the active sentences seem more basic, but is there any firmer reason for doing things this way? The answer is yes. Consider the three sentences:

(30) a) Jack took advantage of Bill

b) Advantage was taken of Bill by Jack

c) Bill was taken advantage of by Jack

Suppose we were trying to explain where the word "advantage" can be used in English. This would be something English speakers know about their language, so we would want to include it in our grammar. If we assume that initially we start out with active sentences, and derive the passive ones, we could say

(31) The word "advantage" may appear in the slot "take ______ of".

We could then account for sentences like (30b) and (30c) by assuming that they were generated by the passive rule. But if we assume that initially we start out with passive sentences and derive the active ones, we would start out with both (30b) and (30c). The position of "advantage" in (30c) can be accounted for by rule (31), but we would need an extra rule, (32), to account for (30b).

(32) The word "advantage" may also appear as the subject of a sentence, provided the main verb is "be taken of".

But to have two rules like this, both (31) and (32), is in effect to say that there is no relation between the facts they describe. To put it another way, it would be equivalent to saying that it was a coincidence that advantage works both ways. But of course we know this is not true, and that really rules (31) and (32) are missing the generalization that in both cases "advantage" is really part of the phrase "take advantage of". So assuming that we start out with passive rather than active sentences has caused us to miss a generalization, and hence we take the alternate hypothesis, passive sentences are derived from active ones.

We will not actually state the passive rule. It turns out to be quite difficult to do so, and it is not clear whether there exists a completely satisfactory account of even this seemingly obvious rule. (We will later come back to this point: that it is extraordinarily hard to formulate the rules correctly.) Instead we will depend on the reader's intuition and assume all of us have the same rough idea of what the rule ought to do in particular cases.

Given both the passive rule and the raising rule we can now play some interesting games. We will start with a sentence we saw earlier, (25a), repeated here as (33).

(33) Sue believes that he won the contest

First, we can apply the passive rule to the lower sentence to get:

(33_p) Sue believes that the contest was won by him.

To make things easier to keep track of, we have labelled this sentence (33_p) to show that it was sentence (33) with the passive rule applied. As we have already seen, we can apply raising to (33), but we can also apply raising to (33_p). What we get are the sentences:

(33_r) Sue believes him to have won the contest

(33_{pr}) Sue believes the contest to have been won by him

Finally, we can apply the passive rule to the upper sentence of each (33_r) and (33_{pr}). We get:

(33_{rp}) He is believed by Sue to have won the contest

(33_{prp}) The contest is believed by Sue to have been won by him

There are several aspects of all this which deserve attention. The first, and most obvious, is that rules like passive must be allowed to apply to the various levels of a sentence. Furthermore, it is important that passive be allowed to apply to the lower levels of a sentence prior to applying to the upper levels. This allows the production of a sentence like (33_{prp}). In this sentence it is important that "contest" is first brought into subject position of the lower sentence so it can subsequently be raised and then passivized in the upper sentence.

To account for facts like these we have what is called the "cycle". Some transformational rules like passive are placed in the cycle, which means that they are successively applied to higher and higher SENTENCE nodes of the sentence. To be a bit more precise, first every rule in the cycle is given a chance to apply to the lowest SENTENCE node, then every rule is given a chance to apply to the next highest node, etc. Furthermore, although we will not go into it at all, some rules are not placed in the cycle, but rather either before or after it, and hence they are called "pre-cyclic" rules and "post-cyclic" rules respectively.

Notice by the way that raising should also be a cyclic rule, since it too can apply to different levels within the sentence. Furthermore, it must be ordered before passive within the cycle, since in (33_{rp}) and (33_{prp}) it was important to first raise the subject of the lower sentence, and then passivize. (Naturally raising does not apply on the first cycle since by its very nature raising must work on two sentence levels at the same time, the level from which the noun phrase is being raised, and the level it is raised to.)

III WHAT IS A TRANSFORMATIONAL GRAMMAR?

This ends our brief excursion into some of the more common transformational rules. Now we will go back and once again ask the question, exactly what is a transformational grammar?

Early on we said that a transformational grammar in some sense accounts for the knowledge speakers of English have which non-speakers do not. In particular we were concerned with the knowledge which enabled them to distinguish grammatical from non-grammatical sentences. To account for this knowledge we were going to produce a set of rules which "generated" all the grammatical sentences, but none of the ungrammatical ones. Notice that we never made the claim that people actually use such rules to produce sentences. Now was any claim made that, a computer, say, could use the rules profitably. (Since the goal is to formulate the rules very explicitly a computer would be able to use them in some sense, but no attempt was made to show that this way of formulating the rules was better than others for a computer.) Instead, the goal was simply to systematize our knowledge of the rules of grammar in a reasonably convenient way, without direct concern with their use, either by men or machines.

We then decided to "generate" the grammatical sentences by starting with a subset of sentences and using transformation rules to "generate" the rest of them, like "generating" the passive sentences from the active ones. Of course, along the way we saw how structuring sentences as phrase markers helped us to more easily formulate our transformational rules, so we changed the ground rules slightly, so that now we started with a comparatively small set of phrase markers and "generated" the complete set of phrase markers for all grammatical sentences. The technical terms used here are "deep structure" for a phrase marker we start out with, and "surface structure" for a phrase marker we end up with.

The important point here is that in general we "generate" many surface structures from a single deep structure, as for example deriving both the active and passive forms when the deep structure is always in the active form.

We can diagram this process as:

(34)

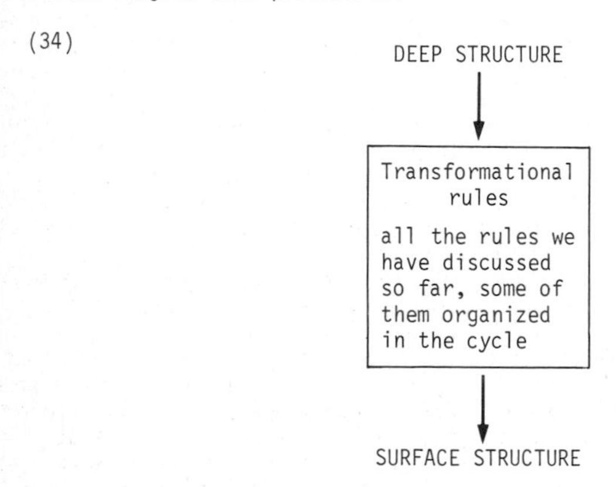

Remember that in reality there will also be many intermediate structures between deep structure and surface structure, since each transformation rule slightly changes the phrase marker.

Now the reader probably has not failed to notice the quotation marks which were placed around the word "generate" when we spoke of a transformational grammar "generating" surface structures from deep structures. The quote marks were there because technically transformational grammars simply describe the relationship between deep structures and surface structures, and we could equally well talk of "generating" deep structures from surface structures. This would correspond to reversing the arrows in the above diagram. If you like, we could think of taking all our transformational rules and reversing the direction in which they operated.

So rather than having a you-deletion rule for imperative sentences, we would have a you-introduction rule for imperative sentences. The point is that nothing in the theory particularly rests on the rules operating in one direction or the other. So while transformational rules are always presented as going from deep structure to surface structure, and hence are thought of as generating surface structures, no particular significance should be assigned to this directionality, or the use of the word "generate".

A word of caution is in order here however. Transformational grammar's indifference to "directionality" only holds providing we do not try to use a transformational grammar either as a psychological theory or as a method for computer comprehension of language. Since transformational theorists in the past have explicitly rejected such use there is no problem. Nevertheless, given the topic of this book, it is surely tempting to try to use these things on a computer. As soon as one tries however, directionality raises its ugly head; for while a transformational grammar can be plausibly used to produce sentences on a computer, they have been uniformly unsuccessful at "parsing" or analyzing sentences. That is to say, it is difficult to use them in going from an English sentence to its deep structure. So the arrows are not quite so reversible after all.

To see why this is the case remember that in generation we started with a deep structure phrase marker and ended up with a surface structure phrase marker. Notice however that to get a real English sentence we must then delete the phrase marker information leaving only the words. That is, we go from (35a) to (35b).

(35) a)

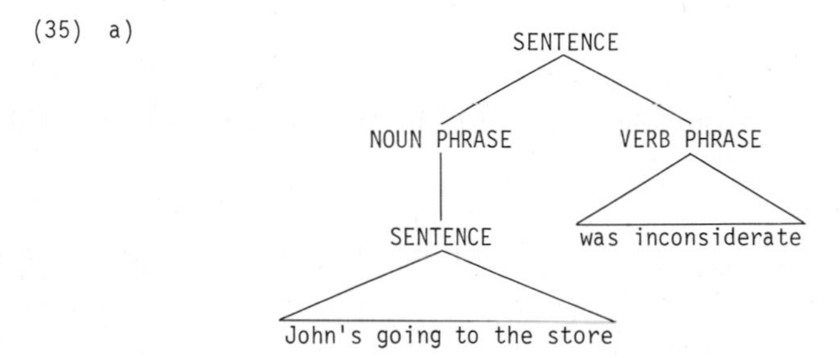

(35) b) John's going to the store was inconsiderate

In going from (35a) to (35b) we lose information. So while (35a) explicitly states that the sentence starts with a subordinate clause, (35b) does not. Hence to reverse the generation process and go from (35b) to its deep structure (i.e. parse (35b)) a major effort must first be made to get from (35b) back to (35a). The experience so far has been that this extra task is the hardest part, and obviously transformational grammar has nothing to say about it.

One thing we have not discussed so far is where the deep structures come from. Originally the theory provided for something called the "base component" which produced the deep structures. The base component is a collection of rules for generating random phrase markers, along with a "lexicon", that is a listing of words along with their relevant grammatical properties. The idea is that after generating (remember those quotation marks) a random phrase marker, words are put in by choosing words with the correct grammatical properties from the lexicon. So to give a trivially simplified example, the base component might contain:

(36)

SENTENCE ⟶ NOUN PHRASE + VERB PHRASE
NOUN PHRASE ⟶ DETERMINER + ADJECTIVE + NOUN
VERB PHRASE ⟶ VERB

along with items in the lexicon, like:

ITEM	CATEGORY
boy	NOUN
laughs	VERB
big	ADJECTIVE
the	DETERMINER

Using these rules we can generate the phrase marker we saw as example (23) repeated here as (37).

(37)

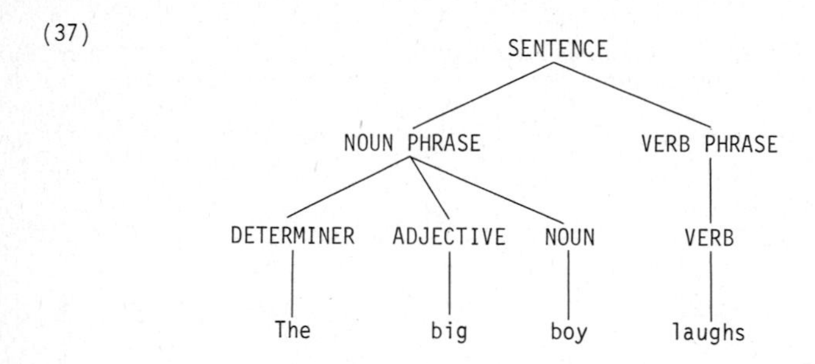

We generate the phrase marker by first generating everything in (37) except for the English words found at the ends of the various branches of the tree (phrase marker). We then substitute in the appropriate items from the lexicon to produce all of (37).

We now extend our diagram (34) to include the complete process of sentence generation.

(38)

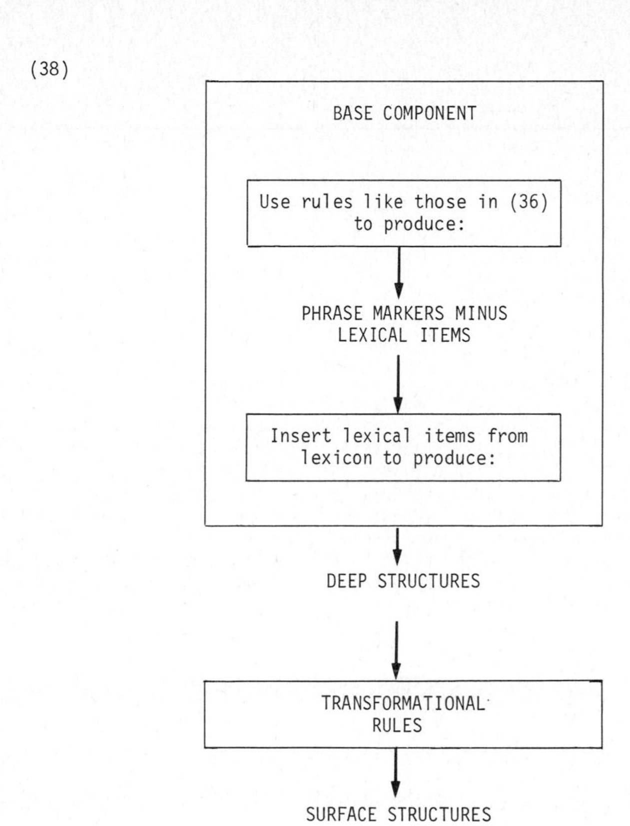

Returning once more to the goal we set out for ourselves at the beginning of this chapter, accounting for the knowledge speakers have that non-speakers do not, one aspect of this knowledge which we have not even mentioned is that a speaker of a language not only knows how to distinguish grammatical sentences from ungrammatical ones, but he knows what the sentences mean. What is needed in (38) then is a theory of meaning. Naturally, the point of fitting a theory of meaning into (38) would be so that not only would the transformational theory predict grammatical sentences, but it would also correlate grammatical sentences with their meanings. There are several conceivable ways this could be done, two of which will be discussed later in this part of the book. A typical, although short-lived proposal was that formulated by Katz and Postal (Katz and Postal 1964) and subsequently adopted by Chomsky in his influential "Aspects of a Theory of Syntax" (Chomsky 1965). This theory generated semantic representations by looking at the deep structures, and performing such tasks as disambiguating word senses, detecting anomolous sentences, etc. In terms of our diagram this would look like:

(39)

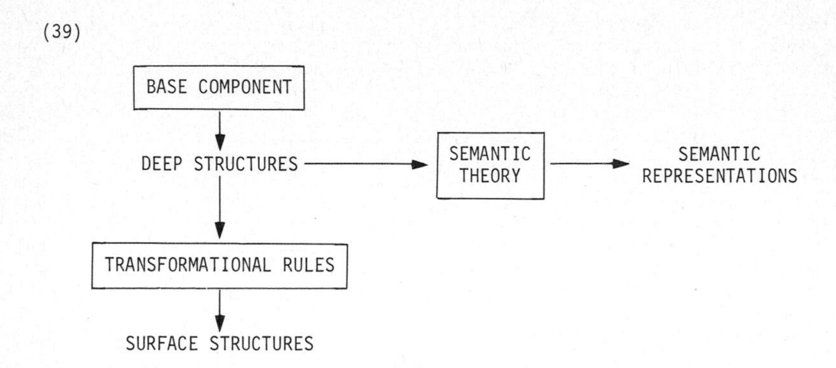

Notice that this organization makes the implicit claim that transformational rules do not affect meaning. If they did then one would not be able to derive the meaning of a sentence from its deep structure, since some optional transformational rule might change its meaning. This claim, as well as almost any other concerning the relation of semantics to syntax is open to dispute. Also note how (39) depends on our earlier observation that transformational grammar should not be interpreted as a theory of how humans do, or computers might, produce sentences. If it were to be interpreted in this light, (39) would imply that one first decides what to say (by the base component producing a deep structure) and only then does one try to figure out what it means.

IV RELATION OF TRANSFORMATIONAL GRAMMAR TO ARTIFICIAL INTELLIGENCE

Much of the artificial intelligence paradigm of language is defined in opposition to the transformational grammar paradigm. (See Chapter 6 for more on this point.) Nevertheless this section will argue that both disciplines have something to learn from each other.

To many AI language workers it is not obvious what we can learn from transformational grammar. For one thing, many, if not most, AI workers do not consider grammaticality a very important phenomenon. After all, we want to get machines to understand what we tell them whether or not the sentences are grammatical. Why go out of our way to give the machine rules to reject sentences which do not live up to its high standard of good English. To make matters even worse, as was pointed out at the beginning, transformational grammar has very few rules which are not discredited, much less undisputed. So, the argument goes, even if we were interested in grammaticality, transformational grammar couldn't help us.

The rebuttal to this argument goes in two stages. In the first, let us assume for the sake of argument that we in AI could use good transformational rules if they were available. Given that they are not, do we in AI have anything better? The answer is no. Furthermore, given the numerical superiority of linguists over AI researchers, linguists have spent a lot more time on the transformational rules than we in AI would be willing to spend. The point is, assuming syntactic rules are useful, the admittedly flawed rules found in transformational syntax are certainly better than any you or I could come up within a short period of time.

But are such rules useful? Again, the answer seems to be yes. To show this it is first necessary to distinguish two possible uses such rules could have. While this text is primarily concerned with getting computers to understand language, there is also the problem of getting them to produce it. The point here is that rules such as we find in transformational grammar are most easily justified in terms of computer production of language. After all, while we might not care for a computer which was too choosy about what it would understand, it would certainly be better to have the machine produce standard grammatical English itself. To do this, rules such as we saw in the first few sections of this paper could certainly be useful. One possible argument against this position (Schank personal communication) is that for most purposes computers could make do with a much more limited repetoire of grammatical constructions, and hence rules like, say, raising, would not be needed. It is hard to argue against this position since nobody has ever really made a study of how few grammatical forms one could get away with and still sound natural, but it is possible that this position underestimates the number needed. Let us just consider one example to illustrate the point.

It is commonly assumed amongst transformational grammarians that the deep structure for (40a) is something like (40b).

(40) a) Mike is likely to win the contest

b)

```
                        SENTENCE
                       /        \
            NOUN PHRASE          VERB PHRASE
                 |                   /\
             SENTENCE            is likely
            /        \
   NOUN PHRASE    VERB PHRASE
        |              /\
      Mike      to win the contest
```

Most people in AI would go along with this at least on the point that "likely" is interpreted as a predicate over the statement "Mike win the contest", which is all that is important for the current argument. With a transformational grammar, to get (40a) out of (40b) it is necessary to apply a rule which is also called raising, but which we will call raising2 to avoid confusion with the rule we introduced earlier. (Raising, you may remember, raised a lower subject noun phrase to the object position of the next higher sentence.) Raising2 takes the lower noun phrase ("Mike") and swings it up into subject position of the higher sentence, while taking the lower verb phrase and moving it to the end of the higher sentence.

Now it is true that we could express the same content as (40a) without resort to the rule raising2. For example:

(41) That Mike will win the contest is likely

Here we started with the phrase structure (40b) but did not apply raising2. However, there are cases where we cannot make the circumlocution we used in (41). For example:

(42) a) *That Mike is winning the contest seems

b) Mike seems to be winning the contest

Here the structure corresponding to (41) is ungrammatical, so we are likely to fall back on (42b) which uses raising2. This is not to say that there is no other way to express the content of (42b) than to use raising2, but it is certainly convenient. For example, we could say:

(43) It seems that Mike is winning the contest

(Of course, here we need yet another rule (called it-insertion).) But in some circumstances we would virtually always use (42b) rather than (43). For example, if somebody said to you that Jones is winning, and you wished to disagree, (42b) would be much more natural than (43). So the point of all of this is that while perhaps not every rule, like raising, is needed, some, like raising2 are very handy to have.

Actually, a small deception has been played on the reader. It turns out that the rule we earlier called raising, and the new rule raising2 are almost certainly the same rule, despite their very different appearance. Arguing this in detail would take too much time. The general idea depends on a fact which you will encounter in the chapter on Fillmore's case grammar. This fact (which is much more secure than case grammar as a whole) is that the position "subject" and "object" do not appear in the deep structure but rather there are rules like subject-creation which make one noun phrase into the subject. The difference between raising and raising2 is simply that in raising2 the noun phrase that is raised undergoes subject creation, while in the rule we called raising it did not. (If you do not see this immediately, don't worry. What we have presented is not so much an explanation as an exercise for the reader. Go back to the examples of raising and try to see how the two rules could be the same.)

We have played this little game for two reasons. First, it shows that a rule like raising plays a much more important role than one would normally suspect. Hence one should be suspicious of one's intuitions that normal sounding English can be produced over a wide range of situations without the use of such rules. Secondly, this sort of interesting insight, that raising and raising2 are really the same rule in spite of their different appearance, is the sort of thing one sometimes finds in transformational grammar, but almost never in artificial intelligence. It is yet another reason for taking AI criticism of transformational grammar less seriously.

So far we have been arguing that transformational rules are useful for computer generation of natural language. However, as should be clear from the topics covered in this book, AI workers are much less concerned with the generation of language than its comprehension. Now let us see if transformational rules are also useful in the comprehension of language. In doing this, however, we must keep in mind the earlier observation that transformational rules cannot be used directly for analyzing sentences. Hence the argument here is rather that they can be suggestive in our search for rules to use to parse natural language.

One obvious example comes from our reflexivization rule. We saw how for a sentence like (44) to be grammatical, "him" could not refer to Jack.

(44) Jack washed him

In a system which was trying to get the pronoun references correct, this would be a valuable clue in the understanding of (44).

Of course, the reflexivization rule was a fairly simple one, and hardly unique to transformational grammar, but a case can even be made that raising is useful in language comprehension. Consider a sentence like (45).

(45) Jack was believed by the boy to have won the contest

This is quite similar to earlier sentences where we saw how the subject of the lower sentence was raised and then passivization moved it to the front of the sentence. A system which knows about such rules would presumably not have any trouble understanding how "Jack" was really the subject of "won the contest" in spite of the fact that it had migrated to the front of the sentence. Notice that the system cannot simply observe that "won the contest" does not have a subject, and hence conclude that "Jack" must be its subject, for it would then be confused by:

(46) Jack was believed by the boy that won the contest

It is clear that the subject of "won the contest" is "the boy". To make things even more confusing, we would not want our system to be confused by (46) and (47).

(47) It was believed by the boy that Jack won the contest

This is not to suggest that any system which understood (45) - (47) correctly would necessarily have our raising rule. There are presumably many ways the same facts could be expressed, so the system might not have anything which looked superficially like the raising rule. What I am suggesting is that in such a case we should first look to see if the two formulations are not really equivalent, and if not then see which is better. In other words, AI programs are going to need knowledge of syntax, anyway, so why not use sources at hand.

This is why artificial intelligence could learn something from transformational grammar, but what could transformational grammarians learn from AI? The answer to this question stems from the aforementioned lack of unchallenged rules in transformational grammar. To get some idea of how serious this problem is in the field, let me quote Postal, a prominent transformational grammarian (Postal 1972, p.160-1):

"It is worth remarking, for example, that after more than a dozen years of generative study of English grammar by dozens and dozens of people, we remain with hardly a single reasonably articulated analysis of any component of the grammar which even approaches relative stability or unchallengeability. Proposal after proposal, from the auxiliary analysis, to selectional features, to noun-phrase conjunction, to cyclic pronominalization, to cross-over constraints, has collapsed or slid into the murk of competing claims and contradictory evidence.

"... To take just one example, the argument given by Ross (1969a) for the transformational cycle as a basis for English pronominalization is a brilliant analysis, one which simply seems to demand immediate agreement. It has, however, quite typically collapsed and no one can now take seriously the idea that pronominalization is governed by a transformational rule as there described or believe that the cyclic principle explains the facts there noted. The point is that not just bad ideas or poor, unsupported analyses fall down. The system seems to resist the best work as well as the rest."

Now it would be nice to say that AI has the solution to Postal's problem, but it doesn't. No present artificial intelligence work sheds any new light on why some constructions are grammatical while others are not, which, when all is said and done remains the fundamental problem in transformational grammar. What artificial intelligence does offer is the opportunity to attack the real fundamental problem, language comprehension, without worrying so much about sentence grammaticality. Naturally, this statement cannot be justified here. If you come to believe it at all it will have to be on the basis of the accumulated evidence provided throughout this book. As already indicated, it seems unlikely that the problems of sentence grammaticality will somehow go away. What does seem to be a reasonable hope is that with a better understanding of understanding, the problems of grammaticality will be seen in a different, and presumably clearer, light.

E. Charniak and Y. Wilks (eds.), Computational Semantics

SEMANTIC MARKERS AND SELECTIONAL RESTRICTIONS

Philip Hayes

In 1963, the first serious attempt was made to incorporate semantics into the theory of transformational grammar. It came in the influential paper by Katz and Fodor, "The Structure of a Semantic Theory", (Katz and Fodor 1963). Their effort was prompted by the observation that transformational grammar as put forward by Chomsky (1957) is not a complete description of a language. It does not account for meaning.

WHAT A SEMANTIC THEORY MUST ACCOUNT FOR

In the view of Katz and Fodor (hereafter K & F), the scope of a language description covers the knowledge of a fluent speaker "about the structure of his language that enables him to use and understand its sentences". (p.482 op.cit.) The scope of a semantic theory is then the part of such a description not covered by a theory of syntax (in their case, transformational grammar). They, however, go on to exclude from such a description any ability to use and understand sentences that depends on the "setting" of the sentences, i.e. the linguistic and/or physical context in which the sentences occur. Setting, as illustrated by K&F's own examples, can refer to:

a) discourse setting:

The shooting of the hunters was terrible

is unambiguous if it is an answer to the question:

How good was the shooting of the hunters?

b) socio-physical setting:

This is the happiest night of my life

is anomalous if spoken at midday.

c) any other use of "non-linguistic" knowledge:

"Take back" is being used in very different ways in the sentences:

Should we take the lion back to the zoo.

Should we take the bus back to the zoo.

Reserving any judgment on the appropriateness of K & F's view of a semantic theory, we can look at the four language phenomena that they felt such a definition obliged a semantic theory to account for. (We will use K & F's own illustrative examples.)

First, there are sentences which can be described syntactically in only one way, and yet have two or more different meanings. One such is:

The bill is large.

This can mean that an invoice is for a large amount of money or that either an invoice or the beak of a bird is physically large.

Secondly, potential ambiguities in the meanings of words can sometimes be eliminated because of relations the ambiguous word bears to other parts of a sentence in which it appears. For example, in:

The bill is large but need not be paid

an invoice and not the beak of a bird is being referred to, since the payment of a bird's beak does not make sense.

Thirdly, there are sentences which are syntactically well-formed but which do not make sense or are in some way self-contradictory. One such is:

He painted the walls with silent paint.

In this example the combination "silent paint" does not make sense. A more famous example due to Chomsky is:

Colorless green ideas sleep furiously.

Fourthly, some sentences which are unrelated grammatically have the same meaning. Such a pair is:

Two chairs are in the room.

There are at least two things in the room and both are chairs.

THE SHAPE OF K & F'S SEMANTIC THEORY

To account for these phenomena, K & F propose an interpretive semantic theory. Given a grammatical description, i.e. a phrase marker (see Chapter 2), for a sentence, the theory interprets the description to produce "readings" for the sentence. Such an interpretive semantic theory has no influence on which phrase markers are produced, but only interprets those that the syntactic theory provides it with. Each reading produced corresponds to a different meaning of the sentence. The number of readings is to be exactly the same as the number of meanings that would be assigned by a speaker of the language considering the sentence in isolation, and not using "non-linguistic" information. For a given sentence there may thus be one, more than one or no readings.

In K & F's theory, the readings for a sentence are built up from the meanings of the words in the sentence. They believe that the meaning of the whole is the sum of the parts. They justify this compositional approach by the observation that native speakers can understand indefinitely many sentences that they have never encountered before, and must therefore be assigning a meaning to the sentences by using those meaning conveying units that they are familiar with, i.e. words. (There is, of course, no a priori reason why the familiar units should not be larger or smaller than words, and in reality they can be both, but this is not a complication that need concern us here.) The argument that meaning is compositional cannot, of course, be an argument in support of the particular way in which K&F's theory says that meanings should be put together. (For other methods of composition see Part III.)

K & F's theory has two components. First, a dictionary in which the meanings of individual words are listed together with, in appropriate cases, restrictions on how words can meaningfully combine with others. These restrictions are called "selectional restrictions" because they select the senses of a word that may combine with a given sense of another word. Secondly, a set of rules defining how the meaning of a sentence may be built up from its component words, using the information about them contained in the dictionary.

Such a theory would, if carried through in full detail, account for the four points quite neatly. The first and third phenomena correspond to those situations in which the same sentences receive more than one and no readings respectively. The fourth corresponds to the case in which two different phrase markers receive the same reading. The second is explained by the elimination of certain combinations of word senses through the restrictions mentioned above. It is, in fact, these selectional restrictions and the objects known as "semantic markers", (described below) which are used to specify them, that form the basis of the whole theory. In getting a rough idea of how the restrictions work, one can thus understand the substance of the theory.

The basic idea is very simple. It rests on the observation that some word senses which are fundamentally predicates or relations may only predicate on or relate objects having certain properties. Thus the sense of "green" predicating color may only apply to physical objects, the sense predicating inexperience only to people and the sense predicating unripeness only to fruit. Such information can be used to disambiguate the phrase "the green ball". Only the color sense of "green" can combine with the spherical object sense of "ball" and no sense of "green" can apply to the other sense of "ball", a formal dance. The six meanings of the phrase possible on a purely combinatorial basis are thus reduced to one. K & F describe properties specifying such selectional restrictions by what they call semantic markers, which are represented by the name of the property enclosed in round brackets. Thus the sorts of objects that the various senses of "green" could apply to would be specified by semantic markers such as (physical object), (human), (fruit).

Such selectional restrictions are not only useful with adjectives, like "green", but can also restrict possible arguments to a verb. "Kick", for example, in its transitive sense of propel by use of a foot or hoof must take an (animal) as subject and a (physical object) as object. Thus in:

The page kicks the ball

the meaning of "page" as a leaf of a book is eliminated, since this sense does not refer to an (animal) leaving only the possibility that "page" is being used to mean a type of servant. As in the previous example, the dance sense of "ball" is eliminated by the (physical object) restriction.

K & F'S FORMAL THEORY

In K & F's formal theory not only the selectional restrictions, but also the meaning of individual words, are expressed in terms of semantic markers. Thus, to take one of their own examples the dictionary entry for "ball" would contain:

Ball → concrete noun → (social activity) → (large) → (assembly) → [dance]

Ball → concrete noun → (physical object) → [sphere]

Ball → concrete noun → (physical object) → [cannon-ball]

As can be seen from the above entries, besides semantic information in the form of semantic markers, syntactic and semantic information in other forms is included in the dictionary entries. Each sense of "ball" listed above thus has associated with it the syntactic information that it is a concrete noun. In the full entry for "ball" there would be other entries which were not concrete nouns (as in, for example, "the children are playing ball"), but only the concrete noun senses will be needed for the sample which will shortly follow and so only those are given.

Each entry is terminated by what K & F call a distinguisher (indicated by square brackets). Distinguishers are intended to contain the remnant of the meaning of a particular word sense not conveyed by the semantic markers in the entry for that sense. They are thus supposed to account for all other aspects of meaning that cannot be accounted for by the markers. Distinguishers, however, play no part in the process of interpretation of phrase markers, although they are present in the resulting semantic representations. For this reason they can in no way account for any of the four abilities which the theory set out to account for with the exception of paraphrasing. Since they are present in the final meaning representation of sentences they must clearly play a part in determining whether the meaning representations of two sentences are the same, and thus whether they are paraphrases of each other. However we will not consider in any detail the ability of the theory to account for paraphrases, so we have adopted the policy of abbreviating distinguishers to the point where they are just sufficient to distinguish the various senses for the reader.

The following dictionary entries for "colorful" show how selectional restrictions are represented in dictionary entries:

colorful ⟶ adjective ⟶ (color) ⟶ [brightly colored] <(physical object) or (social activity)>

colorful ⟶ adjective ⟶ (evaluative) ⟶ [distinctive] <(aesthetic object) or (social activity)>

In each case the type of objects the adjective can modify is indicated by angle brackets.

It will now be instructive to follow through an example of the assignments of readings to a phrase marker. The example given by K & F concerns the phrase marker:

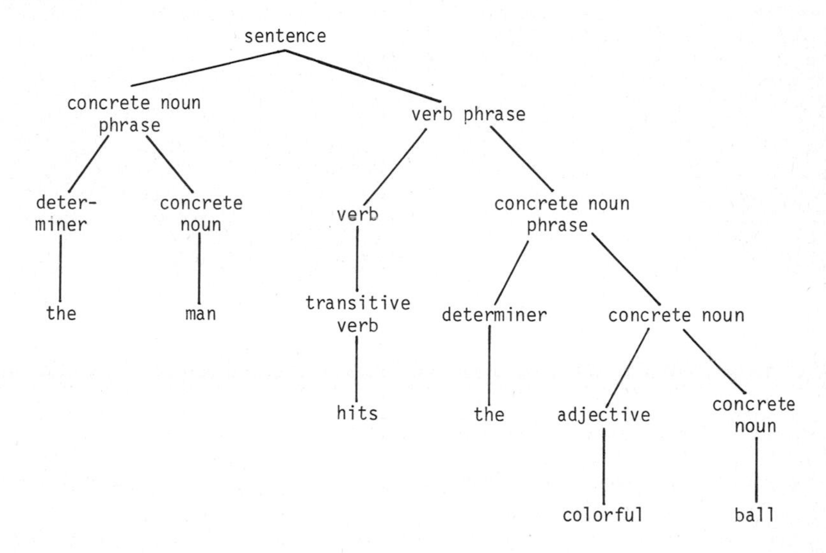

The procedure of assigning readings to this phrase marker is described by K & F in terms of formal rules operating on the appropriate dictionary entries. This formality contributes only confusion to the explanation and we will make do with a less formal summary.

A preliminary step is to select, from the dictionary entries for each word in the sentence represented by the phrase marker, those senses which have the syntactic roles indicated for them by the phrase marker. Thus in the case of "ball", all senses of "ball" that were concrete nouns would be selected. While in the case of "hits", the senses would be all those that were transitive verbs. This procedure results in a tree that looks like:

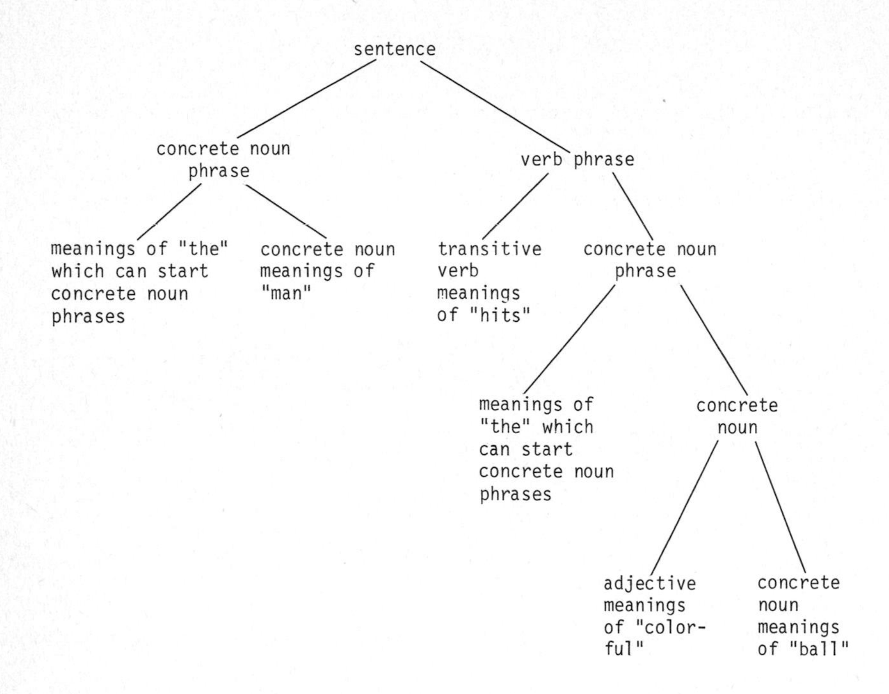

After this initial step, the procedure is in essence to work from the bottom to the top of the phrase marker, amalgamating the sets of meanings of terminal nodes that are immediate descendants of the same node, and replacing that node by the combined set of meanings. This combined set of meanings contains all the meanings obtainable by combining each member of one set with each member of the other, but excludes those combinations forbidden by selectional restrictions. It may thus contain one, more than one or no meanings.

In the above phrase marker, the amalgamations could start either with those of the meanings of "the" with "man" or of "colorful" with "ball". The result of the amalgamation would replace the dominating concrete noun phrase or concrete noun node respectively. This process would continue until an amalgamation was made to replace the sentence node. The meanings produced by this amalgamation would be the readings of the phrase marker.

The amalgamation of the meanings of "colorful" and "ball" as one can see from the dictionary entries already given, produces four meanings for their dominating concrete noun node. They correspond to the brightly colored sense of "colorful" applied to all three senses of "ball", plus the distinctive sense of "colorful" applied to the dance sense of "ball". The combinations of the distinctive sense of "colorful" with the two physical object senses of "ball" are ruled out by the selectional restrictions. As an example of the resulting representations, the last allowable combination mentioned is represented by:

colorful + ball ⟶ concrete noun ⟶ (social activity) ⟶ (large) ⟶ (assembly) ⟶ (evaluative) ⟶ [[distinctive][dance]]

It should be noted that the semantic markers of the appropriate senses of both "ball" and "colorful" are present in this representation. This will be important when we come to combine the meanings of "the colorful ball" with those of "hits".

There is only one meaning in the sets for "man" and for "the". No selectional restrictions operate when the set for "the" is combined either with the set for "man" or with the set just obtained for "colorful ball". Thus, meaning sets with the full possible number of elements result from both these amalgamations. The only result is the addition from "the" of a distinguisher [some definite] to the meaning representations of the concrete nouns. So the example previously quoted would become:

the + colorful + ball ⟶ concrete noun phrase ⟶ [some definite] ⟶ (social activity) ⟶ (large) ⟶ (assembly) ⟶ (evaluative) ⟶ [[distinctive][dance]]

By this stage the phrase marker has been reduced to:

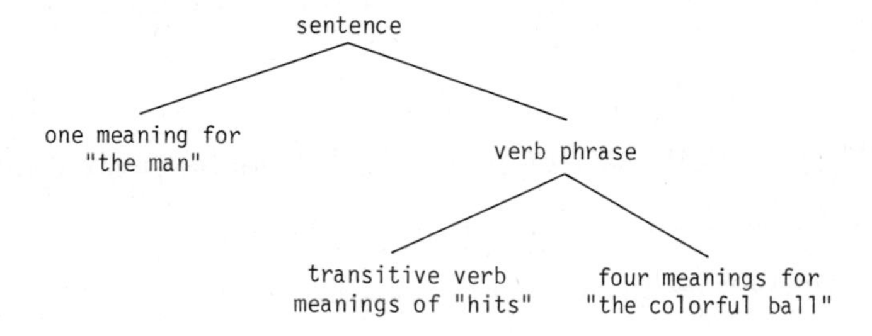

K & F give the following two dictionary entries for transitive senses of "hits":

hits ⟶ verb ⟶ transitive verb ⟶ (action) ⟶ (instancy) ⟶ (intensity) ⟶ [collides with]<SUBJECT: (physical object), OBJECT: (physical object)>

hits ⟶ verb ⟶ transitive verb ⟶ (action) ⟶ (instancy) ⟶ (intensity) ⟶ [strikes]<SUBJECT: (human) or (higher animal), OBJECT: (physical object)>

Combining the nodes for "hits" and "the colorful ball" yields four combinations out of the possible eight, since the two meanings of "the colorful ball" based on the dance sense of "ball" do not satisfy the (physical object) restriction on the object of both senses of "hits".

Making the final amalgamation of the set of four meanings of "hits the colorful ball" with the one-member set for "the man" yields the full four possible combinations, since the one meaning for "the man", being (human), satisfies the subject restrictions of both senses of "hit". One of the four resulting meaning representations for the sentence is:

the + man + hits + the + colorful + ball → sentence → [some definite] →
(physical object) → (human) → (adult) → (male) → (action) →
(instancy) → (intensity) → [collides with] → [some definite] →
(physical object) → (color) → [[brightly colored][sphere]]

The phrase marker we have been discussing is thus shown to have four readings corresponding to:

$$\text{The man} \begin{Bmatrix}\text{collides with}\\ \text{strikes}\end{Bmatrix} \text{the brightly colored} \begin{Bmatrix}\text{sphere}\\ \text{cannonball}\end{Bmatrix}$$

as opposed to the 2 x 2 x 3 = 12 possible on a simple combinatorial interpretation without regard to selectional restrictions.

HOW THE SEMANTIC THEORY RELATES TO THE SYNTACTIC ONE

At this stage we might reflect on how such an interpretive theory fits into the framework of transformational grammar. As was described in Chapter 2, the syntactic component of transformational grammar (as it was at the time K & F's paper was written) falls into two parts: a base component which generates the deep structure phrase markers, plus a transformational component which from these deep structure phrase markers generates the phrase markers of all the other sentences of the language. In rough terms, deep structures correspond to simple declarative sentences, while the sentences produced by the transformational component are more complicated forms such as passives and interrogatives.

The combination rules which K & F described were intended to account for the meaning of the deep structures. This left the question of how meanings should be assigned to the sentences resulting from transformations. K & F postulated rules of a second type which could produce a semantic interpretation of a transformed sentence, given the semantic interpretation of the deep sentence from which it was derived and the transformation used to derive it.

They did, however, note that most transformations, like the passive, preserved meaning, i.e. the sentence resulting from the transformation always meant the same as the underlying sentence. Only for a few transformations viz. the negative, the interrogative and the imperative did this seem not to be the case. K & F commented on how tidy things would become if these transformations could somehow be shown to be meaning preserving as well, since it would eliminate the need for any rules of their second type to interpret phrase markers produced by transformations that did not preserve meaning.

The position that all transformations should be meaning preserving was adopted by Katz and Postal (1964). Since a transformation which changes a declarative sentence into its interrogative form clearly cannot be meaning preserving, their solution was to make their base component generate different phrase markers for the declarative and interrogative versions of the same sentence. (The phrase marker of the question version was, in fact, identical to the indicative version except for the addition of a special tag to say it was a question.) The same was done for negative and imperative sentences, and the only three non-meaning-preserving transformations were thus disposed of.

It is interesting to note that the major part of Katz and Postal's book on the topic is not concerned with justifying this change in terms of the simplification it effected in their semantic theory, but rather with justifying it on syntactic grounds. They felt that a simplification of the semantic theory was not sufficient reason in itself to change the syntactic theory. This attitude on the part of Katz and Postal demonstrates very clearly the role of a semantic theory as an appendage to the syntactic theory in the eyes of transformational grammarians of the time. The debate on the meaning-preservingness of transformations continues to this day, but this is not the place to go into it.

THE ADEQUACY OF K & F'S THEORY

After this digression into the realms of the theology of syntax, we should return to an examination of how adequately K & F's semantic theory fulfils its stated goals. No arguments that can be brought forward against it are conclusive, since K & F did not set out a complete theory, but only indicated the shape they thought one should take. Some interesting points can still, however, be made.

Consider the sentence:

(1) The stock tasted good.

Most native speakers will report that in isolation the sentence is unambiguous. The sense of "stock" being used is that of a sort of soup. Using K & F type selectional restrictions, this disambiguation could be effected by specifying the semantic marker (food) in the restriction on the subject of the particular intransitive sense of "taste" being used in the above example. However, such a course of action runs into problems when one considers:

(2) Fred licked his rifle all over and found that the stock tasted good.

This sentence is also unambiguous but the same sense of "taste" is being used with quite a different sense of "stock" (the wooden part of a rifle). The action being described is somewhat bizarre, but is nevertheless perfectly understandable. Since K & F's theory is compositional they must now insist that (1) was ambiguous all along. For, if the reading of (1) in which "stock" is part of a rifle was not possible in isolation, in a compositional theory, the embedding of (1) in another sentence to form (2) cannot introduce it. That (1) is ambiguous is still just about a tenable position since a native speaker would probably admit this ambiguity of (1) if it was pointed out to him. Holding this position does, however, mean that the proposed restriction on the subject of this sense of "taste" must be weakened to (physical object).

Our first attempt to specify a selectional restriction on the subject of the sense of "taste" we are considering, was based on normality, i.e. we specified (food) since that is what in reality is normally tasted, and is therefore what people normally write and talk about being tasted. This restriction based on normality was shown to be too tight by a description of an abnormal (though perfectly comprehensible and possible) action in which the object tasted was not a food. The counterexample forced us to revise our restriction to correspond to what is actually physically possible, i.e. that virtually any physical object can be tasted. In revising the restriction we, however, lost the ability to make the disambiguation of (1) that humans make, presumably on the basis of the normality criterion just mentioned.

This example illustrates a problem apparently inherent in selectional restrictions. If the restrictions are made too strong, i.e. too specific, they can be shown to over-select by constructing descriptions of unusual situations in which they eliminate the correct reading. If they are made too weak, i.e. too general, they fail to make selections typically made by humans on the grounds of normality.

So far we have seen that K & F cannot account for the lack of ambiguity in (1), but they also have trouble in accounting for the lack of ambiguity in (2). It is very difficult to see how any combination rule of the type discussed above could do it, even if it were possible to represent the relation between "rifle" and "stock" through semantic markers, which in itself is not an easy task. K & F's only defense seems to be to claim that the knowledge people use to disambiguate (2) (i.e. that "stock" can refer to part of a rifle) is non-linguistic, that it is part of the knowledge of the world that they are at such pains to exclude from the scope of their semantic theory. It is not, however, clear why this particular piece of knowledge is any more about the world and any less about language than any of the other pieces of knowledge encoded in semantic markers such as (human), (male), (young), etc.

Bolinger (1965) makes the point even more clearly when he objects to K & F's own example illustrating the sort of disambiguations they do not wish to account for. They claim that accounting for the difference between:

Our store sells alligator shoes

and

Our store sells horse shoes

rests on the knowledge that horses wear shoes and alligators do not, and that shoes are often made out of alligators, but rarely, if ever, out of horses. Indeed it does, but their claim that this sort of knowledge does not fall within the bounds of a semantic theory is countered by Bolinger's question of why (shoe-wearing) is any less of a semantic marker than (young). Why indeed?

Allowing such a widening of the scope of a semantic theory would presumably be regarded by K & F as an opening of the floodgates of world knowledge. They would be quite right, but the thin end of the wedge was already inserted into these floodgates as soon as they started to build a theory that accounted for semantics. They ruled out a semantic theory that takes into account all the knowledge that humans bring to bear in understanding language, on the grounds that this is no less than their entire knowledge of the world. Indeed it is, but if there is a sharp dividing line between purely linguistic semantic knowledge and general world knowledge, K & F failed to draw it. It is commonly assumed by AI researchers that there is no such line and that a semantic theory of language must show how general world knowledge can influence the interpretation of sentences. Such a theory does not actually require that all world knowledge be systematized, but only a demonstration that such a systematization is possible and an indication of how such systematized knowledge can influence sentence meaning.

Much of the linguistic criticism of K & F stemmed from their representation of word meanings by means of semantic markers and distinguishers. The argument is that the dichotomy is arbitrary and corresponds to nothing actually present in natural language. Bolinger makes this point very well in considering K & F's definitions of four senses of "bachelor". (As an unmarried man, a person with a degree, an apprentice knight, and a young fur seal without a mate during the breeding season.) By a series of examples, he shows that every fact mentioned in the four distinguishers K & F give can be necessary for a proper disambiguation and should therefore be represented by a semantic marker. The details of this argument would be out of place here since it is not directly relevant to the adequacy of K & F's theory to account for their four phenomena. What is, however, relevant is that, just as in (2), even after Bolinger has included the information necessary to make a disambiguation as a semantic marker in the definition of the appropriate sense of "bachelor", there is no obvious way that selectional restrictions can be formulated which effect the disambiguation. Thus, in Bolinger's example:

(3) At some time in his life every man is a bachelor

"bachelor" can only mean unmarried man. It is not hard to see how the sense of "bachelor" as a seal can be eliminated, since "bachelor" is the complement of "man" in (3) and a selectional restriction could clearly use the marker, (human), of "man" and the marker, (animal), of the seal sense of "bachelor" to make the required selection. The reason that the apprentice knight and the degreed person senses of "bachelor" are also ruled out is that both refer to a status which, as it happens, is not attained by every man during his life. To account for this disambiguation, Bolinger proposes a semantic marker, (hierarchic), indicating such a status. Even if a simple marker such as (hierarchic) can encapsulate the appropriate fact about the two senses of "bachelor" in question, it is not at all clear how selectional restrictions could be formulated using such a marker to make the required disambiguation.

As a parenthetical remark, it is interesting to note an oddity in the example above. (3) is only unambiguous if it is assumed to be true. If this assumption were not made the occurrence of "bachelor" in (3) would be ambiguous between all three human senses. The sense of "bachelor" as a seal might still of course be ruled out.

We have not yet considered the ability of K & F's theory to account for paraphrases, the fourth task they set for it. A simple example shows the sort of difficulties that can arise. The two sentences:

John sold a book to Mary

and

Mary bought a book from John

are certainly paraphrases, but it is very hard to see how a theory with the sorts of selectional rules described above could produce the same meaning representation for them both. K & F, in fact, did not give any worked examples in which the same meaning representation was assigned by their theory to different phrase markers.

While the above arguments suggest that K & F's scheme of semantic markers and selectional restrictions is not an adequate base for a complete semantic theory of natural language, it does not suggest it is valueless. On the contrary, as far as it goes it is a very useful contribution to such a theory. All that is suggested by the above arguments is that it is not the complete semantic story.

USE OF SEMANTIC MARKERS AND SELECTIONAL RESTRICTIONS IN AI

In most AI natural language understanding systems, semantic markers and selectional restrictions are used, but are not expected to bear the entire semantic burden. They are usually used in conjunction with other less well-defined, but nevertheless powerful semantic tools. In Winograd's well known system (Winograd 1972), for instance, the semantic markers used are very few and refer to very general categories such as (physical), (animate), (human), (abstract). (For more details see Chapter 6.) Even such categories are sufficient for selectional restrictions to reduce the six meanings of "green ball" possible on a combinatorial basis to one.

Winograd's is one of the AI systems most based on syntax, but he still does not use selectional restrictions in the same rigidly interpretive way as K & F. Instead of waiting until he gets one or more complete syntactic structures from a sentence and then applying selectional restrictions to the finished product, he applies selectional restrictions as he goes along. In this way he detects immediately any syntactic misinterpretations that lead to semantic anomalies. The anomaly, for instance, in the incorrect parsing of:

I saw Mont Blanc flying to Zürich

can be detected as soon as an attempt is made to make "Mont Blanc" the subject of "fly", thus preventing time and effort being wasted in building a complete syntactic structure for such a semantic anomaly. This argument is not a theoretical one, but one of computational efficiency, since the same final result would be obtained whenever interpretation is done. Such considerations are nevertheless extremely important if such semantic theories as K & F's are ever to be applied.

There is no need for AI systems to be based on the interpretation of syntactic phrase markers for them to make use of semantic markers. Riesbeck's parser (Riesbeck 1974), for example, never attempts to construct syntactic phrase markers for the sentences it analyzes. Its behavior on the following two sentences is however completely dependent on the semantic markers (physical object) of "book" and (human) of "Mary":

(4) John gave Mary a book

(5) John gave a book to Mary

It works on a word by word basis, and its behavior after processing "gave" depends on the semantic markers of what it encounters next. Since "Mary" is (human), it concludes in (4) that "Mary" cannot be what is being given and so must be the recipient of the gift. In (5), however, "book" is a non-human (physical object) which can be given and so is taken to be the object of the giving. In this parser, semantic information as provided by semantic markers and selectional restrictions is used to bypass the traditional role of syntactic phrase markers in parsing.

In both of the above mentioned systems, selectional restrictions are used in the absolute manner indicated by K & F, i.e. any readings eliminated by selectional restrictions are completely eliminated from any further consideration. It is for this reason that the semantic markers used by these systems are so general. As we have seen, problems arise when one tries to use markers that are very specific in a rigid way. More specific markers are much more useful if they are used on a less rigid basis. Thus the marker (food) could be used to disambiguate (1), "the stock tasted good", in the manner suggested earlier, if it was used by a rule that was less hard and fast, and could be overridden, if the need arose, by other influences such as occur in (2) where the rifle is introduced. Such a rule could be formulated as a preference for rather than a restriction on the subject of the sense of "taste" in question.

The parsing system of Wilks (1973a) treats all restrictions merely as preferences (see Chapter 9 for more details). His philosophy of parsing is to prefer the normal, but accept the bizarre or unexpected. Such an approach has considerable justification, since apparently obvious selectional restrictions are routinely violated in everyday prose. Consider, for example:

> While the famous composer was working out on deck, a sudden gust of wind blew the second movement of his symphony over the side of the ship.

This sentence violates the obvious restriction, (physical object), on the object of the sense of "blow" it uses.

An additional point about Wilks' system concerns its use of trees of semantic markers. These structures allow the meanings of semantic markers to be combined in a more complex way than the simple union expressed by the lists of semantic markers in K & F's theory. They thus permit, for the same repertoire of basic semantic markers, the encoding of more complex meanings and the formulation of more complex selectional or preference restrictions. Such codings of meaning are also evident in the work of the Generative Semanticists (see Chapter 5).

To conclude, let us look at some of the other methods, alluded to above, which are used by AI type systems, in addition to selectional restrictions, to effect disambiguations.

Recency: If an occurrence of "ball" is apparently ambiguous in one sentence, but was used in the preceding sentence unambiguously in its sphere sense, then it would be taken to mean sphere in the sentence under consideration.

Topic: If the topic being discussed is dancing, then in the absence of any conflicting information, an occurrence of "ball" would be taken to refer to a dance. Topic or just general association of ideas can also effect disambiguations within single sentences. In the sentence:

> The gardener picked some stock

the sense of "stock" being used would be taken as that of a kind of sweet smelling plant, presumably because of the association between plants and the profession of gardener (assuming, of course, this sense of "stock" is known). Again in:

> The rancher picked some stock

"stock" would be taken to refer to cattle because of the parallel association between cattle and the profession of rancher.

Physical constraints: While "pen" in:

> The man picked up the pen

is ambiguous between a writing implement and a baby's play pen, in:

> The baby picked up the pen

it can only refer to a writing implement, because it is beyond the strength of a normal baby to pick up a properly designed play pen.

In this example, something analogous to a selectional restriction is being used. The main difference is that the restriction involves a relation between the subject and the object of "pick up", viz. that the physical strength of the subject must be adequate to cope with the weight of the object. In all the selectional restrictions we considered before, the restrictions on the subject and object of the verb were totally independent. In addition, it is not clear that it would be possible to state the appropriate restrictions in terms of semantic markers.

None of these methods of disambiguation can, however, be applied in an absolute way. Indeed, it can often happen that two of these influences will produce contradictory disambiguations of the same sentence. For example, by the topic criterion, in:

The hunter went out with five bucks in his pocket

"bucks" should be taken to mean male deer. However, the physical constraint that a normal-sized male deer will not fit into a normal-sized pocket will make the correct disambiguation. The way such methods of disambiguation interact is a very complex and as yet unresolved problem.

A purely linguistic theory of natural language without regard to setting may not feel itself required to account for the effects on the meaning of sentences of such phenomena as recency, topic or physical constraints. Any AI theory which seeks to account for the way in which language is used and understood can take no such liberty.

CONCLUSION

A semantic theory based on semantic markers and selectional restrictions does not seem to be adequate even for the purely linguistic semantic theory that K & F tried to outline. It can, however, still provide a useful component of an AI theory of natural language comprehension.

E. Charniak and Y. Wilks (eds.), Computational Semantics

CASE GRAMMAR

Wolfgang Samlowski

Case Grammar is another approach among transformational linguistic theories of semantics having an important influence on AI. We shall present Fillmore's approach to Case Grammar in this chapter, not only because he is the most important representative of Case Grammar theorists, but also because several leading researchers within AI explicitly refer to him, though not always with justification.

WHY IS CASE A PROBLEM?

Within traditional linguistics, the notion of case was mostly concerned with morphological analysis of nouns, e.g. the noun endings in German: Kind-Ø, Kind-es, Kind-e, Kind-Ø, or Russian: dom-Ø, dom-a, dom-u, dom-Ø, dom-om, dom-e, etc.

Fillmore, in his famous "Case for Case" (1968), showed that this identification is narrow-minded and restrictive. His point is that the purpose these noun endings serve is the same as that of lexical surface structures, such as prepositions, syntactic structures, intonation patterns, etc., namely to show the semantic relationship between nouns, or noun phrases (NP's), and verbs in the sentence. Consequently, Fillmore holds that the notion of case has to be reconstructed to account for all these phenomena. To do this, he distinguishes the underlying functions, i.e. the semantic case relationship between NP's and verbs from the relationship's <u>expression</u> in particular languages as surface phenomena (which we will call "case forms", as Fillmore does). (From now on we shall call all NP's in case relation and the real world objects they stand for by the name "participant".)

The following examples show what is meant:

(1) Peter hit the boy

is the same as Russian

(2) Petr udaril molodoyčika

and German

(3) Peter schlug den Jungen.

The semantic case function of "Peter" is in (1) - (3) something like the person initiating the action ("the agent") and that of "boy" something like the person affected by the action ("the patient"). However, the case function of "boy" is expressed by three different case forms: in English, the case form is the postverbal position. In German the case form is a word ending, in this example the accusative ending, -en. In Russian, the case form of "boy" is again a noun ending, however in a different case form, genitive. The reader should not worry about the precise definition of the case names, genitive, etc., as nothing essential depends on them.

Now, in Russian and German one could express the same proposition as (2) and (3) with "the boy" and "Peter" exchanged, as in:

(4) Molodoyčika udaril Petr

and

(5) Den Jungen schlug Peter.

In (4) and (5) the relation between the participants (Peter, boy) and the action (hit) is identical to that asserted in (1) - (3), although in (4) and (5) the (surface) syntax has been changed. But in English the case function of nouns is expressed by positional case forms, and such a positional change requires a change of the participants' involvement in the action - see (1) and

The boy hit Peter

where "Peter" is now "the patient" and "the boy" is "the actor". The above examples show that if one wants to specify semantic structure then case forms and case functions have to be distinguished from each other.

THEORETICAL BACKGROUND

Fillmore, then, considers morphological case forms and sentence positions of nouns, prepositions, etc. as indicating one single underlying structure: a system of syntactic-semantic relations. He considers the case functions to be expressed in the deep structure of a generative transformational grammar. Fillmore claims that the traditional categories "subject" and "object" are only surface realizations of the more basic case functions, thus denying a basic assumption of standard transformational grammar. His argument for this change is based on the observation of sentences like (6) to (8):

(6) Peter broke the window with the hammer

(7) The hammer broke the window

(8) The window broke

These examples show that the case form subject can be filled by three different participants involved in this same action. To put it differently, the three participants, Peter, hammer and window, have different functions in this action, but they can take the same syntactic position, e.g. "subject".

Fillmore's rejection of subject and object as underlying universal syntactic-semantic relations has an important consequence: if the syntactic base component of transformational grammar, considered as the "deepest" structure, contains the case forms, subject-object, then it is not the deepest, but an intermediate structure. It is necessary then that a still more abstract base component must underly it, which no longer contains such language-dependent categories but language-free case functions.

Fillmore's Case Grammar: General Assumptions

In his "Case for Case" (1968) Fillmore started from the following general assumptions:

a) Simple sentences of a language consist of a proposition and a modality component. The modality component includes modalities such as negation, tense, aspect, etc. which operate over the whole sentence.

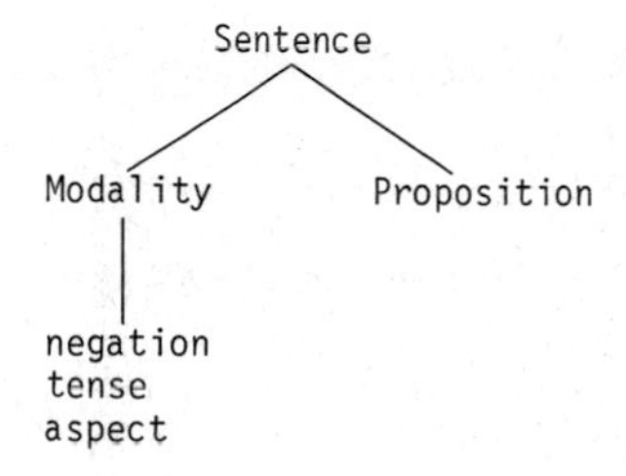

For example, in the sentence (9):

(9) Peter will not steal the dog

the proposition is:

Peter steal the dog

and the modality consists of:

future + negative.

b) A proposition consists of a verb and a set of participants:

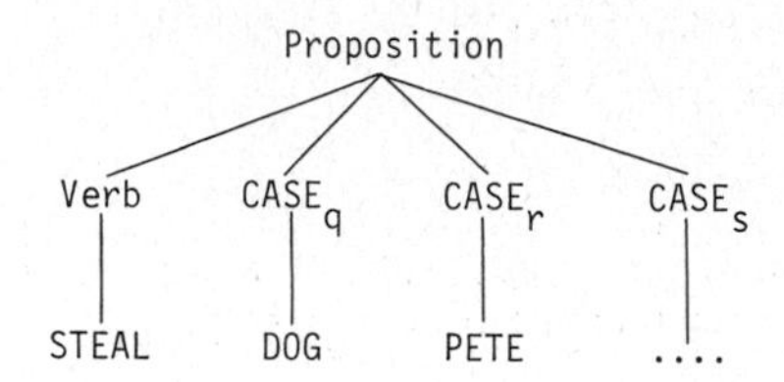

Each case will normally appear on the surface as a noun phrase.

c) The cases used in a sentence with a specific verb have to be selected from a finite, specifiable, and small set of cases.

d) In each proposition each case appears only once (semantic singleness rule).

e) The set of cases a verb might accept is called a case frame, e.g. the verb "hit" has the case frame (Agent, Object, Instrument). This "frame" is not to be identified with the Minsky's "frame" which is mentioned later in this book.

Fillmore believed that one set of case functions operates in all languages, and is presumably innate. He assumed that the following cases (i.e. deep case functions) are necessary:

"AGENTIVE (A), the case of the typically animate perceived instigator of the action identified by the verb.

INSTRUMENTAL (I), the case of the inanimate force or object causally involved in the action or state identified by the verb.

DATIVE (D), the case of the animate being affected by the state or action identified by the verb.

FACTITIVE (F), the case of the object or being resulting from the action or state identified by the verb, or understood as a part of the meaning of the verb.

OBJECTIVE (O), the semantically most neutral case, the case of anything representable by a noun whose role in the action or state identified by the verb is identified by the semantic interpretation of the verb itself; conceivably the concept should be limited to things which are affected by the action or state identified by the verb. The term is not to be confused with the notion of direct object, nor with the name of the surface case synonymous with accusative." (Case for Case, p.24-25.)

In addition, Fillmore considers a LOCATIVE case to be necessary:

(L) "The list of cases includes L, but nothing corresponding to what might be called directional. There is a certain amount of evidence that locational and directional elements do not contrast but are superficial differences determined either by the constituent structure or by the character of the associated verb." (Case for Case, p.25.)

He believed that other cases will probably be necessary. Fillmore gave the following examples:

(10) John opened the door

(11) The door was opened by John

Thus, Agentive is as much John in (10) as in (11).

(12) The key opened the door

(13) John opened the door with the key

(14) John used the key to open the door

The Instrumental is the key as much in (12) as (13) or (14).

(15) John believed that he would win

(16) We persuaded John that he would win

(17) It was apparent to John that he would win

The Dative is John in (15), (16) and (17).

(18) Chicago is windy

(19) It is windy in Chicago (Case for Case, p.25)

The Locative is Chicago in (18) and (19). Objective would be representable as "the door" in:

(20) John sees the door

Factitive role would be filled by "dream" in (21) and (22):

(21) John had a dream about Mary

(22) John dreamed a dream about Mary

Each language chooses its way of expressing these underlying cases by typical case forms, such as subjectivalization, objectivalization, word order, prepositions, affixes, etc. On the use of prepositions in English, Fillmore says:

> "The Agentive preposition is _by_; the Instrumental preposition is _by_ if there is no Agentive, otherwise it is _with_; the Objective and Factitive prepositions are typically zero, the Benefactive preposition is _for_; the Dative preposition is typically _to_ ..." (Case for Case, p.32)

WHAT FILLMORE'S CASE GRAMMAR CAN DO

Fillmore's case grammar provides solutions for the following problems, each of which will be considered in turn.

1. How does one choose the subject of a sentence?
2. Why are sentences with two agents or two instruments ungrammatical?
3. Do verbs like "see" and "show" have something in common?

We have already suggested the need for rules which take us from (deep structure) case functions to (surface structure) case forms. As "subject" is a case form, one of these rules selects, under normal circumstances, the surface subjects (the "subject selection rule"), namely:

(23) If there is an Agentive, it becomes the subject; otherwise if there is an Instrumental, it becomes the subject; otherwise the subject is the Objective. (Case for Case, p.33)

How does this rule work? Consider the following example, the simplest case of subject choice:

(24) The door opened

As we mentioned earlier, the case frame for a verb indicates which case it takes. The case frame for "open" would look like:

(25) (______ O, (I), (A))

The details of this notation need not concern us, except that (25) indicates that "open" takes one obligatory case, the Object, and two optional cases, Agent and Instrument - where "( )" indicates that the case is optional. That the object is obligatory stems from the ungrammaticality of:

(26) *John opened with the key

The phrase marker (PM) for (24) is as follows (27), where K is the symbol Fillmore uses to dominate every preposition in deep structure. In this example the preposition is the "zero preposition", Ø:

(27)

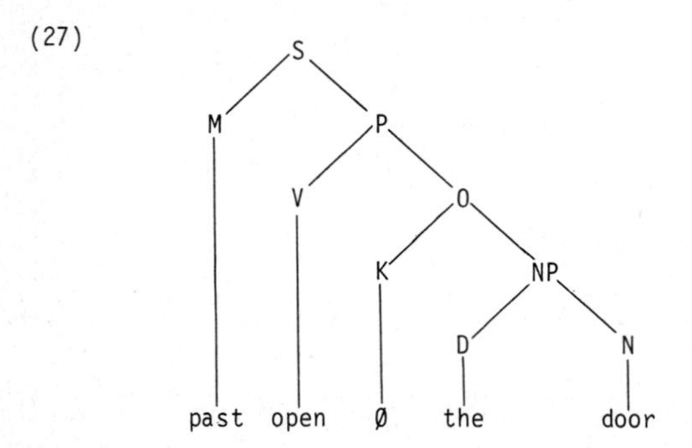

How is the subject chosen from this PM? Since there is only one case in this PM, it becomes obligatorily the subject of the sentence and is shifted into the front position. The resulting PM is this:

(28)

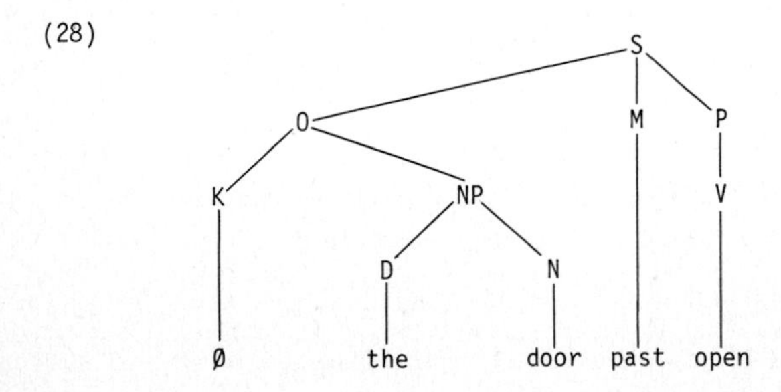

The next transformations are the deletion of the subject preposition and its marker (K), and the collapsing of Modality and Verb. The resulting PM is then:

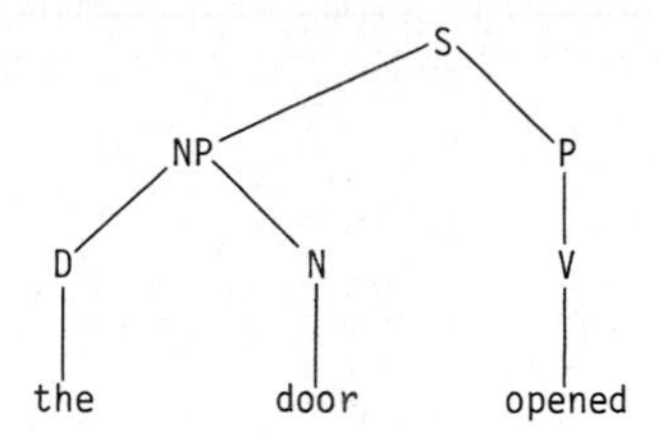

If there is more than one case in the deep structure, things get more complicated. Which case will then be selected? Consider the sentence:

(29) Peter opened the door with the key

which initially has the PM:

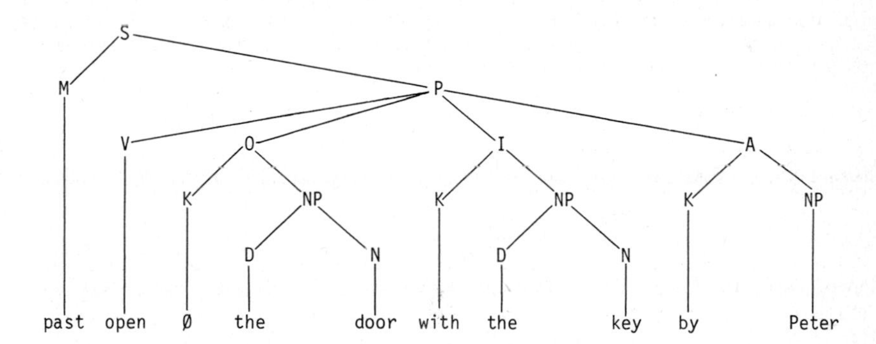

Since A is present, it is chosen as subject by the subject selection rule (23). It is shifted left to the front end. Its preposition (which is by for Agentive) is zeroed and node K is deleted. The resulting PM is:

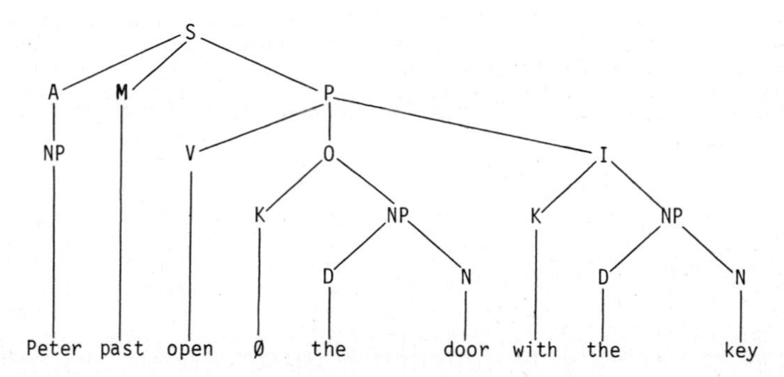

The remaining transformations delete the zero case labels still present (the Objective's case label), together with their markers, and collapses M onto V. The final PM is the following one:

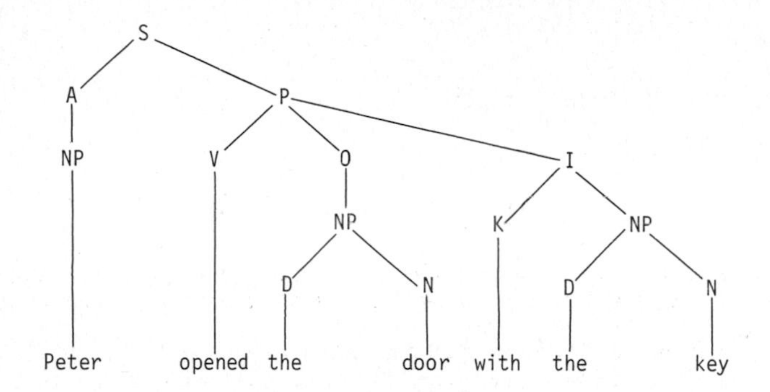

An interesting postulate of case grammar is that each case cannot appear more than once in any case frame. So, for example, "open" cannot have the case frame (_____ (A), I, I, D). This constraint accounts for the oddness of sentences like:

* The key opened the door with a file

A second constraint is that only noun phrases in the same case may be conjoined. Hence the oddness of:

(30) * John and a hammer broke the window

The third point to be mentioned here is the ability of case grammar to provide a means to recognize the two following sentences as being partially synonymous, and, moreover, to give an explanation of what the synonymy is based on.

Peter saw the book

Mary showed Peter the book

The basic assumption of case grammar that there are case functions underlying case forms helps to explain this type of synonymy. The synonymy here consists in the fact that both verbs, "see" and "show", have two participants in common, namely D (Peter) and O (Book), whereas "show" has also an A (Mary) with it, which "see" does not have. So, the underlying common case structure would, then, be (_____ O, D, (A)), whereas the optional A would be realized only when the verb "show" was intended.

The verbs "see" and "look" have a slightly different sort of partial synonymy which one could describe by saying that both have the same basic verb, with the frame (_____ O, D) for "see" and (_____ O, A) for "look", though Fillmore does not actually make use of the notion of basic verb, since he considers verbs defined by their frames alone. Notice that both verbs describe the notion of observation, and hence both require an animate subject, but "look" implies that the "looker" is actively seeking to observe something, while "see" does not necessarily so imply. We have accounted for this in the following way: in "look" the observer is in the Agentive case (implying he is actively observing) while in "see" the observer is in the Dative (implying a passive observation).

What we have just outlined is the version of case grammar presented in (Fillmore, 1968). Fillmore revised this theory in later papers, especially with respect to the list of necessary cases. We have restricted ourselves to the earlier paper, however, as historically it has proved to be the most influential one, both in linguistics and AI.

ARTIFICIAL INTELLIGENCE CASE SYSTEMS

This section will look at three case systems in AI work (those of Simmons, Schank and Wilks) and briefly compare these systems with that of Fillmore.

Simmons

The first case system to be discussed here is that of Simmons because of the three it is the one closest to Fillmore's. (For fuller details of Simmons' network system, see Chapter 7.)

Napoleon was defeated by Wellington at Waterloo

is represented by Simmons in the following way (Simmons 1973):

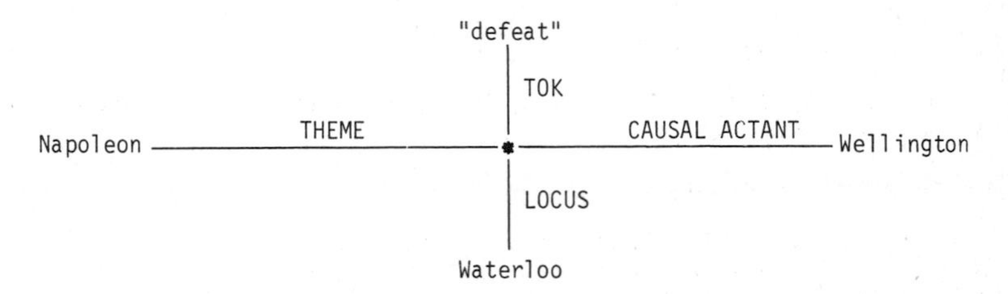

We are interested here in the type of relation between the instance of the concept "defeat" (* in diagram) and the participants involved, i.e. Napoleon, Wellington and Waterloo. The instantiation relation between "*" and the word "defeat" is marked TOK (token) in the diagram.

The reader should not concern himself with the precise definition of the relation TOK; it is sufficient for our purposes to note that the other relations in the diagram are closely parallel to Fillmore's cases in that Simmons' cases hang off "*" in roughly the same fashion as Fillmore's hang off "P" (sentence).

Like Fillmore, Simmons used different case systems in the course of time. The early ones are closely related to Fillmore's cases of the Case for Case and contain AGT, OBJ, INST, SOURCE, GOAL, DATIVE, and THEME (some kind of objective). More recently he has been working with a reduced system of five cases: CAUSAL ACTANT (CA), THEME (TH), LOCUS (L), SOURCE (S), and GOAL (G).

Simmons gives no explicit definitions for these cases, and we have to infer the domain covered by their respective definitions from examples. Causal Actant is the animate instigator of an action, for example, "John" in (31):

(31) John hits the window

But there is another definition for Causal Actant, namely the instrumental cause of an action, such as, for example, "hammer" in (32):

(32) The hammer broke the window

Simmons, therefore, allows two possible Causal Actants within one sentence, as is shown by (33):

(33) John hit the window with the hammer

whose case structure is: John = CA1, window = TH, hammer = CA2.

The reader will see from considering:

(34) The hammer hit the window with John

that although Simmons calls CAUSAL ACTANT a single case, he must in effect have two sets of semantic criteria rigidly connected with the labels CA1 and CA2, and, probably equivalent to Fillmore's Agentive and Instrumental, if he is to recognize that (33) and (34) must have different representations. A similar problem arises with other Simmons' cases.

Theme is the object acted upon by the action, such as, for example, "window" in (31). Theme can also be an animate being which is acted upon, such as Bonaparte in:

Bonaparte was defeated at Waterloo

A sentence may not only have two Causal Actants, but also two Themes, such as, for example, "ape" and "animal" in:

An ape is an animal

Besides the double occurrences of the mentioned cases we have also a double Locus, such as L1, the animate, which serves as the location for some object, and L2, the location at which the event takes place. For example "Peter" and "street" in:

Peter wore a hat in the street

In (35) and (36) we find two cases, Source and Goal, which are defined as the starting and ending points of an action respectively, so Jack would be in the Goal case and Mary in the Source case.

(35) Mary sold Jack a book

(36) Jack bought a book from Mary

Goal, and probably also Source, can be interpreted also in terms of location; for example "office" is the Goal of the movement in:

(37) Peter walked to the office

Furthermore, in (37) we find "Peter" both in the Causal Agent and the Theme case. In Simmons' semantic network we would have the following representation of sentence (37):

(38)

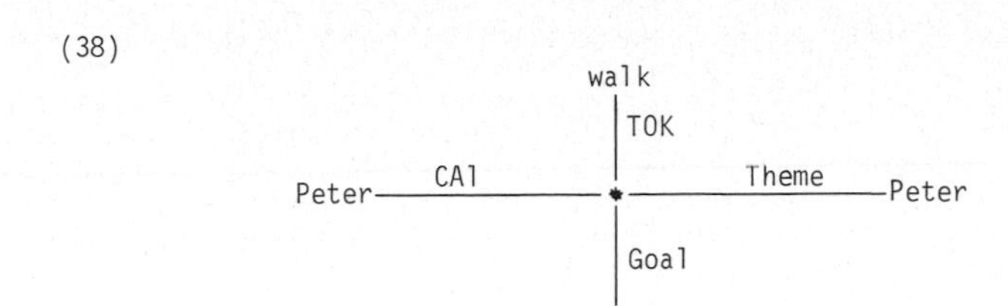

In examples of this general type, Simmons, in some of his papers at least, wishes to assign a second Causal Agent not mentioned in the sentence itself. Thus he tries to differentiate the different uses of "run" in (39) - (42) only by specifying the CA2 (instrument) as "legs", "motors" or "gravity" while leaving the rest unchanged.

(39) John ran to school

(40) John ran the machine

(41) The machine ran

(42) The brook ran

So while in many respects Simmons uses a Fillmorian case system, there are two significant places where he differs. First, Simmons allows a single surface participant to fill two cases, as in (38) where Peter was both CA1 (instigator of walking) and Theme (Object which underwent change). Fillmore did not allow this. Secondly, in examples (39) to (41) CA2 (Instrument) is filled with participants such as "gravity" and "motor" which did not appear in the surface structure at all, again a position counter to Fillmore's (although in earlier papers Simmons did not allow this either).

This same set of "run" examples, (39) - (42), also seems to commit Simmons to breaking down verbs like "run" into more primitive elements, since if "run" becomes "go" with "legs" as instrument then "drive" must be "go" with "car" as instrument. However, Simmons does not comment on this and it is hard to be sure what his position is.

In trying to compare the actual case sets used by Fillmore and Simmons we immediately encounter a fact which we see constantly repeated - the comparison is extraordinarily complex as there is little in common. To take only one example consider the case of a participant that is described as being either in some state or affected by some action. Fillmore uses Dative and Objective while Simmons uses Theme and Locus. However, the comparison is complicated by the fact that both authors include $\pm$ animate as a factor. The following diagram shows the relations:

	ANIMATE	INANIMATE
ACTED-ON	Bonaparte was defeated Fillmore: Dative Simmons: Theme	The window broke Fillmore: Objective Simmons: Theme
IN STATE	Mary wore a sweater Fillmore: Dative Simmons: Locus	The book lay on the table Fillmore: Objective Simmons: Theme

Neither Fillmore nor Simmons suggests any reason for dividing these the way they do.

Schank

Schank (1973b) believes that there are the following conceptual cases between actions (A) and nominals (N). In the Schank notation on the right the case is indicated by the shape of the arrow and its label.

ACTOR	The Actor is the agent or performer of an action.	N ⇐⇒ A
OBJECTIVE	The Objective is the case denominating the object acted on by the particular action.	A ←O— N
RECIPIENT	The Recipient case is used to denote the transition in possession of the object from the originator to the recipient.	A ←R— [→ N / ← N]
DIRECTIVE	The Directive case indicates the starting and ending point of a directional action.	A ←D— [→ N / ← N]
INSTRUMENT	This conceptual case is the conceptual correlate to an instrumentally used nominal. It is always a whole conceptualization, say, "person move stick" and never a simple concept, such as "stick".	A ←I— ⇕

For example, "Peter" in (43) is an Actor:

(43) Peter hits Mary

The "stick" in (44) is in the Objective case:

(44) John hit Mary by throwing a stick at her

In the same example (44), "Mary" and "John" are the ending and starting points of the underlying Directive case. In representing:

(45) Peter is running

the whole conceptualization (46) fills the role of Instrumental in (47):

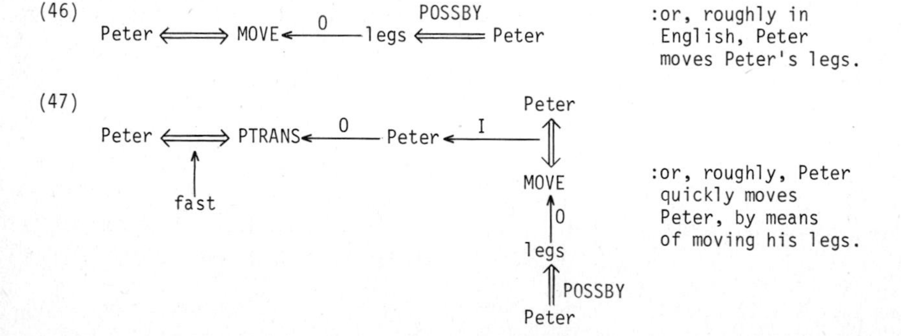

Here PTRANS is a primitive act meaning "moves physically in space".

Example (45) had no explicit instrument but an instrument can, of course, be realised by a prepositional phrase, as in (48):

(48) Peter hit the window with a hammer

The main action is simply

(49)

Peter ⟺ DO ←O— window ←I— (50) :or, roughly, Peter does something to window by means of (50).

where the instrumental action is actually:

(50)

Peter ⟺ PTRANS ←O— hammer ←D— [→ window / ← ?] :or, roughly, Peter moved the hammer to the window, from somewhere.

A brief comparison, at a detailed level, of the Schank cases covering the same ground as Fillmore's Dative case (written D_F(NP) where NP is the Dative participant) is included here for illustrative purposes. In the Schank diagrams on the right, D, of course, still stands for Directional.

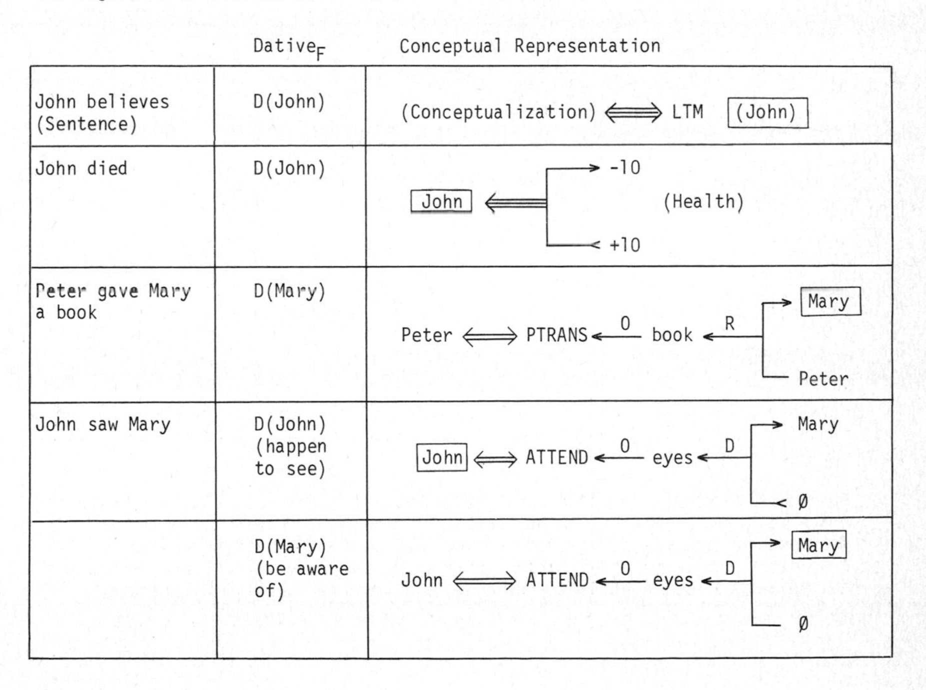

	$Dative_F$	Conceptual Representation
John believes (Sentence)	D(John)	(Conceptualization) ⟺ LTM [(John)]
John died	D(John)	[John] ⟸ [→ -10 / ← +10] (Health)
Peter gave Mary a book	D(Mary)	Peter ⟺ PTRANS ←O— book ←R— [→ [Mary] / — Peter]
John saw Mary	D(John) (happen to see)	[John] ⟺ ATTEND ←O— eyes ←D— [→ Mary / ← Ø]
	D(Mary) (be aware of)	John ⟺ ATTEND ←O— eyes ←D— [→ [Mary] / — Ø]

But the differences in specific cases are not the most important contrasts. Three suggest themselves immediately:

1. Fillmore's case frames are for surface verbs, as we saw. Schank, however, specifies case frames for each of his twelve basic verbs which he calls primitive acts (of which we saw examples: MOVE, PTRANS, etc.)

2. Fillmore's cases, in frames, can, as we saw, be either obligatory or optional. Schank insists that for any primitive act, its associated cases are obligatory.

3. As we would expect from 2, since all the cases for a given act must be filled in a conceptualization, this will mean the insertion of participants not necessarily mentioned in the surface sentence. Fillmore restricts his representations to mentioned participants.

Wilks

Wilks has two sorts of item in his system that must be mentioned in order to illustrate his case system. First, there are formulas which are tree structures of primitive elements, and which represent word senses.

As one sense of "grasp", namely the sense of "pick up a physical object", we have the structure:

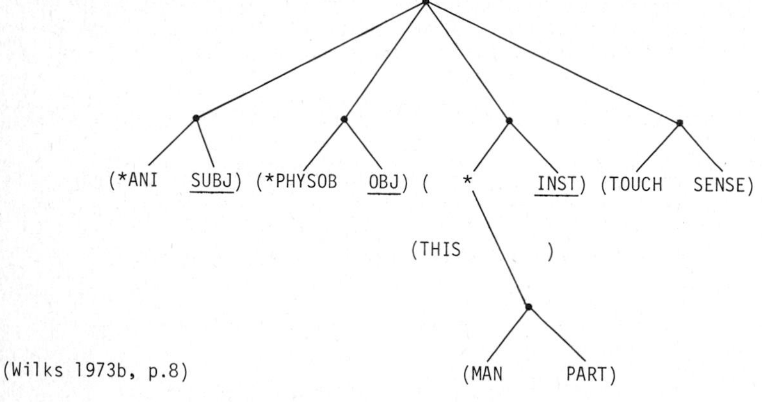

(Wilks 1973b, p.8)

(Animate being touch physical object with body part)

The underlined terminal nodes are those elements of the formula structure we are interested in here: SUBJ, OBJE, INST. Thus, cases occur as part of the meaning structure of a word in a formula.

Like Fillmore, and unlike Schank, the cases INST, SUBJ and OBJE are to be thought of as tied primarily to the surface verb "grasp", rather than as part of a case frame for the basic, or head, action SENSE. They occur where they do in order to define the meaning of "grasp", and therefore would be expected to contain at least the equivalents of the obligatory cases in a Fillmorian frame for "grasp".

Secondly Wilks has templates, out of which a semantic representation is built: these correspond to assertion-like entities which always contain an agent, action and object formula in that order. We shall, for ease of reading, write a template in square brackets, thus, the template for:

Peter grasps the ball

we will write simply as

[Peter grasp the+ball]

where "grasp" in that form stands for the whole tree formula for the action "grasp", and so on for "Peter", etc.

We have mentioned templates because case relations also appear as ties between templates to form higher order clusters. Thus, we could write:

(51) I put the key in the lock

as two templates:

(52) [I put the+key]

(53) [DTHIS in the+lock]

where DTHIS is a dummy holding the "agent place" in (53) and the second (action) place points to a range of structures, each corresponding to a case, that can be realized by the English preposition "in". These structures, called the paraplates for "in" need not detain us, except to note that they specify the case ambiguity of "in", and the result of applying them to the formulas in templates (52) and (53) will provide a case tie, labelled CONT, for containment, that will tie template (53) to the central, action, node of (52) in the representation of (51). The inventory of cases is the same in formulas and paraplates, and is as follows, where we give first the natural language name of the case, then, in upper case, its system name. After this comes the definition of the case, in the form of a question the answer to which defines the participants in the action. This is followed by one example in natural language, and lastly, its representation in Preference Semantics notation as a sub-formula.

"Subject	SUBJ Who did this? "the boy"	((YOUNG MAN)SUBJ)
Object	OBJE Who/what was this done to? "the ball"	((ROUND THING)OBJE)
Recipient	FOR What/who to? What/who for? "for a woman"	((FEM MAN)FOR)
Instrument	INST What with? By what means? "with a stick"	((LINE THING)INST)
Direction	DIRE, TO, FROM, UP Where to? Where from? At what? "from the top"	((UP POINT)FROM)

Possessive	POSS Who owns the thing mentioned? "owned by a man"	((MAL MAN)POSS)
Location	LOCA When? Where? Where at? By what? In what time? During when? Before when? "at that time"	((THIS(WHEN POINT))LOCA)
Containment	IN In what? "in a glass"	(((((FLOW STUFF)OBJE)WRAP)THING)IN)
Source	SOUR Out of what? From what? "out of wood"	((PLANT STUFF)SOUR)
Goal	GOAL To what end? For what purpose? "so as to strike a woman"	((((FEM MAN)OBJE)STRIK)GOAL)
Accompaniment	WITH Accompanied by what/who? With what/whom? Without what/whom? "with a glass"	(((((FLOW STUFF)OBJE)WRAP)THING)WITH)

(Wilks 1973b, p.10/11)

Some of the cases used by Wilks have also negative forms, which, therefore, expand the list of cases: for example, NOTFOR, NOTPOSS, NOTIN, NOTWITH.

Not all of these would be categorized by Fillmore as cases, but would be treated in another way, or not dealt with at all. So, $POSS_W$ and $WITH_W$, for example, do not concern verb-participant-relation and are therefore not cases in Fillmore's sense, and $SOUR_W$, which would still fall under the verb-actant relation, is simply not mentioned or included somewhere else.

The main use to which the cases are put, for Wilks as for Schank, is to make later inferences about entities not specifically mentioned in the corresponding surface sentence. Thus from the "grasp" formula, for example, an instrument can be postulated. Moreover, since the system knows from that formula that the instrument of grasping is preferably a human part, it knows explicitly from the representation what sort of entity it is looking for to fill the slot "instrument of the current act of grasping". In Schank's system, the work of deciding what sort of entity must be the filler is done by the parser (see Chapter 9), and the information necessary is not carried by the representation itself.

As we saw, in so far as the formulas can be seen as a case frame, they are more like a Fillmorian one for the surface verb associated with the formula. However, the paraplate functions which link the templates together by case ties have more the role of a Schankian case frame for a primitive action. So, for example, the paraplate structures for "in" that tie (52) to (53) as a CONTainment dependency have to specify all the cases, realized on the surface by "in", that can be tied to action, whose head is SENSE, and so on for each of the 20 basic elements that are heads of actions. Similarly the paraplates for "by", for example, will specify all the cases realized as "by" that can depend on SENSE, as well as all the other action heads. Thus the paraplates of the system as a whole constitute case frames for the basic head actions, but which are classified under the surface prepositions of English.

CONCLUSION

There are two essential aspects of Fillmore's case theory. The first is, as we saw at the beginning of the chapter, that the old idea of deep structure as containing privileged positions for subject and object must be rejected in favor of a representation more like that of a predicate and its arguments. Hence at some point on the path to surface structure one of the arguments is made into the subject. This idea is fairly well accepted now, and is well supported by syntactic evidence, some of which we discussed when looking at Fillmore's analysis in "Case for Case".

The second aspect, and by far the more problematic one, is that the participants in an action relate to the action in one of a small number of well-defined ways, namely those described by a list of cases. To make a case well-defined we must be able to give a set of rules which are of the form, "If a participant is in case C it must have the following properties..." So, for example, a participant in the agentive (or actor) case must be animate, the instigator of the action, must have instigated the action deliberately, etc.

That this is problematic is suggested by the wide range of current case systems of which we have seen a few in this paper. There is very little agreement on what the best list of cases looks like. It is hence no accident that in giving an example of a well-defined case we choose "agentive", as it is one of the few which is widely agreed upon.

The three AI workers discussed are among many others who have made the formal shift to a case system, one that leads to representations which, whatever their superficial form (i.e. trees in Wilks' system), are really the grouping of case functions around an action (or in the most abstract terms, as we said above: a predicate and its arguments). An open and difficult question is whether AI workers accept the strong notion of well-defined given above, or whether they only accept the weaker claims that case is a convenient formal structure, and a convenient way of specifying the likenesses and differences between actions. It might be possible to accept those claims without accepting that there really was, say, a well-defined Agentive, in the sense of a set of properties that all agents, of all actions, had in common. Fillmore, though, is committed to this stronger claim.

It was clear that Simmons regards his own work as closely connected with that of Fillmore, but, even so, differences in approach began to appear. For Fillmore case frames are attached to surface verbs; for Simmons, case frames are attached not to the surface verb, but to the concept of which that verb is an instance, and therefore, sometimes at least, Simmons seems to postulate a single, more primitive, verb underlying two or more semantically connected surface verbs.

Schank sees all surface verbs as decomposable into a very limited set of primitive verbs (ACTS), and thus case frames are attached to the primitive acts rather than to the surface verbs. Wilks, on the other hand, attaches case frames specifically to surface verbs, at his formula level, and tries to cope with the case behavior of primitives with what he calls paraplates.

Of course, all three use very different cases. To some degree this is related to the decision to attach case frames to primitive vs. surface verbs, but much of the difference is due to dispute about what should be explained by case. So Wilks includes Possessive (John's book) as a case, but Fillmore and Schank would account for it by other means. Wilks and Fillmore include Location (at the store) as a case, but not Schank. Obviously one's cases will be affected by such decisions, but little has been written on how such points are to be resolved.

We mentioned earlier that some AI workers undoubtedly take a more practical and less universal approach to case than Fillmore: because the mere fact that the case system is to be used within a program forces the AI worker to commit himself to a particular set and to precise definitions of individual cases.

Of course, the existence of a program does not guarantee that the cases be well-defined semantically in any sense. Imagine, to take an absurd case, a program with 26 cases, which assigned a case to participants depending on the first letter of the head noun. No programs do anything like this, of course, but neither do they supply or even lay claim to the "perfect" list of cases. We must admit, in the final analysis, that it is an open question whether there really exists a small set of well-defined cases which cover everything that can be said.

What has been illustrated in this chapter is the nature of the constant interaction between work in theoretical linguistics and in AI, and the way AI can suggest a pragmatic test bed for otherwise untested theories of linguistics.

E. Charniak and Y. Wilks (eds.), Computational Semantics

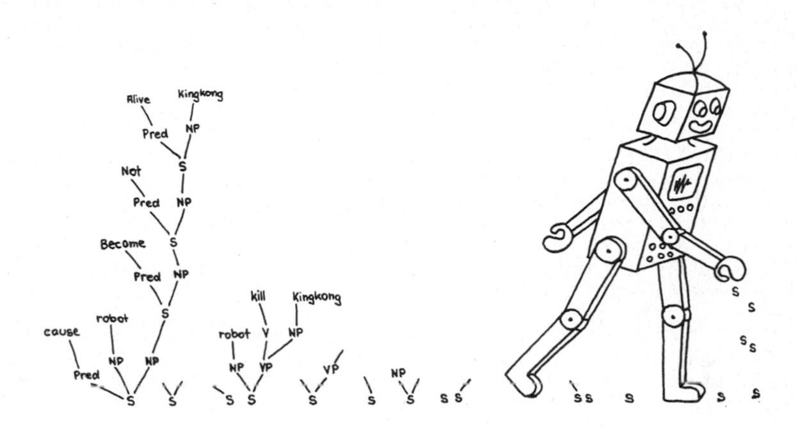

GENERATIVE SEMANTICS

Margaret King

INTRODUCTION

This chapter falls into two sections. The first section attempts to display the Generative Semantics position, by reporting, without much criticism or comment, arguments which are believed by their authors to justify that position. Those linguists who would accept the label "generative semanticist" in fact hold diverse views in many areas. But many of them came to their respective positions initially at least through a reaction against some of the basic tenets of the early transformational grammarians. The exposition in this first section therefore starts from the position which provoked reaction.

In the second section some aspects of the Generative Semantics position will be considered more critically, and it is in this second section chiefly that we shall be concerned with the relationship between Generative Semantics and AI. This relationship, it will be argued, is a rather peculiar one, in that much of the activity of the Generative Semanticists, especially in the more recent stages of their development, while it is basically misconceived as an activity within traditional linguistics, would nonetheless be a perfectly sensible activity within the general area of work in AI.

SECTION I

Historical Background

For our purposes history can begin with Chomsky's Syntactic Structures which, published in 1957, first introduced transformational grammar. Chomsky's 1957 account of grammar is essentially purely syntactic. The role of semantics within grammar is scarcely discussed at all, and indeed meaning is explicitly rejected as a possible basis for formal description:

"It is of course impossible to prove that semantic notions are of no use in grammar, just as it is impossible to prove the irrelevance of any other given set of notions. Investigation of such proposals however seems to lead to the conclusion that only a purely formal basis can provide a firm and constructive foundation for the construction of grammatical theory". (Chomsky (1957), p.100.)

On the other hand Chomsky seems to accept meaning as relevant in the evaluation of grammar:

"In other words we should like the syntactic framework of the language that is isolated and exhibited by the grammar to be able to support semantic description, and we shall naturally rate more highly a theory of formal structure that leads to grammars that meet this requirement more thoroughly". (Ibid., p.102.)

However, the first attempt to see how a theory of meaning might be incorporated into transformational grammar had to await Katz and Fodor's 1963 paper, The Structure of a Semantic Theory.

In Chapter 3 the Chomsky-Katz-Postal model (henceforward CKP model) has already been discussed. It is only necessary here to remember that when they say that the semantic component "interprets" the underlying phrase markers, they mean that its only function is to assign a semantic interpretation to the phrase markers. It can play no role in distinguishing grammatical from ungrammatical sentences. Thus the semantic component for them as for Chomsky is still secondary: it can block some anomalous readings, but it cannot function in the creation of deep structures. This feeling that the semantic component has somehow been "tacked on" to a much more important syntactic component comes out also in Chomsky's comment on Katz and Postal's proposal that transformations should be meaning-preserving, where he makes it quite clear that semantic proposals are only acceptable insofar as there are independent syntactic grounds for accepting them:

"The justification for the principle is not that it simplifies semantic theory, but rather that in every case where it was apparently violated, syntactic arguments can be produced to show that the analysis was in error on internal, syntactic grounds. In the light of this observation, it is reasonable to formulate the principle tentatively as a general property of grammar". (Chomsky, 1966.)

In Chapter 2 and Chapter 3, the question of meaning-preserving transformations has already been discussed. Chomsky's comment is quoted here simply to point out that as far as he is concerned, linguistic proposals in general must be syntactically justified. Katz and Postal too seem to accept this, since a major part of their book is devoted to showing that apparent counter examples of their (semantic) proposals can be rejected on purely syntactic grounds.

The CKP model became generally accepted by the TG community when it was incorporated into Chomsky's revised version of Transformational Grammar in Aspects of the Theory of Syntax (1965). This very influential book can be thought of as the jumping off point for the Generative Semanticists.

Reaction to the Interpretive Position and Development of Generative Semantics

In the ensuing two or three years however several criticisms of the "Aspects" theory developed. Many of these criticisms were based on a central idea - that syntax and semantics could not be separated. It should be noted, however, that the Generative Semanticists themselves were, at least originally, working within the same framework as that assumed by the CKP model. Therefore at first they felt it necessary to provide syntactic arguments to support their attacks. It is only comparatively recently that semantic or logical arguments have been thought to be sufficient in themselves. What follows is an attempt to summarize the major differences between the interpretive and generative positions by reporting, briefly, some of the arguments against the interpretive position based on this central idea.

a. The Status of Deep Structure

No-one disputes that sentences have both a semantic representation and a syntactic surface representation. The CKP model however postulates the existence of an intermediate level, the "deep structure", appearing between the base component and the transformational component. This "deep level" can be defined in many ways. However, in the CKP model one of its chief properties was to separate all those operations which take account of semantic information from those which are purely syntactic. In other words, the semantic reading of the sentence has already been determined by the time that phrase markers are input to the transformational component. (cf. Chapter 3).

McCawley (1968) in a post-script to a paper which, in its main body, accepts the CKP model, attacks this position. He claims that there are phenomena which demand the abolition of a distinct syntax and semantics. Explaining these phenomena in traditional terms causes one to miss a significant generalization. He thus argues that the separate semantic and syntactic components of the CKP model must be replaced by a single system of rules converting semantic representations into surface syntactic representations by a series of intermediate steps. If there is just one set of rules which takes semantic structures and generates from them surface syntactic structures, the semantic component has become a part of the generative mechanism of the grammar, instead of playing a purely interpretive role as in the CKP model. It is from this new generative capacity of the semantic component that generative semantics gets its name.

The second argument against the existence of a separate level of deep structure appears in a later paper of McCawley's (Meaning and the Description of Language). He points out there that linguists working within the CKP tradition found themselves forced to postulate ever more abstract structures as the deep structures of sentences. Thus, Lakoff (1965) presented arguments that the deep structure of the apparently simple sentence "John opened the door" contained two embedded sentences:

```
                S
           /        \
         NP          VP
         |         /     \
       John       V        NP
                  |         |
            (causative)     S
                         /     \
                       NP       VP
                       |         |
                       S         V
                    /     \       |
                  NP       VP   (inchoative)
                 /  \     /  \
               det   N   V    adj
                |    |   |     |
               the door  be   open
```

(Inchoative in this diagram is the abstract element which combines with adjectives to form verbs of change, e.g. "Mary's face reddened" = "Mary's face became red".)

This analysis, if it seems at first sight unnatural, can be made more plausible by considering a sentence like "Floyd melted the glass, though it surprised me that it would do so" where neither of the two surface level noun phrases can provide an antecedent for the "do so" in the "though... "clause. An analysis of this sentence similar to that given for "John opened the door" will provide an antecedent, since there will be a constituent (roughly "glass become molten") to serve as referent.

McCawley further claims that Rosenbaum's (1965) analysis of verbs such as "seem" provides another example of very abstract deep structure. This analysis involves postulating that "seem" is an intransitive verb with a sentence as its subject. The deep structure proposed for "John seems to know the answer" is then:

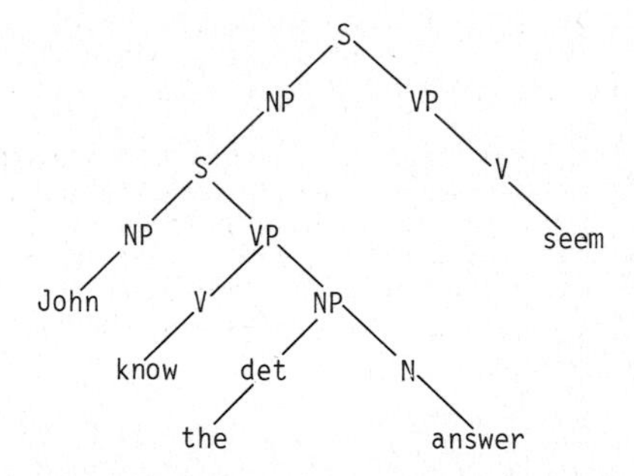

For McCawley it seems clear from the structure itself that such deep structures are very far removed indeed from the corresponding surface syntactic structure. McCawley argues too that they closely approach the "meaning" of the surface structure, i.e. that "John opened the door" <u>means</u> "John caused the door to be open". Thus he claims that underlying deep structure is a semantic structure, and that this in itself casts doubt on the existence of a separate deep structure, placing the burden of proof on those who claim that it exists.

b. The Homogeneity of Semantic and Syntactic Structures

The claim that semantic structures have the same formal nature as syntactic structures is usually summed up in the claim that a semantic structure is a labelled tree. Furthermore the labels on the non-terminal nodes of the sentence structure, like S, NP, VP, etc. are the same categories as those familiar in trees defining surface syntactic structures. The only formal difference is the labels at the terminal nodes. In surface structure the terminal nodes are the words of the language in question, in semantic structures some kind of semantic units, usually parallel to variables, constants, predicates and operators.

Clearly this claim can be broken down into several parts. First it must be shown that semantic structures are in fact trees, i.e. that the semantic structure must be able to show how smaller units can be combined into larger units. (The reader should not imagine that it is the term "tree" which is of crucial importance here. Any representation which allows combination of units to be clearly shown would do just as well, so tree could be replaced throughout by (for example) "labelled bracketing" without making any difference to the sense or the strength of the argument). McCawley (1972) argues that this point is sufficiently made by sentences such as Lakoff's (1965) example:

"John doesn't beat his wife because he loves her"

This sentence is ambiguous. Its two readings differ in the scope of the negation (reading 1: NOT (John beats his wife), reading 2: NOT (John beats his wife because he loves her)). Clearly each of these readings has the same semantic units, but has them grouped differently. The semantic representation then must be able to show these different groupings; that is, semantic structure must involve constituent structure. Ross, in a remark reported in the same paper points out that the same point is made by pairs of unambiguous sentences:

"John tried to begin to solve the problem"

"John began to try to solve the problem"

Secondly, for a grammarian still working inside the traditional transformationalist framework, it must be shown that the categories which label the non-terminal nodes of the semantic deep structure are precisely the basic categories which are independently needed for syntactic description. The first step in this argument is to demonstrate that the number of basic categories required for syntactic description is smaller than had previously been thought, since, to the proponents of this argument, it seemed intuitively clear that the number of categories needed for semantic description was small. (FOPC, for example, uses three - formula, predicate and argument.) Clearly if the same categories are to be used for both semantic and syntactic description, a fortiori the same number of categories will be used.

It was shown by linguists working within the transformational grammar tradition that many syntactic categories were derived rather than basic. For example, the categories PREDP, AUX and MODAL which appear in Chomsky (1965) can be treated simply as verbs which (like "seem" in the Rosenbaum analysis above) trigger a VP-promotion transformation (probably the same transformation as the raising transformation mentioned in Chapter 2) which detaches the VP from the embedded sentence and puts it after the verb in question. On this analysis the deep structure of "John is sleeping" would be as described in McCawley (1970):

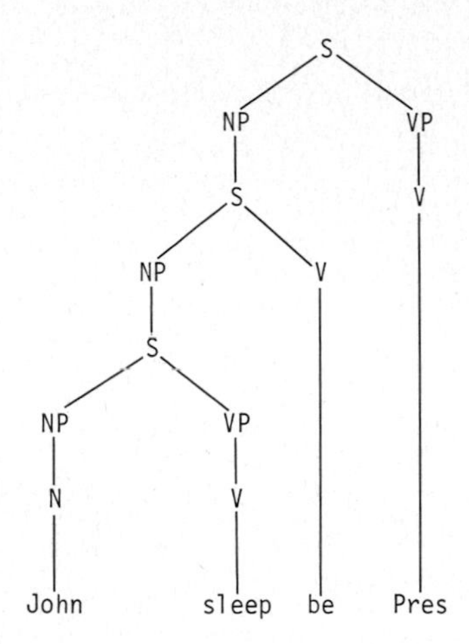

which, after the VP promotion transformation has been applied becomes:

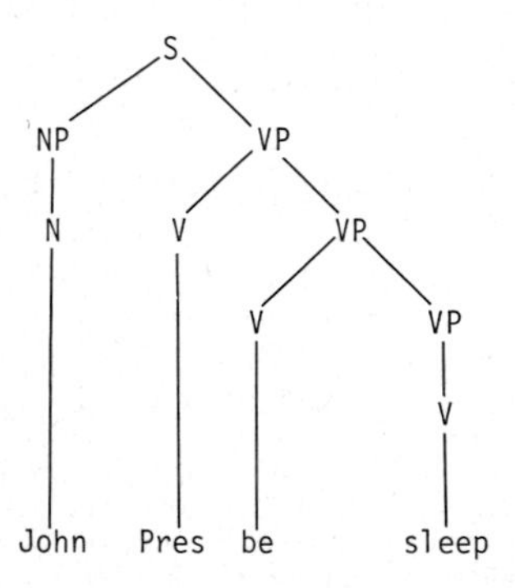

A further argument which also reduces the number of categories required for syntactic description appears in Bach (1968) where he claims that the traditional distinction between nouns, verbs and adjectives is mistaken and that "all three categories are represented by one in the base component". He claims that the underlying structures of the following pairs of sentences,

1. The man is working
2. The one who is working is a man
3. The man is large
4. The one who is large is a man

are much more similar than the traditional analysis would allow. Bach's suggested underlying structure for each of these sentences is:

1. The one who is a man is working
2. The one who is working is a man
3. The one who is a man is large
4. The one who is large is a man

The differences in the surface structures are then attributable to the operation of transformation rules rather than to differences in the base component.

As a result of these and similar arguments the inventory of categories is held to be very small. McCawley (1970) gives it as consisting only of Sentence, NP, VP and "contentive". (Contentive is Bach's name for the category which includes nouns, adjectives and verbs.) A further proposal of Fillmore's (1968) would reduce the inventory still further, in that VP would be regarded as a derived category. If these arguments hold then we have reduced the categories required to S, NP, "contentive", (which correspond to the traditional logical categories, formula, predicate and argument). These McCawley felt intuitively to be exactly the categories needed for semantic description.

As the above comparison with FOPC might suggest, the Generative Semanticists also claim that there is a strong correspondence between such categories and the categories of formal logic. We shall come back to this point later when we discuss the relationship between semantic representation and logic.

c. The Homogeneity of Semantic and Syntactic Rules

It seems intuitively likely that anyone who holds the position that semantic and syntactic structures are essentially of the same nature would also want to hold that the rules of grammar which determine well-formedness are not distinct from rules needed to determine what a well-formed sentence might mean. It is not surprising then that the Generative Semanticists hold precisely that.

The argument presented here in support of this position is one of several in Lakoff (1972). The point of the argument is not that a CKP model could not deal with the phenomena discussed (it could), only that such phenomena show, under Lakoff's analysis, the same rule functioning on one occasion as a syntactic rule, and thus determining well-formedness, on another occasion as a semantic rule, blocking one particular reading.

Adverb-preposing is a rule which moves an adverb to the front of a higher clause, as in the pair of sentences:

(1) a. Sam smoked pot last night.

b. Last night, Sam smoked pot. (Lakoff's numbering in examples)

However there are constraints on adverb preposing imposed by the verb or adjective in the higher clause. When these constraints are violated, the result is an ungrammatical sentence:

(5) a. It is mistaken that Sam smoked pot last night.

b. *Last night, it is mistaken that Sam smoked pot.

Adverb preposing then must be a rule of grammar, since it helps to distinguish grammatical from ungrammatical sentences.

But precisely the same rule in some cases helps to block a particular interpretation of a sentence. Consider the pair:

(6) a. I mentioned that Sam smoked pot last night.

b. Last night, I mentioned that Sam smoked pot.

(6)b is not a paraphrase of (6)a, since (6)a is ambiguous: "last night" could modify either "mentioned" or "smoked". In (6)b, "last night" can only modify "mentioned". That is, "last night" must have originated in the same clause as "mentioned" and has moved to the front of its own clause. If a similar sentence is written excluding the possibility that the modifier originates in the same clause as "mentioned", adverb preposing produces an ungrammatical sentence.

(6') a. I mentioned that Sam will smoke pot tomorrow.

b. *Tomorrow, I mentioned that Sam will smoke pot.

So here we have a case where the same rule with the same constraint yields in (6')b an ungrammatical sentence, but in (6)b only blocks a particular interpretation. This suggests that rules specifying well-formedness are not distinct from rules determining meaning.

d. Lexical Insertion

Earlier, when the formal nature of semantic and syntactic structures was being discussed, it was said that the non-terminal nodes of trees representing semantic structure were the same as the non-terminal nodes of trees representing surface syntactic structure. As this might imply, the Generative Semanticists hold that the terminal nodes are different. So note that if it were the case that the intermediate stages of a derivation split into two groups, one group with semantic items at the terminal nodes, the other with lexical items, it would still be possible (and sensible) to assert the existence of a level of deep structure separating the two groups. If this were so, the insertion of lexical items at the terminal nodes would all take place at one point in the derivational history of each sentence. It is worth remembering that this definition of deep structure as "the stage of the derivation immediately after all lexical insertions have been made and immediately before input to the transformational component" is the only definition which all transformational grammarians at that time would accept. But in fact it has been convincingly argued (McCawley, Meaning and the Description of Language) that lexical insertion does not all take place at one point. Consider as one example that discussed by McCawley (p.53):

> "It is obvious to John that Bill is a fool, and the former dislikes the latter"

The structure from which this is derived must have "Bill is a fool" as the subject of "It is obvious to John". Thus, at this level, "Bill" precedes "John". But in the surface representation "former" refers to "John" and "latter" to "Bill". The insertion of "former" and "latter" cannot therefore take place until after the transformation which changes the word order. (Unless, as Chomsky now believes, transformations are allowed to change meaning or unless lexical insertion is done at the very end of the derivational history, a position which Chomsky would not accept.)

e. Lexical Decomposition

The CKP model contains in the semantic component a dictionary which provides lexical items with various readings, which are to be interpreted by projection rules. Since the Generative Semantics paradigm sees semantic structure as primary, the role of lexical insertion is inverted: lexical insertion consists in replacing semantic elements by lexical items. However, this replacement is not necessarily one for one in that often several semantic elements will be replaced by a single lexical item. In this sense lexical items are decomposable into more primitive semantic units.

Although lexical decomposition is one of the features of the generative semantics position which is used also by AI workers, it is not, for that or any other reason, uncontentious. Lakoff (1974) points out that lexical decomposition was in fact the main focus of contention between the generativists and the interpretivists for some considerable period of time, since the function and structure of the lexicon seemed one of the few areas in which the two schools shared sufficient common assumptions for argument to be possible.

Postal (1971) argues that the surface verb "remind" (in the sense of "Harry reminds me of Fred Astaire") cannot correspond to any single verb element in deep structure. Rather, he argues, it must be analyzed in terms of two elements, one a main verb with properties like those of the verb "strike" in sentences like "Harry strikes me as being incompetent", the other the verbal of a complement sentence with properties like the verbal/adjectival forms in sentences like:

Max is like my brother.

Pete resembles his father.

That suggestion is similar to Max's idea.

On Postal's analysis the sentence "Max reminded me of Pete" would have an underlying structure:

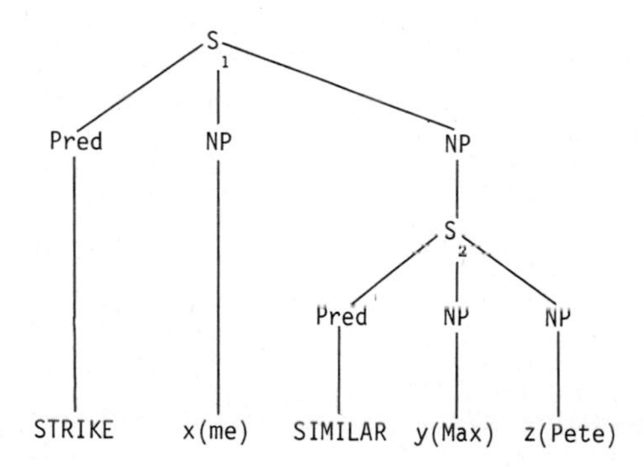

and the lexical item "remind" would not be inserted until after certain definite transformation rules have been applied in order to bring the semantic elements STRIKE and SIMILAR together into one constituent where they can be replaced by the lexical item. Postal's argumentation is too long and too complex to repeat here. But it is worth noting that if correct, it not only entails, according to Postal, that the terminal nodes of the semantic representation cannot be lexical items, as in the CKP model, but also reinforces the position in (d) above, that since lexical insertion cannot take place all at once prior to all transformations, it makes no sense to speak of a separate level of deep structure corresponding to the point after all lexical insertions have been made and before input to the transformational component.

As was said earlier this notion of lexical decomposition (the decomposition of lexical items into more primitive semantic units) has been widely used in AI. No more will be said about that here except to notice that Schank's and Wilks' work, for example, depend critically on the validity of lexical decomposition. But despite their use of lexical decomposition neither Schank nor Wilks would accept any of the arguments put forward by either side in the Generative Semantics vs. Interpretive Semantics debate as having a bearing on the issue of the validity of lexical decomposition, because the debate has been conducted solely in terms of what makes the transition from deep structure to surface structure easiest.

f. Identification of Semantic Structure with Logical Form

Very early in the development of generative semantics a claim began to appear that the apparatus required to describe the semantic structure of a sentence was closely related to the apparatus of symbolic logic. Thus Bach (1968) argues that "a system of quantifiers and variables is worth exploring as a possible part of the base rules" although he notes that the particular operators postulated for the base cannot be exactly those of symbolic logic, since (for example) in natural language, unlike logic p can entail $\sim p$. (e.g. "Some people have red hair" entails "some people do not have red hair".) McCawley (1968) complements this discussion by proposing that English must have at least two kinds of universal quantifier, the normal one and a "set exhaustion" quantifier which is involved in such sentences as "The men courted the women" which implies not that "Every man courted every woman" but rather that "Every (or almost every) man courted one or more women and that every (or almost every) woman was courted by at least one man".

Whether or not one agrees with these analyses is not really the point here: often the "logic" used is shaky, to say the least. It is enough to recognize that an interest in using some sort of logic as a technique to represent semantic structures was developed rapidly.

The same interest shows itself in McCawley (1970) where he argues explicitly that symbolic logic (with modifications) provides an appropriate system for semantic representation. He argues first that the syntactic categories needed in deep structure form a small finite set (the argument which was referred to in point (b) earlier) and then that the members of this set correspond closely to the categories of logic, especially when quantifiers are re-interpreted as two place predicates. With this correspondence accepted, he goes on to argue that the rules governing the way in which "deep" syntactic categories can be combined correspond exactly to the formation rules of symbolic logic which define a well formed formula. For example, the rule that a sentence consists of a contentive (in Bach's sense) plus a sequence of noun phrases corresponds to the formation rule in logic that a proposition consists of an n-place predicate plus an argument for each of the n-places in the predicate. (The sentence "John loves Mary" in Bach's term consists of the contentive "loves" plus the two noun phrases John and Mary, and is closely parallel to the standard logic text book example Lxy where L is the predicate "loves" and "John" and "Mary" supply the values for the place holders x and y to give a proposition.)

Summary of Section I

In this first section a number of topics has been discussed, all of them very briefly. The result has been, we hope, an outline sketch of the motivations behind the generative semantics movement and of the general position adopted by that school. The fact that topics have been introduced without criticism or argument should not mislead the reader into thinking that there is no contention about these topics. On the contrary, the literature of linguistics in the last few years is full of dispute about such matters. But to attempt to review the arguments involved would go beyond the scope of this chapter both in length and in the degree of technicality involved. In section 2, therefore, only some topics in which the Generative Semanticist position seems particularly dubious or confused will be discussed a little more critically. Before turning to this more detailed discussion, let us briefly summarize the Generative Semanticist position as we have defined it so far, using the summary offered by McCawley (1971). (The reader should not be worried by point 4. We have not covered the rather complicated question of derivational constraints. The point is left in the quotation only for completeness.)

"(1) Semantic structures are claimed to be of the same formal nature as syntactic structures, namely labelled trees whose non-terminal node labels are the same set of labels that appear in the surface structure.

(2) The notion of "deep structure" which separates syntax from semantics and a distinction between "transformation" and "semantic interpretation rules" are given up in favor of a single system of rules which relates semantic structure and surface structure via intermediate stages which deserve the name "syntactic" no more and no less that "semantic".

(3) It is held that the rules needed to determine what a grammatical sentence may mean are also needed to determine what is grammatical at all.

(4) A grammar is taken not to generate a set of surface structures but a set of derivations, and to consist of a set of "derivational constraints": constraints on what combinations of elements may occur in semantic structure, on what combinations of elements may occur in surface structure, and on how the different stages of a derivation may differ from each other.

Subsequent papers have argued that it is necessary to allow derivational constraints to mention non-consecutive stages of derivations and have elaborated and clarified the notion of semantic structure and its relation to logic and provided reasons for taking "semantic structure" to be the level of linguistic structure to which logical rules of inference apply (so that it can appropriately be called "logical structure"), provided that "logic" is taken in a sense which is broad with regard to what it covers."

SECTION 2

Natural Logic and AI

The quotation from McCawley (1971) which closed section I was very unfairly cut off at the point where McCawley was about to expand what the sense of "natural logic" must be. Let us start this section by finishing the quotation:

"..., provided that "logic" is taken in a sense which is broad with regard to what it covers (i.e. its scope includes not only inference, but other relations between the contents of sentences, not only the study of declarative sentences but of the full range of sentences in natural languages, and not only the logical properties of and, or, not, if, all, and some, to which logicians have been unduly attached, but the logical properties of all elements of content) and narrow with respect to the linguistic constraints on the entities that are recognized (e.g. rather than the "atomic predicates" being allowed to be arbitrary functions, as in the work of most logicians, the existence and atomicity of putative "atomic predicates" must be linguistically justified). I will use the term natural logic (following Lakoff) to refer to logic in this sense."

We noticed in section I that from the beginning it was recognized that logic, in the sense, presumably, of first-order predicate calculus, was not adequate to deal with natural language. But the suggestions about what extensions to symbolic logic may be needed given by McCawley in the quotation above are very considerable indeed: it is a little difficult to see how the result could be regarded as any sort of "modification" of standard symbolic logic. And the demands made on this natural logic by later work have extended the term still further.

An early demand was that natural logic should be able to deal with presupposition. Quite what is meant by presupposition here is extremely unclear. Most linguists quote Strawson (1952) as the source of the notion of presupposition, and, although he did not introduce the term, certainly his treatment has been by far the most influential. His prime example is the statement made by the sentence "All John's children are asleep", which, he says, presupposes the truth of the statement "John has children". If John has no children then the statement "All John's children are asleep" fails to be either true or false. Note that the statement conveyed by the negated sentence "Not all John's children are asleep" can have a truth value if and only if the statement "John has children" is true. This is an important part of the definition of presupposition since it serves to distinguish presupposition and entailment.

But the use of the term presupposition by linguists is not (or at least not usually) Strawson's use. Fillmore (1969) talks of uses of the noun "bachelor" when used as a predicate as presupposing that "the entities being described are human, male and adult". Thus the sentence "That person is not a bachelor" is only used as a claim that the person is or has been married, never as a claim that the person is a female or child. That is, "it is simply not appropriate to use this sentence, or its non-negative counterpart, when speaking of anyone who is not a human male adult". This cannot be presupposition in Strawson's sense, and not only because it is the use of the word bachelor which is said to convey presupposition: but also because we should hesitate to say, if this sentence were used of a female, that the sentence thereby had no truth value (as Strawson's definition would require us to do). The most that we might want to say is that the statement is misleading - or obviously true.

In the same paper Fillmore distinguishes two other categories of presuppositions: the first category is rather like what Searle (1969) calls "normal input output conditions" in that they have to do with "the fact that the hearer must understand English, be believed by the speaker to be awake, not totally paralyzed, etc., which have to do with "questions of good faith" in speech communication". It seems reasonable to accept these as normal pre-conditions for the successful performance of uttering any sentence, that is for achieving by its utterance whatever it was that one meant to achieve (without bothering too much here about all the different sorts of things one might want to achieve by different utterances of the same sentence on different occasions). But such pre-conditions cannot be matters of grammar, except in the rather trivial sense that grammatical analysis has to assume that they have been fulfilled.

The second category has to do, he says, with "the use of the definite article" in such sentences as "Please open the door", and are to do with such matters as the existence and specificity of the door. The debate about referring expressions has been raging in philosophical circles for some time, and it would not be appropriate to enter it here. For our purposes it is enough to note once again that our reactions when such a presupposition is violated are not to regard the sentence as non-sensical (imperative sentences cannot lack a truth value), but simply to ask for more information (which door?) or to feel that we have been badly misled if no door turns out to exist.

All these senses of presupposition, and more, have been used by Generative Semanticists. For Lakoff (1972) the term presupposition seems to be very broad indeed, since he introduces his section on presupposition by saying "Natural language is used for communication in a context, and every time a speaker uses a sentence of his language to perform a speech act he is making certain assumptions about that context" and then goes on to give some very strange examples of presupposition. Take his example (22) (Lakoff's numbering):

"Sue pretended that her boss realized that she had an IQ of 180"

which Lakoff claims presupposes "She had an IQ of 180". It may be lack of imagination on my part that prevents me from seeing what logically prevents someone with an IQ of 140 pretending that someone else realized that she had an IQ of 180 - out of self-aggrandizement, honest mistake or whatever. And certainly I cannot see that the "Sue pretended..." sentence fails to have a truth value if "She had an IQ of 180" is false.

(Although Lakoff is not consistent about what definition of presupposition he is using, his footnote on p.655 (ibid.) seems to imply that he takes something like the Strawsonian definition to be basic: "I take the term "presupposition" as meaning what must be true in order for a sentence to be either true or false".)

It is perhaps a little unfair to castigate Lakoff for his treatment of presupposition in this paper, since he himself acknowledges in a footnote (ibid. p.658) that his treatment of presupposition is woefully inadequate. But he does not seem to have drawn from this the conclusion that presupposition (in the sense used in his paper) covers too wide an area to be dealt with adequately in a grammar. Rather he seems to have gone on to widen it. Thus in Lakoff (1974) we find:

"The term "presupposition" has been used (confusingly) to cover two very different concepts. (1) Logical presupposition: a relation holding between two logical structures. We can further define an extended sense of logical presupposition as a relation holding between two surface structures just in case the logical structure of the one logically presupposes the logical structure of the other. (2) Pragmatic presupposition: a relation holding between an individual and a proposition... I assume the study of logical presuppositions is part of the study of natural logic. I take pragmatic presuppositions as being handled by transderivational syntactic rules, which will take into account logical, syntactic, lexical and phonological facts of the language in question".

This seems to make quite clear a demand implicit in Lakoff (1972) that grammar should take account of the speaker's assumption in making an utterance. It is therefore legitimate to ask what kind of a grammar this would have to be. Since speaker's assumptions are innumerable, frequently wrong, uncertain, misguided or downright perverse, it cannot be grammar in any normal sense.

The problem here comes, perhaps, from a deliberate ambiguity about the purpose of a grammar, an ambiguity inherited by the Generative Semanticists from the transformational school. Most proponents of transformational grammar would claim that a grammar is intended as much to analyze sentences as to generate them, despite the fact that analysis presents particular problems of a more difficult nature than those of generation (cf. Chapter 2).

The problems of analysis are even more acute for the Generative Semanticists, since they want to incorporate into the grammar matters which are inaccessible to the understander. The understander, and hence an analysis system, cannot with certainty get at a speaker's intentions and assumptions, for example. Of course, a system can say that on the basis of an utterance the speaker could normally be taken to have particular assumptions and intentions. But this is not to say that the speaker must in fact have those assumptions and intentions. Anybody with a little linguistic ingenuity can concoct situations in which the "normal" assumptions do not hold. Thus it is not possible to incorporate rules within an analysis grammar which define what a speaker's assumptions and intentions must be, as the Generative Semanticists seem to wish.

It might be thought that the same problem would affect AI natural language understanding systems. But this is not actually so. AI systems typically work within a fixed context (the context of the text being analyzed) and thus limit the problem to discovery of what is meant within that context, and, at the same time, work with uncertain assumptions. That is to say that an AI system knows that it is guessing at what is being assumed, is prepared to revise its assumptions and is prepared to back up and correct those assumptions which turn out to be wrong. There is a theoretical point surfacing here too concerning the purpose of a grammar. A grammar can only coherently be designed on the basis that, when used for analysis, it is to be used to determine what the text, independent of any particular speaker's assumptions or intentions, can properly be taken to mean. Any attempt to design a grammar or any other criterion is doomed to fail, simply because it will be attempting to account for factors which are in principle inaccessible to the analyzer.

The situation when a grammar is being used to generate sentences is rather different. It seems here clear that speaker's beliefs can be incorporated into the grammar since those beliefs and the means of accessing them are defined within the system. But the situation is not as clear as it seems, in that the specification of the rules involved is extraordinarily complex. Even with what are apparently the most transparent examples it is possible to find a counter example. "All John's children are asleep" seems to commit the speaker to believing that John has children. But perhaps the speaker only believes that his hearer believes that the children in the next room are John's (although in fact they are not) and simply speaks so to avoid confusion.

So far I have attempted to make an outline case against generative semantics, at least in its later manifestations, by pointing out that the attempt to include presupposition, in a very broad sense, in a grammatical system leads to a situation where grammar breaks down, both because of the magnitude of the task, and, more importantly, because grammars are not the sort of thing which can correct assumptions which turn out to be wrong.

This latter charge can be directed against the entire generative semantics enterprise. It is a natural property of transformational grammars that during the course of a derivation no decision is made that the derivation has in some way gone wrong, and that it is necessary to backtrack to correct the derivation. When a grammar is a syntactic device this can be regarded as relatively unimportant. The grammaticality of the sentence is determined by the system itself. However, once a demand is made that the grammar should contain and take account of knowledge of states of affairs in a world external to the grammar itself, the acceptability of the sentence is not determinable solely within the system. Thus the ability to recognize a mistake in one's knowledge which has led to a "wrong" derivation becomes of crucial importance.

As we noted earlier, many AI systems are designed in such a way as to make possible the formation of tentative assumptions. Systems designed in this way are not vulnerable to the same theoretical criticism. Such tentative assumptions are typically based on very general inductive knowledge about facts in the world. Ideally the system may, later, correct the assumptions in the light of further knowledge.

It is possible, of course, to redefine grammar in such a way that it must be able to make tentative assumptions and correct them. But it should be clear that this redefined sense of grammar is not a definition of some sort of mechanism which can decide whether a sentence is grammatical in the usual sense of grammatical for most speakers independent of context. It is the definition of a design criterion for an AI system in which what is aimed at is understanding the sentence, and grammaticality, in the sense defined above, is of at best secondary importance. Existing AI systems do attempt to meet this criterion. Thus some systems, like Wilks', may reject the use of a conventional grammar completely, using only semantic notions in the analysis of texts, while others, like Charniak's, may concentrate almost exclusively on the assumptions used in understanding a sentence. (The two approaches are not so far apart as may appear from this brief account, since Wilks also makes extensive use of inference mechanisms in analysis.)

The criticisms of the generative semantics position based on its treatment of presupposition hold true of the generative semantics treatment of logic in general. For, says Lakoff (1974):

"Natural logic is the study of reasoning in natural language. As such it differs from classical logic in many respects. First, its scope is much broader. Classical logic concerned itself with concepts like and, or, if then, not, every and some. More recently logicians have attempted to deal with a handful of other concepts, such as logical necessity, obligation, belief, knowledge, certain adverbs, many, few, etc. - mostly in isolation as minor extensions of classical logic. A complete natural logic would have to deal with all of these concepts together, plus hundreds and perhaps thousands more - depending on how many primitive concepts natural language can be reduced to. In short it is the full study of the conceptual resources of natural language."

To see how impossible a demand this is to make of any kind of deductive logic, the reader need only think for a short time of what must be meant by "the full study of the conceptual resources of natural language". Natural language reasoning is rarely strictly logical: the conceptual resources of natural language must presumably include the mystical but wierdly rational language of the schizophrenic and the intuitive ability a good psychiatrist shows to construct a whole framework from hundreds of scattered verbal clues, as well as the ordered argument of the scientist making a case. The only kind of logic which might possibly deal with such disparate matter is, again, a logic which works on probability and induction, which can make likely assumptions and change its assumptions when necessary. Again, the resulting paradigm is not that of classical logic, no matter how extended, but that of artificial intelligence with its direct and explicit concern to investigate "the conceptual resources of natural language". (For a much fuller discussion of this topic, see Wilks (1972b).)

As a footnote to this argument it is worth pointing out that only within the AI paradigm does Lakoff's (and others') notion of grammaticality make sense. In Lakoff (1974b) he says:

"I don't think that one can in general say that sentences in isolation are grammatical or not. Instead one has to ask whether a given sentence can be paired with a given logical structure in a given context. If one views grammars as generating relations between sentences, contexts and logical structures, the notion "grammaticality" has no meaning. In its place there is the concept of the degree of well-formedness of quadruples of the form (sentence, logical structure, context, conveyed meaning)".

It is this position which allows him sometimes to draw conclusions based on forms which occur only in a particular dialect, as well as to mark as unacceptable sentences which seem perfectly normal but which he considers to be logically inappropriate in a particular context. Within linguistics such arguments make no sense. Grammar is, or should be, concerned with the set of sentences which are acceptable to most speakers of the standard form of that language, independent of context. We have already seen that insisting that context must be taken into account leads to a definition of grammar which is not viable. To see what a strange position accepting conclusions based on a particular dialect leads one into one need only consider some of the odder sentences found in some dialects. For example, in the dialect of English in which the author was brought up, sentences like "Given birth to a boy she has, isn't it?" are extremely common, but surely no one can seriously believe that it is possible to make general judgments about English based on such forms?

Within the AI paradigm however it makes sense, as we saw earlier, to demand that context be taken into account. It is also possible within the same paradigm to set up a particular grammar for a particular subset of a language and to legislate that anything which the system can understand is grammatical.

CONCLUSION

The whole of this last section can be summarized very briefly: the demand that grammar should take into account not only well-formedness and semantic acceptability but also all possible aspects of the context of use of a sentence renders the production of a grammar in any normal sense of the term impossible, since grammar can no longer be understood as a means of determining which sentences are grammatical for the majority of speakers of the standard form of the language. On the other hand, such a demand does provide an intelligible and coherent basis for work within the paradigm of artificial intelligence. The reader needs only to look at the other chapters in this book to see that this is so.

E. Charniak and Y. Wilks (eds.), Computational Semantics

PARSING ENGLISH I

Yorick Wilks

In each of the preceding chapters, the reader has encountered some formal structure, proposed by someone as the appropriate structure for some sentence, or sentences, of natural language: transformational derivations, predicate calculus, the trees of Generative Semantics, and so on.

Given any proposed structure for natural language, syntactic, semantic or whatever, we may distinguish between the structure itself, and its correlation with pieces of language. Among such correlations we may distinguish between parsings and assignments. By "parsing" here is meant the provision of definite procedures of application, and by "assignment", the provision of no more than a list of correspondences, between chunks of language and formal structures. Logicians often tell us that, say, the structure of the sentence "John loves his wife's sister" is of the form EXISTS(X) EXISTS(Y) EXISTS(Z) (X = JOHN AND Y = WIFE(X) AND Z = SISTER(Y) AND LOVES(X,Y)), but they rarely, if ever, provide a parsing of that structure onto the sentence, for the procedure is considered either obvious or outside their field. That is what I mean by an assignment, or the provision of a list of correspondences between sentences and structures.

At this point let me try and say a little what a parsing is rather than what it is not. Let us consider the structure specified by one of the simplest grammars: a content-free phrase structure grammar (see Chapter 2). This might contain a set of rules like the following:

S ⟶ NP VP

NP ⟶ Determiner Noun

VP ⟶ Verb NP

Determiner ⟶ The, the

Noun ⟶ dog, cat

Verb ⟶ likes

Sentence: The dog likes the cat

This sentence "The dog likes the cat" is considered to be produced by the listed rewrite rules of this grammar. The grammar is thought of as implicitly defining a procedure; starting with the symbol S, (the left hand side of the rule), and rewriting it by its corresponding right hand side, giving new symbols which in turn are rewritten using other rules (although the same rule can be used again if it is possible to do so, providing that only one symbol is rewritten each time a rule is applied). The production of this sentence is usually represented by a phrase-structure tree as follows (also called a phrase-marker) where every production of branches from a node corresponds to the application of one of these rewrite rules, as just described. Eventually symbols are written that are actually words of English, and the process can go no further when every node is an English word.

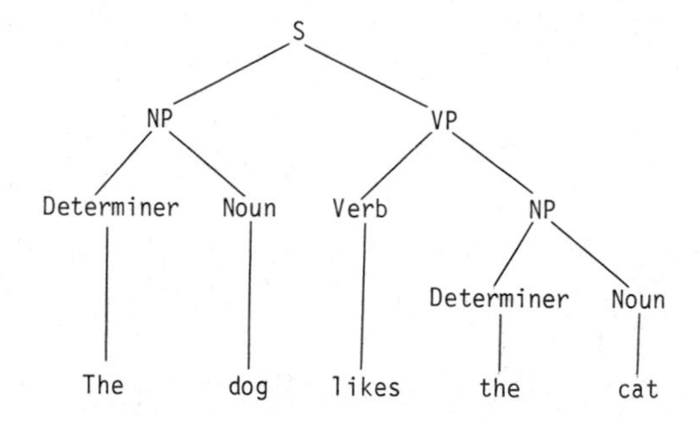

The tree diagram above might be held to reflect certain syntactic relationships between the words of the sentence. Thus in this structure, "The" has been tied to "dog" by the application of the rule "NP ⟶ Determiner Noun" and that relation of "The" to "dog" is the dependence of a determiner on the noun it determines. However, the generation process, just described, would only be a parsing process if, by good fortune, the sentence we generated happened to be the one we were trying to parse.

Those who advocate the use of phrase-structure grammars for parsing would want to start with the sentence and end up with the tree structure above. Let us see how they might do this.

For the purpose of phrase-structure parsing we think of each word in the sentence to be parsed as attached to one or more grammatical categories: in this case, as we see from the rules, "dog" is attached to a single category "Noun". There are two ways of doing the parsing: top-down and bottom-up. Bottom-up is the more straightforward way, and is illustrated by the next figure. The words of the sentence are listed and starting from the left of the sentence, we attempt to replace each one by its category, and then to rewrite successively pairs of category symbols by reversing the grammar's rewrite rules, until we reach the final sentence symbol S. The lines of the derivation (the tree above upside down, in fact) can then be considered as the parsing:

The dog likes the cat

Determiner dog likes the cat

Determiner Noun likes the cat

NP likes the cat

NP Verb the cat

NP Verb Determiner cat

NP Verb Determiner Noun

NP Verb NP

NP VP

S

Top-down parsing starts, not with the words and their categories, but simply with the symbol S which is then rewritten with our rules as described initially. The procedure continues to generate sequences of categories until it finds one that will match directly onto the leftmost word of the sentence, "The". This procedure continues, as illustrated by the next diagram, until the last word at the right is reached and then once again the lines of the procedure are the parsing.

Looking for: S : | the dog likes the cat

Looking for: NP | VP : | the dog likes the cat

Looking for: Determiner | Noun VP : | the dog likes the cat

Looking for: Noun | VP : the | dog likes the cat

Looking for: VP : the dog | likes the cat

Looking for: Verb | NP : the dog | likes the cat

Looking for: NP : the dog likes | the cat

Looking for: Determiner | Noun : the dog likes | the cat

Looking for: Noun : the dog likes the | cat

Looking for: the dog likes the cat |

The two derivations (bottom-up and top-down) are formally equivalent. The | marker in the above diagram indicates the point in the sentence reached.

Several things should be noted here: parses do not have to be left to right, they could easily be the other way round. The structure is rarely as trivial as this one, and usually a word will have several possible categories assigned to it in the dictionary and part of the job of the parsing process is to find out which of those roles the word has in any particular sentence. So "run" has a Verb category in "I run for a bus" but a Noun category in "I built a new chicken run", (a run is a cage for chickens). So, if we used either of the above processes to parse "I run for a bus", we would find that we produce the correct structure:

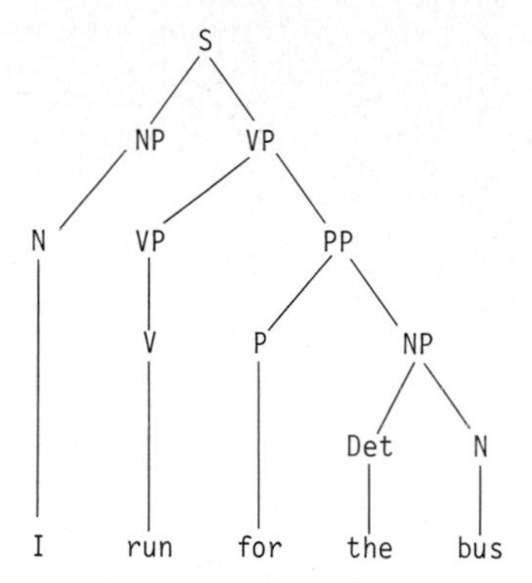

but never a structure where "run" had its N (Noun) category, because there is no sequence of proper grammar rule applications that could produce a tree for that sentence with the node above "run" labelled N. In particular, there is a rule:

VP ⟶ V (and then V ⟶ run)

but no rule:

VP ⟶ N (and then N ⟶ run)

So one reading of "run" is excluded by the parsing of this sentence.

At this point, another important pair of technical terms enters: "breadth-first" and "depth-first" parsings. Breadth-first is the parallel treatment of all possible alternative structures at a given time, none is given any precedence. They are all developed until one or more reach the success symbol S (if the parsing is bottom-up). In depth-first parses the alternative structures are treated sequentially, and if one combination is no longer a possible success (because, in this grammar no more rewrites of a string are possible even though the parsing has not been completed), then the system must back-track (see Chapter 1), which means going back and continuing one of the alternative structures that had not yet been tested. Thus, for example, if "run" had been considered with its N category in the sentence above, then, on the bottom-up strategy, "I run" would be replaced by "N N" and, in the grammar we have, there is no rule which rewrites "N N" as anything else. It is discovering that which causes a back-track and the replacement of N by, in this case, a V category for "run".

In the case of transformational structures in particular, a sentence is often parsed so as to produce a structure quite different from the original form of the sentence. So, to take a classic example, a passive sentence like "I was given the money last week" might be given a parsed structure representing it, whose form was actually that of "Someone gave me the money last week", as regards the order of its principal constituents. So we may say that a parsing may produce a structure quite different from the superficial form of the input sentence. Grammatical parsing programs of this sort were a growth industry in the Sixties, but they will not be discussed in any detail here beyond the introduction of the basic notions. That is because one of the assumptions of this book is that grammatical (or syntactic) parsing of the sort described is not fundamental, and that it need not be even a preliminary to assigning a useful meaning structure to sentences. However, that will be argued only indirectly, and much later on.

Parsing, then, has been introduced in a very general way, without discussing whether or not a given structure is an interesting one, in the sense of being worth assigning to a sentence. Moreover, certain kinds of structures, such as logical ones, have a life of their own, as it were, independently of their being parsed onto sentences. Let me make a second distinction at this point that will be important in the examination of systems that follows. It is between AI language systems that are primarily content-motivated and those which are primarily structurally-motivated. It will not be claimed that the systems discussed are of one sort or the other, since there is as always a continuum in these matters, but we will ask readers to keep the distinction in mind during the description and discussion of systems.

Structurally-motivated systems are those which, whatever their natural language capacities, are set up in order to solve problems that are essentially non-linguistic, and are concerned with the relation of the proposed representation of structure to other structures. To put it another way, structurally motivated systems are those which have a fairly narrow and non-linguistic problem in mind, and only bother extracting the content of the input natural language to the limited degree that it is relevant to the problem being considered.

A paradigm of this would be Bobrow's early STUDENT (Bobrow 1968) (but done in 1964) that solved elementary algebra problems. It did indeed take in a form of restricted English but only kept track of certain algebraic relations, such as "the sum of", etc. This program also illustrates another property of structurally motivated systems - namely that the structures they parse into are justified by their function within the problem domain rather than their ability to represent the content that language can express. So STUDENT used linear equations as its "semantic representation" since they were most suitable for algebra problems. Similarly, it could be argued that the Predicate Calculus representation used in many early systems was justified primarily by its compatability with the simple logical problems the systems dealt with, rather than its ability to represent the content of language.

Content is, in a strong sense, the problem of natural language understanding. It is the problem that has dogged mechanical language analysis since its inception in the Fifties, and it centres on the problem of systematic ambiguity. A brief, but tendentious, historical sketch will make this point: the "machine translation era" of the Fifties and early Sixties was a bold attempt to do an enormous task: extract the content of natural language utterances. It failed, and for three main reasons: word sense ambiguity or polysemy, structural ambiguity (where we will concern ourselves only with case ambiguity as illustrated by the ambiguity of prepositions) and referential ambiguity (the ambiguity of pronouns). It failed to develop and implement structures to deal with these features of even non-metaphorical natural language. Generative linguistics was born partly in response to this failure: it has provided complex structures, but has lost the sense of any definite task to be performed, and the most recent sign of this failure of nerve has been a retreat from any relation to parsing, and towards the doctrine that the true structure of language is its logical structure (see Chapter 4).

And so we come to the AI approach, which represents a return to definite tasks and procedures and now, slowly but surely, a withdrawal from the structurally-motivated approach. Most early work on language within AI was highly structurally motivated: the importance of the Predicate Calculus as the basic form of representation of language was simply taken for granted by many leading AI workers. What they were interested in was proving theorems via the derivation of one predicate calculus representation from another, and as far as they were concerned there simply was no "problem of language" for the three "intractables" of language ambiguity listed above were just ignored. They really did seem to believe that natural language was a projection of some underlying logical format. Slowly but surely, reality has crept in. Most recently, in a survey of AI language systems, Terry Winograd (Winograd 1973) has distinguished between "first" and "second" generation AI language systems, modestly placing his own (which I shall discuss below) at the end of the first generation. This distinction will not be examined in any detail, but it does draw a line almost exactly where AI language systems were described above as emerging from a wholly structurally-motivated approach.

WINOGRAD'S UNDERSTANDING SYSTEM

To get a better look at some of these issues, probably the best place to start is with Winograd's own program. His system runs as a dialogue, in real time, between a human operator who types in messages, and the system proper, called SHRDLU, which displays on a screen pictures of a closed world of colored blocks and pyramids, a box into which they can be put, and an arm or crane that can move the objects about. SHRDLU displays its replies to the operator by writing on the same screen.

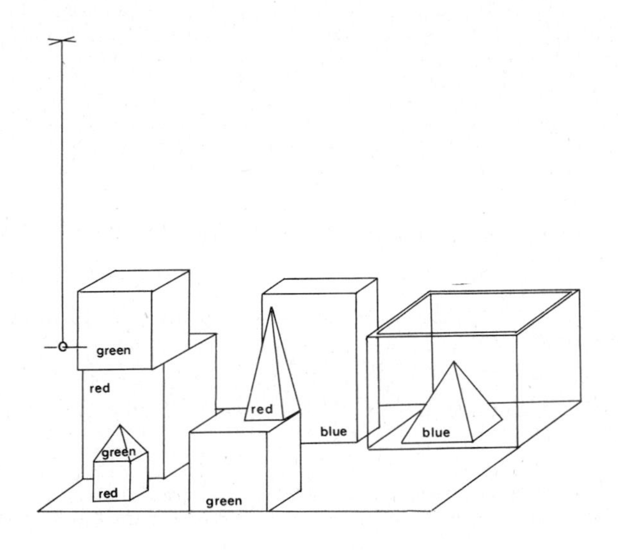

Winograd's blocks world

The following is a discontinuous sample of the dialogue Winograd gives in his book. SHRDLU's replies are in upper case:

pick up the big red block

OK

find a block which is taller than the one you are holding and put it into the box

BY 'IT', I ASSUME YOU MEAN THE BLOCK WHICH IS TALLER THAN THE ONE I AM HOLDING
OK

what does the box contain?

THE BLUE PYRAMID AND THE BLUE BLOCK

had you touched any pyramid before you put the green one on the little cube?

YES, THE GREEN ONE

when did you pick it up?

WHILE I WAS STACKING UP THE RED CUBE, A LARGE RED BLOCK AND A LARGE GREEN CUBE

why?

TO GET RID OF IT

This ingenious program was also able (to a limited extent) to accept new definitions of words, such as "steeple"; to make use of what it knew about the properties of the objects described, such as that a block could have its top cleared off, but a pyramid could not; and also to remember what it had done before, as in the sample above.

The syntactic analysis program was written in PROGRAMMAR, a procedural language related to PLANNER (see Chapter 1). This means that a familiar phrase structure rule such as

$$S \longrightarrow NP + VP$$

(to be interpreted: a sentence consists of a noun phrase followed by a verb phrase) would be expressed as:

```
(PDEFINE SENTENCE
   (((PARSE NP) NIL FAIL)
    ((PARSE VP) FAIL FAIL RETURN)))
```

The details of the notation need not detain us at this point; what is important is that Winograd's grammar is not the conventional list of rules, but small sub-programs like the lines above, that actually represent procedures for imposing the desired grammatical structure.

The first level of linguistic procedures in the system applies a "systemic grammar", due to M. A. K. Halliday (1970), which imposes a hierarchical structure of clauses on the input sentences, which seem to be drawn from a vocabulary of about 175 words.

In terms of the notions set out earlier Winograd's parsing is top-down, and depth-first, with no automatic back-up. The parsing program for each grammatical category is a functional definition in PROGRAMMAR, which can be stated either as above for SENTENCE, or as a flow-chart as below for VP:

DEFINE program VP

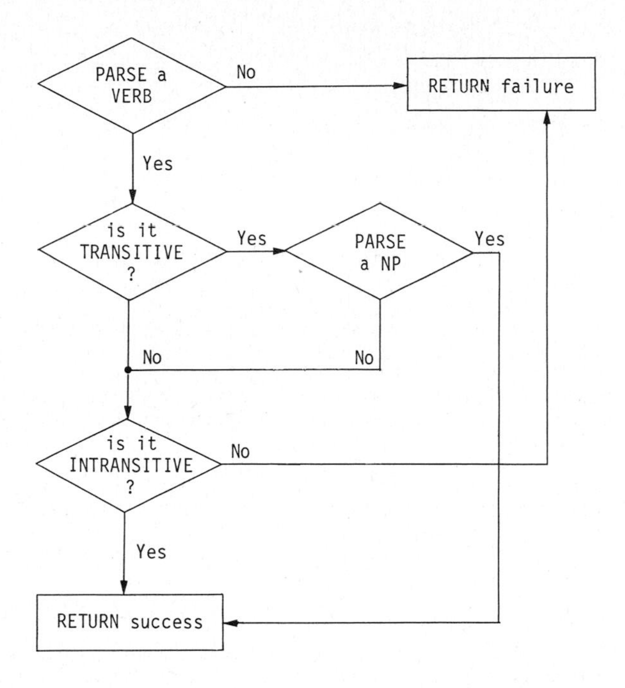

Here is Winograd's own account of the start of this top-down parsing procedure for the sentence "Pick up a red block" (where the material in [ ] is added explanation and not Winograd's own):

"The CLAUSE program looks at the first word to decide what unit the CLAUSE begins with. If it sees an adverb, it assumes the sentence begins with a single-word modifier [slowly, Jack lifted the book]: if it sees a preposition, it looks for an initial PREPG [on the top of the hill stood a tree]. If it sees a BINDER, it calls the CLAUSE program to look for a BOUND CLAUSE [before you got there, we left]. In English (and possibly all languages) the first word of a construction often gives a very good clue as to what that construction will be. In this case, "pick" is a verb, and indicates that we may have an IMPERATIVE CLAUSE. The program starts the VG program with the initial VG feature list (VG IMPER), looking for a VG of this type. This must either begin with some form of the verb "do" [do not call me!] or with the main verb itself [call me!]. Since the next word is not "do" it checks the next word in the input (in this case still the first word) to see whether it is the infinitive form of a verb. If so, it is to be attached to the parsing tree, and given the additional feature MVB (main verb). The current structure can be diagrammed as:

```
(CLAUSE MAJOR)
    (VG IMPER)
        (VB MVB INF TRANS VPRT) ----- pick
```

TRANS and VPRT came from the definition of the word "pick" when we called the function PARSE for a word".

After this syntactic parsing, a number of "semantic specialists" attach semantic structures to specific syntactic ones. In the case of "a red cube", the following structure is built up by an NP "semantic specialist":

```
        (GOAL (IS ?X BLOCK))
        (GOAL (COLOR ?X RED))
        (EQDIM ?X) ------------- PLANNER description
    (BLOCK MANIP PHYSOB THING) --------- markers
```

The first three lines will eventually form the bulk of a Micro-Planner program which, when evaluated, will seek an object X that is a block, is equidimensional (EQDIM) and is red (where "red" itself has a definition in the system that restricts its application to objects with the feature PHYSOB). The last line of the figure is a set of "semantic features" read off right to left from the following "feature tree" (see Chapter 3):

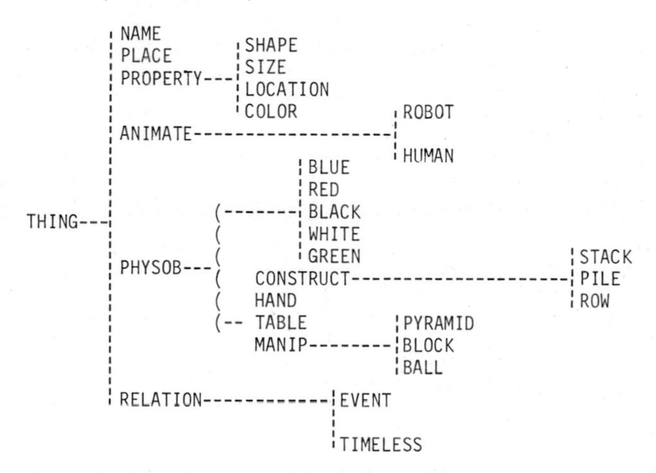

The semantic structure of "the red cube" can be used by the deductive component of the system, before evaluation resulting in the actual picking up, to see if such an object is possible. If it were not, (an "equidimensional pyramid" would not be), the system could go back and try to re-parse the sentence.

The meaning of verbs in SHRDLU is more complex. The semantic component has access to a definition for "pick up" just as it does for "red" and "block", and this definition will enable SHRDLU to translate "pick up statements" into Microplanner in a manner analogous to that for noun phrases.

There are two complications here. Firstly, "pick up", unlike "red", is defined in terms of other concepts in the system: in particular, in terms of GRASP and RAISEHAND, which are two of the three basic actions in the system. Secondly, there are two types of verb definition, semantic and inferential. Winograd does not give the semantic definition for "pick up", but here is the one for "grasp", which is a closely related verb.

```
(CMEANS ((((ANIMATE))((MANIP)))
        (EVAL (COND ((PROGRESSIVE)
                     (QUOTE (GRASPING 2 *TIME)))
                    (T (QUOTE (GRASP 2 *TIME)))))
        NIL))
```

which says essentially that grasping is something done by an animate entity to a manipulable one (first line). More of the real content of such actions is found in their inferential definition. Here is the one for "pick up":

```
(CONSE TC-PICKUP
        (X)
        (PICKUP ?X)
        (GOAL (GRASP ?X) THEOREMS)
        (GOAL (RAISEHAND) THEOREMS))
```

This definition allows the program to actually carry out the "pick up" command - if it is possible to do so in the simulated world, as it would not be, for example, if there were already a block on top of the red one. PICKUP is being defined in terms of a number of more primitive sub-actions, such as GRASP and RAISEHAND, each of which must be carried out in order that something may indeed be picked up. These sub-actions themselves have inferential definitions: the one given for "GRASP", for example, is somewhat different from its "CMEANS" definition given above, although the inferential definitions are also, in some sense, definitions of meaning as well as programs for actually carrying out the associated commands.

One reason for the enormous impact of this work was that, prior to its appearance, AI work was not very linguistically interesting, while the systems of the linguists had no place for the use of inference and real world knowledge. Thus a very limited union between the two techniques was able to breed considerable results. Before Winograd there were few programs in AI that could take a reasonably complex English sentence and ascribe any structure whatever to it. In early classics of "natural language understanding" in AI, such as Bobrow's STUDENT (1968) problem solver for simple algebra, input sentences had to be short and of stereotyped form, such as "What is the sum of ....?"

Conversely, in linguistics, there was, until very recently, little speculation on how we understand the reference of pronouns in such elementary sentences as "The soldiers fired at the women and I saw _several_ fall", where it is clear that the answer is both definite, and that finding it requires some inferential manipulation of generalizations about the world. The reader should ask himself at this point _how_ he knows the referent of the pronoun in that sentence.

SOME DISCUSSION OF SHRDLU

So far, there has been little or no critical discussion of Winograd's work. What would critics find to attack if they were so minded? Firstly, that Winograd's linguistic system is highly conservative, and that the three-way distinction between "syntax" and "semantics" and "deduction" may not be necessary at all. Systems that do not make these distinctions will be discussed below, and Schank's has already been introduced in Chapters 5 and 6. Secondly, that his semantics is tied to the simple referential world of the blocks in a way that would make it inextensible to any general, real world, situation. Suppose "block" were allowed to mean "an obstruction" and "a mental inhibition", as well as "a cubic object". It is doubtful whether Winograd's features and rules could express the ambiguity, and, more importantly, whether the simple structures he manipulated could decide correctly between the alternative meanings in any given context of use. Again, far more sophisticated and systematic case structures than those he used might be needed to resolve the ambiguity of "in" in "He ran the mile in five minutes", and "He ran the mile in a paper bag", as well as the combination of case with word sense ambiguity in "He put the key in the lock" (door lock) and "He threw the key in the lock" (river lock).

The blocks world is also strongly deductive and logically closed. If gravity were introduced into it, then anything supported that was pushed in a certain way would have, logically have, to fall. But the common sense world, of ordinary language, is not like that: in the "women and soldiers" example given earlier, the pronoun "several" can be said to be resolved using some generalization such as "things shot at and hurt tend to fall". There are no logical "have to's" there, even though the meaning of the pronoun is perfectly clear.

Indeed, it might be argued that, in a sense, and as regards its semantics, Winograd's system is not about natural language at all, but about the other technical question of how goals and sub-goals are to be organized in a problem-solving system capable of manipulating simple physical objects. If one glances back at the definition of "pick up" quoted above, one can see that it is in fact an expression of a procedure for picking up an object in the SHRDLU system. Nothing about it, for example, would help one understand the perfectly ordinary sentence "I picked up my bags from the platform and ran for the train", let alone any sentence not about a physical action performable by the hearer. One could put the point so: what we are given in the PLANNER code is not a sense of "pick up" but a case of its use, just as "John picked up the volunteer from the audience by leaning over the edge of the stage and drawing her up by means of a rope clenched in his teeth" is not so much a sense of the verb as a use of it.

In this book there is no discussion, beyond the very brief mention here, of the excellent and widely known work of Woods (1972). His system, based on what is called an "augmented state transition network grammar", is undoubtedly one of the most robust in actual use, in that it is less sensitive to the PARTICULAR input questions it encounters than its rivals. The reason for not treating it in depth is that both Woods and Winograd have argued in print that their two systems are essentially equivalent (Winograd 1971), (Woods 1973), and so, if they are right, there is no need to discuss both, and Winograd's is, within the AI community at least, the better known of the two.

Their equivalence arguments are probably correct: both are grammar-based deductive systems, operating within a question-answering environment in a highly limited domain of discourse. Winograd's system of hints on how to proceed within his PROGRAMMAR grammar, is, as he himself points out, formally equivalent to an augmented state transition net-work, and in particular to the ordering of choices at nodes in Woods' system.

There is a low-level problem about the equivalence of Woods' and Winograd's systems, if we consider what we might call the received common-sense view of their work. Consider the following three assertions:

(1) Woods' system is in some sense an implementation of a transformational grammar

(2) Winograd's work has shown the irrelevance of transformational grammar

for language analysis - a view widely held by reviews of his work.

(3) Woods' and Winograd's systems are formally equivalent - a view held by both of them.

There is clearly something of an inconsistent triad amongst those three widely held beliefs. The trouble probably centers on the exact sense which Woods' work is formally equivalent to a transformational grammar - not a question that need detain us here, but one worth pointing out before passing to the further topics in Chapter 9.

E. Charniak and Y. Wilks (eds.), Computational Semantics

SEMANTIC NETS AS MEMORY MODELS

Greg Scragg

INTRODUCTION

In Chapters 1 and 6 it was argued that there is a need for world knowledge in the understanding of language. There must of course be some sort of representation for this knowledge. We refer to the problems of designing structures for representing knowledge as the problems of memory. However, it is necessary to discuss how to get at information while discussing what it looks like. One cannot divorce structure from function. We refer to these two aspects as the active and static aspects of memory respectively, and discussion of the two will be intertwined.

"Memory" is used by people in related disciplines in slightly different ways from that we are using here. It will help clarify what we mean when we refer to memory if we first rule out some things that we do not mean. Obviously we are not referring here to the usual computer science definition of memory as the place where information is stored in a computer. And we are not referring to the "man on the street" definition which equates memory with the ability to remember. From a psychological point of view we will not be discussing the various hypothesized "memories", but rather we will restrict memory here to refer to long term memory representations (see Chapter 10 for long term - short term distinction) together with the low level processes which access that representation. Finally, it is not necessary to discuss how the information actually came to be stored in memory (learned) in the first place, so this too will not be discussed.

This is primarily a chapter on representation of "memory" as opposed to "language". However, the author believes that there is little (if any) difference between such a representation and the representation of language at the deepest level. True, there are a number of things that must be in memory but which are hard (if possible at all) to express in natural language, such as the smell of a rose or how to ride a bike. But presumably all things expressable in language must be representable in memory. For this reason we will not hesitate to include in this chapter some work aimed at representing language, but which is equally applicable to the representation of memory.

The first question we will attack is that of "low level structure". That is, how can we represent information at all? How can we represent a simple fact? In chapter 1, we showed briefly how the predicate calculus could be used to represent knowledge. It provides both a representation (FOPC formulas) and a method for inferring new facts from old (theorem proving). In addition it has the advantage that it is a notation that should already be familiar to most people in computer science and related fields, and for which there is an extensive metatheory already developed. There is however another representation format that has proved even more popular with AI researchers in recent years. That is the "semantic net". In what follows we will use the semantic net as the principle model of memory, referring to other forms to make points that are not applicable to semantic nets.

SEMANTIC NETS

Quillian (1968) is generally credited with developing the concept of a semantic net (although the structure used in Raphael's SIR (1964) (as seen in Chapter 1) has much the same appearance and we will talk about it as if it were a semantic net). In its simplest form, a semantic net is a collection of points, called nodes; each can be thought of as representing a concept (the exact definition of concept is not important at this point. It will suffice to think of it as an entity about which information is stored). Each node may have a name, such as "boy" or "gift". Nodes without names generally will correspond to concepts that are not representable by simple English names, such as "the cute little girl with the long blond curls who lives around the corner". A node may be connected by a directed arc (arrow if you prefer), called a relation, to any other node in the net. This relation will have a label. Graphically we might have:

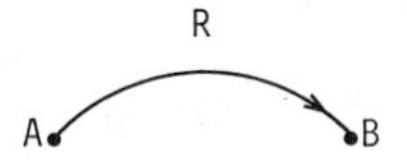

which would be read as R connects A to B. The intended interpretation of this structure is that relation R holds between A and B or A stands in relation R to B. Note that B does not necessarily stand in relation R to A. This is why the arc must be directed and is represented by an arrow. For example, if A is Anna, B is Bill and R is LIKES, we have:

Bill may not be the least bit interested in Anna, so we cannot assume:

Any node may be related to an arbitrary number of other nodes, each of those nodes to any number of other nodes, and so on. As more and more nodes and arcs are added, the graphical representation starts to look like a network of lines, thus giving it the name Semantic Net (Semantic, because historically such nets were first used to represent meanings of natural language expressions).

The network can be built up to represent very complicated inter-relationships. In:

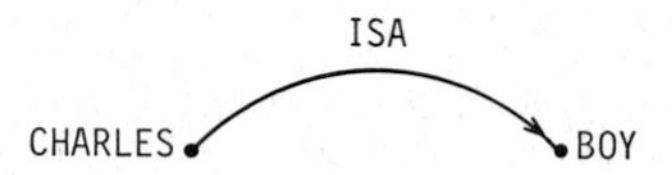

CHARLES represents a particular member of the set of all boys.

Charles hit the blond haired girl

could be represented as:

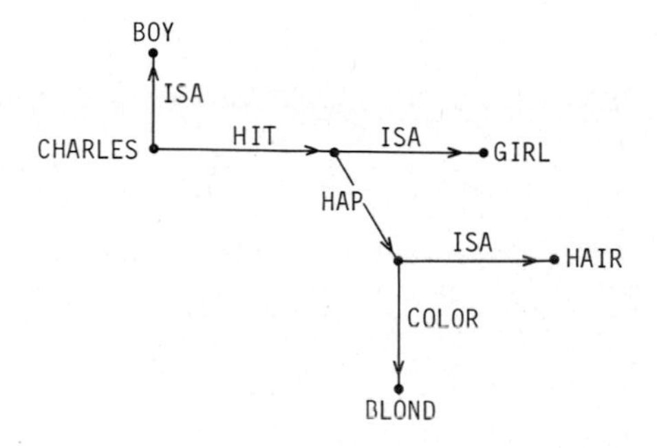

where HAP means has-as-part. Note that there are unnamed nodes representing the girl and her hair. (Such unnamed nodes will sometimes be given arbitrary symbols like C1, C2, etc. for internal reference.) If the additional information that the girl was tall were added, the node representing the girl would be expanded to:

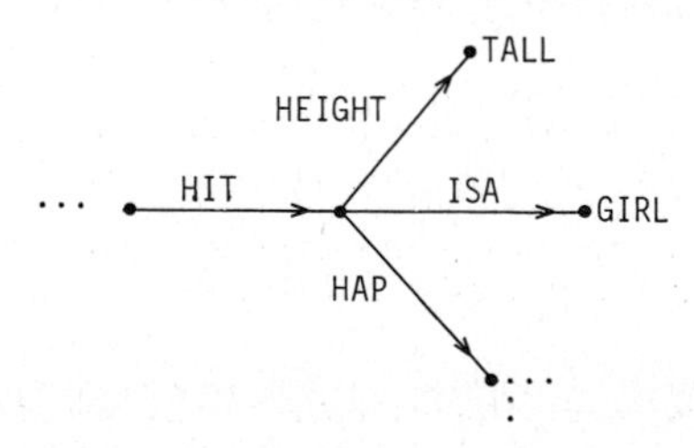

The smallest unit of information in a semantic net is the triple A R B. But the basic unit is the node or concept. A concept has information content only because it is related to other nodes. The information can be thought of as existing in the relations. A concept with no relations attached to it is empty of content and presumably inaccessible. It is a concept about which nothing is known (which is a strange concept indeed).

The word "concept" is usually used to refer to both general and specific concepts. A specific concept, like this piece of paper, or the particular boy who hit the blond girl in our last example, will be called a "token". The non-specific concepts will be called "types". Often non-specific concepts will be class types like GIRL and HAIR. In other cases they could possibly be interpreted as classes (TALL = the class of tall things?) but we find such interpretations strained and will not insist that all "types" are classes. (The reader who is familiar with Quillian's original paper may notice that the usage we are making of type and token here is slightly different from that of Quillian.) We saw in our last diagram how a token (the blond girl) was connected to its type (girl) by the relation ISA (IS-A and ELEMENT have also been used to express this relation). In these cases we can say that the token node (blond girl) is a "token of" its type node (girl). Types (girl) which are sub-types of other types (human) may be connected to the larger type by the relation SUPERSET (or S.S. or some other equivalent).

It is important to emphasize the type - token distinction. Systems which fail to do so will usually get into trouble because they cannot tell the difference between an entity(token) and a set (type) which has no members. To see this suppose we had the (improper) structure (1) as:

(1)

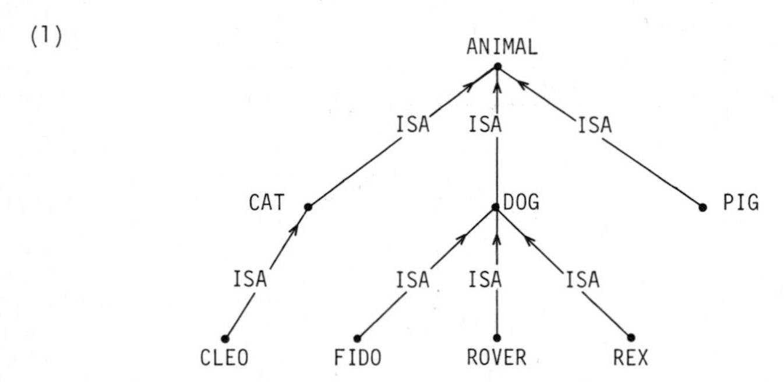

a substructure of a data base. If the system using this data base were asked the question:

How many animals do you know about?

it could answer "three" by counting the immediate subsets of animal. Or it could answer "five" by following all chains of ISA's to their ends (CLEO, FIDO, ROVER, REX and PIG). But there is no way to recognize that there are actually four distinct animals (Cleo, Fido, Rover, Rex) without flagging the types and tokens in some way, such as using two different relations - ISA and SUPERSET. An alternate method would be to flag every node with a label to indicate whether it is a class or a token.

With this last example we have for the first time entered into a discussion of the active aspect of memory. In that example we needed to discuss information retrieval (find out how many animals you know about) in order to make a point about the form a net should take (the need for a type - token distinction). Indeed, much of the early popularity of nets was due to its ability to make certain kinds of retrieval and inference easy. In particular it can nicely handle inferences of the "Socrates is a man, all men are mortal" variety. Here the example is "a canary is a bird, all birds have wings".

```
CANARY ----S.S.----> BIRD ----S.S.----> ANIMAL
   \                   \                  \
   COLOR               HAP                HAP
      \                   \                  \
      YELLOW              WING               SKIN
```

If this were part of a net, the color of canary can be found by simply following the COLOR arrow from CANARY to YELLOW. To determine if a canary has wings (note that HAP doesn't connect CANARY to WING here) it is only necessary to notice that BIRD HAP WING and CANARY S.S. BIRD so canaries must also have wings. Similarly it can be seen that canaries have skin by repeating the syllogistic argument once more. Thus semantic nets provide an implicit method of inference for some situations.

There are two more properties of semantic nets which contributed to their early popularity. First, semantic nets suggest certain ways to reduce the amount of information it is necessary to store. It is not necessary to note that canaries have wings and crows have wings and robins have wings and ducks have wings. Each such property need only be related to the most general type node which has the common property (bird in this case). This representation has further appeal in that it explicitly shows what most birds have in common. The second fact which gave impetus to the semantic net idea was the results of psychological experiments that implied that human information storage might also be of this form (Collins and Quillian (1968) but see Chapter 10 for later results). It was noted that human reaction time increased steadily as questions sought properties which were more and more general (e.g. canaries are yellow, have wings, have skin, etc.) This is exactly what semantic nets would predict because more general properties are further from the specific tokens, so more nodes must be examined to find them.

Generalizing Nets

Originally semantic nets seemed to offer something for everyone, a real panacea for the psychologist and the computer scientist. However, later psychological results suggested that they were not inherently good psychological models and computer scientists soon found formal problems with the model in that as more complicated data was considered, the nets used in early systems rapidly became insufficient: restrictions or additions were needed in the basic structure to make them continue to be viable models.

Some of these formal problems are dealt with in a memory model being developed by Norman, Linsey and Rumelhart (see Norman & Rumelhart 1975) as the nucleus of a comprehensive psychological model. Their memory contains several improvements or extensions to the basic notion of a semantic net.

One problem with the representation we have developed so far is how it handles facts like "John hit Mary", which would be represented as:

One problem with this is that it does not allow one to add additional information about the event such as when he hit her, where (both location of the blow on the body and location where the entire action occurred), if a stick was used, etc. This problem can be solved by introducing concept nodes for events as well as objects. Doing this we get:

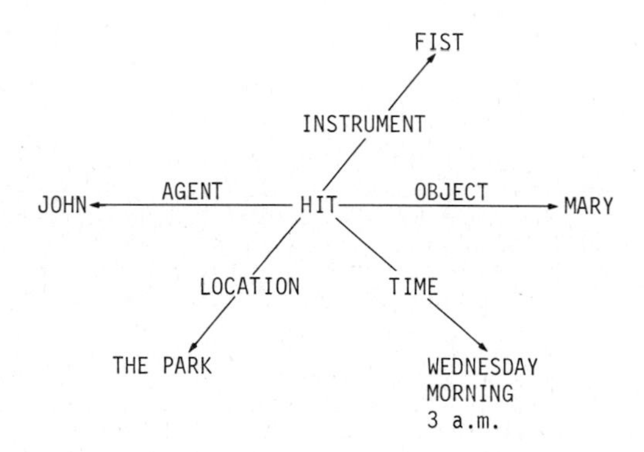

Notice that while before we distinguished who hit whom by locating one at the tail of the relation arrow and one at the head, this is no longer possible as now John and Mary each have their own arrow. Instead we distinguish by calling one the agent and the other the object, giving the representation a case-like appearance.

But this representation still has problems. Consider the representation for the following:

John hit Mary and Bill hit Sue.

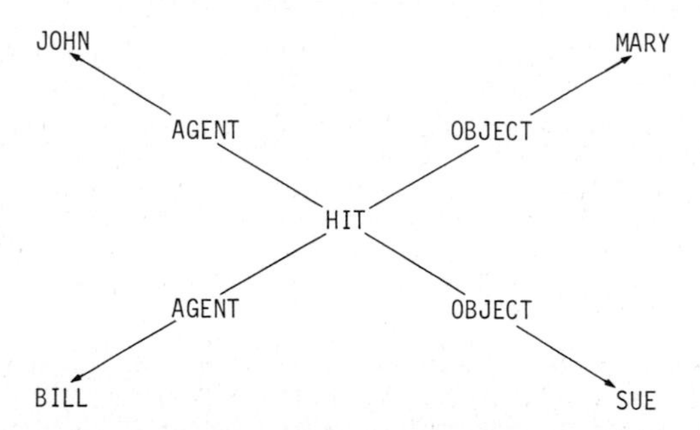

Now it is not clear who hit whom and how many acts of hitting actually occurred. (Nor can we simply allow two HIT nodes because, having the same name, there would be no way to distinguish them for accessing purposes.) To avoid this problem we must distinguish particular acts of hitting from the notion of "hitting in general". Doing this gives us:

(2)

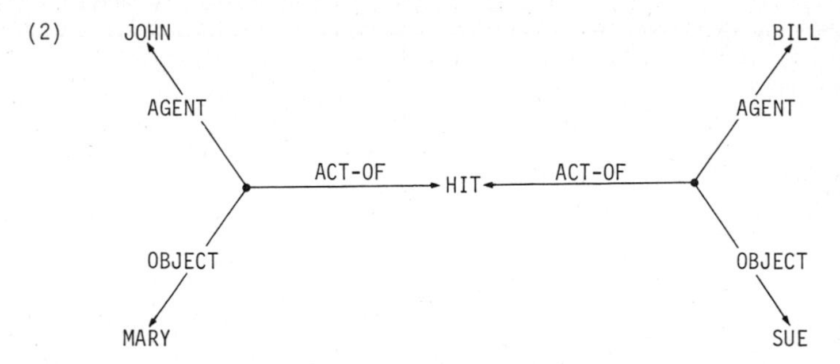

The node HIT in the center represents the concept of hitting. The two occurrences of someone being hit are related to the general notion, HIT, by the relation ACT-OF. The ACT-OF relation between action concepts is parallel to the ISA relation between object concepts.

The node HIT in (2) could be expanded to include:

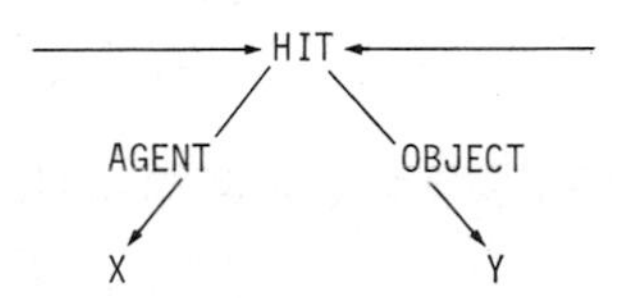

This information is descriptive of the general concept of hitting as its location indicates. It implies that the notion is incomplete (or even unimaginable) without an AGENT and OBJECT. (Hence each of the instances (ACT-OF's) of HIT must have both an AGENT and an OBJECT.) Such required attributes can be thought of as parallel to the case relations discussed in Chapter 4, except that here they are requirements on memory and not directly on language structure. Note that a semantic net representation strongly suggests that a case-like structure should be used instead of a positional structure as in a predicate calculus representation. So while before predicates like "hit" were links between nodes (or more formally <u>relations</u> between nodes) now they are nodes themselves. Since originally in our representation all predicates were relations we could use the terms pretty much interchangeably. But now we can't. So we will continue to use the term <u>relation</u> to indicate the links between nodes, while <u>predicate</u> will now refer to the general concept nodes like HIT. Furthermore, we will call structures like (2) "<u>predicate structures</u>" to emphasize the fact that therein HIT is a node (predicate) rather than a link.

This change from link to node will have a number of important effects on the use of semantic nets which will become apparent as we progress. For now, note that relations like AGENT will be among the most common in the net. Every instance of (essentially) every action will have an AGENT (or ACTANT or whatever - the wording is not intended to imply the use of any particular case system such as we saw in Chapter 4.)

One result of the introduction of predicate structures is that the equivalent of any N-ary FOPC predicate (see Chapter 1) can now be represented in a semantic net. Prior to this addition, only two place predicates had semantic net equivalents, i.e. a relation arc. The price of these new advantages is the increased size of the data base and probably an increase in retrieval cost. We should warn the reader, however, that in spite of the fact that all modern semantic nets have something like the predicate structures described, the authors of such systems continue to talk as if they didn't and use the old notation as an abbreviation for the new. We will do so here also. However, when an arc is drawn that really represents a node, it will be distinguished by a circle node in the center of the arc. Thus:

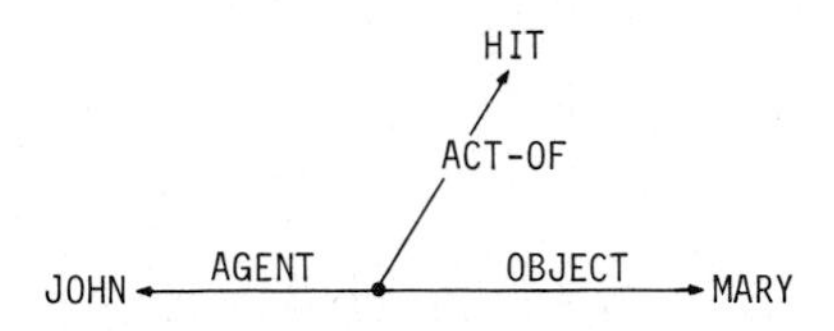

becomes:

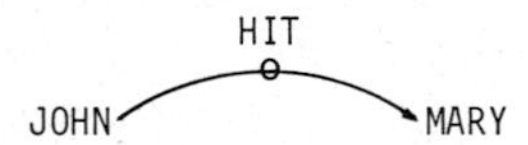

It is occasionally necessary to represent items in a data base which are not known to be true, or even that are known to be false. For example, to represent:

Peter said that he went to the store

requires that

He went to the store

be represented in some way even though it may be known to be false. One way to do this is to tag every predicate node with a truth value of TRUE, FALSE or UNKNOWN. Thus "Peter said that he went to the store" could be represented as:

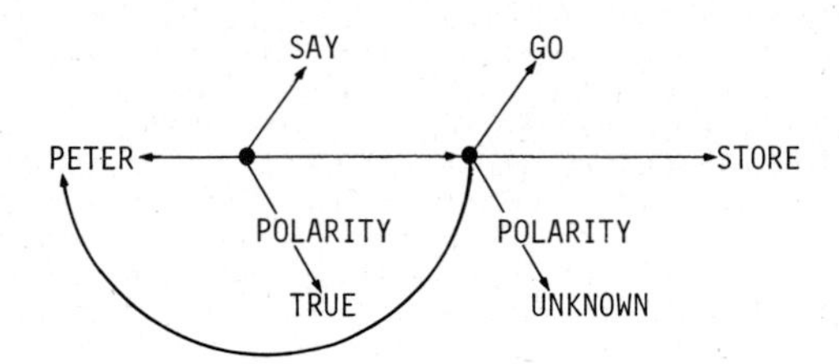

Here we know that Peter said this but not whether he actually went. However, this convention is not sufficient. Consider:

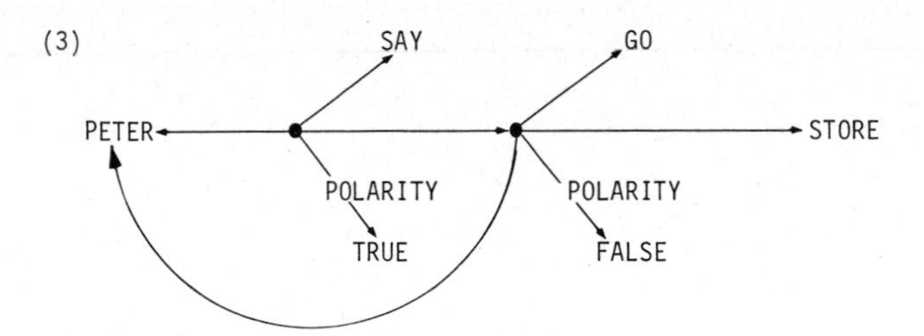

This is actually ambiguous between:

Peter said that he went to the store, but he really didn't

and:

Peter said that he didn't go to the store.

One convention that avoids this problem was created by Schubert (1975). He uses the logical operator NOT as a predicate. Thus:

Peter didn't go to the store

is represented by:

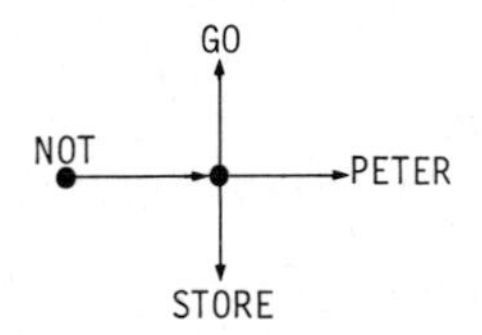

He adds the additional convention that a node is actually asserted (claimed to be true) in the data base if and only if no arrow in the diagram points at it. Thus in the last diagram the negation is asserted but the affirmative statement is not. In this way the two meanings of (3) would be represented.

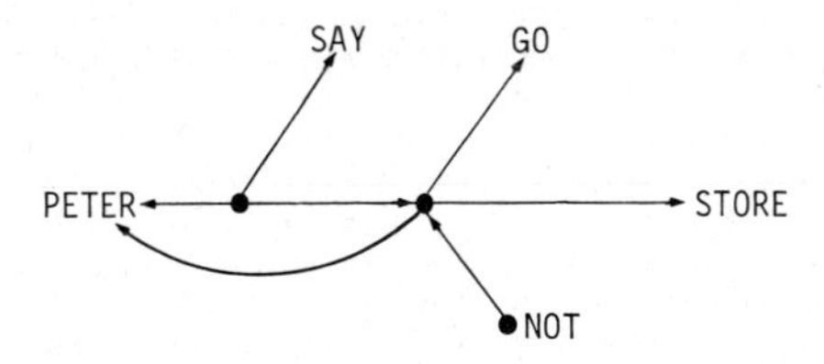

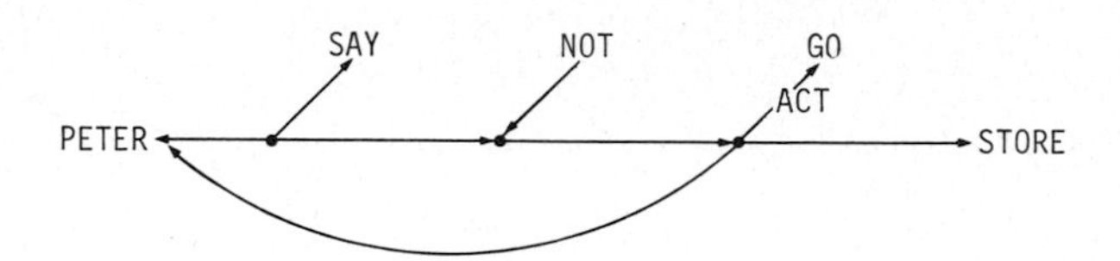

Implementation

A note is in order regarding conversion of semantic nets to computer representations. Until now we have tried to discuss semantic nets without considering the problems of actually representing them in a computer. There is at least one important question which is not obvious from discussions of semantic nets as a graph, but which is forced upon us if we actually try to implement a semantic net based system. We cannot actually store lines and nodes in a digital computer, so we must select some alternate representational scheme. We have two basic choices:

List, for each node, all the relations which apply to it (along with the names of the nodes to which the relations point.) That is:

<u>JOHN</u>
HIT BILL
LOVES MARY

List, for each relation concept, all of the pairs of nodes that are connected by that relation.

<u>LOVE</u>
JOHN, MARY
JOAN, FRANK

(It would, of course, be possible to do redundantly both of these or perhaps some combination.) The second choice used alone is essentially unworkable, because the effect would be to provide a storage where all occurrences of a given relation are grouped together. This would not be too bad if our relations were of the type described earlier (and used above) such as LOVE and HIT. To see if JOHN LOVEs anyone, we could simply look under the relation LOVE where there would be a list of all pairs (A,B) such that A love B is true. If JOHN appeared on the left in the list, then we assume that he loves someone (in particular, the person matched with him on the list). However, recall that LOVE is now represented by a predicate structure and the relations are things like AGENT and OBJECT. Because most (or all) predicates have an AGENT, searching the list of AGENT relations would be equivalent to searching through every predicate in the data base to see if JOHN was ever an agent and then checking to see if the predicate is an ACT-OF LOVE. Even after this exhaustive search, we would not know who was the OBJECT of his LOVE.

On the other hand, if everything were indexed by node and we wanted to answer the above questions, we would look at the node for JOHN to see if he were the AGENT of any predicate:

```
JOHN                     LOVE7

  AGENT LOVE7              ACT-OF LOVE
      :                    HAS-AGENT JOHN
      :                    HAS-OBJECT JILL
JILL

  OBJECT LOVE7
```

If any such predicate is an ACT-OF LOVE, then we know that he does love someone. Note that LOVE7 (an instance of LOVE) is also a node so there will be an index of relations in which it appears. To find out who JOHN LOVEs simply look at the HAS-OBJECT relation on LOVE7. Thus, it is essential that the data be stored in (at least) the node format.

Notice that in the above illustration of indexing we actually were storing redundant information. To express the fact that John loves Jill we used five entries where in theory we could have done with three, say the three listed under LOVE7. In practice, however, this is not a viable option as such a scheme would require that any time we wanted to know if John loved anybody the system would have to look through every node to see if it had the properties attributed to LOVE7 above. Obviously in such a case, saving on (redundant) index entries only to be forced into such a search would be false economy. But in other cases the situation is not so clear. Consider the relation SUBSET. A complete indexing would not only store under A that it is a SUBSET of B, but also under B that it is a SUPERSET of A. Again, this is redundant information, but as we have seen it is sometimes much faster to retrieve a fact if the inverse of a relation is explicitly stored. If we only index under A in A SUBSET B, then it will be very hard to find all the SUBSETs of a node and vice versa. On the other hand, it seems improbably that people always have both SUBSET and SUPERSET stored. Notice that the question:

Dachshunds are ____ ?

is easily answered with "dogs", so presumably (DACHSHUND SUBSET DOG) or some equivalent is stored under DACHSHUND. But:

Name ten kinds of dogs

is much harder. (You probably do know ten, but unless you are especially knowledgeable about dogs it will take you a while.) This would argue that DOG does not have all its subsets listed under it. But exactly when both relations and their inverses should be stored is an unsolved problem.

A Quick Comparison of Nets and Calculi

An apparent advantage of using a predicate calculus representation is that the entire power of FOPC is made available to make deductions on the data base without further effort. The FOPC provides a means for representing quantifiers and other concepts, not easily expressed in semantic nets. Try to represent the equivalent of:

EXISTS(X) (P(X) AND Q(X) IMPLIES R(X))

One problem with FOPC as a data representation is its lack of a good organization for facts (see Chapter 1). Anyone who has attempted to do proofs in the FOPC knows that it is not always easy to select the formulas and deduction rules for calculating a specific fact. The techniques currently employed in theorem proving programs are even less efficient than people at selecting the most relevant material. There is no reason in principle, of course, that many of the organizational features of a semantic net could not be introduced into FOPC (indeed many of them have) but we must recognize nevertheless that FOPC has not proved as suggestive as semantic nets with respect to good organizational methods.

Although we have described semantic nets as if this were an essentially different method of representing memory from the FOPC (and, indeed, we think they really are different in intent), they can be shown to be essentially equivalent in expressive power, although not necessarily in convenience of use.

To see that this is so in an intuitive way, note the similarity between a collection of two argument FOPC predicates and the computer representation of a semantic net described in the previous section (i.e. concept-relation-concept triples). However, there are problems with any attempt to show that they are exactly equivalent. Most of these center around the question of quantification. How does one quantify relations in a semantic net? Most advocates of semantic nets are vague or even inconsistent when they describe the meaning of their relations in terms of quantification. For example, if

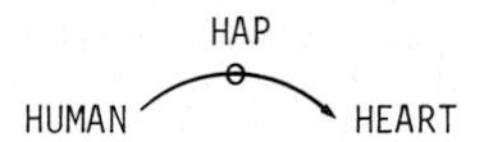

is a substructure of the data base, the usual interpretation is that all HUMANs have HEARTs. But if

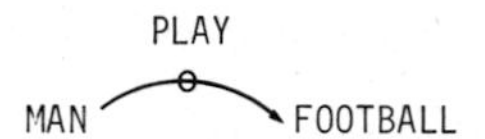

is part of the data base, we are usually told that it means that men sometimes play football. (Or, more precisely, while we assume every human has a heart unless being told specifically otherwise, we would only assume that some people play football.) It turns out that it is impossible to simply assign an interpretation to relations which would cover all possible quantifications of the relation. To see this note that there are six unique quantifications for a two place predicate in the predicate calculus:

(4) a) FOR-ALL(X) (FOR-ALL(Y) (RX,Y))

b) FOR-ALL(X) (EXISTS(Y) (RX,Y))

c) FOR-ALL(Y) (EXISTS(X) (RX,Y))

d) EXISTS(X) (FOR-ALL(Y) (RX,Y))

e) EXISTS(Y) (FOR-ALL(X) (RX,Y))

f) EXISTS(X) (EXISTS(Y) (RX,Y))

However, in a semantic net, there are only four possible quantifications obtainable by appending a quantifier to each end of a relational arc:

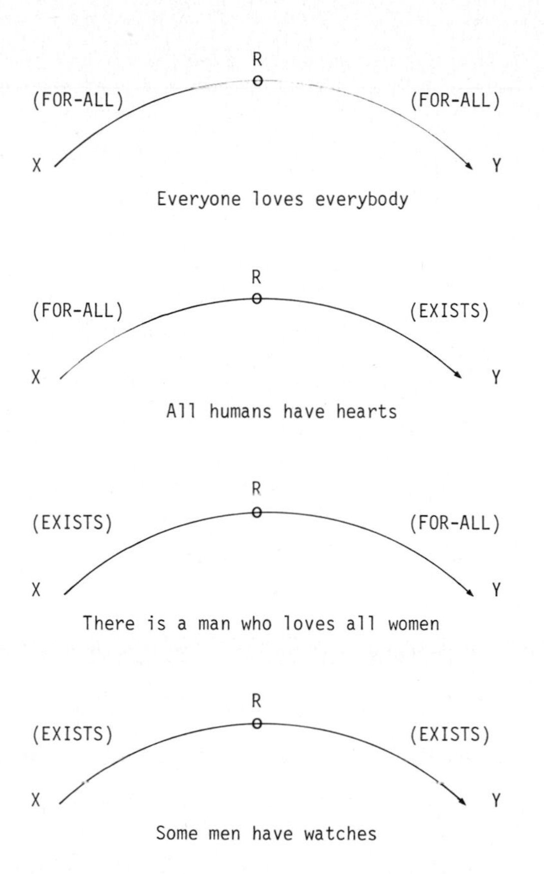

If a semantic net is to have all the quantificational power of the FOPC, then some further (more complicated) structural rules must be found.

Schubert (1975) has shown one way of constructing most of the structures available in the FOPC in a semantic net. To do this he first puts the predicate calculus representation of the statement into Skolem form (described in Chapter 1), a form which has no existential quantifiers and all universal quantifiers are outside of the body of the expression. In his graph, nodes that are universally quantified are specially flagged (he used a dashed circle). Any node that corresponds to a skolem function which depends on a universally quantified node is connected (by a dashed arc) to that governing node.

For example:

Every man loves a woman

has two interpretations, representable in the FOPC as:

FOR-ALL(X) (EXISTS(Y) (MAN(X)IMPLIES(WOMAN(Y)AND LOVE(X,Y))))

and EXISTS(Y) (FOR-ALL(X) (WOMAN(Y)AND(MAN(X)IMPLIES LOVE(X,Y))))

In Skolem form these are:

FOR-ALL(X) (MAN X IMPLIES WOMAN(MANS-WOMAN(X)) AND LOVE(X,MANS-WOMAN(X)))

FOR-ALL(X) (WOMAN(A) AND(MAN(X)IMPLIES LOVE(X,A)))

(A is a constant)

In a semantic net, these can be diagrammed as

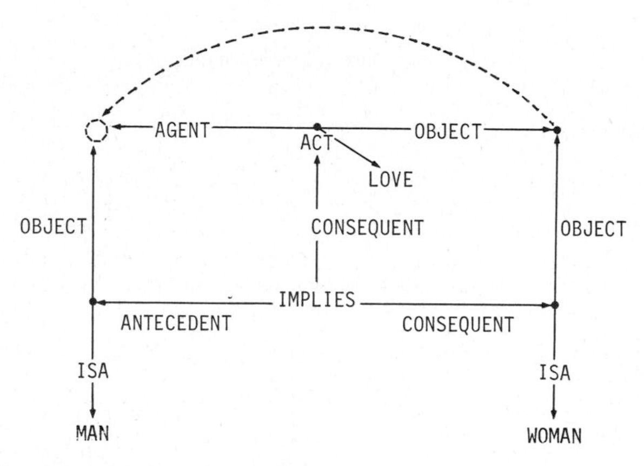

(6) Every man has a woman to love

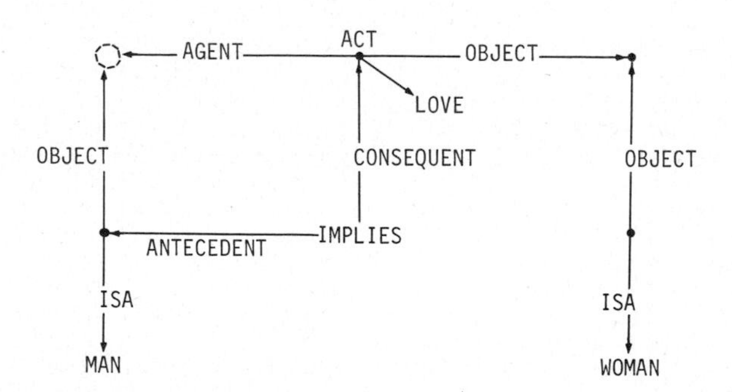

(7) There is a woman and every man loves her

The nodes drawn as dashed circles are universally quantified. The dashed arrow indicates the Skolem function dependence of the woman loved on the man doing the loving. Note that in (6) the only asserted relation is the implication, but that in (7) the existence of the woman is also asserted.

A little thought will probably convince you that by such techniques the entire representational power of the FOPC can be mimicked in the semantic net. (Similarly any link in a semantic net may be thought of as a binary predicate of the FOPC. So, semantic nets and the predicate calculus can be thought of as having equivalent representational powers.)

This is nice enough in theory. But in practice, Schubert's constructs are much too bulky. In the above examples, if it were also known that Max was a man, and we wished to determine if he loved a woman, there would be no less than eight links which would have to be traversed in the shortest path from Max to woman, as can be seen in the following simplified diagram:

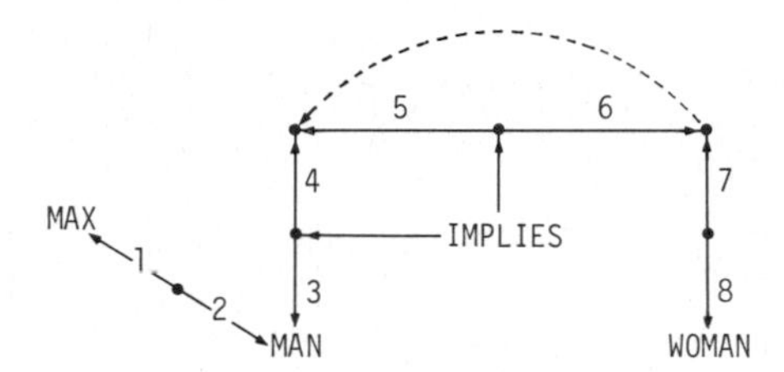

Note that Schubert found it necessary to represent class relations such as (ISA MAN) as predicate structures. That is, while previously "Fred is a man" would have looked like:

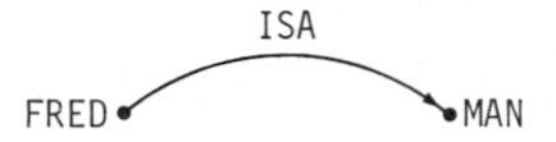

now it will be

OBJECT ISA
FRED MAN

In general any program to deduce simple facts such as ISA relations would be much more complicated than one would like. The reader should be able to verify for himself that such a deduction would require two steps in the original nets and four in the expanded (predicate structure) nets.

So far we have looked at how one might modify a net to incorporate predicate calculus features, but there has also been some work on FOPC representation which has had the effect of bringing it close to nets, for example Sandewall (1970). Sandewall notes that if one uses traditional predicate notation in FOPC one runs into problems. So suppose we represented the fact that John loves Mary as follows:

LOVES (JOHN, MARY)

There is no way now within FOPC to express "Bill believes that John loves Mary", as,

BELIEVE (BILL, LOVES (JOHN, MARY))

is not legal FOPC. (We saw in Chapter 1 that predicates were not allowed to be arguments to other predicates.) Sandewall proposes two ways to overcome this problem within FOPC, one of which is to handle this last example as follows:

VERB (E1, BELIEVE)
SUBJECT (E1, BILL)
OBJECT (E1, E2)
VERB (E2, LOVES)
SUBJECT (E2, JOHN)
OBJECT (E2, MARY)

If this looks at all familiar, it is because it is essentially the same solution as was proposed for the similar problem we saw with nets earlier in this chapter when we made verbs into predicate structures and introduced cases.

Sometimes combining nets and FOPC also includes an attempt to bridge the gap between the FOPC advocates who want a strict formalism which is always provably correct in its deductions and those who feel that this strict formalism imposes too tight a restriction on the facts which can be represented and the deductions which can be made from them. Two attempts to represent quantification in semantic nets so as to allow for less formal and more intuitive deductions and/or representations were made by Palme and Scragg. Neither of these really ensured that all possible combinations of quantifiers could be represented, but were nontheless instructive. Scragg attempted to simply ignore the formal constraints of FOPC and marry the problems of quantification to those of representing the vaguer quantifiers that we use all the time like many, more, some (meaning a few but not all), etc. Palme, on the other hand, created a new quantifier, ITS.

Scragg (1973) tried to patch up the problems by being deliberately vague about the meaning of quantified relations and making a few simple observations about the nature of real world quantification. All relations were unquantified and it was assumed that the proper quantification could be determined whenever needed. This determination could be made in a number of ways.

1. Relations between tokens are never quantified. Relations between a token and a type cannot be quantified with respect to the token. So we need only worry about quantification with respect to type nodes (takes care of (4d, e, f)).

2. Doubly universally quantified relations are rare in everyday (non-scientific) knowledge. We do not often assert facts such as "All men love all women". Therefore, if we treat these as being non-existent we will not lose much (takes care of (4a)).

3. We can apply a principle of locality of information. By that, we mean simply that when two facts which are inconsistent are encountered, the problem can be avoided by regarding the more local (close) to be the dominant. Thus, if the net includes:

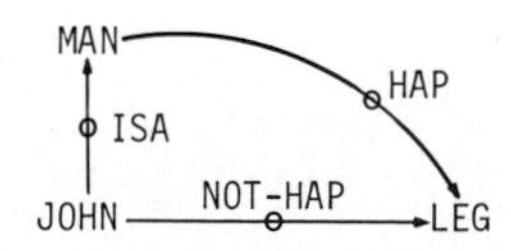

We can regard this as the consistent statement that men in general (most) have legs but that at least one (John) does not. Note that the statement that John does not have legs is more local to the node John than is the fact that men do have legs. (This implies that searches for information should be done by examining all closely related information first and looking further only when it is not available locally.)

4. Some relations, such as HAP, are always quantified as FOR-ALL,EXISTS. When such a relation is applied to a type node, the meaning is that for each item in the first class there is a unique item in the second class related to the first by the given relation (i.e. there exists a function to find it). Thus MAN HAP HEART means that for each man there is a heart. The astute reader will observe this is the remaining two cases (4b, c) and that it is of course the same situation for which Schubert needed the Skolem functions. Such relations are assumed to be universally quantified at the tail and existentially at the head. "Every man loves some woman" becomes simply:

Note that "Every woman is loved by some man" would be

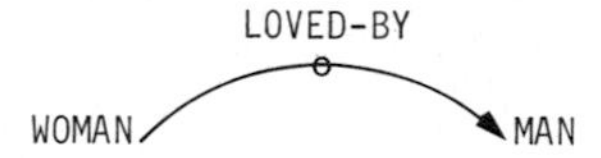

Since the two English statements are not equivalent, we must assume that LOVE and LOVED-BY are not exactly inverses if this convention is used. This duplication, of course, could become a problem. It is still not clear how to show that a particular relation holds from every member of a restricted subset to every member of another restricted subset. (For example, "Every boy in the class loves every girl in the class".)

Palme (1973) tried to represent quantification by introducing a third quantifier, ITS. ITS can be thought of as meaning the possessive pronoun "its". Not surprisingly, ITS is used in the same situations where Schubert and Scragg had to provide special features: the FOR-ALL x EXISTS y situations. With three quantifiers, he now could define six separate relations for each previous relation: quantifying with FOR-ALL or EXISTS on the left and FOR-ALL, EXISTS or ITS on the right. The above example becomes:

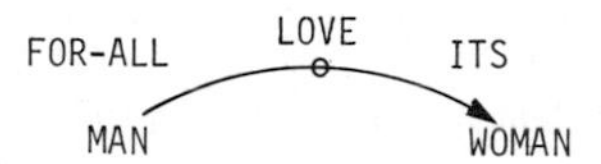

A little arithmetic shows that Palme has six possible combinations for quantifications, just enough to satisfy all the cases of (4).

TWO SEMANTIC NET SYSTEMS

Up to this point we have discussed only the problems of how to represent information on a very low and general level. We will now briefly examine two particular systems, namely those of Schank and Simmons, (which we saw briefly in Chapter 4) and note two very different courses that they took, both using semantic nets that obeyed essentially the same rules that we have set down here.

Schank

There is a continuing debate over the need for a primitive representation, that is one in which all concepts can be broken down into some small finite set of component concepts. Two of the leading exponents of the use of such primitives are Wilks (described in Chapters 4 and 9) and Schank. Schank's theory, known as conceptual dependency, is one of the most thorough attempts to establish a set of rules dictating exactly what can appear in a semantic net-like representation. In its present version, called MARGIE (Schank et al 1973) Schank's system has an analyser of English due to Riesbeck (1974), a semantic memory component due to Rieger (1974), and a generator of English due to Goldman (1974). MARGIE produces output in two modes: the PARAPHRASE mode and the INFERENCE mode. The system's inferencing capabilities will be discussed in the next chapter. In paraphrase mode a typical example is:

INPUT: John killed Mary by choking Mary

OUTPUT: John strangled Mary

John choked Mary and she died because she could not breathe.

Mary died because she was unable to inhale some air and she was unable to inhale some air because John grabbed her neck.

Schank's aim has been to provide a representation of meaning in terms of which these and other tasks, such as machine translation, could be carried out; a representation, moreover, that was to be independent of any particular languages, and of syntax, and indeed of all surface structures whatever. (This makes it very close to a model of memory representation.)

The formal structure of Schank's graphs is that of dependency grammar (Hays 1964) and the items (nodes) in the graph are of four types, or conceptual categories. They are symbolized as PP, ACT, PA and AA, which are acronyms, but which correspond roughly to those of a noun, verb, adjective and adverb respectively. This is a considerable oversimplification, however, made only to give a brief and self-contained description. In fact, many English nouns are represented as ACTs in conceptual dependency, such as "hunt". These units are combined to form the basic structure, a "conceptualization" which corresponds very closely to predicate structures. The conceptualization for "The man took a book" would roughly look like:

(8) Man $\overset{P}{\Longleftrightarrow}$ take $\overset{0}{\longleftarrow}$ book

We have already seen Schank's case notation in Chapter 4. To briefly remind you, $\Longleftrightarrow$ indicates that "Man" is in the ACTOR case, while $\overset{0}{\longleftarrow}$ indicates the objective case. Both man and book are said to be dependent on the central ACT (take). Finally, the "P" indicates past tense. There is a carefully constructed syntax of linkages between the conceptual categories, that will be described only in part in what follows.

Note the similarity between (8) and (9).

(9)

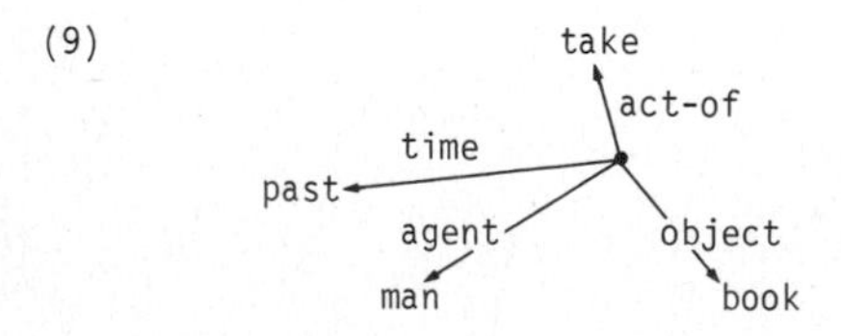

The major difference in appearance is that (9) uses a predicate structure while (8) does not, but in fact the actual implementation of (8) uses predicate structures for the reasons mentioned earlier in the chapter.

The heart of Schank's notation is his 11 basic or "primitive" actions. They are: PROPEL, MOVE, INGEST, EXPEL, GRASP, PTRANS, MTRANS, ATRANS, SPEAK, ATTEND and MBUILD. There is also a default action DO. The precise number here is not crucial as it changes occasionally. What is important is that the number is quite small. Schank holds that these are sufficient along with a small (but so far unspecified) number of states to represent the meanings of all verbs. Probably the best way to get a feel for how the notation works would be to see a few examples (of increasing complexity).

Our earlier example (8) ("The man took a book") would really look like:

man ⟺ PTRANS ←O— book ←D— [→ man ; ←]

This roughly corresponds to: The man Physically TRANSferred the book from some unknown location to himself.

John killed his teacher

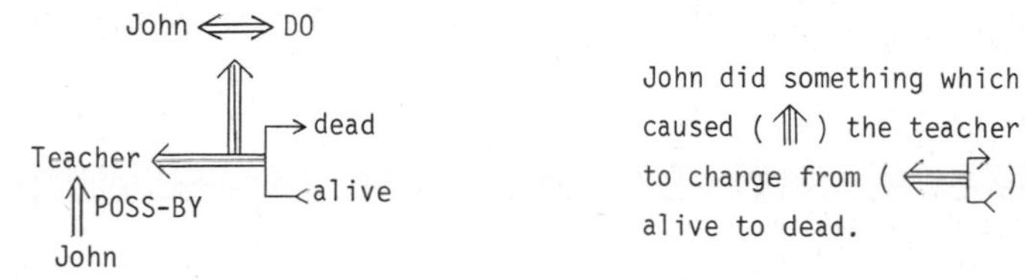

The comparison between this and the generative semantic analysis, "cause to be dead" should be clear.

I saw John eating soup

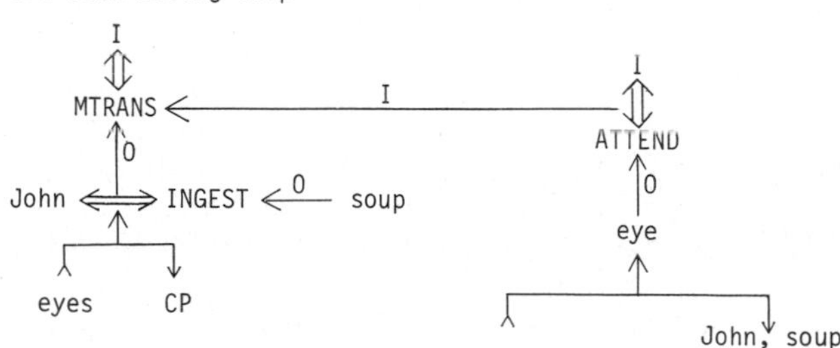

To follow the above first look at the left half. It says, in effect, that I Mentally TRANSferred information from my eye to my Conceptual Processor (CP) and the information which was transferred was John's eating soup. The right half says that the way this information transfer was accomplished was by ATTENDing my eye from some unknown location to John and the soup.

Schank has developed rules which specify well formed conceptualizations. So, for example, the primitive act INGEST must have as its instrument the act PTRANS. There are also inferences which must be true of any ACT classified as an INGEST action, such as: the thing ingested changes its form, that if the thing ingested is edible the ingester becomes "more nourished", etc. To see how these rules work, let us see how complete conceptualizations are built up.

John ate a fig

The basic definition for "eat" is:

$$X \Longleftrightarrow \text{INGEST} \xleftarrow{O} Y$$

We can consider this as an active object with slots that it seeks to fill in from the context in which it is activated. Thus in our sentence the variables will be filled in, producing:

$$\text{John} \Longleftrightarrow \text{INGEST} \xleftarrow{O} \text{fig}$$

However, this is not all. One rule specifying well formed conceptualizations states that all acts have instruments, which the above diagram does not. Furthermore, INGEST specifies that its instrument is always PTRANSing Y to the mouth of X (or less likely, moving the mouth to the object). This would give us:

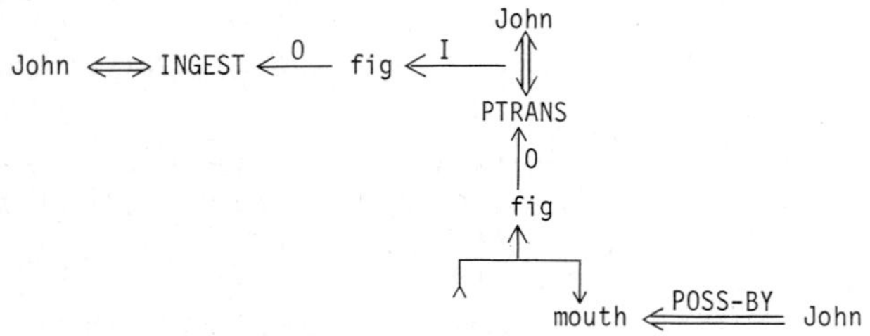

```
                                      John
John <==> INGEST <--O-- fig <--I--     ^
                                       ||
                                       v
                                     PTRANS
                                       ^
                                       |O
                                      fig
                                       ^
                                  _____|_____
                                 |           |
                                 ^           v
                                           mouth <==POSS-BY== John
```

From this we could, if we choose, go on to make further inferences of the sort mentioned above. What is important to notice about this completed conceptualization is how far removed it is from the original sentence.

Simmons

Unlike Schank, Simmons does not believe that all descriptions must be broken down into primitives. But he does place a very definite structure on his nets, much of which is due to his specific case system (as described in Chapter 4). A typical example sentence is:

John broke the window with a hammer

He represents this as a network of nodes C1, C2, C3, C4 corresponding to the appropriate senses of "John", "break", "window" and "hammer" respectively. The relations between the nodes are labelled by one of the "deep case relations": CAUSAL-ACTANT (CA1, CA2), THEME, LOCUS, SOURCE and GOAL. So, in (10) John is the first causal actant (CA1) of the breaking, the hammer is considered the second causal actant (CA2) of that breaking, and the window is the theme of the breaking. Thus, the heart of the analysis could be represented by a diagram as follows:

(10)

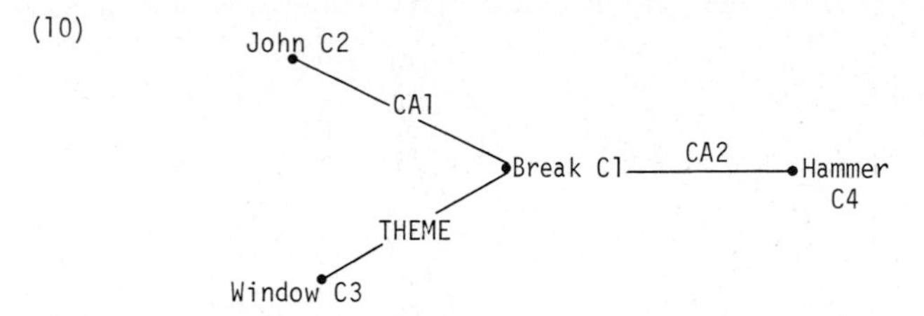

or (internally) by a set of relational triples:

(C1 CA1 C2) (C1 CA2 C4) (C1 THEME C3)

However, this is not the full representation, and our addition of the word labels to the diagram is misleading, since the nodes are intended to be something like what we earlier called tokens. (Simmons says that a node represents a "contextual meaning of a word".) These tokens are related to particular word senses by the relation TOK (for token) which is very roughly equivalent to ISA. That is, mention of "the bank" (in the sense of a banking institution) would be represented in the net by, say, C55, which would be related by TOK to the word sense of "bank" corresponding to the place where one often saves money. It would not, of course, be directly related to the word "bank", which, after all, is ambiguous. In an implementation the word senses would be separate lexical entries and would be given arbitrary names, such as L97. For a particular sense of "apple" Simmons suggests an associated set of syntactic and semantic features:

NBR (number) - S (singular)

SHAPE - spherical

COLOR - red

PRINTIMAGE - apple

THEME - eat

SYNTACTIC-CATEGORY - noun

etc.

Returning to our example of "John broke the window", a complete representation including TOK relations would go as follows:

(C1 TOK break) (C1 CA1 C2) (C1 THEME C3) (C1 CA2 C4)

(C2 TOK John) (C2 DET Def) (C2 NBR S)

(C3 TOK window) (C3 DET Def) (C3 NBR S)

(C4 TOK hammer) (C4 DET Indef) (C4 NBR S) (C4 PREP with)

The equivalent net form would be:

(12)

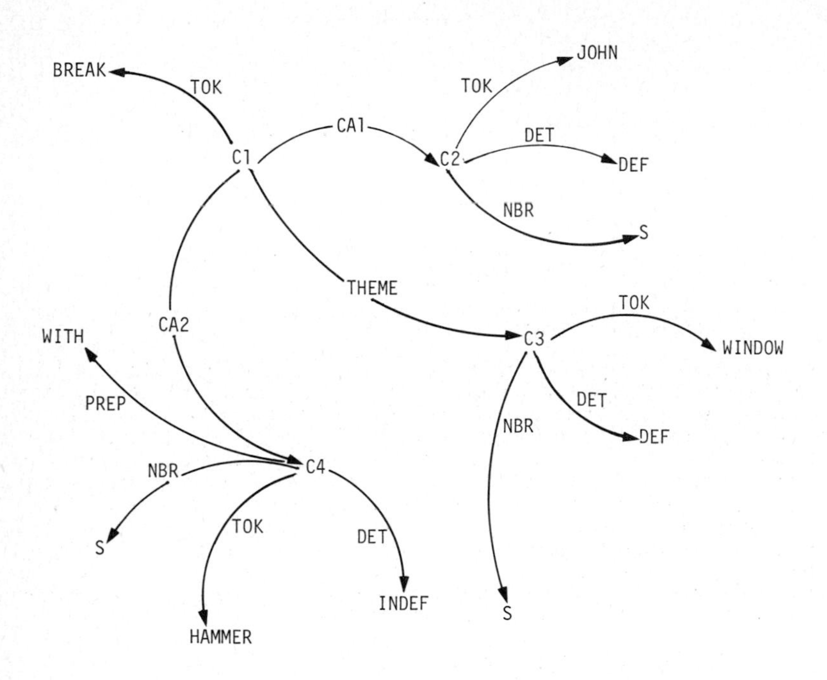

The network in (12) is also a representation of the following sentences, which can be thought of as surface variants of a single "underlying" structure:

John broke the window with a hammer

John broke the window

The hammer broke the window

The window broke

It will be clear that Simmons' method of ascribing a node to each word-sense is not in any way a primitive system, like Schank's. Simmons uses, however, a system of paraphrase rules that would map from one network to another in a way that he claims is equivalent to a system of primitives. Thus in (Simmons 1973) he considers the sentences:

John bought the boat from Mary

Mary sold the boat to John

which would normally be considered approximate paraphrases of each other. However his system would represent them differently.

C1 TOK buy, SOURCE (Mary), GOAL (John), THEME (boat)

C1 TOK sell, SOURCE (Mary), GOAL (John), THEME (boat)

Using Simmons' notation the single representation for both sentences with the primitive action "transfer" would be as follows:

C1 TOK and, Args C2, C3

C2 TOK transfer, SOURCE (John), GOAL (Mary), THEME (money)

C3 TOK transfer, SOURCE (Mary), GOAL (John), THEME (boat)

Simmons opts for the first form of representation, with paraphrase rules to derive one from the other.

It should be clear that Simmons' representation is much closer to natural language than Schank's. Not only does he shun primitives, but he sees his tokens as tokens of lexical entries. This sometimes leads to strange problems. Look back at (11). There are features attached to "apple" which describe apple, features which describe computer characteristics, such as PRINT-IMAGE, and features which describe the role it plays in syntax. Simmons is certainly not the only one to lump such disparate items together. However, we suspect that such a policy can only lead to trouble. If we ask for information about an apple, we certainly don't want to be told PRINT-IMAGEs.

ORGANIZATION

The extensions discussed so far have been on a very local basis. What can be said about the overall organization of memory and the representation of more complex ideas, such as descriptions of physical objects or a series of events?

The various opinions expressed by different individuals about the higher level organization of memory seem to reflect the computational or psychological bias of the holder of the opinion. That is, organization is influenced by inference mechanism considerations as well as the desire to model humans closely. To start with a simple example, consider what might be a possible representation for the notion of "a large block". One would expect that such a simple thing wouldn't be too controversial. But, two possible constructions for the above notion come to mind:

(13)

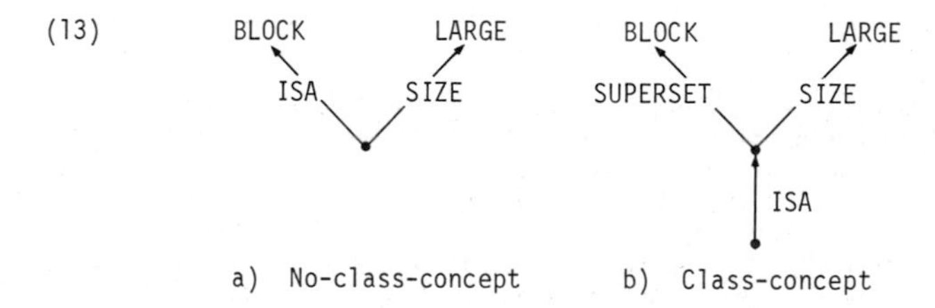

a) No-class-concept b) Class-concept

The major distinction is that (13b) assumes the existence of a concept of "large block" as a class of things, while (13a) does not. And the number of possible representations becomes even larger when we add more adjectives. In the no-class-concept theory, "a large red block" is represented in the obvio, way:

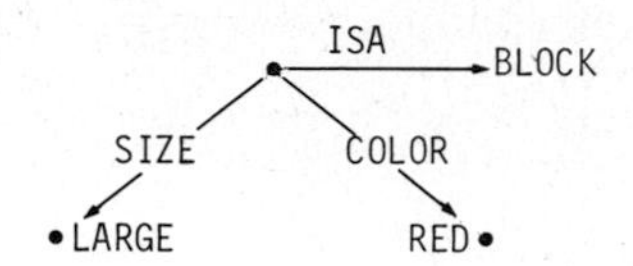

Using class-concepts, however, allows for three other possibilities.

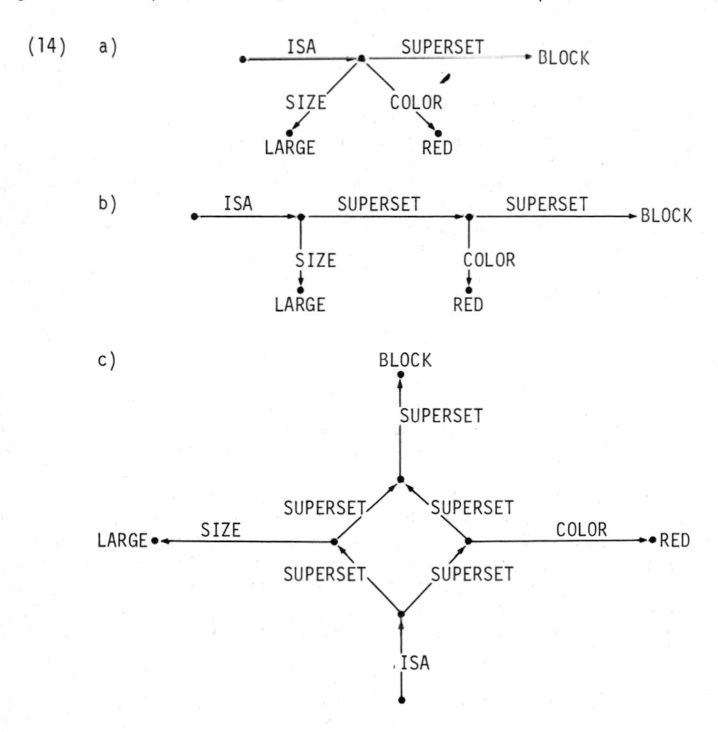

None of these structures is flawless. (14a) fails to relate the concept for "large red block" to the concept for "large block". The author for one believes that these concepts should be related explicitly. (14b) recognizes that the block is in fact a red block, but fails to be symmetrical by recognizing that it is a "large block" in the same way. As more than two defining properties are added (14c) either runs into a combinatorial explosion or faces the system designer with a very complex problem of deciding which possible subset relations must be made explicit.

A related problem that is found in both the class and non-class representations occurs when a subset is defined by two properties which are not independent of each other. For example, a block which in fact is multi-colored could be represented as:

(15)

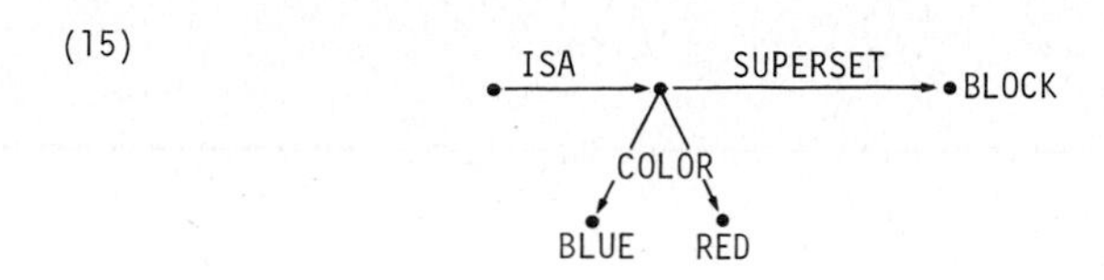

But this seems to imply by the conventions that have been used so far that the block is (all) red and (all) blue. One way out of this problem is to represent "blue and red block" as

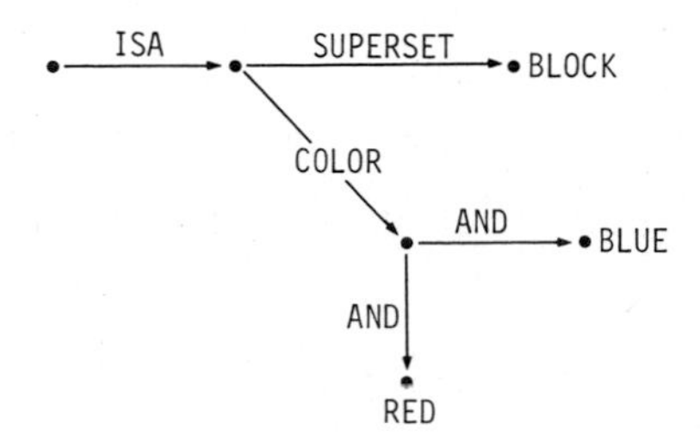

Alternatively, if (15) is used for "blue and red block", a rule could be introduced to the effect that certain related properties (such as identical ones) do not apply to a node when taken individually.

The representational question is clouded even further by idioms or slight variants of general concepts. A "very red nose" must have a representation that shows that it is in fact a "red nose" but that there is something special about its redness. "Black men" does not refer to the set of men who are black in color but to those with a particular set of characteristics, which does not necessarily include blackness. (Probably this is really a parsing problem.)

Events also combine in groups to form more complicated events. What higher level organization has been proposed for complicated events? In order to talk about such organization let us suppose for the moment that we have a representation for actions and simple constructs, say that of Schank. That means that we have specified what relations we will allow and in what combinations and the names of our primitive actions. Furthermore, let us assume that we have agreed on the translations of "everyday concepts" into this representation. That is we have a structure for "sweet", one for "buy", etc. What we need now is a theory of more complex actions. For example, how do we link the descriptions of the various substeps of the process of cakemaking into a single description of the overall action of making a cake.

Norman defines complicated actions within a semantic net by describing them as an ordered list of the substeps necessary for the performance of that action. Interestingly enough he can also describe in this way actions which manipulate the data base. For example, the definition of "establish", (his procedure to ensure that the triple "a r b" is in the data base) is the following net:

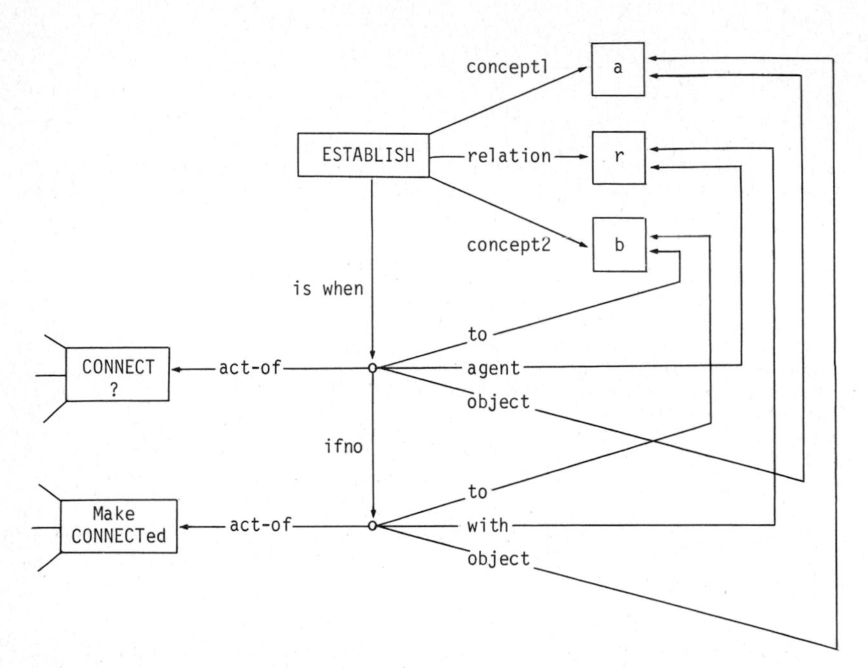

The interpretation of this net is a program for the defined concept ESTABLISH. The program accepts three parameters a, r and b. The definition (iswhen) is that the program first uses CONNECT? to see if r already connects a to b in the data base. If it does not (ifno) a is connected (using make-CONNECT) to b with r. Note what this has done. Within a semantic net representation, a procedure has been defined which manipulates the semantic net. Not only is it possible to describe events in a semantic net, but all questions of how to use the data (inference mechanisms) may also be specified in the net. While the description of ESTABLISH is data because it is represented in a semantic net, it is also a procedure.

This is a backwards way of introducing a controversy about data representation. There are those who claim that all knowledge is stored in the form of procedures and those who claim that it is stored as a collection of facts. (This controversy has been mentioned previously in Chapter 6). In Norman's system this distinction is deliberately blurred (and the author thinks it should be). Various researchers take one extreme view or the other and produce many examples favoring their point of view. One prototypical example is that of the definition of an arch. On the one hand, the pro-procedure people suggest that the way to represent knowledge about an arch is to have a program, say, for recognizing one. The pro-data people think you should simply have a description of a generalized arch. Looked at from a slightly different view point the Simmons - Schank differences are in fact a variant of this fight. Schank wants an all-purpose representation while Simmons wants to have procedures to get from one representation to another.

Of well known programs, Winograd's is probably the most dependent on procedural knowledge (see Chapter 6). Early use of semantic nets was probably one of the most data directed approaches. The opinion taken here is that, in general, information should be stored in whatever form is the most convenient. For the most part data stored as procedures tends to be stored with too much specificity of purpose. It is better to store that a table is red than to store how to determine that a table is red. For example, what if we also need to know if a table were green? What about alternative methods (for a blind man for instance)? There are exceptions to this rather sweeping generality. One is the situation such as in Norman where both forms exist together as different ways of viewing the same representation. Another is information about actions.

In the LUIGI system (Scragg 1974) ambiguous (data or procedure) representations are used to store information about actions. The system was built within Norman's MEMOD system. LUIGI knew how to perform (actually, simulate) various human actions such as toasting bread, making spaghetti or cleaning up the kitchen. The information about how to perform these actions was stored as procedures. However, these procedures could be used as data by other parts of the system to answer such questions as "How do you make a ham and cheese sandwich?", "How many utensils do you use if you make a mushroom omelette?", "Why did Don use a knife?" or even the question "Did anyone do anything which would have moved the bread?" which is self-generated after LUIGI fails to answer "Where is the bread?" by simpler means. Because all of the simulation procedures are readily available to processing routines they can be examined in detail to predict their side effects and even to calculate prerequisites if they are not explicitly mentioned.

For example, to answer the question:

How do you make a ham and cheese sandwich?

LUIGI must examine his own program that he would use if he were commanded to make a sandwich. At each step of the program, he must determine if the step is one that should be mentioned. He then generates a description of the step, noting that the system would be the actor and that the sandwich would be made of ham and cheese. His ultimate output is:

IF I WERE TO MAKE A SANDWICH

THEN I WOULD DO THE FOLLOWING THINGS:

I PLACE SLICE OF BREAD ON THE COUNTER

I SPREAD MUSTARD ON THE BREAD

I PLACE HAM ON THE BREAD

I PLACE CHEESE ON THE BREAD

I PLACE LETTUCE ON THE BREAD

I PLACE SECOND PIECE OF BREAD ON THE BREAD

The major claim here is that a single representation, which is both data and procedural, can be used to describe complex actions in a way suitable for multiple purposes. Recently (Scragg 1975) this sort of representation has been expanded into a net, which includes alternate methods and independent ordering of steps as well as cause and effect information and tie-ins to the rest of the data base. The expanded net is to be coupled with an interpreter which does not require a fixed ordering for the steps, but can select one either randomly or with some motivation. Not having a fixed algorithm will probably make the problem solver more human like than in the original LUIGI system. But now we are getting into fairly high level data structures, a topic which the next chapter will cover in much greater detail.

E. Charniak and Y. Wilks (eds.), Computational Semantics

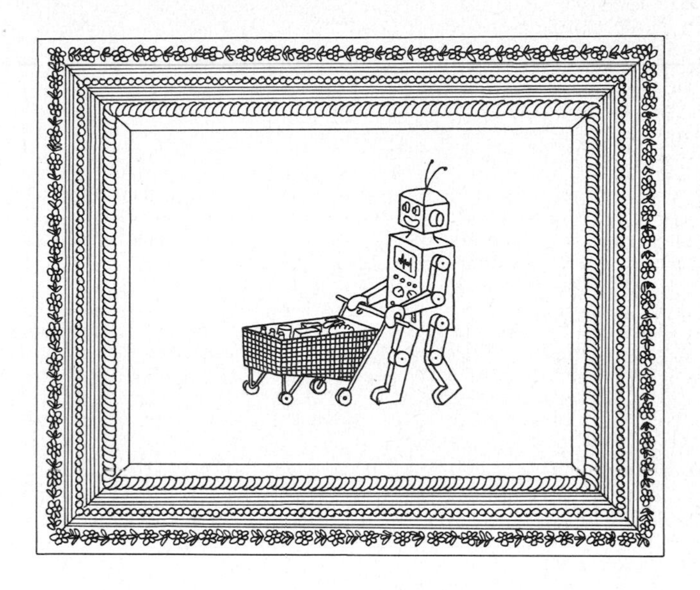

INFERENCE AND KNOWLEDGE PART 2

Eugene Charniak

A DEMON BASED SYSTEM

At the end of Chapter 1 we encountered the programming language PLANNER. At the same time we noted, however, that it constituted a proposed solution to the problems of inference and knowledge. But how good a solution is it? Well, we have seen one problem with PLANNER already. Since it is a programming language, as well as a theory of fact use, it is possible to use PLANNER in so many ways that it is hard to pin down exactly what PLANNER commits one to. Such flexibility is desirable in a programming language, but in a theory it constitutes vagueness. So the first problem with PLANNER as a theory of knowledge and inference is that it is a vague theory.

Naturally, this first problem makes it quite difficult to find other problems. To do so we will have to stop looking at PLANNER itself, and instead look at some of the ways it has been used. In particular we will look at Charniak's work on children's stories (Charniak 1972). It will then be suggested that some of the problems we see in this model are really problems with PLANNER itself.

The problem this model (or system) is concerned with is one which was referred to throughout Chapter 1, namely answering reasonable questions on the basis of a piece of simple narration (or children's story). So consider:

> Janet needed some money. She got her piggybank (PB), and started to shake it. Finally some money came out.

Some typical questions would be:

> Why did Janet get the PB?
>
> Did Janet get the money?
>
> Why was the PB shaken?

The reader should be sufficiently attuned by this point to recognize that to answer these questions real world knowledge is needed. The model is solely concerned with the problem of using the necessary real world knowledge to make inferences and it does not explicitly consider problems of natural language per se. In particular it does not deal with syntax, and while it does deal to some degree with those problems at the boundary between syntax and inference (like determination of noun phrase reference), these will not be considered here.

We will assume that as the story comes into the program it is immediately translated into a semantic representation which is convenient for doing inference. The semantic representation of a sentence will be a group of MICRO-PLANNER assertions. The model will try to "fill in the blanks" of the story on a line by line basis. That is, as it goes along, it will try to make connections between events in the story (usually causal connections) and fill in missing facts which seem important.

Demons and Base Routines

Consider a fact like:

(1) If "it is (or will be) raining" and if "person P is outside" then "P will get wet".

We have an intuitive belief that (1) is a fact about "rain", rather than, say, a fact about "outside". Many things happen outside, and getting wet is only one of them. On the other hand only a limited number of things happen when it rains.

We will embody this belief in our system by associating (1) with "rain" so that only when "rain" comes up in the story will we even consider using rule (1). We will say that rain is the "topic concept" of (1). To put this another way, when a concept is brought up in a story, the facts associated with it are "made available" for use in making inferences. (We will also say that the facts are "put in" or "asserted".) So, if "circus", say, has never come up, the program will not be able to make inferences using those facts associated only with "circus".

Note however that we are not saying that "rain" has to be mentioned explicitly in the story before we can use (1). It is only necessary that there be a "rain" assertion put into the data base. Other parts of the story may provide facts which cause the program to assert that it is raining. For example:

> One afternoon Jack was outside playing with Bill. Bill looked up and noticed that the sky was getting dark. "I think we should stop" said Bill. "We will get wet if we keep playing".

Here, the sky's getting dark in the afternoon suggests that it is going to rain. If this is put into the data base it will be sufficient to bring in facts associated with "rain".

Also note that a topic concept need not be a single "key word". A fact may not become available to the system until a complex set of relations appears in the data base. A fact may be arbitrarily complex, and in particular may activate other facts depending on the presence or absence of certain relations in the story.

Looking Forward, Looking Back. When a fact is made available we might not have all the information needed to make use of the fact. Since we are making inferences as we go, if the necessary information comes in after the rule has been asserted we want to make the inference when the information comes in. So we might have:

(2) Jack was outside. It was raining.

(3) It was raining. Jack was outside.

In (2) there is no problem. When we introduce "rain" we have sufficient information to use (1) and infer that Jack is going to get wet. But in (3), we only learn that Jack is outside after we mentioned rain. If we want to use (1) we will need some way to have our fact "look forward" in the story. To do this we will represent facts by PLANNER ANTEcedent theorems, so a fact will have two parts, a pattern and body (an arbitrary PLANNER program). We execute the body of an ANTE only when an assertion is put in the data base which matches the pattern. In (1) the pattern would be "someone outside". Then in (3) when we introduce (1) no assertion matches the pattern. But the next line creates a matching assertion, so the fact will be executed. We will say that a fact is "looking forward" when its topic concept appears before the assertion which matches the pattern. When the assertion which matches the pattern comes first we will say that the fact is "looking backward" (as in (2)). (This is a slight extension over MICRO-PLANNER antecedent theorems which can only look forward.)

We can see how important looking forward is with a few examples.

(4) "Janet was thinking of getting Jack a ball for his birthday. When she told Penny, Penny said, "Don't do that. Jack has a ball."
Here we interpreted the line "Jack has a ball" as meaning that he did not want another. The common sense knowledge is the fact that in many cases having an X means that one will not want another X. This piece of information would probably be filed under "things to consider when about to get something for somebody else". Naturally it was an earlier line which mentioned that Janet was thinking of getting Jack a ball.

(5) "Bill offered to trade his pocket knife for Jack's dog Tip. Jack said "I will ask Janet. Tip is her dog too."
The last line is interpreted as the reason Jack will ask Janet because of information about the relation between trading and ownership.

(6) "Janet wanted to get some money. She found her piggybank and started to shake it. She didn't hear anything".
The last line means that there was nothing in the piggybank on the basis of facts about piggybanks.

In each of these cases it is an earlier line which contains the information which is used to assign the interpretation. So in (4) there is nothing inherent in the line "Jack has a ball" which means "don't get him another". If there were, something in the line would also have to trigger a check for the following situations:

Bill and Dick wanted to play baseball. When Jack came by Bill said, "There is Jack. He has a ball."

> Tom asked his father if he would buy him a ball. "Jack has a ball" said Tom.
>
> Bill's ball of string was stuck in the tree. He asked Jane how he could get it out. Jane said, "You should hit it with something. Here comes Jack. He has a ball."

Facts were formulated as antecedent theorems because of the clear need to "look forward". However, rather than continue calling the facts antecedent theorems, we call them "demons" since it is a shorter and more mnemonic name.

Specification and Removal of Demons. It should be emphasized that the model does not "learn" the information contained in the demons. This information is put in by the model maker. On the other hand, the demons are not specific to the story in the sense that they mention Jack, or "the red ball". Rather, they talk about "a person X" who at one point in the story could be Jack, at another, Bill. We will assume a mechanism for binding some of the variables of the demon ("specifying" the demon) at the time the demon is asserted.

We want demons to be active only while they are relevant to the story. A story may start by talking about getting a present for Jack, but ultimately revolve around the games played at his party. We will need some way to remove the "present getting" demons when they have outlived their usefulness. (An irrelevant but active demon not only wastes time and space, but can cause us to misinterpret a new line.) As a first approximation we will assume that a demon is declared irrelevant after a given number of lines have gone by.

Base Routines. So far we have said that demons are asserted when the proper concept has been mentioned. But this implies that there is something attached to the concept telling us what demons should be put in.

If we look at a particular example, say (5), it is Bill's offer to trade which sets up the context for the rest of the fragment. We will assume that the information to do so is in the form of a program. Such routines, which are available to set up demons, will be called "base routines".

The relation between base routines and demons can be represented as:

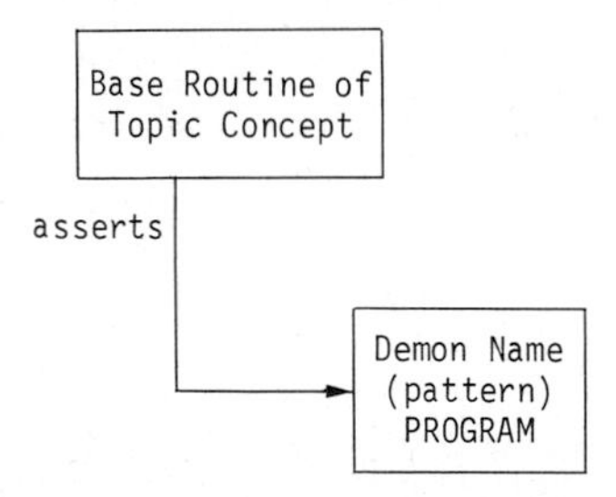

These base routines will be responsible for more than setting up demons. Suppose we are told that Jack had a ball, and Bill a top. Then Jack traded his ball to Bill for the top. One question we might ask is "Who now has the top?" Naturally, since questions of "who has what" are important in understanding stories we will want to keep tabs on such information. In this particular case, it must again be the "trade" statement which tells us to switch possession of the objects. Every time a trade occurs we will want to exchange objects, so whenever we see "trade" we execute the "trade" base routine. Of course, the program can't be too simple-minded, since it must also handle "I will trade..." and perhaps even "Will you trade...?"

A good test as to whether a given fact should be part of a base routine or a demon is whether we need several lines to set it up or whether we can illustrate the fact by presenting a single line. (Naturally several lines could be made into one by putting "and's" between them, but this is dodging the point. This is only an intuitive test.) So we saw that "Jack has a ball" was not enough by itself to tell us that Jack does not want another ball. Hence this relation is embodied by a demon, not a base routine.

Bookkeeping and Fact Finders

Updating and Bookkeeping. Up to this point we have introduced two parts of the model, demons and base routines. In this section we will introduce the remaining two parts.

Again let us consider the situation when Jack had a ball, Bill a top, and they traded. When we say that Bill now has the ball, it implies that Jack no longer does. That is to say, we must somehow remove the fact that Jack has the ball from the data base. Actually we don't want to remove it, since we may be asked "Who had the ball before Bill did?" Instead, we want to mark the assertion in some way to indicate that it has been updated. We will assume that there is a separate section, pretty much independent of the rest of the model, which is responsible for doing such updating. We will call this section "bookkeeping".

Fact Finders. But even deciding that one statement updates another requires special knowledge. Suppose we have:

(7) Jack was in the house. Sometime later he was at the store.

If we ask "Is Jack in the house?" we want to answer "No, he is at the store." But how is bookkeeping going to figure this out? There is a simple rule which says that (<state> A B) updates (<state> A C) where C is not the same as B. So (AT JACK FARM) would update (AT JACK NEW-YORK). But in (7) we can't simply look for Jack AT <someplace which is not the store>, since he is IN the house. To make things even worse, we could have:

Jack was in the house. Sometime later he was in the kitchen.

To solve this problem we will need:

(8) To establish that PERSON is not at location LOC

Find out where PERSON is, call it X.
If X = LOC, then theorem is false so return "No".
If X is part of LOC then return "No".
If LOC is part of X, then try to find a different X.
Else return "Yes".

In (7) the bookkeeping would try to prove that Jack is not at the store, and it would succeed by using (8) and the statement that Jack is in the house. Bookkeeper would then mark the earlier statement as updated. Theorems like (8) will be called "fact finders". Fact finders are represented as MICRO-PLANNER CONSEquent theorems. (In particular (8), expressed however as an ANTE, appeared in Chapter 1.)

The basic idea behind fact finders is that they are used to establish facts which are comparatively unimportant, so that we do not want to assert them and hence have them in the data base. So in (7) we do not want to assert "Jack is not in the house" as well as "Jack is at the store". In the same way we will have a fact finder which is able to derive "<person> knows <fact>" by asking such questions as "was the <person> there when <fact> was mentioned or took place?" Again, this information is easily derivable, and not all that important, so there would seem to be no reason to include it explicitly in the data base.

Then, we can represent our model as:

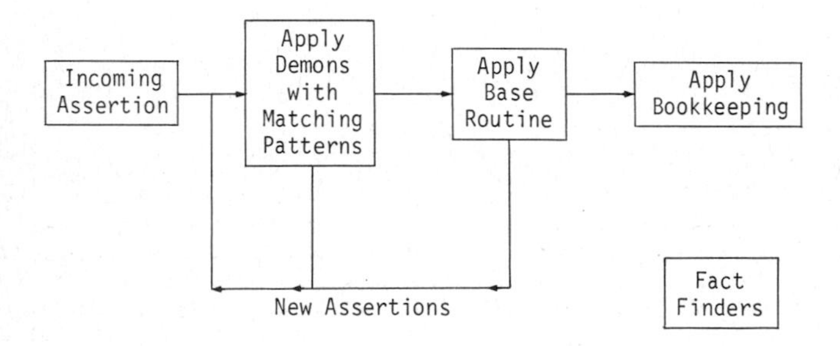

THE FIVE QUESTIONS

To summarize this, let us return to our five questions and see what answers this model gives. In answering them however we will have to be careful, since in a peculiar way the model just presented (and the ones we will consider henceforth) answers all of them. Since this model was made into a computer program, and since one has to specify everything in a program, the model must have some answer to each of the questions. Yet, very little was said in the preceding pages about, say, semantic representation, and the model is really not intended to say anything about semantic representation at all.

The way out of this peculiar contradiction is to make a distinction between a computer program and the theory a computer program embodies. There has been much written on the relation between programs and theories, and the last thing we want to do is add to this literature, but some distinction of this sort is necessary. The distinction we will make is quite simple. If person P writes an AI program which performs task T, we will say that P's theory of T is those parts of the program which P considers significant. This definition has as a consequence that a single program could embody two different theories. This could happen, for example, if two people wrote a single program, but held different opinions about which portions of the program were significant.

So with this distinction in mind, what answers does the above theory provide?

SEMANTIC REPRESENTATION. It says very little about semantic representation. Indeed the only statement which the preceding commits one to is that a semantic representation with <u>only</u> a small number of primitives is wrong. For example, the model used more specific concepts like "rain", "piggybank" and "present giving".

This might seem to contradict the "primitive" position seen in the last chapter in the work of Schank (see also the work of Wilks in Chapter 9). But while the "primitive" position implies breaking things down into primitives, one may still use higher level concepts. And, in fact, neither of the authors mentioned denies that higher level concepts might be useful.

INFERENCE TRIGGERING. The model is firmly committed to making non-problem occasioned inferences at read time, and for the reasons we went into in the section discussing when we make inferences. This was the entire point of the demon apparatus.

ORGANIZATION. By and large the theory just presented is a theory of organization. In particular it states that given a particular assertion, the way we find those facts which we should use to make inferences from the assertion is to look firstly in the base routine for assertions of that form, and secondly for any demons which happen to have been activated which are looking for assertions of that form. To put this slightly differently, the system presented states that the PLANNER mechanism of pattern directed invocation is the way facts are located.

INFERENCE MECHANISM. The theory assumes that the inference mechanism is MICRO-PLANNER demons (or the equivalent in some other language). We will subsequently argue against this assumption, and by implication the organizational assumptions as well.

CONTENT. As presented the model said nothing about content in that it makes no claim about exactly what it is we know about piggybanks, or anything else. One might use this model to make claims about what it is we know of these topics, but nothing in the presentation here does so.

Problems with the Model

There are many places where one could find fault with the model just proposed, but we will pick one issue which seems important because it touches on the more general issue of the role of high level programming languages as vehicles for theories of knowledge and inference.

Consider a fact like:

(9) Umbrellas are used to keep rain off one's head

To fit such a fact into the model just presented, we would most naturally treat it as follows:

(10) Base routine which activates demon: Possibility of rain

Pattern: Person gets umbrella

Program: If person might be caught in rain he got the umbrella to prevent getting wet

This will work quite well for stories like:

It looked like rain. Jack got his umbrella.

It would even be possible, using mechanisms in the model which were not explained previously, to handle a story like:

As Jack was leaving the house he heard on the radio that it might rain. He went to the closet.

If asked why he did this we would respond that he was probably getting an umbrella. (It would be also possible to answer that he was getting his raincoat, but this is not important since "raincoat" would also have information connecting it to rain.) The extra mechanism which is needed here is the ability to put the "expectation" of getting an umbrella together with our knowledge of where umbrellas are normally kept, to conclude that he is going to get his umbrella in spite of the fact that the word "umbrella" was never mentioned.

The trouble with this solution is that it would not account for the following story:

(11) Jack began to worry when he realized that everyone on the street was carrying an umbrella.

Question: What was Jack worrying about?

Answer: That it might rain, and he was without an umbrella.

While it is intuitively clear that a fact like (9) comes into play here, the formulation in (10), as vague as it is, is incapable of accounting for (11). The problem is that since (11) never mentioned rain, the demon expressed in (10) would never have been activated. To put this in terms of pointers, the fact in (10) only allows a pointer from "rain" to "umbrella", it does not allow a pointer from "umbrella" to "rain", and hence cannot be used to help us conclude in (11) that the problem is rain. Now it is not hard to come up with solutions to this problem. For example,

(12)

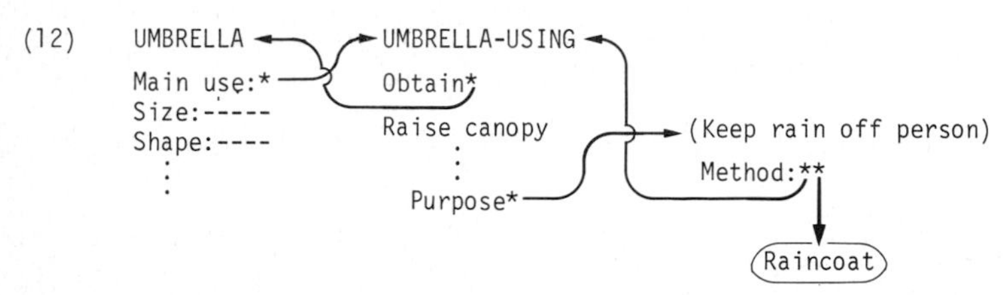

What (12) says is that there is a heading under "umbrella" which indicates the use of umbrellas by pointing to a set of facts about umbrella usage. Umbrella usage naturally points right back at umbrella because to use an umbrella you must have one. It also notes that the purpose of using an umbrella is to keep rain off one, and keeping rain off one notes that one standard way to accomplish this end is to use an umbrella. Now with the possible exception of the facts listed under "umbrella-using" none of this looks very much like a program, or a demon. It is rather a complex set of pointers, which is just another way to say "data structure". Furthermore, it is argued in (Charniak 1975a) that even umbrella-using cannot be considered to be "program" but rather looks like "data".

Now all this argument is highly speculative. First, we are arguing that the proper representation for fact (9) looks more like data than program, and from that conclusion we wish to argue against PLANNER, and the "proceduralist" (see Chapter 7) view in general. Both phases of the argument can be attacked. For one thing, it is conceivable that we could change demon (10) so that it could also be activated by "umbrella". This would not be easy since it would require that the program take into account under which circumstances it was activated, but it could be conceivably done. The response, of course, is the same one we gave concerning FOPC. When we have to subvert the natural inclinations of a system there is probably something wrong. (It is also true that there is no hard line between what might be considered program, and what data. One of the factors which helps determine whether we consider a particular structure as one or the other is to what degree the structure determines how it is to be used. By allowing programs to become usable in more than one way we are making them slightly less "program-like". One must watch for the possibility that in gradually modifying one's program to account for cases like (11), it becomes "data" without one's realizing it.)

Also note that by giving up the use of demons to represent individual facts like (9) we are implicitly giving up the mechanism of pattern directed invocation as our means of locating useful facts. That is, since we no longer represent (9) as a demon there is no longer the pattern-program distinction which makes the concept of pattern directed invocation meaningful.

But saying that (9) is better expressed in a data format like (12) than a demon format like (10) is not necessarily to say that knowledge should not be expressed in PLANNER. As we noted earlier, PLANNER is a programming language and hence has a certain amount of flexibility. To consider only one possibility, we could agree that (9) should not be expressed as a distinct demon, while arguing instead that it is better expressed as part of a program which, say, includes all of the information expressed in (12), but unlike (12) is written in PLANNER. The objection is simply what by now has become an old refrain: we should be suspicious when we have to manoeuvre around the problems inherent in a formalism.

TWO NATURAL LANGUAGE REASONING PROGRAMS

In a field like this, where very little is known, and most work is of the form, well let's try this and see how it works, there is a natural tendency simply to list those doing work within the approved paradigm. This has been avoided so far, but we will relax a bit here and go into the work of two people whose work seems of particular interest. We will keep up the implicit comparisons offered by the answers to the five questions, but otherwise their work will be presented in an non-unified manner.

McDermott

McDermott's program TOPLE (1974) differs in a subtle, yet interesting way from the other work presented here. The other work, as, say, represented by that on children's stories has been primarily concerned with inference as a necessity for question answering. TOPLE's main concern is not so much making inferences, or question answering, but rather "believing". That is to say McDermott wants to answer the question: How does one come to _believe_ something? The intuitive answer is that it is a function of the authority behind the statement, and how well it fits into the rest of one's beliefs. McDermott starts from the common sense view and tries to expand on it. That the process manifestly requires inference as a component is the reason his work is so relevant here.

Much of what follows is in the form of an expanded explanation of McDermott's main example. McDermott's TOPLE only handles sentences which describe a simple world consisting of a monkey and experimenter in a single room - a narrow situation ("_micro-world_"), similar to Winograd's SHRDLU. SHRDLU's situation was the "blocks world", while TOPLE's is one inspired by McCarthy's "Monkey and Bananas" problem. McCarthy's original problem was concerned with axiomitizing the knowledge needed by a monkey trying to get some bananas suspended from the ceiling and out of his direct reach. However, a box is provided which can be moved under the bananas allowing the monkey to reach them. McDermott was not concerned with this problem in particular, but simply considered it a subject familiar to his audience.

TOPLE accepts a present tense account of what is happening in the monkey's room and tries to believe everything it is told by seeing how the new fact relates to what it already knows. Unlike the blocks world, which was rigidly determined (see Chapter 6), TOPLE allows some vagueness into its world, such as precisely where things are located in the room, or why the monkey performed a particular action. But the best way to see all of this is to go through a few lines of an example handled by the program.

Like Charniak, McDermott was not specifically concerned with parsing language but was concerned with reference and ambiguity problems, and he adopts the same solution of inputting not English, but a semantic representation which deliberately allows for ambiguities which are to be figured out by the program. We will simply give the input in English equivalents however.

"The banana is under the table, by the ball."

This is handled as two statements, the first of which is of no particular concern to us. The second is of some interest since, as McDermott points out, it is ambiguous between at least two situations, namely those corresponding to (13) and (14).

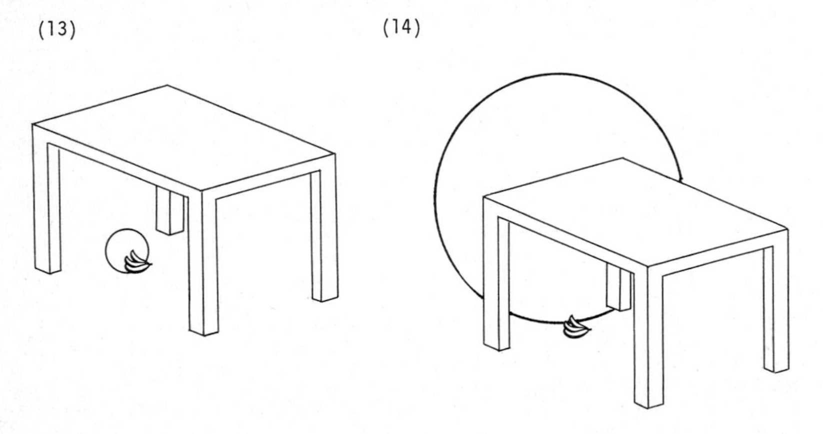

Clearly (14) is odd, because balls seldom are so large, but note that if we had said "by the floor lamp", situation (15), corresponding to (14) would be quite reasonable. TOPLE chooses (13) as its idea of what the room looks like on the basis of likely size for a ball.

(15)

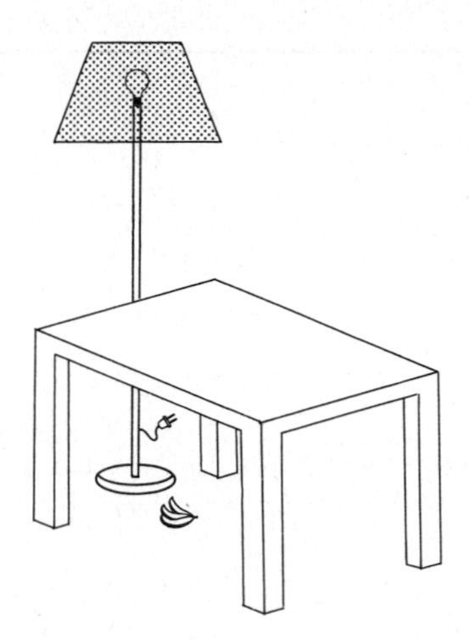

A more interesting example of the program's behavior is its response to the sentence,

"The monkey goes over to the table."

TOPLE wants to believe this statement. The program for GO states that to do so it must establish that the monkey can and wants to perform this action. The former is no problem, but the program does not know why Spiro wants to go to the table. A good reason would be because he is interested in something at that location, namely the table, ball, or banana. TOPLE cannot imagine Spiro being interested in the table, but he could play with the ball, or eat the banana. The uncertainty between these two is reflected in the fact that TOPLE generates two alternative versions of what Spiro wants and what he will do. (The representation used here is not McDermott's, which is more complex. Since we will not be discussing any issues which make the more complex notation relevant, we have simplified it for ease of presentation.)

In situation 0:

(WANT SPIRO (HOLD SPIRO BAN1))

(WANT SPIRO (EAT SPIRO BAN1))

(HUNGRY SPIRO)

(GO SPIRO TAB1)

In situation 1:

(AT SPIRO TAB1)

(PICK-UP SPIRO BAN1)

In situation 2:

(HOLD SPIRO BAN1)

In situation 3:

(EAT SPIRO BAN1)

In situation 4:

BAN1 ceases to exist

OR in situation 0':

(WANT SPIRO (HOLD SPIRO BALL1))
(WANT SPIRO (PLAY SPIRO BALL1))
(GO SPIRO TAB1)

In situation 5:

(AT SPIRO TAB1)

In situation 6:

(PLAY SPIRO BALL1)
(PICK-UP SPIRO BALL1)

In situation 7:

(HOLD SPIRO BALL1)

"Each situation referred to here is a separate state of the world, which represents a state incrementally different from its predecessor as a result of some action. These two sequences of situations are mutually exclusive: situations 1 and 5 are both possible successors to state 0. (Notice that there are two different versions of state 0 which the system keeps in mind.) The sequences are generated by simulating Spiro with the goals corresponding to his respective WANTs. (HUNGRY SPIRO) in situation 0 or (WANT SPIRO (PLAY SPIRO BALL1)) in situation 0' are the crucial assumptions shown - they were introduced to explain the monkey's behavior."

At this point the program has created two "possible worlds" — one in which Spiro is hungry and one in which he wants to play. Furthermore each world has been elaborated with actions to be expected given the assumption about Spiro's desires. What is needed now is some evidence to support one possibility over the other. The next sentence is "Spiro picks up the banana" and this provides the evidence needed. In particular this will match a predicted action in situation 1, and hence serves to confirm the entire series of situations 0 to 4. Of course, really only events up to situation 2 have been mentioned; that Spiro will eat the banana as claimed in situation 3 is a prediction TOPLE makes. The unrealized possible world consisting of situations 0' and 4 to 7 will simply be thrown away.

As we have come to expect from a language understanding system TOPLE holds many beliefs which are not in any sense deduced from what it has heard, but are guessed, so it must keep track of its reasons for believing what it believes. What makes TOPLE different from other systems discussed here is that if later information conflicts with its guesses, it has some ability to find new hypotheses which account for both old and new data.

This ability is due to TOPLE's "belief ring" device. To take a slight variation on one of McDermott's admittedly artificial examples, (one that certainly does not come up in the monkey and bananas world) suppose we know that Fred is a bird, but that he does not fly. To try to believe both of these statements at the same time forces one to make up some hypothesis explaining the discrepancy. So, for example, we might suppose that Fred is a penguin. To support this hypothesis, we might look to see where Fred lives, hoping it is in the Antarctic. Let us suppose however that all we can find is that Fred lives in the southern hemisphere. This supports the hypothesis that Fred lives in Antarctica, but hardly confirms it. Using belief rings, we would represent our current state of knowledge as follows:

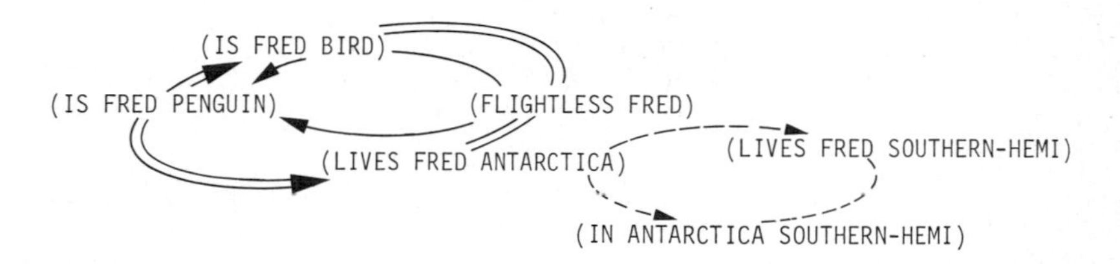

First look only at the single solid arrows. This ring represents our initial situation. The arrows point from the problematic statements to the hypothesis which solves the problem. But assuming Fred was a penguin was problematic, we looked for support by assuming he lived in Antarctica, and this is the double lined ring. This in turn was an unjustified assumption, and in looking for support we found the southern hemisphere statement which, as the dotted ring indicates, supports belief in Antarctica. Associated with each ring, but not shown above, is a program which helps in case there is reason to doubt any of the elements of the ring. So, for example, if we learned that Fred lived in Sidney we would have to doubt that he lived in the Antarctic. To overcome this we could either start believing that Fred was an ostrich, or that he lived in a zoo.

What is especially interesting about all of this is that it gives the program a good measure of how unplausible a particular fact is, namely, how many unjustified assumptions does the program have to make in order that the unplausible fact seems plausible. This in turn is of interest because in using our real world knowledge to, say, decide pronoun reference, we generally make our choice not because one possible referent would lead to an impossible situation, but rather because choosing one referent will lead to a slightly more plausible situation than another (see Chapter 9 for more on reference determination).

Turning to our five questions, there are several aspects of McDermott's program which deserve notice. With regard to why and when inferences are made (inference triggering) McDermott's program differs from the others (as we have already noted) in that it assumes inferences are made to help believe what one is told, rather than simply fill in blanks of a story. This seems to have some interesting ramifications with respect to reference determination, as already seen. However, the entire area of justified belief is so unexplored that this aspect of the program offers little that can be compared to other work. One area where it does have interesting contrasts is that of organization.

When a new assertion comes into the system there are two places in TOPLE where one should look for facts which should be combined with it to make new inferences. The most obvious place is a series of routines which are keyed to the main predicate and very roughly correspond to Charniak's base routines. (This is a very rough approximation since, in fact, McDermott also uses these routines as fact finders.) So, for example, we saw how it was the routine for GO which started the system on the trail which lead to setting up the two possible worlds, each based on a different assumption about why Spiro went to the table. The other place where the incoming assertion should look is in the multiple world structure. We saw how depending on whether we thought Spiro was going for the banana or the ball, TOPLE predicted two different possible continuations of the story. Each continuation is given its own "world", i.e. separate data base, but each data base is connected to the "real world" in that the facts known in the real world are assumed in both possible worlds. So we have three data bases at that point, arranged as follows:

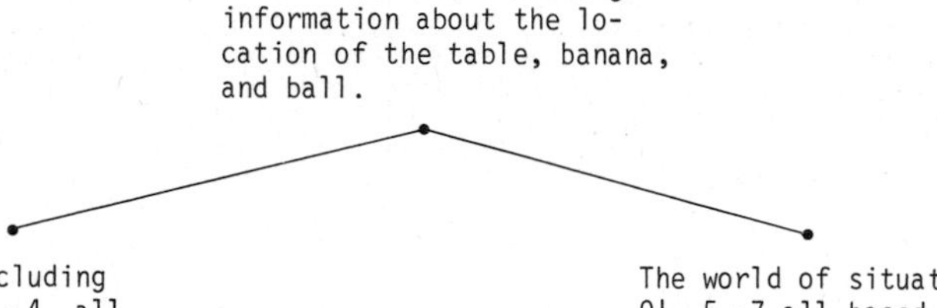

Now remember that when the next sentence came in (Spiro picked up the banana) this matched one of the statements in the left hand world, and hence it was chosen as the true successor to the "real world" and the right hand continuation was dropped. In doing this we were making inferences. In particular, we infer that Spiro went over to the table so as to pick up the banana and eat it.

Again, roughly speaking, this multiple world structure serves McDermott in the same capacity as demons did for Charniak. They enable the program to look forward to what might happen, and recognize confirmation when it occurs. However, the two mechanisms are by no means formally equivalent. For one thing, multiple worlds have a hard time with situations where at some point several alternatives might happen, but which occurs has no effect on the continuing action. For example, we know that when a person exchanges something at the store he could get, a) his money back, b) a credit slip, c) another thing of the same type, d) something different, but costing the same. It is not hard to imagine a single demon accepting any of these possibilities, but offhand it would seem that TOPLE would have to split into four worlds. A multiple worlds system could handle this more reasonably if we allowed assertions with variables, so that one "world" could accept several slightly different outcomes. Of course, in allowing variables we would be extending McDermott's concept, and still further extensions would be needed for multiple worlds to replace demons. So we are back to our usual situation of asking at what point one should give up extending and look instead for a different formalism.

On the other hand, the multiple world structure is much more convenient than demons for modelling predictions of a series of actions over time. And finally, in one way McDermott's model is similar to Charniak's in that his system would have the same problem concerning missing a generalization about using an umbrella.

Rieger

The work of Rieger would be of interest if only because it is the first attempt to use Schank's conceptual dependency theory within a theory of inference and knowledge. However, it is probably the case that Rieger's work owes little to conceptual dependency theory, as will be seen by the fact that further description of his work will hardly mention it. On the other hand, the work is perfectly capable of standing on its own intrinsic merit, so it need not be viewed as an extension of conceptual dependency theory.

Rieger's program, which he did not name, has as its primary purpose the making of reasonable inference from the input it is given. The input, like both Charniak and McDermott, is expressed not in natural language, but in a suitable formalism, in this case conceptual dependency representation.

One problem in describing Rieger's work is that he attempted to cover so much ground that it would not be possible to go through a short example which would demonstrate a significant number of his program's capabilities. However, a typical example would be something like:

John hit Mary.

From this input the program would make inferences like:

(16) John probably used his hand.

(17) Mary was probably hurt.

(18) John probably wanted to hurt Mary.

(19) John might have been angry at Mary.

(20) John and Mary are near each other.

Mary now wants to feel better.

John probably wants Mary to feel better.

This example is typical in that, a) The inferences are based upon a single sentence. There are some examples of three or four line "stories", but the overwhelming majority of examples are inferences made from one or two lines of text. b) The topic of the sentence is some relatively simple action like hitting, rather than more complex activities like birthday parties, or getting around in a supermarket. c) The program will often go too far in making inferences, so that the last inference above is odd. The program made the inference because it believes that Mary's wanting to feel better is a result of John's hitting her, while at the same time believing that John wants all the conceivable results of his action. While Rieger would admit that this particular inference is a mistake, his philosophy is that at this point in time it is better to write programs that err on the side of inferring too much, rather than too little.

Given the scope of the program (besides simply making inferences, it is also designed to understand stories, engage in dialogue, use inference to help figure out reference and word sense ambiguity, and answer questions based not on a story, but rather about the way the world normally is) to try to simply describe its workings would inevitably lead to a large amount of detail and little enlightenment. Instead let us use our five questions to structure the description. In doing so, however, we are leaving out a large amount and concentrating on those aspects of the program which we consider theoretically most interesting. That is to say, (using the program-theory distinction mentioned in the last section) what will be presented is Charniak's theory of Rieger's program, not Rieger's.

SEMANTIC REPRESENTATION. As already mentioned Rieger uses conceptual dependency theory, which is, of course, a theory of semantic representation.

INFERENCE TRIGGERING. Much of what is most interesting, if not to say controversial, in Rieger's work falls under this heading. For example, on the important question of how much inference is done at read time Rieger takes what is at the moment an extreme view, namely that the number of inferences is huge. Of course, no-one really has any idea of how many inferences need be made, so saying that the number is huge in itself does not mean much, but when coupled with Rieger's examples of inferences which ought to be made, and his overall view of the status of inference making, it becomes clear that he is thinking of several orders of magnitude more inferences than, say, McDermott or Charniak would be prepared to admit. For example, Rieger holds that inferences are a "reflex" and are made in an almost completely unguided way upon hearing a sentence. The purpose of all this unguided inference is to find connections between what was just said and other information already in memory. To use his analogy, the incoming sentences form points in "inference space" and the purpose of the unguided inference is to make expanding spheres around those points in inference space until one sphere comes in contact with others. By comparison, both Charniak's and McDermott's models make inferences only to fill specific "gaps", presumably because both think that the number of inferences which would be produced in an unguided search would be so huge as to preclude the spheres meeting in a reasonable time. Another way to see this disagreement would be to note that for Rieger, the following would be reasonable inferences to make at read time.

Input: John told Mary that Bill wants a book.

Responses: Bill wants to possess a book.
John believes that Bill wants a book.
Mary now knows that Bill wants a book.
Bill probably wants to read a book.
Bill might want to know the concepts contained in the book.
Bill might get himself a book.
John might give Bill a book.
Mary might give Bill a book.
John may want Mary to give Bill a book.
John and Mary may have been together recently.

Of all of these, only the first seems reasonable to usually infer. (That is, there are special circumstances where any of the above might be inferred. For example, if we knew that the book in question was one where Mary had several extra copies, we might wish to infer the second to last. But this is clearly an exception rather than a general rule.) Other topics which fall under the heading of inference triggering are Rieger's discussion of the relation between inference and reference (see Chapter 9) and his classification of inference types (which we will discuss next). The classification is according to what one is trying to learn by making the inference. (If you do not see how a classification of inference types falls under the heading of Inference Triggering, wait, it will be justified later.)

It would not be possible to discuss all of Rieger's inference types (Rieger spends about 150 pages doing so) so we will simply present Rieger's listing of the types which are reasonably self-explanatory. (With the exception of type 1, what follows is Rieger's wording.)

1. Specification inferences: A conceptual dependency representation for an action has certain slots for information which must be filled in (specified). So, for example, it required an inference to infer that if John hit Mary a hand was used to do the hitting (16).

2. Causative inferences: What were the likely causes of an action or state? For example, (19).

3. Resultative inferences: What are the likely results (effects on the world) of an action or state? (17).

4. Motivational inferences: Why did (or would) an actor want to perform an action? What were his intentions? (18).

5. Enablement inferences: What states of the world must be (must have been) true in order for some action to occur? (20).

6. Function inferences: Why do people desire to possess objects?

7. Enablement-prediction inferences: If a person wants a particular state of the world to exist, is it because of some predictable action that state would enable?

8. Missing enablement inferences: If a person cannot perform some action he desires, can it be explained by some missing pre-requisite state of the world?

9. Intervention inferences: If an action in the world is causing (or will cause) undesired results, what might an actor do to prevent or curtail the action?

10. Action-prediction inferences: Knowing a person's needs and desires, what actions is he likely to perform to attain those desires?

11. Knowledge-propagation inferences: Knowing that a person knows certain things, what other things can he also be predicted to know?

12. Normative inferences: Relative to a knowledge of what is normal in the world, determine how strongly a piece of information should be believed in the absence of specific knowledge.

13. State-duration inferences: Approximately how long can some state or protracted action be predicted to last?

14. Feature inferences: Knowing some features of an entity, and the situations in which that entity occurs, what additional things can be predicted about that entity?

15. Situation inferences: What other information surrounding some familiar situation can be imagined (inferred)?

16. Utterance-intent inferences: What can be inferred from the way in which something was said? Why did the speaker say it?

So looking at 7, enablement-prediction inferences, a typical example would be:

Andy blew on the hot meat.

Here we would assume that Andy intended to eat the meat. Presumably our reasoning would be that blowing on the meat will cool it, and food being at a reasonable temperature is a usual pre-requisite (or, to use Rieger's term, "enabling condition") for eating it. So from Andy's desire to obtain the enabling state we infer his desire for the action.

But why do we need such a classification? We need it to help limit the number of inferences the system makes. That is, Rieger and the other authors discussed in this chapter believe that many, if not most, of the inferences a comprehension program must make are done while the system is reading the text rather than after a question has been asked. Given however that in general an infinite number of inferences may be drawn from a line of text, we must, at the very least, classify inferences into two classes: those the system will draw immediately, and those it will only make if asked a question which requires the inference. (This is where inference triggering comes in.) But presumably which inferences should be made immediately will depend on the circumstances, such as what the system is trying to get out of the text. So we cannot simply classify inferences into two groups, but rather must make a much finer classification which will also tell us how the boundaries of the "make inference while reading" class will change with circumstances. Hence we need a classification of inferences.

And, indeed, Rieger uses his classification in precisely this way, but given that he already argued that one should not limit the number of inferences significantly (remember the expanding inference spheres) his argument for using the inference types is not very convincing, and hence his classification never seems very useful. Furthermore, he only uses four of the sixteen types, in any way whatsoever. That he spends so much time on the classification without ever giving convincing evidence of how it is to be used is one of the major problems of the work.

ORGANIZATION. Rieger's organization can be explained using the terminology developed in the description of Charniak's work. Inference making information is organized into clusters which Rieger calls inference molecules, which in turn correspond to base routines. Fact-finders have their parallel in Rieger's Normality molecules (although since Rieger believes that most inferences should be made at read time presumably his normality molecules are used much less than Charniak's fact-finders). Rieger does not have anything corresponding to demons, and in fact explicitly argues against their use, claiming instead that it would be better to simply go ahead and make the inference immediately, rather than waiting for confirming evidence as a demon does. This is somewhat plausible in cases like, if Jack is hungry, assert that he will likely eat. The alternative suggested by the demon approach would be to put in a demon looking for evidence of eating. In this case both alternatives seem reasonable, but in other cases Rieger's lack of demons (or the equivalent) leads to problems. So, if Janet gets her piggybank, the demon approach would suggest looking for evidence both that money was in it, and that there was no money in it; would Rieger assert both of these? Notice that McDermott would handle this by using alternate possible worlds, which we have already noted accomplish much of the same things as demons, but Rieger does not have alternate worlds in his model.

INFERENCE MECHANISM. The inference molecules, which we earlier identified as bearing the main load of inference making, are actually LISP programs. However, some facts, like the main use of an object, (the main use of telephone is to communicate information) are represented as "data". Nevertheless most facts are represented as programs and Rieger explicitly argues for procedural representation.

CONTENT. Essentially nothing.

FRAMES

Much of the current work on the problems discussed in this chapter is taking place with the terminology and ideas developed by Minsky in his so-called "Frames paper" (Minsky 1975). This is a complex paper, but the basic idea is quite simple; the units of knowledge manipulated by understanding programs should be much larger than the units used by any of the systems we have looked at so far in this chapter. As such, we will consider the frames idea as a statement about organization, as opposed to the other four issues we have been concerned with. However, it should be emphasized that Minsky's paper has many other aspects to it which we will not even consider.

Minsky's Formulation of Frames

Minsky's starting point is not language at all, but rather the problem of accounting for the ability to see. The problem for Minsky, as well as anyone who wishes to enable a serial digital computer (i.e., a machine which only has one process going at a time) to see, is people's ability to walk into a room, or anywhere else, and seemingly take everything in at a glance. If people are indeed capable of this it would argue that they were not working serially, but rather were able to process many different portions of the scene at the same time (that is, they were working in "parallel"). Minsky proposes instead that the "all at a glance" ability is illusory, and in fact seeing is an extended process. But he still must explain how everything happens so smoothly and quickly. He does this by proposing that prior to walking into a room, say, we have a good idea of what it is we are about to see. If the room is one we are familiar with, our foreknowledge will include details like furniture arrangement, floor covering, etc. If we assume we can bring all of this knowledge to our "attention" in a unit, it is only necessary when we walk into the room to check a few things to see what, if anything, has changed from our expectations. Minsky calls this chunk of knowledge a "frame". But even if we are walking into a strange room, we still have a lot of knowledge about what to expect. At the very least the type of door will indicate that we are walking into a room rather than an auditorium or outdoors. Furthermore, we will usually have a good idea of what sort of room, be it a living room, office, or classroom, and in each case there will be a frame which tells us what in general we should be expecting, so that "seeing" the room only requires noting how the particular room in front of us compares to the usual case. A frame then is a data structure for representing a sterotyped visual situation. When we move on to language we will simply drop the word "visual".

Keeping to the paradigm situation of describing our knowledge of a room, what do we need to represent this knowledge? If it is a room we know well, we will need to indicate the objects in it. Each object will be represented by a "terminal" of the frame. The terminal will describe the object in the sense that it will specify the properties the object has. In the case of a stereotyped room, such as the typical office, the terminals will not be so much specific objects, but, naturally enough, prototypic objects, such as "the standard desk". These terminals will be described by the properties the object typically has. Minsky assumes that in fact people do assign a specific object to such prototypic terminals (as a "default" value) which becomes in effect our personal idea of the standard desk. But actually, little in the theory depends on whether the terminal simply describes a vague desk which we can instantiate when we walk into the office, or whether instead the terminal also gives a specific standard desk which must be modified to fit the particular instance in front of us.

Besides the terminals we also need relations between objects, as well as information on how to use the frame. Furthermore, each frame will have pointers to other frames which describe the same place, but from a different point of view. So when we walk into a room the wall behind us will not be visible, and hence according to Minsky will not be in the frame describing what we expect to see. However, there will be related frames which will describe this wall. To avoid needless duplication of descriptions between related frames it is assumed that frames may share terminal nodes. That is, supposing we only had four views for a room (one aimed at each wall) most objects in the center of the room would appear in all four, and each wall would appear in three of the four. By sharing terminals we need not give the descriptions of each object anew in each frame.

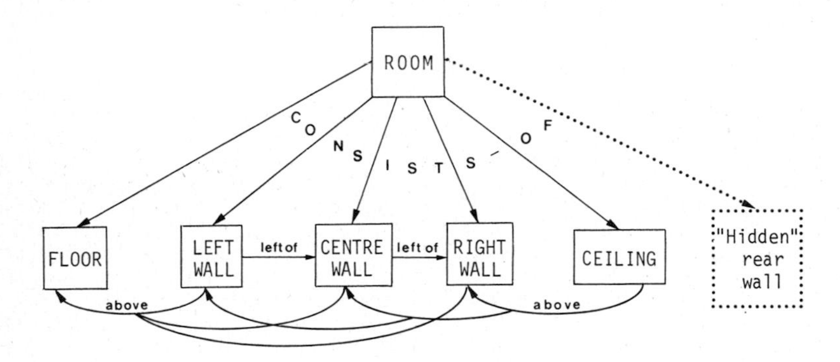

A FRAME FOR A BARE ROOM

We have started our discussion of frames with their application to vision because it is there that they fit most cleanly. When we move into the problems of language, the frames Minsky proposes become more complicated. For one thing we no longer have a single notion of "frame" but rather four kinds of frames, roughly corresponding to syntactic representation, semantic representation, stereotyped event situation, and communication convention representation. The first two should be reasonably self explanatory. The last of the four concerns our knowledge of the way stories are told, conversations held, or scientific articles proceed. To look at stories, one can typically expect one or more main protagonists, a setting, and some overriding goal. The "story frame" would then specify what our conventions are for telling a story. There have been many attempts to specify this, (indeed much literary analysis can be thought of in this light) but as of yet nothing has been proposed specific enough to help us in the analysis of stories.

It is, however, the third of the four frame types, "stereotyped events", or what Minsky calls "scenario frames", which is of most interest to us here. Minsky is never very specific about what a scenario frame looks like, but one of his examples should give some idea of what he has in mind. What follows is a schematic outline of the birthday party frame. This could be used to comprehend stories of the simple variety we have been considering in this chapter. In particular, that a present is required, as mentioned below, would be necessary information to understand a story like:

> Jane was invited to Jack's birthday party. She wondered if he would like a kite.

DRESS.................Sunday best.

PRESENT...............Must please host.
Must be bought and gift-wrapped.

GAMES.................Hide and seek. Pin tail on donkey.

DECOR.................Balloons, favors, crepe-paper.

PARTY-MEAL............Cake, ice-cream, soda, hot-dogs.

CAKE..................Candles, blow-out, wish, sing birthday song.

ICE-CREAM.............Standard three-flavor.

This frame fits reasonably well into the model established for the case of vision, in the sense that the left hand column can be considered a list of frame terminals, while the right gives the default fillers for those terminals. However, slightly later in the paper Minsky opts for considering the terminals to be "the most serious problems and questions commonly associated with (the topic of the frame)". And he gives a slightly different analysis of the same frame.

Y must get P for X....Choose P!

X must like P.........Will X like P?

Buy P.................Where to buy P? } Sub-questions of the "present" frame?

Get money to buy P....Where to get money? }

Y must dress up.......What should Y wear?

In comparing the two versions, notice that the former resembles something like a "static" description of what makes up a birthday party, while the latter reads more like a series of instructions one might give to somebody who had to attend a party, and who never had before. Notice, for example, that the second version does not mention decorations. One might imagine a second series of instructions (a second frame), but this one for a party _giver_, which did mention the problem of choosing decorations.

Further Work in the Frames Paradigm

Minsky never notes the shift which occurred between his two party frames, but some subsequent work has tended to favor the second version over the first. In particular, two recent papers, one by Schank and Abelson (1975) and the other by Charniak (1975b) describe formal objects much like Minsky's scenario frames, and in both cases the frames take the form of instructions to an individual about how to do something. In the Schank and Abelson paper the formal objects are called "scripts" deriving from previous work of Abelson (1973) which we have not had space to discuss. The script they present is how to eat at a restaurant. Charniak calls his information clusters "scenario frames" after Minsky, and outlines how to shop at a supermarket. What follows is Charniak's analysis in that the examples and terminology are his, but there seem to be no significant differences between his frames and Schank and Abelson's scripts.

As Minsky, a scenario frame (henceforth simply "frame") is a data structure about one stereotyped topic, such as shopping at the supermarket, taking a bath, or using a piggybank. Each frame is primarily made up of many statements about the frame topic, called "_frame statements_" (henceforth abbreviated to FS). FS's correspond roughly to Minsky's terminals, especially when terminals are taken to be questions about the frame topic. (Questions can be viewed as notational variants on statements, and nothing in (Minsky 1975) really argues against considering them as such.) The FS's are expressed in a suitable semantic representation, although we will simply express them here in ordinary English.

The primary mechanism of understanding a line of a story is to see it as instantiating one or more FS's. So, for example, a particular FS in the shopping at the supermarket frame would be:

(21) SHOPPER obtain use of BASKET.

(SHOPPER, BASKET, and in general any part of an FS written in upper case is a variable. These variables must be restricted so that SHOPPER is probably human, and certainly animate, while BASKET should only be bound to baskets, as opposed to, say, pockets.) This FS would be instantiated by the second line of story (22).

(22) Jack was going to get some things at the supermarket.
The basket he took was the last one left.

Here we assume that part of the second line will be represented by the story statement:

(23) Jack1 obtain use of basket1.

(Again, both (21) and (23) would really be represented in some more abstract internal representation.) That (23) is an instantiation of (21) would be recorded with a special pointer from the story statement to the FS it instantiates.

The supermarket frame will contain other FS's which refer to (21), such as:

(24) (21) usually occurs before (25).

(25) SHOPPER obtains PURCHASE-ITEMS.

Any modification (like (24)) of a particular FS (like (21)) will be assumed true of all SS's (story statements) which instantiate that FS (like (23)), unless there is evidence to the contrary. Hence, using (24) we could conclude that Jack has not yet finished his shopping in (22). Other modifications of (21) would tell us that Jack was probably already in the supermarket when he obtained the basket, and that he got the basket to use during shopping.

The variable SHOPPER in (21) also appears in (25), and in general a single variable will appear in many FS's. Hence the scope of these variables must be at least that of the frame in which they appear. When an SS instantiates an FS the variables in the FS will be bound. Naturally, it is necessary to keep track of such bindings. For example, failure to do so would cause the system to fail to detect the oddness in:

> Jack went to the supermarket. He got a cart and started up and down the aisles. Bill took the goods to the check-out counter and left.

It is probably a bad idea to actually change the frame to keep track of such bindings. Instead we assume that the frame remains pure, and that the variable bindings are recorded in a separate data structure called a "frame image" (abbreviated FI). For frames which describe some action, like our shopping at supermarket frame, we will create a separate FI for each instance of someone performing the action. So two different people shopping at the same time, or the same person shopping on two different occasions, would require two FI's to record those particulars which distinguish one instance of supermarket shopping from all others.

Much of this information will be stored in the variable bindings (shopper, purchase items, store, shopping cart used, etc.). However the variable bindings do not exhaust the information we wish to store in the FI; for example, it will probably prove necessary to have pointers from the FI to some, if not all, of the SS's which instantiate FS's of the frame in question. Of slightly more interest is that the FI of a frame describing an action will keep track of how far the activity has progressed. So, for example, we would find the following story odd:

> Jack drove to the supermarket. He got what he needed,
> and took it to his car. He then got a shopping cart.

We have already said that FS's are modified by time ordering statements, so to note the oddity here it is only necessary to have one or more <u>progress pointers</u> in the FI to the most time-wise advanced FS yet mentioned in the story.

To give the reader some more concrete idea of what such a frame would look like we include the following example, recognizing that it is first simply a fragment of a complete supermarket frame, and secondly that it is probably incorrect in many particulars.

```
(26)    Goal:  SHOPPER owns PURCHASE-ITEMS
        SHOPPER decide if to use basket, if so set up cart-carry FI
  (a)   SHOPPER obtain BASKET *cart-carry
        SHOPPER obtain PURCHASE-ITEMS
          |  method - suggested
          └─>Do for all ITEM ∈ PURCHASE-ITEMS
                SHOPPER choose ITEM ∈ PURCHASE-ITEMS - COLLECTED
                SHOPPER at ITEM
                  side-condition COLLECTED at ITEM also
                    |  method - suggested
  (b)               └─>cart-carry (SHOPPER, BASKET, COLLECTED, ITEM)
                SHOPPER hold ITEM
  (c)           ITEM in BASKET *cart-carry
                COLLECTED ← COLLECTED + ITEM
             End
        SHOPPER at CHECK-OUT-COUNTER
        SHOPPER pay for PURCHASE-ITEMS
        SHOPPER leave SUPERMARKET
```

We will not explain the notation, which at a superficial level should be fairly obvious, but there are two points which deserve mention. The first is that the frame calls a sub-frame ("cart-carry" (line (b))) which tells how to use a shopping cart. Furthermore, lines (a) and (c) are specially marked in the frame indicating that they are also FS's in the cart-carry frame and hence (i) only apply if the cart-carry frame is active, and (ii) gain much of their significance from their position in the cart-carry frame (for example, it is in the cart-carry frame where it will be made explicit exactly why one puts the groceries into the cart).

Frames vs. Demons

To gain some perspective on frames, let us see how they compare to the demons we saw earlier in this chapter. Actually, we have already seen one such comparison already. The problem with handling a fact about umbrellas which we brought up concerning the demon model leads to a reformulation of the facts in terms of the diagram (12). The reader is encouraged to go back to that diagram and convince himself that it can be seen as fitting into the frames model quite easily (especially "umbrella-using").

There are, however, other advantages of frames over demons. To see them, let us first note the analogy between FS's on one hand, and demons on the other. This analogy works because FS's accomplish precisely what demons were designed to do - assign significance to a line of text due to the context it is in. So we notice how the following lines will be given significance by the supermarket frame not because they match a demon, but because they match an FS.

> Jack got a cart.
>
> Jack picked up a carton of milk.
>
> Jack walked further down the aisle.
>
> Jack walked to the front of the store. He put the groceries on the counter.

What is interesting in this comparison is that one demon usually has a minimum of three or four statements, whereas obviously a single FS is only one statement. FS's seem then to have a considerable conciseness to them, at least when compared to demons. The reason for this is not hard to see. Demons being independent facts must bind their own variables, and much of the size of a demon is due to checks to make sure that the variable bindings are correct (for example, BASKET must be a basket, and not a carton of milk). These same things must be checked in a frame, but since the scope of the variable is the entire frame, rather than a single FS, the overhead, so to speak, is shared. Furthermore, the inferences about a given FS are stored implicitly in the structure of the frame, whereas they had to be stated explicitly in the demon. So a second advantage of the frames approach over demons is the conceptual economy one obtains in the expression of facts.

The analogy between FS's and demons also points to a third way in which the frames approach seems superior. One problem which bothers many people about the demon approach is that it seemingly calls for large numbers of demons to be activated every time a given topic is mentioned in the story, although it is unlikely that more than a small fraction of the demons will ever be used. There are two possible reasons why people feel this is a problem. One is that so many active demons might make it hard to locate those demons which really should apply. Frames does not help with this problem since there will be equal numbers of FS's.

To see the second reason why activating large numbers of demons is problematic, note that if it took no time at all to set up a demon, setting up many of them would seem less bad. But of course it does take time to set up a demon, and it becomes a problem to justify this computation in light of the unlikeliness of the demon ever being used. Frames offers a potential solution to this second problem because with frames, rather than supermarket activating many demons, we need only create a frame image for one frame (i.e. supermarket). This would take much less time and hence would be better, but it should be noted that we pay a price. In particular most of the work involved in setting up a demon is to index our storage of active demons so that retrieving the ones needed will be reasonably easy. By comparison, looking through frames to find matching FS's promises to be a time consuming task unless we do something similar. On the other hand, the frames approach allows one to trade more time for locating an FS in return for less time to set up a new topic (frame), and the specter of all those never to be used demons makes one inclined to accept this trade.

Finally, the frames presented here have no problem handling time relations between FS's. The same cannot be said of demons. (This was hinted at when we noted that McDermott's possible worlds handled time relations better than did demons.) We saw earlier in this section how frames might use a progress pointer to allow the program to notice actions which were out of sequence. What could be the equivalent in the demon model of the progress pointer? For one thing, where would such a pointer be stored? Short of giving every demon a pointer to the progress pointer, an inelegant solution at best, it is not clear what one could do. Furthermore, where would the time ordering information be stored? Notice that time ordering information is much more complex than a simple string, or even lattice, which indicates the time orderings of actions. For example, some time orderings are "strict" in the sense that one cannot possibly do things any other way, while others are "suggested" in the sense that it is a good idea to do the actions in a given order, but possible to do them some other way, while yet others are "regulatory" in the sense that it is possible, but illegal, to do the actions in the opposite order (Charniak 1975a). In the frames model one can store time ordering statements in the frame along with the rest. It is by no means obvious what to do in the demon model. This is not to say that one could not do it, but again one would be circumventing the natural properties of the model.

CONCLUSION

Frames may well be better than demons, but this should not fool the reader into thinking that we know the answers to all of the questions we proposed long ago in Chapter 1. Let us consider just a few problems which we did not even mention in our analysis of frames.

One problem is formalizing under what circumstances a frame will be activated (in the sense of a frame image being created for it). A first order solution is that each frame will be activated by certain key words, like "supermarket". But this is clearly insufficient. For one thing, often we will mention "supermarket" but not want to activate the shopping frame, as when one is describing a city block and mentioning each kind of store in the block. At the same time we may well want to activate the supermarket frame without any obvious key words being mentioned. For example:

> As Jack walked down the aisle he picked up a can of tunafish and put it in his basket.

How we are to handle such situations is an open question.

Even more important, frames only handle "stereotyped" situations. Such situations are the backbone of all stories, but obviously a story must move beyond the stereotype or else it will be quite boring. We have not said how frames are to be used in understanding the unusual twists which occur in all stories, and in real life for that matter.

One could multiply such problems several times over, but let us conclude with a problem which affects all of the systems mentioned in this chapter — that of content. It probably has not escaped the reader's notice that each time in our analysis by means of our five questions, when we came to "content" the answer was always the same. In none of the systems had the author attempted to formalize an appreciable amount of the knowledge we need to understand even the simplest stories. Many reasons can be given for this, but two stand out. First, the problem of content is tough. (Charniak 1974) attempts to analyze the information needed to understand the last line of story (16) in Chapter 1 ("He will make you take it back"). In something like 100 pages he comes up with an admittedly incomplete analysis. Secondly, one cannot really get very far on the problem of content until one has at least some idea of what one's representation looks like, else one is left writing a list of English sentences, which hardly solves the problem. Hence it is not until one has some faith in one's representation that one can even try formalizing a sizable chunk of world knowledge.

On the other hand, the picture is not as bleak as the preceding paragraphs might make it seem. Our state of knowledge is steadily improving, even if our goal is still far off. Compare the frame analysis to, say, Raphael's SIR (Chapter 1). Raphael's system was quite limited, as was inevitable at that time. SIR handled "A man has two hands. A hand has five fingers. How many fingers does a man have?", but it is not clear how to extend that to understanding the point of getting a basket in a supermarket. The new systems understand language to a degree unimaginable in these earlier systems, and that is some sort of progress.

E. Charniak and Y. Wilks (eds.), Computational Semantics

PARSING ENGLISH II

Yorick Wilks

This chapter continues the discussion of systems that aim to represent the structure of natural language, and to parse those structures onto natural language. At the end of the survey, the systems discussed, in this and other chapters, will be contrasted and compared along several dimensions.

One important thing to bear in mind in what follows is that "parsing" is being used not only in its standard sense in mathematical and computational linguistics: a sense which is completely neutral about the content, value, or interest of the structure which is parsed onto natural language. So, for example, the general notion of parsing was illustrated in Chapter 7 by means of a phrase structure grammar, but the reader will have gathered already that the whole argument of this book is that far richer meaning and knowledge structures than those produced by phrase structure grammars are needed if we are to do anything interesting. So then, "parsing" in what follows is not neutral about what Charniak in Chapter 1 called the content of representations, but rather assumes that to be worth parsing they should have something to say about what, in Chapter 7, were called the intractables of systematic ambiguity in natural language: namely, word sense ambiguity, structural case ambiguity, and ambiguity of pronoun reference.

Second Generation Systems

To understand what Winograd meant when he contrasted his own with what he called second generation systems, we have to remember, as often in this subject, that the generations are of fashion, not chronology or inheritance of ideas. He described the work of Simmons, Schank and Wilks among others in his survey of new approaches, even though the foundations and terminology of those approaches were set out in print in 1966, 1968 and 1967 respectively. What those approaches, and others, have in common is the belief that understanding systems must be able to manipulate very complex linguistic objects, or semantic structures, and that no simplistic approaches to understanding language with computers will work.

It was suggested in Chapter 7 that, as a first approximation only, such second generation approaches could be seen as within what Minsky has called the "frame approach", as described in Chapter 8.

The key point about any structures that are to be called frame-like is that they attempt to specify in advance what is going to be said, and how the world encountered is going to be organized. The structures, and the inference rules that apply to them, are also expressions of something not present in first generation systems, namely "partial information" (in McCarthy's phrase, and meaning rules like "people try to get what they want": rules which express inductive generalizations that are useful but not always true). As was shown earlier in Chapter 7, with the "women and soldiers" example, such loose inductive information, seeking confirmation from the surrounding context, is required for very simple sentences. In psychological and visual terms, frame approaches envisage an understander as at least as much a looker as a seer.

The reader should notice that the characterization of frame-like systems just given is far more general than that set out by Charniak in Chapter 8, and is intended to serve only to introduce three more systems: Colby's, Riesbeck's implementation of Schank, and Wilks'. After that the more general and more specific characterizations of "frame" will be drawn together.

Colby

Colby (Colby et al 1971), (Enea and Colby 1973), (Colby and Parkison 1974) has developed over a period of several years an on-line dialogue system that simulates a paranoid patient called PARRY. A measure of its success is that it is perhaps the most used AI program in existence; used, that is, by those outside the research project that developed it. Here is a discontinuous sample of its output, again with the system's responses in the upper case:

Have you been hospitalised before?

THIS IS THE FIRST TIME.

How long have you been there?

ABOUT TWO WEEKS.

Any headaches?

MY HEALTH IS FINE.

Are you having any difficulty with your memory?

NO.

Then perhaps you can tell me who is the President of the United States?

NIXON IS PRESIDENT.

What day is it today?

TODAY IS THURSDAY.

What season is it?

LET'S GET ON WITH THE INTERVIEW.

Colby's aim was to produce a system that was not, in his word, "fragile" in the way that most AI systems are: one that did not break down, or give up, if the input was not exactly what it expected, but one that carried on somehow in all circumstances, in the way that conversing humans do.

Fragility is avoided by having no conventional syntax analyser, and by not even attempting to take account of all the words in the input. This is a considerable aid, since any parser that begins to parse a more than usually polite request such as "Would you be so kind as to..." is going to be in trouble. British English speakers arriving in the U.S. quickly learn not to use such phrases, since they cause great confusion to human listeners in stores.

The input text is segmented by a heuristic that breaks it at any occurrence of a range of key words. Patterns are then matched with each segment. There are at present about 1,700 patterns on a list (Colby and Parkison, in press) that is stored and matched, not against any syntactic or semantic representations of words (except to deal with contractions and misspellings), but against the input word string direct, and by a process of sequential deletion. So, for example, "What is your main problem?" has a root verb "BE" substituted, and a generic "YOU" for "YOUR", to become

WHAT BE YOU MAIN PROBLEM

It is then matched successively against the stored pattern list in the following forms, each of which is formed by deleting one word from the original string:

BE YOU MAIN PROBLEM

WHAT YOU MAIN PROBLEM

WHAT BE MAIN PROBLEM

WHAT BE YOU PROBLEM

WHAT BE YOU MAIN

Only the _penultimate_ line exists as one of the stored patterns, and it is therefore matched by what we might call this _minimal parsing procedure_.

Stored in the same format as the patterns are rules expressing the consequences for the "patient" of detecting aggression and over-friendliness in the interviewer's questions and remarks. The matched patterns found are then tied directly, or via these inference rules, to response patterns which are generated.

Enormous ingenuity has gone into the heuristics of this system, as its popularity testifies. The system has also changed considerably: it is now called PARRY2 and contains the above pattern matching, rather than earlier key word, heuristics. It has the partial, or what some would call "pragmatic", rules about expectation and intention, and these alone might qualify it as "second generation" on some interpretations of the phrase. A generator is also being installed to avoid the production of only "canned" responses.

Colby and his associates have put considerable energy into actually trying to find out whether or not psychiatrists can distinguish PARRY's responses from those of a patient (Colby and Hilf 1973). This is probably the first attempt actually to apply Turing's suggested (1951) test for machine-person distinguishability by comparing outputs. There are statistical difficulties about interpreting the results but, by and large, the result is that the sample of psychiatrists questioned cannot distinguish the two. Even so, there are many who still, on principle, believe that PARRY is not a simulation because, in their terms, it "does not understand". People who argue that way sometimes implicitly use very high standards for what it is to understand. One could extend their case ironically by pointing out that very few people _understand_ the content of sentences in the depth and detail that an analytic philosopher does, and a very good thing too. But there can be no doubt that many people on many occasions DO seem to understand in the way that PARRY does.

When it was said earlier that PARRY was "robust" as regards the way it dealt with unusual or unexpected input, that did not mean that one would get a very sensible reply if one typed in "***", but, of course, doing things like that is not a very sinsible way to test a language program. What is clear is that, because of its very simple construction, PARRY has been much easier to extend to cover new input than most programs.

The real defect of PARRY is that it is "fragile" in a more general way, namely that much of its "understanding" is due to the particular environment of the imitation of _paranoid_ behavior. The user of the program tends to tolerate evident "refusals to co-operate" and abrupt "changes of subject" by the program, on the ground that a paranoid might well behave like that, although, in language understanding terms, this behavior is the result of the system being unable to make any sense (in terms of effective pattern matching) of the input it is receiving.

Wilks

This system constructs a semantic representation for small natural language texts: the basic representation is applied directly to the text and can then be "massaged" by various forms of inference to become as deep as is necessary for tasks intended to demonstrate understanding. It is a uniform representation, in that information that might conventionally be considered as syntactic, semantic, factual or inferential is all expressed within a single type of structure. The fundamental unit of this meaning representation is the _template_, which corresponds to an intuitive notion of a _basic message_ of agent-action-object form. Templates are constructed from more basic building blocks called _formulas_, which correspond to senses of individual words. In order to construct a complete text representation (called a _semantic block_) templates are bound together by two kinds of higher level structures called _paraplates_ and _inference rules_. The templates themselves are built up as the construction of the representation proceeds, but the formulas, paraplates and inference rules are all present in the system at the outset, and each of these three types of pre-stored structure is ultimately constructed from an inventory of eighty _semantic primitive elements_, and from functions and predicates ranging over those elements.

The system runs on-line as a package of LISP (see Chapter 12), MLISP and MLISP2 programs, the two latter languages being expanded LISP languages that have a command structure and pattern matching capacities. It takes as input small paragraphs of English, that can be made up by the user from a vocabulary of about 600 word-senses, and produces a good French translation as output for a considerable range of input texts. This environment provides a pretty clear test of language understanding, because French translations for everyday prose are in general either right or wrong, and can be seen to be so while, at the same time, the major difficulties of understanding programs — word sense ambiguity, case ambiguity, difficult pronoun reference, etc. — can all be represented within a machine translation environment by, for example, choosing the words of an input sentence containing a difficult pronoun reference in such a way that the possible alternative references have different genders in French. In that way the French output makes quite clear whether or not the program has made the correct inferences in order to understand what it is translating. The program is reasonably robust in actual performance, and will even tolerate a certain amount of bad grammar in the input, since it does not perform a syntax analysis in the conventional sense, but seeks message forms representable in the semantic structures employed.

Typical input would be a sentence such as "John lives out of town and drinks his wine out of a bottle. He then throws the bottles out of the window." The program will produce French sentences with different output for each of the three occurrences of "out of", since it realizes that they function quite differently on the three occasions of use, and that the difference must be reflected in the French. A sentence such as "Give the monkeys bananas although they are not ripe because they are very hungry" produces a translation with different equivalents for the two occurrences of "they", because the system correctly realizes, from what will be described below as preference considerations, that the most sensible interpretation is one in which the first "they" refers to the bananas and the second to the monkeys, and bananas and monkeys have different genders in French. These two examples are dealt with in the "basic mode" of the system (Wilks 1973a). In many cases it cannot resolve pronoun ambiguities by the sort of straightforward "preference considerations" used in the last example, where, roughly speaking, "ripeness" prefers to be predicated of plant-like things, and hunger of animate things. Even in a sentence as simple as "John drank the wine on the table and it was good", such considerations are inadequate to resolve the ambiguity of "it", between wine and table, since both may be good things. In such cases of inability to resolve within its basic mode, the program deepens the representation of the text so as to try and set up chains of inference that will reach, and so prefer, only one of the possible referents.

The system contains no explicitly syntactic information at all: what it knows about any English word sense is its formula. This is a tree structure of semantic primitives, and is to be interpreted formally using dependency relations. The main element in any formula is the rightmost, called its head, and that is the fundamental category to which the formula belongs. In the formulas for actions, for example, the head will always be one of the primitives PICK, CAUSE, CHANGE, FEEL, HAVE, PLEASE, PAIR, SENSE, USE, WANT, TELL, BE, DO, FORCE, MOVE, WRAP, THINK, FLOW, MAKE, DROP, STRIK, FUNC or HAPN.

Thus:

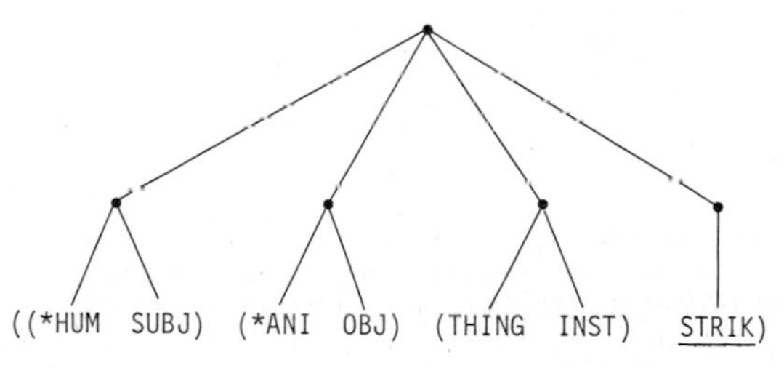

is the formula for the action sense of "beat", and is an action preferable of STRIKing, normally done with an INSTrument (see Chapter 5 on case elements) that is a THING, preferably to an ANImate OBJect, and preferably by a HUMan agent. Asterisks in front of elements (like *HUM) indicate that a class of elements is in question; in this case *HUM covers MAN and FOLK (for human groups). The tree structure is largely superficial so as to get a particular LISP representation and the same semantic entity could be written as Chapter 5 showed Simmons writing his Fillmorian case dependencies, thus:

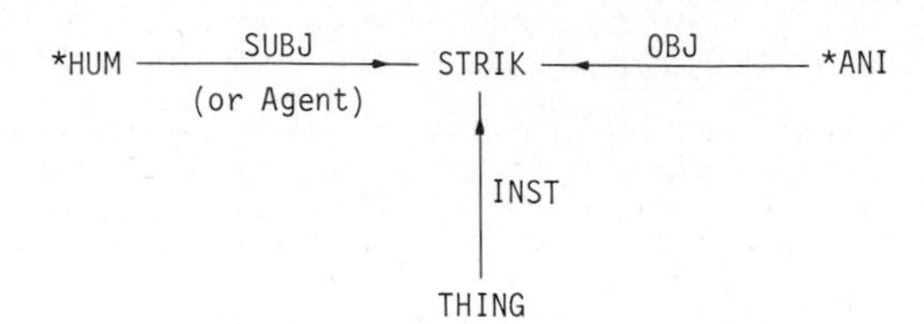

This form emphasizes that the three case parts at the "top level" of the formula are in some fundamental relation to the basic action, or head of the formula (always its right-most member and underlined here). However there are limitations to this re-picturing, as with all picturings. For example, it makes little sense for formula trees representing noun senses, since the head of such a tree (say, THING for a tree for "needle", or STUFF for a tree for "water") will not have case subparts depending on it in the straightforward way that the head of an action tree, like the above one for "beat", does.

The case subparts of a formula can themselves contain case-subparts and even action elements, down to whatever level is thought necessary by the dictionary maker. So, for example, the formula for "sew" would contain an instrument subpart which would specify that the preferred instrument was a linear object (LINE THING) accompanied by an aperture (THRU PART) — that is, of course, a needle. This sub-tree (of the whole tree for "sew") might look like:

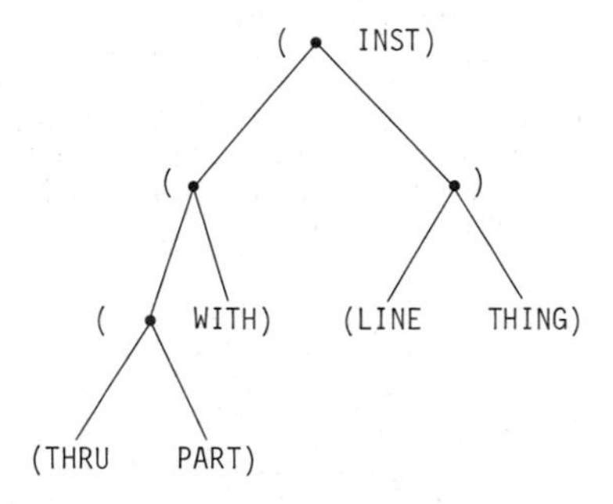

where we have an accompaniment case specification inside an instrumental specification. This form of representation allows order to be of critical importance, which it cannot be in the pictorial-graph style, and it allows far more flexibility in expressing the meaning of noun-senses than can be achieved by the Fodor-Katz method (see Chapter 3) which has no case or action elements (Schank's system is a variant of that method, see Weber (1972)).

Template structures, which actually represent sentences and their parts are built up as networks of formulas like the one above. Templates always consist of an agent node, and action node and an object node, and other nodes that may depend on these. So, in building a template for "John beat the carpet", the whole of the above tree-formula for "beat" would be placed at the action node, another tree structure for "John" at the agent node and so on. The complexity of the system comes from the way in which the formulas, considered as active entities, dictate how other nodes in the same template should be filled.

Thus, a full template is a complex structure. Here, for example, is one for "John shut the door":

(1)

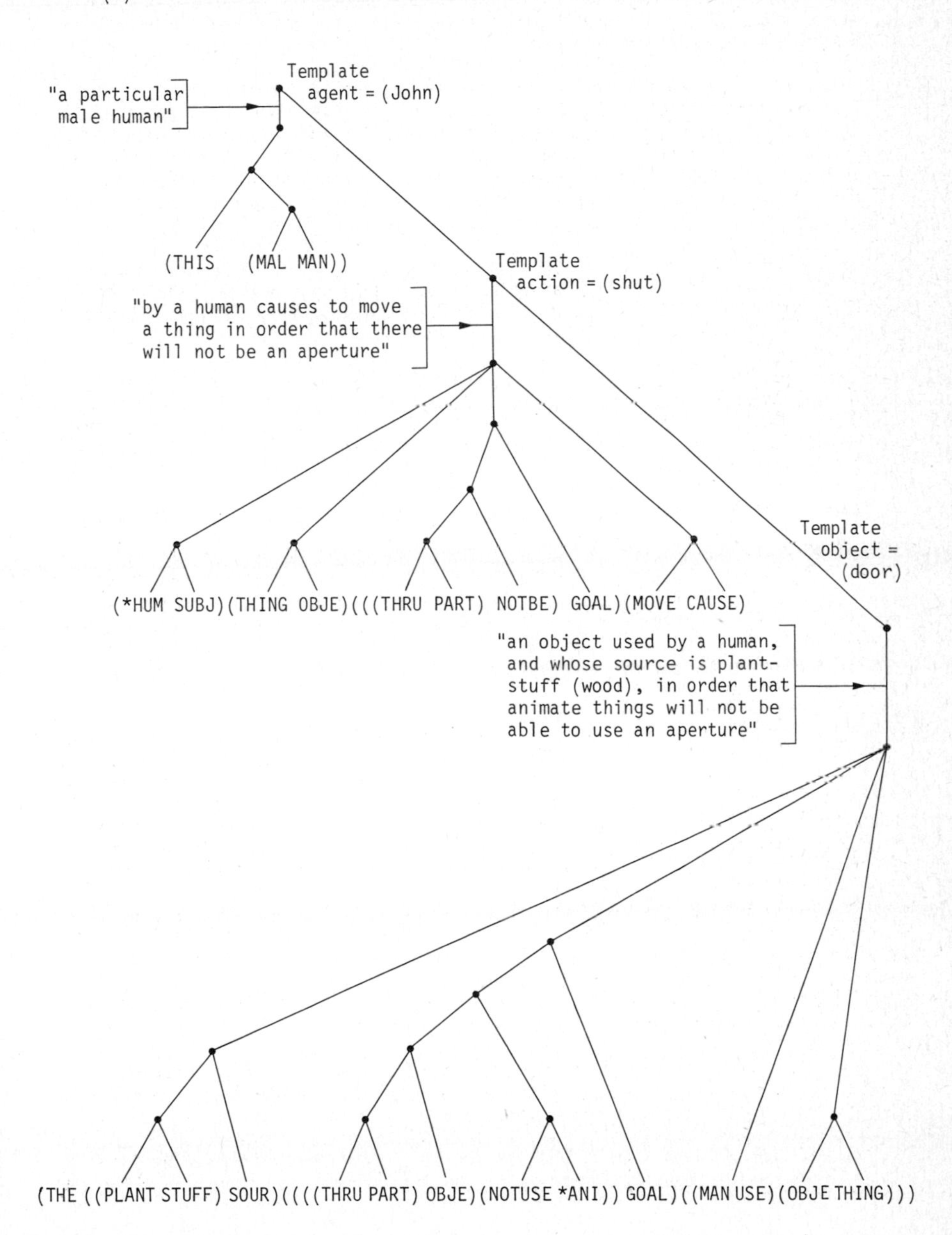

The article "the" is not given special semantic representation, but is simply attached, as shown, to the corresponding formula (as would be a PAST element to the "shut" formula). Although all templates have this basic form of agent-action -object formulas, other formulas can be attached dependently to any of the nodes. So, if the sentence were, "John shut the green door", a formula for "green" would be attached to the object node above.

How are these template structures actually parsed onto text? The process begins with fragmentation: the program goes through a sentence breaking it at key words like prepositions, subjunctions, etc. This is done only on the basis of the list of key words plus the range of semantic formulas for each (non-key) word. A sentence like "The sort of man | that dogs need | is kind" would be fragmented at the two strokes as shown. Even this requires use of the formula semantics, so as to see that the "that" is a relative that, and not a qualifier as it would be in "The dog likes that man".

Normally each fragment of a sentence, produced in this way, has one or more templates matched onto it — though in the case above "The sort of man is kind" would be immediately rejoined into a single fragment.

Next come the procedures for matching templates onto fragments. First the parser goes through the formula combinations (for there will in general be more than one formula for each word, as formulas correspond to word-senses) for a fragment from left to right looking only at the head elements of the formulas. It looks for agent, action and object formulas, in that order initially. So, since all qualifier (adjective) formulas have KIND as their head, this procedure would never take a KIND-headed formula as a possible agent. This process is bare template matching, and is more complex than I have suggested here because fragments of text do not always have their main items in convenient agent-action-object order. So, there is a scale of preferred head sequences. Again, many fragments do not have all three formula types: "John left" has no object, naturally enough, and so that node is filled out by a dummy so as to retain a canonical form of template. Finally, prepositions in English are always assigned to the action node, and so will always have corresponding dummy agent nodes (a point that will be dealt with in detail later).

The matter of matching is also more complicated than suggested initially when it was said that templates were built up from whole formulas during analysis. The whole template for, say, "John shut the door" given above is built up in that way, but the system already knows that a template based on the three ordered heads MAN CAUSE THING is a possible template in a way that KIND CAUSE THING would not be. Thus bare templates (or template types) consisting of just three ordered elements do pre-exist in the system and are indeed matched onto text fragments.

Then comes a more interesting matching process, let us call it preferential expansion. Templates so far have been constructed by assigning formulas to nodes only on the basis of their head elements. Thus in "John shut the case", we would have the "correct" template similar to (1) above, but we would also have one containing a "legal case" formula at its object node, with a different head, GRAIN — meaning a structure, of arguments in this example.

Expansion requires that each possible template for a fragment is taken in turn, and its formulas are examined to see which of their preferences are satisfied in the template in which they find themselves.

Formula subparts were explained earlier as preferring certain semantic entities, not requiring them to be present. Thus the formula for "shut" in (1) prefers a human agent and a physical thing as object. Only the template with the physical object sense of "case" (whose formula head is THING) will satisfy both preferences expressed in the formula for "shut", since a GRAIN formula cannot stand for a physical object. Not only the action formula, but all those making up the template, are examined in this way.

This seeking sorts of agents, objects, etc. is only preferential, in that formulas not satisfying that requirement will be accepted, but only if nothing more satisfactory can be found. The template finally chosen for a fragment of text is the one in which the most formulas have their preferences satisfied. There is a general principle at work here: that the right interpretation "says the least" in information-carrying terms. This very simple device of counting preferences is able to do much of the work of a conventional syntax program as well, since, at the same time as resolving word-sense ambiguity as above, it ensures that "adjective senses" are correctly assigned instead of "noun senses" — in "the green door" — and so on.

The formulas are therefore not just static objects expressing the meaning of words, for in processes like the one just described, they actively dictate how templates are to be constructed. In terms of the bottom-up versus top-down distinction developed earlier, preference methods do not fall neatly into either type, but are a bottom-up selection of a preferred structure which is then applied in a top-down manner.

So far, we have encountered the fragmentation process, followed by two stages of the template matching process. A two stage inferential process then follows, by the end of which a semantic text representation has been constructed. The whole process can be illustrated by a flow chart:

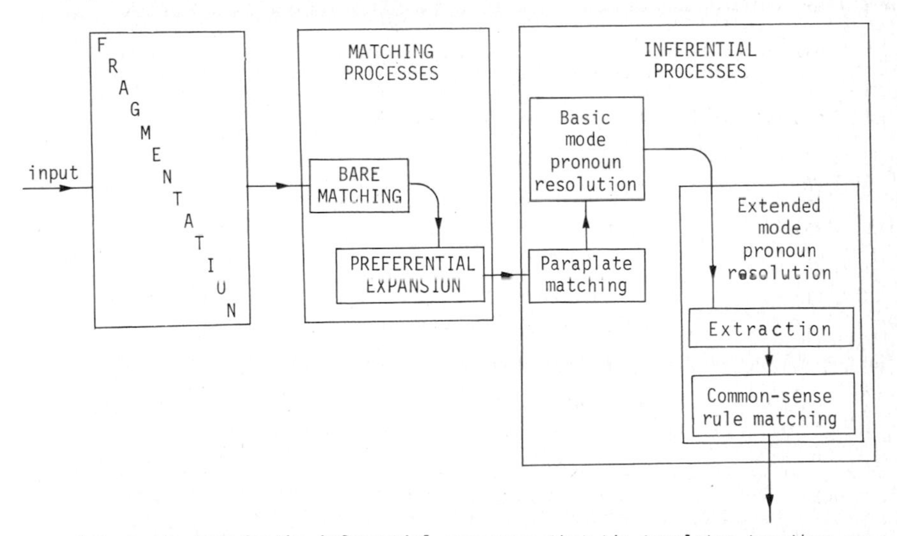

Let us now turn to the inferential processes that tie templates together, so as to produce a semantic block as a text representation — a semantic block is an ordered sequence of templates connected by labelled ties yet to be described. If it can be constructed for a text, then, as far as the system is concerned, all semantic and referential ambiguity has been resolved and the present program will begin to generate French by unwrapping the block again. The generation aspects of this work have been described in (Herskovits 1973). Thus, with the present program, the flow chart above would go on to a French generation program, though it could equally well go to a question-answerer or something of that sort.

From now on, to avoid expressing templates in the detail of (1), they will be written in square brackets containing the English words or dummies for at least the three node-senses. However, it should be remembered that objects in [ ] are complex semantic objects and not the English words they contain.

Paraplates are another type of structure that serves to connect two templates, normally a template representing a main clause and one representing a prepositional phrase. Thus, if we were representing

John left his clothes at the cleaners

which would be represented initially in the system by two templates, the correct paraplate, when applied, would assert a spatial-location case tie (SLOCA) between the two as follows:

```
           [John                 left his+clothes]
SLOCA  ┌──────────────────────────────┘
       └→[( □ = Dummy Agent) at the+cleaners]
```

What is the shape of a paraplate in virtue of which it does this? Each paraplate expresses one of the cases (which is the same inventory as used inside formulas) in this way, and there are many paraplates expressing any particular case. Each paraplate is stored under some English preposition, each of which may of course realize many cases.

Thus let us consider "by", as it functions in the following sentences, all of which may be considered to start with "He left Comano by ...", where I have indicated at the right of each line the apparent case of the last clause and thus the type of paraplate that should connect the two clauses on a given line.

(2)	He left Comano	by courtesy of the police,	SOUR
(3)		by the autostrada,	DIRE (direction case)
(4)		by car,	INST
(5)		by stealth,	WAY (manner case)
(6)		by Monday night,	TLOCA (time location case)
(7)		by following the arrows,	DIRE
(8)		by stealing a boat	INST

Paraplates are in principle six-place entities that are the "skeletons" of a pair of templates, not all of whose places need be filled, corresponding to agent-of-first-template, action-of-first-template, object-of-first-template, and so on for the second template (except that the agent and object of the second are rarely filled). Paraplates, unlike templates, have filtering functions at their nodes that any template pair "matching" a given paraplate must satisfy at every node. Here are four paraplates that should match onto the templates for the sentences with corresponding numbers. Like the sentences above, the paraplates will all have the same left-hand side, which is written only once.

(3')	(*ANI) (MOVE) (WHERE POINT)	—(DIRE)→	□ □	(WHERE LINE)
(4')		—(INST)→	□ □	(*REAL)
(7')		—(DIRE)→	□(*DO)	(WHERE SIGN)
(8')		—(INST)→	□(*DO)	(*REAL)

where *DO covers a wide class of action heads, and the brackets containing formula parts are all to be interpreted as: matches onto corresponding part of a template if the latter has the mentioned subparts of formula. Thus (3') matches (3) because:

the formula for "he"	falls under (has as appropriate subpart)	*ANI
"left"	"	MOVE
"Comano"	"	(WHERE POINT)
"autostrada"	"	(WHERE LINE)

and so on for the other correspondences of sentences and paraplates. The result of the paraplate (3') matching the two templates for (3) is that the case label DIRE on the arrow of (3') is asserted as holding between the two templates that represent (3). In more complex cases there may be two or more templates available for a sentence fragment, and the template that matches with a "more preferred paraplate" will ultimately represent that fragment. As we shall now see, paraplates, for a given preposition, are ordered and "more preferred paraplate" simply means "the paraplate applied earlier".

The above are some of the paraplates attached to "by" and brought in whenever a "by" template is to be tied to others. They are organized under the action element on the left of the paraplate, and the paraplate stack for a given preposition and primitive action is *ordered*, though not simply ordered, as we shall see.

So INST case is largely a default case for MOVE as it is cued in by "by", in the sense that almost any entity can be an instrument here if we have no reason to believe it is something else. Thus the more specific (3') must be applied *before* (4') in order to match direction case for (3) since, if the order were reversed (4') might match with what "ought to" match with (3'). We could imagine some very specific requirement being expressed by a function at the last (sixth) node of (4') — say, one equivalent to "entity for transporting humans" instead of the very wide function (*REAL), meaning any real object or substance, at present in (4'). If that were done then (4') could be put above (3') in the stack and would catch (i.e. the sixth node function would be satisfied by) sentence (4). But if the sentence were "He left Comano by cattle truck" it would fail (4') — since cattle trucks are not normally used for transporting humans — then fail (3'), which is now below (4'), and now there would be no appropriate default paraplate to catch the sentence and assign the default case INST to its internal tie.

This is the sort of reasoning that establishes the need for a preferential order of application paraplates. But it is not a simple (linear) order since, for example, there is no reason why (7') should be ordered with respect to (3'). An order that takes account of that indifference is called a *partial* ordering (which has no connexion with partial *information* as defined earlier).

Thus paraplates have a general structure <template form> → <template form>, and so it is reasonable to call them inferential structures in a wide sense, and this idea will not be strange to readers who will have encountered Schank's system in Chapters 4 and 7 where his case expansions of conceptualizations are called "inferences".

As described at the beginning of the Wilks section, the system has also tied templates together by means of simple preferential substitutions for problem pronouns, as with the "monkeys and bananas" example. Solving that example ties templates in the sense that the process can be thought of as imposing a tie from the "pronoun node" in one template to the "noun node" (the noun that the pronoun refers to, that is) in another template.

A general point should be made here about the treatment of the problem of pronoun reference by the systems described in this book, that is: Winograd's (Chapter 6), Rieger's (Chapter 8, which did a considerable amount of indirect pronoun referencing via Riesbeck's analyzer — see below), Charniak's (Chapter 8, which was originally designed to refer pronouns in the general process of analyzing children's stories) and Wilks', in the present discussion. The point is that none of these systems has a single uniform method for resolving pronouns to the nouns or phrases they refer to, because pronoun reference is not a simply structured problem, and so not open to solution by a uniform method.

For example, it is a convenient fiction, encouraged by almost all systems, that a pronoun refers to some item mentioned earlier (or occasionally later). But this is not so in general, as can be seen from such sentences as "It is hot in here" or "In Italy he drank mineral water in his wine and it tasted good" where, in the last example, the "it" refers to a combination not actually mentioned in the sentence. Again, selection restrictions, preferentially applied or otherwise are sometimes sufficient to resolve pronouns, as in the "bananas and monkeys" example, but it is easy to construct other examples where they are not enough — and we shall turn to several in a moment. There is the well known rule, often half remembered from school, that a pronoun refers to the last mentioned object "of the right sort", and sometimes, usually if we have nothing else to go on, that rule can explain how we normally refer a pronoun, as in "John took the wheel off his bike and then the saddle and left it in the garage", where "it" would normally be taken to be the last thing mentioned, the saddle. But, of course, if we read "The log floated past the tree and then the fish swam under it" we know fairly surely that it was the log the fish swam under and not the, last mentioned, tree.

In this last example we might well want to say that we refer the pronoun as we do because of what we know about floating and swimming, and trees are not normally floating.

What we have, in common sense terms, is a hotch-potch of different ways of referring pronouns in different circumstances. If any of them is offered as the principal rule, it is not too hard to find exceptions to it. The danger is then of going to the other extreme and saying that these various general rules are no use because they don't work in all cases. That too is wrong: norms are not less valuable because they are sometimes violated.

There are roughly two main sorts of approach to the pronoun reference problem to be found in AI systems. On the one hand are those who concentrate on very general manipulations of their systems and hope that much pronoun reference will be dealt with correctly if those manipulations are properly performed. This style emphasizes the central examples rather than the exceptions, and also tends to classify different types of pronoun reference in terms of the operations of the systems themselves, and Wilks' and Schank's systems emphasize this approach.

On the other hand are approaches which emphasize special routines to deal with special sorts of circumstance, and pronoun reference problems arising in connexion with description of those types of circumstance: Winograd's "specialists" (Chapter 6) and Charniak's "demons" (Chapter 8) are examples of such routines. This approach tends not to emphasize the role of the system of representation, and tends to concentrate on difficult, rather than central, examples in that it is interested in examples which violate the norms and seldom in those which conform.

In practice, all working systems are a combination of these two approaches, and none could yet be said to have done more than scratched the surface of this enormous problem.

After this general digression on pronoun reference, let us return to Wilks' system. Many examples are not resolved by the simple preferential methods of his "basic mode" and, in particular, if a word sense ambiguity, or pronoun reference, is still unresolved, then a unique semantic block of templates cannot be constructed and the "extended inferential mode" is entered. In this mode, new template-like forms (called extractions) are inferred from existing ones, and then added to the template pool on which common sense inference rules then operate.

Let us illustrate these final parsing processes by looking at the sentence:

(9) John bought a car in the market and liked it immediately.

The final semantic block for this will be (schematically):

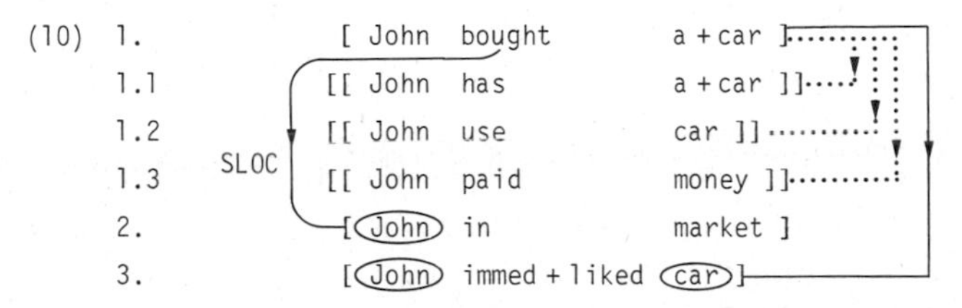

where "car" and "John" are ringed to show that they are the final resolved values of the formulas at those nodes. The "John" nodes have been replaced by simple preferential procedures in the basic mode, and we shall concentrate on the "car" node that replaces "it". This representation is the result of three separate processes operating on the original three templates (# 1, 2, 3) representing the text. First, the SLOC tie has been inserted by paraplates in the way described. Secondly, 1.1, 1.2 and 1.3, in double brackets, are extractions which are added to a representation prior to the application of inference rules. They have been extracted from # 1, as is shown by the dotted arrows connecting them. The main type of extraction is one which comes from the "unpacking" (see below) of each case type (except AGENT and OBJECT) in the formulas of the source template (# 1).

Thus, we have in the formula for "bought" (see below) a GOAL subpart which says that the purpose of buying something is to use it, hence from the template # 1, 1.2 has been extracted by "unpacking" the GOAL subpart. Similarly 1.3 follows by an extraction of the WAY (or manner) case in # 1. 1.1 intuitively is a causal consequence extracted from # 1, since "buy" is basically a GET action, its formula being:

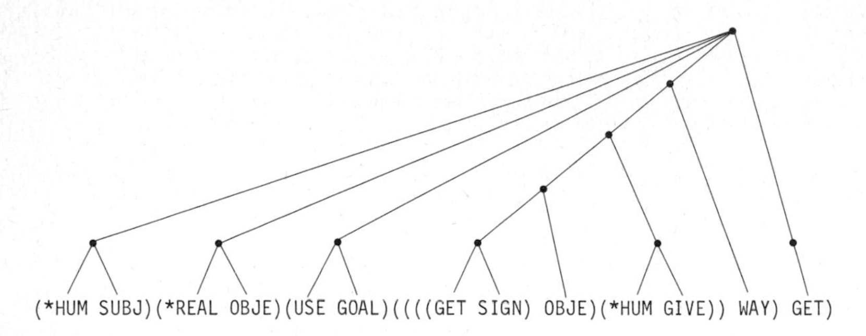

That is to say, in semi-English, buying is a getting, done by humans to real objects in order to use them, the manner being the human giving money = (GET SIGN). Thus, the three extraction arrows in the representation above could in fact be labelled CAUSE, GOAL and WAY respectively.

Extractions, then, are new template-like entities added to a representation to deepen it. They represent information not explicitly present in the original text, information that may not even be necessarily true. After all John may have bought the car (# 1) but may not have it (# 1.1), because he re-sold it immediately. Extractions are produced by "unpacking" the case subparts of formulas and allowing them to produce template-like items *as if all the case preferences in the formula had in fact been satisfied*. Since the formula is installed in a template information can be found, usually in the rest of the template, that shows what exactly such satisfaction would be. That is, if the GOAL of buying is to use something, the system can see from the object node of template # 1 what the something is. Extractions, then, are *generally* local, from within a template.

Thirdly we have common sense inferences (square "template ⟶ template" links in (10)). #3 has been tied to #1 in the representation above by an inference arrow (shown as a *square* line) on the basis of which the ?it in #3 has been correctly replaced by the formula for "car". Inference rules have the form <template> ⟶ <template> but always contain restricted variables. In this case the rule tying #1 to #3 would have been:

[animate 1 cause + self + have realobject 2] ⟶ [1 *judges 2]

where the variable 1 is restricted to be something animate: "*judges" represents a general function satisfied by actions of liking, as in the present example; and the square brackets show that we are dealing with only the "readable shorthand" form of the rule, for its "full form" would be:

((*ANI 1)((SELF HAVE) CAUSE)(*REAL 2)) ⟶ (1 *JUDG 2)

The left-hand side matches onto template #1 and the right-hand side onto #3. Thus resolving ?it at the object node of #3 as the same entity as that filling the variable #2 on the left-hand side, i.e. the car.

It should be noticed that these inference rules are only *partial*: they are not in general consequences that must follow, in any sense. The assumption is that if they can match and so fill "gaps" in this way, then the solution they yield is the correct interpretation of the text. Moreover, the rules can be chained so as to reach from a template (or extraction) containing a problem pronoun to one containing a possible solution, and the "preferential assumption" is that the shortest possible chain of such inferences will be the right one, which is not to deny that some other longer chain of rules would reach the other, less preferred, solution ("market" in the example above). A similar hypothesis of "bridging inferential gaps" by the shortest determinate chain has recently been explored, though from a psychological point of view, by Clark (1975).

There is also a considerable overall similarity of approach to that of the "demon strategy" of Charniak described in Chapter 8, though not as regards the shortest chain preference. In that chapter Charniak's work was described purely in inferential terms, but one of its original purposes in (Charniak 1972) was to resolve pronoun reference in children's stories. Both are "gap filling" approaches, as contrasted with, say, Rieger's (1974) approach where inferences are made without, as here, continually looking for confirmation of them at every stage. Again, both Charniak's and Wilks' systems have rules equivalent to

A IMPLIES B

A IMPLIES NOT B

where an inference rule seeks either an assertion or its negation. In (3) above, the same matching would have taken place if we had been told that John did not like it. These approaches are therefore far more dedicated to relevance and cohesion than to logical form, for the A/B inference pair above would render any system logically trivial, but from a language understanding point of view, no worse for it!

The chief drawback of Wilks' system is that codings consisting entirely of primitives have a considerable amount of both vagueness and redundancy. For example, no reasonable coding in terms of structured primitives could be expected to distinguish, say, "hammer" and "mallet". That may not matter provided the codings can distinguish importantly different senses of words. Again, a template for the sentence "The shepherd tended his flock" would contain considerable repetition, each node of the template trying, as it were, to tell the whole story by itself. Whether or not such a system can remain stable with a considerable vocabulary, of say several thousand words, has yet to be tested.

Again, it remains to be shown that a large body of common sense inference rules can be controlled, and that solutions can be found to pronoun problems without the chains becoming inordinately long. There may also be something inherently implausible about always preferring a rule chain of length, say, 4 to one of length 3. (Though preferring length 4 to length 1 might be clearer and more plausible.) This difficulty may mean that preferences in the system will have to be weighted, in a way they are not at present.

Riesbeck's Implementation of Schank's System

Schank's system of conceptual representation was introduced in Chapters 4 and 7. It was implemented in the MARGIE system (Schank et al. 1973) with a parser by Riesbeck (1974), an inferential memory by Rieger (1974, and see Chapter 8) and a generation system by Goldman (1974). It is with the parser for English that we will be concerned here. The construction of a parser for conceptual dependency notation was certainly no trivial task: the reader will remember from Chapter 6 that, although Schank gives procedures for extending the conceptualizations — case inferences, for example — he does not, in any sense, give procedures for attaching the conceptual structures to natural language, nor does he consider it his task to provide the information to enable this to be done. That does not mean that he ignores problems like word-sense and case ambiguity in sentences, only that he assumes that the application of a correct representation will, necessarily, solve these problems. As we saw in the last section, on Wilks, the semantic information and criteria required to parse case structures, for example, are considerable and Riesbeck has attempted also to provide these. His first step in making Schank's system computable was, of course, to convert the Schank diagrams to explicit linear symbolic form, since diagrams necessarily contain their information in an implicit form.

Riesbeck's parser is, in the terms developed earlier, depth-first. It becomes top-down almost immediately in the parsing process. Not immediately, because the conceptual structures to be parsed onto the text are "cued in" by the appearance of the words of the sentence, examined from left to right. Riesbeck describes these structures as expectations: expectations, that is, about what else will be said, or has already been said, in the text; and these expectations are concretely expressed as requests associated with the appearance of text words. The strongest argument for this approach is that the most appropriate conceptual structures for what appears in a text are utterly unlike the superficial structure, and that these most appropriate structures are best applied as soon as possible in the parsing — rather than, say, after a later process of deepening the representation as in the Wilks system. The best example for showing this is Riesbeck's "John gave Mary a beating" which, of course, has little to do with giving, and we shall work through this example in detail.

In Riesbeck's system the proper structure for this sentence is actually attached to "beating", so that when "beating" is reached, in going through the sentence, that proper conceptualization (based on the primitive action PROPEL, and expressing the movement of John's hand) will, as it were, take over and supplant the request structures already satisfied during the analysis of the first four words of the sentence.

Below is Riesbeck's sequential table of requests associated with the sentence words, as it is parsed from left to right, and expressed here as sequence down the page.

NP here is the familiar grammar category noun-phrase. The table is quite easy to follow if we remember that the numbered requests in the third column remain active (and are thus passed down the third column) if they are not satisfied. The requests 5 and 6 called "true" are simply default requests (of the type found in LISP, see Chapter 12) that will be satisfied automatically if nothing above them is.

What happens with the parsing of this sentence, put very roughly, is that the satisfaction of request 2 makes the parser think, as it were, that it is dealing with a sentence like "John gave Mary a dollar"; hence its expectation about "to" at step 2. It goes on believing this until requests 3 and 4 are reinstated at step 7 and request 4 is satisfied and not request 3, as would have been the case if Mary had been given a dollar.

The action taken at step 7 is to completely restructure the representation and to base it, not on the Schankian primitive act PTRANS (for "give"), but on PROPEL (for "beat").

STEP	WORD READ	REQUESTS WAITING	REQUESTS TRIGGERED	ACTIONS TAKEN
Ø	none	1 - is there an NP?	none	none
1	John	1 - is there an NP?	1	assume "John" is subject of the verb to follow
2	gave	2 - is the current NP a human? 3 - is the current NP an object? 4 - is the current NP an action? 5 - true	5	assume the word "to", if it appears, introduces the recipient of the "giving"
3	Mary	2 - is the current NP a human? 3 - is the current NP an object? 4 - is the current NP an action?	2	assume Mary is the recipient of the "giving"
4	a	3 - is the current NP an object? 4 - is the current NP an action? 6 - true	6	save the current list of requests and replace it with: 7 - does the current word end an NP?
5	beating	7 - does the current word end an NP?	none	none
6	period	7 - does the current word end an NP?	7	build the NP "a beating" and reset the list of requests
7	none	3 - is the current NP an object? 4 - is the current NP an action?	4	assume the NP action is the main action of the clause, the subject (John) is the actor and the recipient (Mary) is the object

This same method is applied to more complex sentences, such as those containing prepositional phrases.

Let us look at the parsing of a prepositional phrase as in "John prevented Mary from leaving by locking her in".

There are three phases in the parsing:

(i) "prevent" generates requests (expectations) for prepositions FROM and BY1. Let me call these objects preposition-forms for the moment. BY1 is what we can think of as a "sense" of the preposition "by". If Riesbeck were using case description, we could say that BY1 is the "manner case" manifestation of "by", as opposed to its other case manifestations.

(ii) FROM itself has very complex requests associated with it such as FROMØ:

```
(T(IMBED ⟸ ((MOD QUOTE((CANNOT)))
    (TIME CHOICE ⟸ TIME)
    (SUBJ CHOICE OBJ))
  ((OR(EQ WORD(QUOTE BY))
    (BREAK_POINT))
 (RESET_ALL)NIL))
 NIL
```

This is clearly a complex object and need not be fully explained to define its role, namely that of tying together two conceptualizations: one for the preventing and one for the leaving, and in that sense its role is analogous to the Wilks paraplates described earlier. It is written out here so that we can see that this request is seeking the preposition "by" to follow it (fourth line from bottom).

(iii) the requests of BY1 are an even more formidable object than that above, but Riesbeck makes clear that it is seeking forms of primitive act to fit a following "by" phrase should it occur, as it does in fact in the example sentence.

One immediate problem here is what is a prepositional-form like FROMØ? Is it a case or not? At one point Riesbeck suggests that it is 'specific to "prevent"' which suggests that it cannot be a case in any general sense, but is some other classification of preposition appearance. Secondly, it is not really made clear what happens if an expectation is not fulfilled, because they always seem to be. So it is never clear where, say, other FROMn's would come into play if FROMØ failed to do the trick.

This last point is part of a general question as to whether there is anything corresponding to Wilks' paraplate preference order in Riesbeck or not. Wilks has argued, perhaps not convincingly, that there has to be some order imposed in case parsing, but Riesbeck says specifically that the requests are not ordered. On the other hand, Riesbeck's strategy as described may imply an ordering: "prevent" calls FROMØ and if that fails and there is a FROM1, say, available, then there is some ordering like that of application of the paraplates. But that might seem inconsistent with his claim that the requests are NOT ordered.

Riesbeck may unconsciously accept a form of what one might call the phenomenological fallacy, which is that people say what is expected of them, and so a preference order of structures is not necessary. But, alas, they all too often don't, and one has actually to attend to what they say..

Again, depending on the exact interpretation of prepositional-forms, the system is highly superficial in a strict sense of the word: it is its verbs that seek prepositions (if FROMØ is a preposition), rather than basic actions seeking cases. This surface method naturally makes it hard to state "significant semantic generalizations", and is particularly odd in a parser that claims to be based on Schank who abhors all processing based on surface correlations. So, in that sense, Riesbeck's parser may be more independent of Schank's system than appears initially.

Another general, and related, problem is that Riesbeck wishes to avoid any intermediate structure (such as Wilks' templates), whether syntactic or semantic, between text words and the final conceptualization. To do this he may, in the end, have to associate different requests with a word corresponding not only to different senses of the word, but to its syntactic positions. Riesbeck's request table shows how closely related requests are to syntactic order. That need not be fatal, even if so, but it would clearly make it hard to state any semantic generalizations that should be the heart of the system, and very hard to specify the word-by-word requests for a sentence of any length or complexity.

Part of this comes from general difficulties about uncontrolled expectation as a parsing mechanism, and the question of whether one can have a wholly depth-first parser, like Riesbeck's, if one has no back up. One might say that depth-first parsing, whether semantic or syntactic, requires a notion of failure and backup: that is to say, a notion of when a current structure has become inapplicable, and then of where, in the previous choices taken, to go back and try again. But almost all contemporary approaches are weak on failure and backup: Winograd's, Wilks' and Riesbeck's. Indeed, part of the point of top-down, frames-like, approach is to make backup much less needed. The tension comes in trying to combine this with a wholly depth-first parsing technique as Riesbeck has done. Or, to put this in slogan form, structures of expectation may have to be explored more than one at a time so as to simulate attention. Systems that do not attend are like people that do not attend but only expect what to hear. In neither case do they communicate or understand.

Exaggerated expectation involves what was earlier called the phenomenological fallacy: when understanding language as human beings we are never conscious of alternative interpretations, the fact that a word we read in context has many senses out of context, etc., therefore a semantic parser should not consider such alternatives either, for, if it has the right conceptual/semantic/preferential/ frame structures in it, it will go directly in a depth-first manner to the correct reading and never consider any other.

The premise of this position is of course true, but the conclusion is totally false, and it is perhaps worth setting out why.

Where it is wrong is in its assumption that the correct interpretation fits and the other possible interpretations do not fit at all. Hence the first path that can be followed will be the right one. The truth of the matter in semantics is that the right interpretation fits better than the others, but to see that we necessarily have to see how well the other possibilities fit.

One detailed example Riesbeck discusses is the parsing of:

"John gave Mary the book"

in which the action "give" generates requests, one of which is that "if what follows the verb immediately is human then assume it is RECIPient case, otherwise assume it is OBJect case." There is nothing in his description that allows any backup to an alternative request should one fail after appearing to succeed and this is consistent with the depth-first no backup position. So, for example, both the following perfectly natural sentences would be wrongly analyzed on such a method:

"John gave Mary to the Imam of Oudh"

"John gave his city his stamp collection"

There is nothing the least tricky or bizarre about such sentences, and the examples show that simple unfettered expectation is not enough unless one can be *sure* one has one's criteria right, *or* one has some breadth-first way of considering alternatives *or* one has complex backup.

PARSING AND "LARGER CHUNKS OF KNOWLEDGE"

In Chapter 8, Charniak introduced a supermarket frame as a representation of a "larger chunk" of our knowledge about the world than the knowledge representations discussed so far in this chapter, even though the three authors surveyed here were described earlier as being within the frames approach too. What we have already then are two "scales" of frame: a smaller and a larger. Wilks' template structures and Schank's conceptualizations would be frame structures on the smaller but not the larger scale, whereas Charniak's frames, as described in Chapter 8, would be larger scale frames. Schank has recently made a transition to the larger scale with structures he calls (after Abelson 1973) "scripts". These will now be described briefly, and their possible relation to parsing will be discussed later.

Schank began the transition, together with Rieger, by developing a new class of causal inferences that deepen the conceptualization diagrams still further. So, in the analysis of "John's cold improved because I gave him an apple" (Schank 1973a) the extended diagram contains at least four yet lower levels of causal arrowing, including one corresponding to the notion of John constructing the idea (MBUILD) that he wants to eat an apple. So we can see that the underlying explication of meaning here is not only in the sense of linguistic primitives, but in terms of a theory of mental acts as well.

A contrast became apparent here between Schank's work and Rieger's: in Rieger's thesis (Rieger 1974) the rules of inference create separate and new subgraphs (see Chapter 8) which may stand in an inferential relation to each other so as to produce conclusions about problems of, say, pronoun reference, etc. But in Schank's corresponding papers the same inferences are not applied to actual problems of language analysis (Schank 1973a) but they only produce more complex conceptual graphs. Then Schank reversed this trend towards ever more complex diagrams (*for individual sentences*) by considering the representation of text. He concluded that the representations of parts of the text must themselves be interconnected by causal arrows, and that, in order to preserve lucidity, the conceptual diagrams for individual sentences and their parts must be abbreviated, as by triples such as PEOPLE PTRANS PEOPLE. Here, some of the surface structure *has* to survive in the representation unless one is prepared to commit oneself to the extreme view that the ordering of sentences in a text is a purely superficial and arbitrary matter. The sense in which this is a welcome reversal of a trend should be clear, because in the "causation inference" development all the consequences and effects of a conceptualization had to be drawn within itself. Thus, in the extreme case, each sentence of a text should have been represented by a diagram containing most or all of the text of which it was a part. Thus the representation of a text would have been impossible on such principles.

Most recently (1975a) Schank has produced a "script" for knowledge about eating in a restaurant. This is no longer a causal sequence developed during the processing of a text, but is, like Charniak's frames (Chapter 8) a structure which precedes any encounter with text. The script begins:

"Scene 1 entering

PTRANS - go into restaurant

MBUILD - find table

PTRANS - go to table

MOVE - sit down

Scene 2 ordering

ATRANS - receive menu

ATTEND - look at it

MBUILD - decide on order

MTRANS - tell order to waitress."

and so on for scenes 3, eating, and 4, exiting. Schank also has a program which will take a paragraph length restaurant story and produce a slightly longer story with the "missing bits" filled in from the script above. So that, if it reads a story like "John went to the restaurant, got angry and left", it can reply with what it assumes to have happened in more detail, such as "John went to the restaurant. He found a table and sat down. He got the menu and ordered the food. When it came he didn't like it, so he got angry with the waitress and left."

As so often in our subject it is hard to see just what claims are being made by such a program, or how to evaluate such output. The sort of consideration that makes it more plausible can be seen from the following genuine newspaper story:

"Mr. Justice Forbes, at Winchester Crown Court yesterday, criticized authorities who charge people with attempted murder without "a scrap of evidence".

Philip Slater, aged 25, was charged with carrying an offensive weapon, attempted murder, and wounding with intent.

After he had pleaded guilty to wounding with intent Mr. Justice Forbes said: "Why was this charge of attempted murder put? There was never the slightest chance that any jury would convict this man on this charge."

The reader should now ask himself whether the man charged was carrying a gun. If the answer is yes, the question arises as to why one thinks so, because the story does not say so. Schank might well argue that we are filling out the story from a "script" of some sort.

Exactly the same considerations are present in Charniak's frames, discussed in Chapter 8, and these two systems with "large scale frames" will be discussed in the next part of the chapter.

We shall now turn to some comparisons and contrasts, under ten connected headings, between the systems discussed in the last four chapters from the point of view of parsing.

Level of Representation

One important line of current dispute among recent approaches concerns the appropriate level of representation for natural language. On the one hand are those like Colby, and in some ways Charniak, who hold that language can be, in effect, self-representing, while on the other hand there are those like Schank and Wilks who hold that the appropriate level of computation for inferences about natural language is in some reduced, or primitive, representation. Charniak holds that his structures are independent of any particular level of representation, or rather, that they could be realized at a number of levels of representation, depending on the subject area. However, there is no doubt that the representation in terms of predicates that he offers in his work appears to be in one-to-one correspondence with English words.

The strongest low-level approach is undoubtedly that of Colby, who straightforwardly faces the enormous mapping problems involved if the structures are at the English word level. It is important to realize that this dispute is ultimately one of degree, since no one would claim that every locution recognized by an intelligent analyzer must be mapped into a "deep" representation. To take an extreme case, any system that mapped "Good Morning" into a deep semantic representation before deciding that the correct response was also "Good Morning" would be making a serious theoretical mistake.

But these disputes are at all times questions of degree: Schank has argued most strongly for the use of primitives but has only produced them for verbs, although work has continued independently on noun primitives for his system (Weber 1972). While on the other hand Wilks has produced primitives for all parts of speech, yet retains access to surface items in his system, unlike Schank, and now (1975c) seems in the process of putting other, less primitive, more superficial, items into his semantic formulas.

However, the most serious argument for a non-superficial representation is not in terms of the avoidance of mapping difficulties, but in terms of theoretical perspicuity of the primitive structures, and this argument is closely tied to the defence of semantic primitives in general, which is a large subject that can only briefly be touched on here. One of the troubles about semantic primitives is that they are open to bad defenses, which decrease rather than increase their plausibility. For example, some users of them for linguistic representation have declared them to have some sort of objective existence, and have implied that there is a "right set" of primitives open to empirical discovery. On that view the essentially linguistic character of structures of primitives is lost, because it is an essential feature of a language that we can change its vocabulary, and be understood via alternative vocabularies. If there was a right primitive vocabulary, that was a list of names of brain-items, that essential feature would be lost. What is the case is that there is a considerable amount of psychological evidence that people are not able to recall either the actual words or the syntactic structure used. There is large literature on this subject, from which two sample references would be (Wettler 1973) and (Johnson-Laird 1974).

These results are, of course, no proof of the existence of semantic primitives but they are undoubtedly supporting evidence of their plausibility, as is, on a different plane, the result from the encoding of the whole Webster's Third International Dictionary at Systems Development Corporation. It was found that a rank-ordered frequency count of the words used to define other words in that vast dictionary was a list (omitting "the" and "a") which corresponded almost item-for-item to the sort of list of semantic primitives used by, and derived a priori by of course, those researchers described here who construct semantic representations.

It is important to distinguish the dispute about level from the, closely connected, topic of the centrality of the knowledge required by a language understanding system

Centrality

The centrality of certain kinds of information concerns not its level of representation but its non-specificity: again a contrast can be drawn between the sorts of information required by Charniak's system, on the one hand, and that required by Schank's and Wilks', on the other. Charniak's examples suggest that the fundamental form of information is highly specific to particular situations, like parties and the giving of presents, while the sorts of information central to Schank's (before scripts) and Wilks' systems are partial assertions about human wants, expectations, and so on, many of which are so general as to be almost vacuous which, one might argue, is why their role in understanding has been ignored for so long.

If one was a reasonably fluent speaker of, say, German, one might well not understand a German conversation about birthday presents unless one had detailed factual information about how Germans organize the giving of presents, which might be considerably different from the way we do it. Conversely, of course, one might understand much of a technical article about a subject in which one was an expert, even though knowing very little of the language in which it was written.

In the end this difference may again turn out to be one of emphasis, and of what is most appropriate to different subject areas, though there may be a very general issue lurking somewhere here. It may not be a foolish question to ask whether much of what appears to be about natural language in AI research is in fact about language at all. Even if it is not that may in no way detract from its value. Newell (Moore, Newell 1973) has argued that AI work is in fact "theoretical psychology", in which case it could hardly be research on natural language. When describing Winograd's work earlier in the chapter, this question was raised in a weak form by asking whether his definition of "pickup" had anything to do with the natural language use of the word, or whether it was rather a description of how his system picked something up, a quite different matter.

Suppose we generalize this query somewhat, by asking the apparently absurd question of what would be wrong with calling, say, Charniak's work an essay on the "Socio-Economic Behavior of American Children under Stress?" In the case of Charniak's work this is a facetious question, asked only in order to make a point, but with an increasing number of systems in AI being designed not essentially to do research on natural language, but in order to have a natural language "front end" to a system that is essentially intended to predict chemical spectra, or play snakes and ladders or whatever, the question becomes a serious one. It seems to be a good time to ask whether we should expect advance in understanding natural language from those tackling the problems head on, or those concerned to build a "front end". It is clearly the case that any piece of knowledge whatever could be essential to the understanding of some story. The question is, does it follow that the specification, organization and formulization of that knowledge is the study of language, because if it is then all human enquiry from physics and history to medicine is a linguistic enterprise. And, of course, that possibility has actually been entertained within certain strains of modern philosophy.

This is not an attempt to breathe fresh life into a philosophical distinction between being about language and not being about language (though see Chapter 11 below), but rather introducing a practical distinction between specific knowledge and central knowledge without which a system could not be said to understand language at all. For example, one might know nothing of the arrangement of American birthday parties, but could not be accused of not understanding English even though one failed to understand some particular children's story. Yet, if one did not have available some very general partial inference such as the one about people being hurt and falling, or one about people endeavoring to possess things that they want, then it is quite possible that one's lack of understanding of quite simple sentences would cause observers to think that one did not understand English. An interesting and difficult question that then arises is whether those who concentrate on central and less central areas of discourse could, in principle, weld their bodies of inferences together in such a way as to create a wider system; whether, to put the matter another way, natural language is a whole that can be built up from parts?

On the other hand, it must be realized that there are undoubtedly linguistic problems that do seem to rest on even more specific real world knowledge than that represented in current systems, as can be seen by contrasting the sentences:

The deer came out of the wood

The grub came out of the wood

where we might safely assume that readers would assign quite different senses to "wood" in the two cases simply on the basis of the two different agents, though no one has yet suggested any general method for tackling such elementary examples.

Phenomenological Level

Another distinction that can be confused with the central-specific one is that of the "phenomenological levels" of inferences in an understanding system. There is nothing daunting in that phrase: consider the action eating which is, as a matter of anatomical fact, quite often an act of bringing the bones of one's ulna and radius (in the arm) close to that of the lower mandible (or jaw). Yet clearly, any system of common sense inferences that considered such a truth when reasoning about eating would be making a mistake. One might say that the phenomenological level of the analysis was wrong even though all the inferences it made were true ones. The same would be true of any AI system that made everyday inferences about physical objects by considering their quantum structure.

Schank's analysis of eating contains the information that it is done by moving the hands to the mouth, and it might be argued that even this is going too far from the "meaning" of eating, whatever that may be, towards generally true information about the act which, if always inferred about all acts of eating, will carry the system unmanageably far.

There is no denying that this sort of information might be useful to have around somewhere; that, in Minsky's terms, the "default" value of the instrument for eating is the hand brought to the mouth, so that, if we have no contrary information, then that is the way to assume that any given act of eating was performed. Nonetheless, there clearly is a danger, and that is all that is being highlighted here, of taking inferences to a phenomenological level beyond that of common sense. A clearer case would be Schank's analysis (1973a) of mental activity in which all actions, such as kicking a ball, say, are preceded by a mental action of conceiving or deciding to kick a ball. This is clearly a level of analysis untrue to common sense, and which could have only harmful effects in a system intended to mimic common sense reasoning and understanding.

Decoupling

Another general issue in dispute concerns decoupling, which is whether or not the actual parsing of text or dialogue into an "understanding system" is essential. Charniak and Minsky believe that this initial "parsing" can be effectively decoupled from the interesting inferential work and simply assumed. But one could argue that many of the later inferences would actually have to be done already, in order to have achieved the initial parsing. For example, in analyzing "He shot her with a colt", we cannot ascribe any structure at all until we can make the inference that guns rather than horses are instruments for shooting, and so such a sentence cannot be inserted into an inference-but-no-parsing structure without assuming that language does not have one of its essential characteristics, namely systematic ambiguity. The essence of decoupling is allowing representational structures to have significance quite independent of their application, and if one does decouple one may be in a situation not essentially different from that of the logician who simply asserts that such-and-such is the "right structure" of some sentence.

Also, the inferences required to resolve word sense ambiguities, and those required to resolve pronoun reference problems, are not of different types; often the two problems occur in a simple sentence and must be resolved together. But Charniak's decoupling has the effect of completely separating these two closely related linguistic phenomena in what might seem to be an unrealistic manner. His system does inferencing to resolve pronoun ambiguities, while sense ambiguity is presumably to be done in the future by some other, ultimately recoupled, system. (Although Charniak would argue that sense ambiguity could be introduced into his system in its present form.)

Another way of pointing up the difference between the attitudes of the systems discussed to decoupling is by describing the role of syntax analysis in them. As we saw, syntax was the heart of Winograd's system, but both scales of frame approach discount syntax analysis, though for very different reasons: Charniak does so because it is part of the initial parsing from which his inferential work has been decoupled. Schank and Wilks do so because they believe a semantic analysis to be fundamental, and that in an actual implementation the results of syntactic analysis can all be achieved by a sufficiently powerful semantic analyzer. And this last assumption is confirmed by the limited degree of success that the two semantic analyzers have actually achieved in operation.

The thesis behind this chapter (and it differs from the views of Chapters 7 and 8) is that parsing is essential to a system, and so it cannot be ultimately decoupled. This goes not only for "representation of knowledge" systems, but equally for those claiming to represent semantic memory. The argument is not only that parsing provides a test of a proposed structure, for that is secondary, but that the parsing procedures define what the significance of the proposed structure is. It will not have escaped the notice of readers that all the knowledge and memory structures proposed and discussed in this section of the book look very like rearranged English. Schank and Wilks claim, in different ways, that the structures are only short-hand for others expressed in terms of primitives, but those in turn look like rearranged, but more bizarre, English. The argument of this chapter is that it is only parsing — the procedural application of these structures to surface text — that gives them significance and thus stops them being just rearranged English.

Application

This point is a generalization of the last two, and concerns the way in which different systems display, in the structures they manipulate, the actual procedures of application of those structures to input text or dialogue. This is a matter different from computer implementation of the system. In the case of Colby's patterns, for example the form of their application to the input English is clear, even though the matching involved could be achieved by many different implementation algorithms. In Wilks' system the same is true of the template structures, even though by the time the input has reached the canonical template form it is considerably different from the input surface structure. The system at the extreme end of any scale of perspicuity of application is Winograd's, where the procedural notation, by its nature, tries to make clear the way in which the structures are applied. At the other end are the systems of Schank and Charniak, where no application is specified, which means that the representations are not only compatible with many implementation algorithms, which does not matter, but are also compatible with many systems of linguistic rules, whose specification is an essential piece of inquiry, and whose subsequent production may cause the basic system to be fundamentally different.

Application is thus different from decoupling, for Schank's system is clearly coupled to language text by Riesbeck's parser, though his structures do not express their own application to language text, as was pointed out in the discussion of Riesbeck's system.

In some of his more recent writings Winograd has begun to develop a view that is considerably stronger than this "application" one: in his view the control structure of an understanding program is itself of theoretical significance, for only in that way, he believes, can natural language programs of great size and complexity remain perspicuous.

Forward Inference

Another outstanding dispute concerns whether one should make massive forward inferences as one goes through a text, keeping all one's expectations intact, as Charniak, Schank and Rieger hold, or whether, as Wilks argues, one should adopt some "laziness hypothesis" about understanding, and generate deeper inferences only when the system is unable to solve, say, a referential problem by more superficial methods. Or, in computer terms, should a system be problem or data-driven?

Although Schank sometimes writes of a system making "all possible" inferences as it proceeds through a text, this is not in fact the heart of the dispute, since no one would want to defend any strong definition of the term "all possible inferences". Charniak's argument is that, unless certain forward inferences are made during an analysis of, say, a story — forward inferences, that is, that are not problem-driven; not made in response to any particular problem of analysis then known to the system — then, as a matter of empirical fact, the system will not in general be able to solve ambiguity or reference problems that arise later, because it will never in fact be possible to locate (while looking backwards at the text, as it were) the points where those forward inferences ought to have been made. This is, in very crude summary (see Chapter 8), Charniak's case against a purely problem-driven inferencer in a natural language understander.

One difficulty with this argument is the location of an example of text that confirms the point in a non-contentious manner. Another is that it is not always clear whether the argument is about what people are thought to do when they understand, or about how one should construct an understanding system. It would be possible, for example, to agree with Charniak's argument and still construct a purely problem-driven inferencer on the ground that, at the moment, this is the only way one can cope with the vast majority of inferences for understanding, since any system of inferences made in response to no particular problem in the text is too hard to control in practice. Rieger (1974), for example, has to resort to a simple arbitrary numerical cut-off of forward inferencing, which seems unsatisfactory. Indeed, it is noticeable that the more recent papers of Schank and Charniak have been considerably less forward-inference oriented than earlier ones. On the other hand, systems that now run without forward inferencing could easily do some: the process Wilks calls extraction for example could easily run as a purely data-driven process.

This dispute is perhaps only one of degree, and about the possibility of defining a degree of forward inference that aids the solution of later semantic problems without going into unnecessary depth. This might be an area where psychological investigations would be of enormous help to workers in AI.

Modularity

Modularity concerns the decomposability of a program or system into (interacting) parts, and the nature of the relationship between the parts. Winograd's program, as we saw, contains syntactic, semantic and deductive segments, which interact in a way he describes as "heterarchic", as opposed to "hierarchic", which means that different segments can be in control at different times.

On the other hand, Schank and Wilks have argued that it is not necessary to observe either the syntactic-semantic, or the semantic-deductive, distinction in an understanding program, and that it may well not be possible to specify the syntactic-semantic distinction in principle either. On this view there is no particular virtue in integrating syntax and semantic routines, since there was no need to separate them.

Charniak, however, would argue that, in some sense, one should make a syntax-semantics distinction here if one can (see Chapter 2). This is consistent with his view on decoupling, and it is convenient to decouple at a module, as it were, such as syntactic analysis; but decoupling and strong modularity are not the same thing. Winograd's program, for example, is modular but not at all decoupled from surface text.

Scale of Representations

This dispute is related to the ones about application and decoupling and concerns the practical function of the larger scale frame representations of knowledge. The point of view of this chapter has been that these representations must be justified in terms of some concrete problem that they solve, such as word-sense or pronoun reference ambiguity, otherwise they may not be essentially connected with the understanding of natural language. That is to say that representation of knowledge as such, and independent of any purpose or problem, is not a task for AI.

In the light of this let us turn back for a moment to the "larger scale" chunks of knowledge: Charniak's frames, which were created as wholes (Chapter 8) or Schank's scripts which were created by "stacking up", in a predetermined order, primitives for individual actions. This development is open to any representation system with forms standing for individual assertions: Wilks, for example, could "stack up" his common sense inferences rules in advance so that they ran not just

```
                  P  IMPLIES  Q
                      but
                  P
        IMPLIES   Q
        IMPLIES   R
        IMPLIES   S
```

where each of the schematic letters stands for a complex object like a template, or one half of a common sense inference rule.

One way of putting a doubt about the role of any structures of so large a scale is to imagine one for a less everyday activity.

Suppose we were considering sentences about a puberty rite in a distant tribe. We might make up a frame as follows in a combination of Schank's and Charniak's (Chapter 8) notation:

```
        Script:  male puberty rite
        Roles:   male child, village elder, helpers, crowd
        Reason:  placing ritual incisions on back of child

    (11) a)  Goal:  CHILD is tattooed
         b)  HELPERS hold CHILD (by both arms)
         c)  ELDER obtain TOOLS
         d)  ELDER exhorts CROWD (on proper behavior)
         e)  (general condition)
             §bad behavior by CROWD ——→ activity halted
         f)  ELDER checks if CHILD properly purified
         g)  (special condition)
             CHILD not purified ——→ activity halted
         h)  ELDER mark CHILD's back
         i)   |  method suggested
              └——→ do for all CUT-MARKS
```

The general idea should be clear without detailed explanation, and the choice of a remote, and imaginary, culture is for a good reason.

Suppose we now have the "story sentence"

(12) Little Kimathi's mother accidentally touched his arm during the puberty rite. The crowd drew back in horror.

If we wish to "understand" this sentence, would we need the "puberty rite frame" given earlier? The frame (11) covers (12) with line (e), given some adequate definition list of bad behaviors in the frame (to which we are directed by "§", let us imagine). And yet it is clear that we do understand (12) perfectly well without (11).

In common sense terms, we could say that we infer from (12) that the mother touching Kimathi during the ceremony was a bad thing; we do not need the frame stating that in order to understand. An earth-frameless Martian would understand (12) provided he knew the meanings of the words and had some smaller scale knowledge about aversion behavior being produced by bad events. Hence the choice of a puberty rite rather than a supermarket for the frame (11), for we are Martians where puberty rites are concerned. If we do understand (12) it cannot be from our associated frame because, presumably, we do not have one.

It is not being argued here that large scale frames have no function, only that, as regards concrete problems of language understanding, their function has not yet been made explicit.

One possible explicit claim about the function of large scale frames (and one almost explicit in (Schank 1975a)) could be put as follows: "In order to understand a story we need to know how basic stories (i.e. frames) of that type go; that is, we only understand, and can only understand, a particular story by judging how it follows, or diverges from, the normal story of that type." We could call this the plot-line hypothesis (PLH) and whether current psychological research is to be taken as confirming or disconfirming this claim is at present a matter of dispute.

Real World Procedures

At the time of Winograd's work and during the early phases of the design of PLANNER (see Chapter 1) there was considerable dispute about the slogan "meanings are procedures". The dispute was about the most appropriate form of intelligent programs and the slogan was intended to support the procedural form, which we saw examples of from Winograd.

This dispute has quietened down, but there is an analogue of it still about in language work, and concerned not with the internal procedures of the computer, but the relation of understanding to real activities in the world. The reader will have noticed that many of the systems described in this book (Winograd's, Charniak's, Scragg's, Rieger (1975)) actually concern themselves with real activities: picking up, cooking, etc., or, more precisely, with simulations of these physical activities. Is this just accident, or is there some real relationship between doing and understanding?

There is an implicit, but pervasive, hypothesis behing much current work that might be called the do-it hypothesis, namely that in representing knowledge, we should concentrate on the representation of human activities that we know how to perform: stacking blocks, eating in restaurants, shopping in supermarkets, cooking food, or, in Rieger's case (1975), the different matter of how a water closet performs its task.

The connexion with natural language comes with the further assumption that one cannot understand language about human activities unless one has performed, or can perform, them. The core of this argument is rather like the one that young school children in class cannot understand the discussions of love in the Shakespeare plays they have to study because they have not experienced the corresponding feeling.

There is clearly something in this argument, but the trouble comes with specifying just what it is that the non-performer does not understand, given that one could answer questions as if one did understand. People can answer a lot of questions about skiing, and certainly appear to understand newspaper stories about it, even when they cannot ski.

A stronger argument is that the relevance of an activity frame to natural language is bound up with the teachability of the activity. This version has the advantages of avoiding asserting the PLH directly, as Schank seems to do, but is weakened by the fact that the frame activities in question (eating in restaurants, shopping in supermarkets) are not, in any obvious sense, taught at all, at least not in the sense that using scissors or typing one's shoe laces are taught.

These are points in dispute, then, between those, like Charniak and Schank, who believe in the function of large scale frame structures, and those who, like Wilks, remain agnostic.

The Justification of Systems

Finally, one might usefully, though briefly, contrast the different modes of justification implicitly appealed to by the systems described earlier in this paper. These seem to reduce to four:

(i) In terms of the power of the inferential system employed. This form of justification has underlain the early predicate calculus-based language programs, and is behind Hayes' (1974) recent demand that any formalism for natural language analysis should admit of a set theoretic semantics (see Chapter 11), so as to gain "intellectual respectability", as he puts it. The same general type of justification is appealed to in some degree by systems with PLANNER-type formalisms.

(ii) In terms of the provision and formalization in any terms, including English, of the sorts of knowledge required to understand areas of discourse.

(iii) In terms of the actual performance of a system, implemented on a computer, at a task agreed to demonstrate understanding.

(iv) In terms of the linguistic and/or psychological plausibility of the proffered system of representation.

Oversimplifying considerably, one might say that Charniak's system appeals mostly to (ii) and somewhat to (i) and (iv); Winograd's to (iii) and somewhat to the other three categories; Colby's (as regards its natural language, rather than psychiatric, aspects) appeals almost entirely to (iii); and Schank's and Wilks' to differing mixtures of (ii), (iii) and (iv).

In the end, of course, only (iii) counts for empiricists, but there is considerable difficulty in getting all parties to agree to the terms of a test. A cynic might say that, in the end, all these systems analyze the sentences that they analyze or, to put the same point a little more theoretically, there is a sense in which systems, those described here and those elsewhere, each define a natural language, namely the one to which it applies. The difficult question is the extent to which those many and small natural languages resemble English.

E. Charniak and Y. Wilks (eds.), Computational Semantics

PSYCHOLOGY OF LANGUAGE AND MEMORY

Walter F. Bischof

INTRODUCTION

The intent of this chapter is twofold: first it should provide the non-psychologist with some basic concepts and some important experimental findings in the field of psycholinguistics and the psychology of memory. The second goal is to take a close look at the nature of psychological arguments and psychological evidence. To understand this second goal one has to realize that there is a growing interest among the AI community in psychology and that psychological arguments are gaining more and more importance in theoretical considerations. It is undeniable that psychology has had some beneficial influence on AI and that psychological evidence may sometimes be useful for the evaluation of AI models. But a closer look at today's psychology and some thoughts about the nature of psychological arguments will show that this psychological evidence is often due to misconceptions and that in general psychological arguments are often overestimated.

The chapter is roughly organized in the following way: after a discussion of association, a concept equally important both for language and memory, some topics in psycholinguistics are reviewed, followed by a discussion of methodological problems. The second section reviews some theories of memory, again followed by a discussion of more general problems. The last section considers the use of psychological findings and theories in AI.

One preliminary point should be made clear: it is not the intent of this chapter to give an encompassing review of the two fields. A few selected topics are discussed, which are either particularly popular in AI or which lead to discussion of more general problems. Good overviews can be found in (Herriot 1970) and (Fillenbaum 1971). For the psychology of memory see, for example, (Norman 1970) and (Postman 1975).

ASSOCIATION

There are a lot of theories and models in the psychology of language and memory, but if one takes a closer look at them, it is astonishing to discover how many of them refer to the concept of association, a term already found in the work of Aristotle more than 2,300 years ago. The concept of association is so ubiquitous that it seems worthwhile to examine it somewhat more closely.

The classical theory of association assumes that associations are formed by contiguity, i.e. when a person is exposed to two stimuli which occur together, then an associative link is built between the two internal representations of the stimuli. And the more frequent they occur together, the stronger the association. This has the effect that when the subject is exposed to only one of the stimuli, the representation of the other is also activated through the associative link.

Probabilistic View of Association

A way to determine the associative strength between two items (e.g. two words) is by means of an association task: a person is given a word and asked to say the first word which then comes into his mind. From the frequency of the different words which are produced by a number of persons, the associative strength between the words is determined. So, for example, the most frequent associations to "needle" are "thread" (16% of responses), "pin" (15.8%), "sharp" (15.2%), "sew" (13.5%) and "sewing" (10.7%).

It is a plausible assumption that the association task reveals some general properties of the language knowledge we have, and that idiosyncratic factors normally play a secondary role (though the association task is also a useful tool in psychoanalysis).

These values for associative strength are computed on the basis of a large number of subjects. Yet if we look at only one person, then we see that a word is associated to several others. So the subject might once answer to "girl" with "pretty" and another time with "boy", etc. This means that the subject has available different associations and has to make some kind of choice during the association task which one he will actually produce. This leads to the next view of association.

Association as Disposition

This view stresses the fact that a stimulus is associated to all potential responses. The fact that there is an association between a and b does not necessarily mean that whenever a is given, b will follow. Which response actually follows depends on some "process conditions". There have been attempts to specify these process conditions, but on the whole one can only say that they were failures.

Contextual Association

There is yet another problem with association. The recall of a previously learned list of items cannot be fully explained by associations between the items.

At least one of these items has to be associated with the general environment stimuli in the presence of which the items are learned. These contextual associations enable the subject to recall the first item in the list.

In conclusion one can say that association is primarily a descriptive term. It only tells us that when a occurs, b will follow with a certain probability. This is no more than an empirical description without any implications for more wide ranging theoretical statements. A clarification of association can only be achieved by outlining the processes which underly it. Nonetheless psychological theories often go no further than this empirical description, believing that they have made theoretical statements.

Association and Language

The concept of association was not primarily used to explain language understanding directly. From the beginnings it was a general conviction among psychologists that this was impossible, simply because language understanding was too complex. Therefore the first requirement was to explain how humans solve "simple" tasks, as, for example, learning a list of words, or a list of word pairs, or the spontaneous production of words (association task) etc. It was claimed that only when we know how people solve the "simple" tasks, we are prepared to study language processes. It is therefore unclear to what degree psychologists really believe that the principles found in such studies with verbal material are useful for an explanation of language.

However, associationist theories of language were attempted, although their "insights" were entirely based on language production, since they had no experimental tools to study language comprehension directly, a problem that will be discussed later on. Such theories will most plausibly conceive language use as a probabilistic process, especially since any deterministic theory of language processes could easily be demonstrated to be false.

Association theory assumes that we have something like a big word-to-word (or concept-to-concept) association network in mind, and that language production is a "random" walk through this network. Since unrelated concepts are very weakly interassociated it is very improbable that people utter meaningless sentences, though it is not impossible (before Chomsky's work appeared this type of argument even was used to explain why we utter grammatical sentences). The associationist's task is therefore to find which concepts are strongly interassociated, i.e. bundled clusters of concepts in the "semantic space" and to find the dimensions of this "semantic space".

PSYCHOLINGUISTICS

Prior to Chomsky, work in psycholinguistics was associationistic in character. However, transformational grammar's growing popularity in linguistics carried over to psychology, and subsequent psycholinguistic research was characterized by its strong dependence on linguistics. Only at the end of the decade and in the Seventies have psycholinguists again begun to work on their own theories of language behavior.

A considerable portion of the psycholinguistic research was oriented toward the assessment of linguistic structures (e.g. the psychological reality of deep and surface structure) and of linguistic processes (e.g. the psychological processes corresponding to transformations). The following sections very briefly describe some of these experiments, mainly to give the reader some flavor of the type of research pursued. A complete description of the experiments, as well as the theoretical disagreements which led to the experiments, would be beyond the scope of this chapter.

The Psychological Reality of Linguistic Constructs

Johnson (1965) was the first to test the psychological reality of phrase-structure rules (see Chapter 6 for an explanation of this type of rule). He supposed that if phrase-structure rules were involved in language understanding, then they probably would have an effect on the subjects' representation of sentences in memory, and this in turn would be reflected in the errors in recalling learned sentences. In particular he supposed that the major clauses would be stored as units in memory and these units would be recalled as a whole (see also the section on organization theory for a further discussion of this idea). Therefore recall errors should most likely occur at the transitions from one major clause to the next. In the experiment Johnson asked his subjects to learn a list of sentences like "The small boy saved the dying woman" or "The house across the street is burning". They remembered sequences like "The tall boy came ...", "The boy helped the woman", etc. He then determined the location of the first error in the reproduction (wrong word, omission of a word, etc.) and calculated the probability of a word being incorrect, given that the previous word was correct. As expected these transition error probabilities were considerably higher at the border of major constituents (e.g. between NP and VP) than within the constituents (see Figure 1).

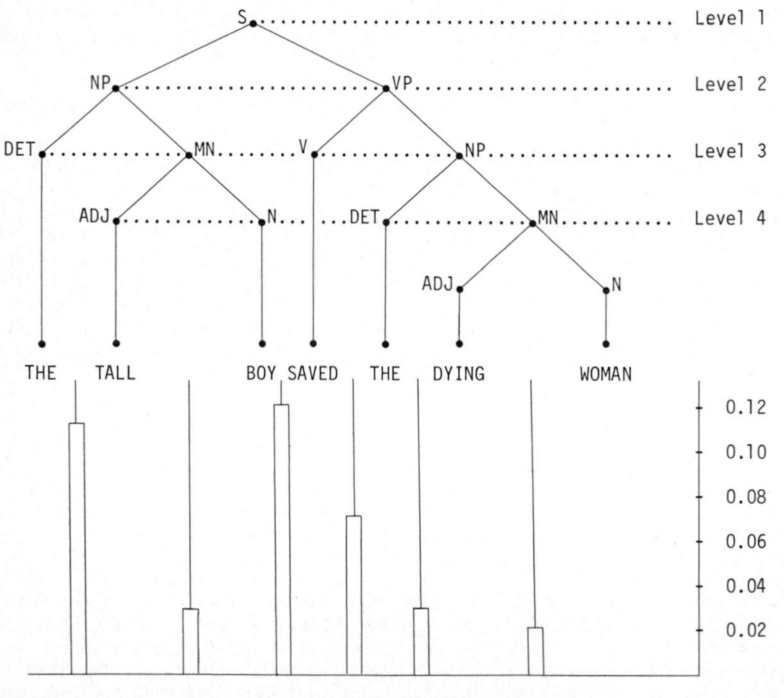

Figure 1 Transition Error Probabilities (Johnson, 1965)

Surprisingly he also found that the error probabilities were not equal between the words within major constituents; Johnson suggested that the likelihood of an error is a function of the level of transition from word to word, where the transition from "boy" to "saved" represents a higher transition than that from "saved" to "the", which in turn is higher than that from "the" to "dying" (again see Figure 1). These "levels" are defined in terms of phrase-structure rules, so by showing a dependence on "level" in the results Johnson gave some evidence for the psychological validity of phrase-structure rules.

Johnson's theory is a surface structure theory of language in that it makes no reference to transformational deep structure, or any other level of structure. Such a theory was further investigated in a famous series of experiments, the so-called "click experiments" by Garret, Fodor, Bever and their colleagues. In these experiments the subjects heard a click in one ear while they were listening to a sentence in the other ear; they then had to report where the click had occurred. The subjects tended to displace the click from its objective position forward or backward toward major constituent borders. The initial findings were quite consistent with the results of Johnson. But more recent findings, where deep structure and surface structure did not coincide, cannot be interpreted only on the basis of surface structure. A particularly interesting result (Bever, Lackner & Kirk, 1969) is the displacement of clicks in the two superficially similar sentences like:

(1) "The corrupt police can't bear criminals to confess very quickly"

(2) "The corrupt police can't force criminals to confess very quickly"

whose underlying syntactic structure according to transformational grammar (ignoring within-clause structure) is:

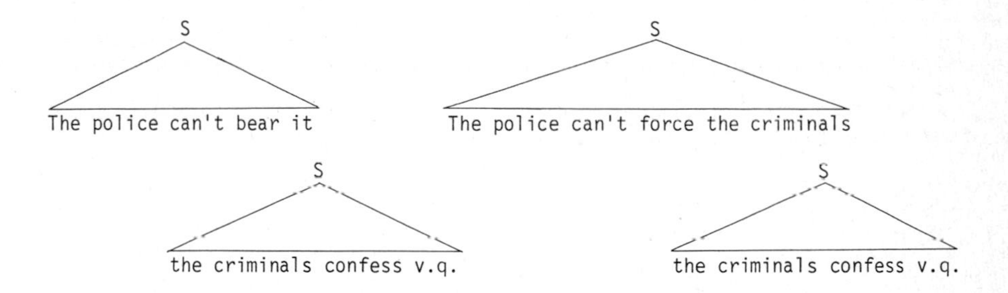

i.e. in sentence (1) the entire embedded clause is the object of the main verb "bear" while in sentence (2) the subject of the embedded clause is simultaneously the object of the main verb "force". While in (1) a click objectively located in "bear" was subjectively located between the verb and the complement, there was no systematic tendency of displacement of the click in (2). We need not be concerned with why clicks are displaced. What is important about these experiments is that whatever the explanation may be, it has to refer to the underlying structure of sentences.

Psychological Reality of Linguistic Processes

Naturally enough, the concern with the validity of transformational constructs, such as deep structure, was matched by concern with the psychological reality of transformational processes. There were two positions on this issue. The correspondence hypothesis states that there is an isomorphy between transformational rules and psychological processes. On the other hand the theory of derivational complexity makes weaker assumptions and claims only that there is a positive relation between human language performance and the length of transformational derivation.

A first source of evidence for the psychological reality of transformational rules was the experiment of McKean, Slobin and Miller (1962) where the subjects were required to transform affirmative sentences into negative, passive and negative-passive ones. The reaction time to do the negative-passive transformation was roughly the sum of the reaction time for the negative and the passive transformation. This suggests that the subjects use transformational rules and that they use them one after the other. A weak point of this experiment, despite its clear-cut results, is that the subjects were explicitly required to transform the sentences. People seem to use transformational rules, if they are required to do so, but it doesn't say that they use them in ordinary language understanding processes. An indirect source of evidence for the psychological reality of the transformational component is Mehler's (1963) experiment where the subjects had to learn simple and transformed sentences. The analysis of the recall errors showed that the sentences were often remembered in a "less-transformed" form and Mehler suggested that sentences are represented in memory as kernels plus markers of their derivational history, i.e. which transformational rules have been used to get the kernel. So the sentence "The old woman wasn't liked by John" would be stored in memory as "John liked the old woman" plus the two markers "passive" and "negative". Recall of the sentences would then consist of remembering the kernel and applying to it those transformations which are remembered.

In Savin & Perchonok's experiment (1965) the subjects had to learn sentences of different complexity plus a number of unrelated words. The recall of these words was negatively correlated with the number of transformations in the sentence, which can be explained by an assumption that the transformations occupy additional space in memory and therefore fewer additional words are recalled.

The experiments reported in the preceding paragraphs give some support for the importance of grammatical factors in human language behavior. But there are some serious doubts about using grammatical factors alone to explain language understanding.

It is a feature of these experiments that they isolated the importance of syntactic information by eliminating all contextual information. They therefore say nothing about the importance of syntactic factors in natural situations. Furthermore all the experimental tasks involved exact reproduction of syntax, something rarely, if ever, required in normal situations. In such cases one must consider the possibility that the subject develops, during the course of the experiment, some ad hoc strategy to solve the task. Such strategies might bear little resemblance to those used in everyday situations where content is more important than syntax.

Semantics in Psycholinguistics

It seems that in the last years the Chomskian paradigm has lost much of its attraction and has been replaced by a growing interest in semantic factors, or more precisely, the belief that semantics is the most important determinant of language behavior. But no adequate elaborated semantic theory yet exists and this is reflected in recent research with its tendency to an atheoretical position. Often it only tries to find interesting relationships between variables and hesitates to assemble a concrete process model of language understanding.

The transition from the Chomskian paradigm to modern work in research on comprehension processes probably starts with the non-transformational deep structure models. Their main idea is that in the process of comprehension of a sentence its deep structure is not recovered via transformations, but rather the important factor is "the degree to which the arrangement of elements in the surface structure provides clues to the relations of elements in deep structure". An illustration of this idea is the finding that sentences like "The shot (which) the soldier (that) the mosquito bit fired missed" were more difficult to paraphrase when the pronouns were left out.

The idea that different perceptual strategies are used in language comprehension has been generalized and developed by Bever (1970). In understanding language we use an undetermined number of heuristic strategies (lexical, syntactic, semantic, etc.) to reveal the underlying actor-action-object relations. One of these heuristics is the use of syntactic clues in the surface structure, another is the "semantic plausibility" strategy: the functional relations (actor, action, object) are not found via recognition and use of syntactic information, but through "semantic short-cuts". The plausibility of this hypothesis has been shown by a number of experiments. Schlesinger (1966) showed that perceptually complex sentences are easier to understand when the subject-verb-object relations are semantically determined as, for example, in the sentence (3) in contrast to (4).

(3) The question the girl the lion bit answered was complex.

(4) The lion the dog the monkey chased bit died.

Slobin (1966) showed that the normally greater complexity of passive sentences is neutralized when the semantic relations help to determine the semantic subject and object, as in (5) and (6), (where it is unlikely that a book would read a professor).

(5) The book was read by the professor.

(6) The professor read the book.

Such sentences are said to be <u>irreversible</u>. But in reversible sentences the passive sentences, like (7), are perceptually more complex than the active ones, like (8).

(7) The brother was hated by the sister.

(8) The sister hated the brother.

We find similar effects in sentences (9) and (10). But in (9) and (10) the semantic irreversibility is due to pragmatic expectations rather than semantic restrictions. (Herriot, 1969).

(9) The doctor treated the patient.

(10) The patient treated the doctor.

In recent years psychologists have come to realize that inference processes play an important role in human language use. This view was not the immediate result of previous experimental evidence, but rather came about due to the growing influence of AI, particularly of Winograd and Schank.

Bransford & Franks (1971) did an experiment on sentence recognition where they found that subjects were unable to distinguish between sentences they had heard during acquisition and closely related sentences they had not. They concluded that the subjects "spontaneously integrate the information expressed by a number of consecutively experienced sentences into wholistic semantic ideas".

Johnson, Bransford & Solomon (1973) used as a recognition task sentences which either made an instrument-inference very likely such as, for example, "The man drove to work" or a result-inference, as, for example, "The spy threw the secret document into the fireplace". In recognition the subjects were very likely to judge the sentences "The man took his car to work" and "The spy burned the secret document" as the sentences they had heard during acquisition.

These experiments show that inferencing processes occur, but proving that people do inferencing while reading — a view which is probably held by most AI workers — is much more difficult. It does not follow from the findings reported above. In fact there are equally good interpretations which explain the results on the basis of characteristics of recall processes (see, e.g. reconstructive memory) and there probably could be other interpretations also.

More successful in this respect was an experiment done by Frederiksen (1975). His essential idea was as follows: if inferences are done during recall of a story to fill "gaps" in memory, then these inferences should gradually disappear with repeated exposure to the story, since the subjects remember more of the original story text. But if these inferences are done while reading, they become an integral part of the representation of the story and the amount of inferences in the reproduction would not be reduced with repeated reading of the story. In the experiment the subjects had to repeatedly read and reproduce a story. The fact that the number of sentences in the reproduction which Frederiksen classified as "inference sentences" remained constant with repeated trials favored the hypothesis that inferencing occurs while reading.

But the best proof of the inferencing-while-reading theory was made by Bransford & Johnson (1972) in an experiment which is impressive solely from the simplicity of its design. Their subjects had to read and recall a story which starts as follows: "The procedure is actually quite simple. First you arrange things into different groups depending on their makeup. Of course, one pile may be sufficient depending on how much there is to do. If you have to go somewhere else due to lack of facilities that is the next step, otherwise you are pretty well set. It is important ..." The subjects who heard the topic of the paragraph after presentation of the text and those who didn't get the topic at all were equally bad in reproducing the text, but those who got the topic (it is about washing clothes) before the passage were significantly better in reproducing the story. This result clearly shows that inferencing and the availability of appropriate knowledge for these inferences are a crucial part of the understanding mechanisms.

Problems of Psycholinguistics

In the previous paragraphs a very small sample of experiments has been reviewed, and only a few theoretical questions have been touched. They have shown that psycholinguistics is potentially relevant for other fields which deal with natural language understanding in that psycholinguistics can give us insights about human understanding which rest upon a more reliable foundation than introspection. But on the other hand, many of the results are obvious — if not trivial. They support views which are taken for granted anyway, or which have already been independently proved to be true. This is, for example, the case with the previously mentioned experiments designed to demonstrate that inferencing occurs during understanding.

But what seems interesting about these experiments is that psycholinguistics has developed its own methods to investigate the process of language understanding. It might seem that these methods would be useful in answering questions about language understanding where other sciences (and perhaps AI) are at a loss. But a closer look at the experimental paradigms available casts doubt upon this thesis. (By paradigm here we mean a class of experiments which share the same overall structure, where the structure involved is seen as, in some sense, defining the theoretical basis of the experiments.)

In most paradigms (remembering sentences and stories, matching sentences with pictures, recognizing sentences, etc.) it is not possible to find adequate means to discriminate between the comprehension process itself and other processes such as memory processes and recall processes. This difficulty in correlating the source of certain effects with a particular, definite, process is a serious limitation in psycholinguistic research. Take as an example the recall of sentences where the syntactic characteristics of the text seem to have some effect on the subjects' recall ability. These effects might be due to the subjects' own processing strategies, or to the way in which syntactic information is stored or to the way in which syntactic information is recalled.

Another problem with some paradigms (judging comprehensibility, judging grammaticality, transforming sentences, etc.) is that their relation to the process of language understanding is far from clear. There is no indisputable method by which we can infer the characteristics of language understanding strategies from such activities: indeed it is not certain that they are based on the same cognitive strategies as language understanding at all.

A third problem is that it is difficult, within the experimental situation, to control or to maintain the degree to which the subject is able or required to process the information given to him (for example, straightforward recall of a sentence probably requires less intensive processing of the sentence than does a demand that the subject should relate that sentence to the wider context of a picture or a story.) This is not to say that no control is possible; the imposition of time limitations or giving instructions that the subject should concentrate on content or on exact syntactic structure can be used to a limited extent to enforce levels of comprehension. But it is difficult, given that such methods are necessarily inexact, to compare the results of different experiments. Let us give here just two examples of types of experiments where difficulty in control of levels of comprehension can lead to incomparable or mistaken results. First, consider recall experiments. The more deeply information has been processed, the more resistant that information is to forgetting. If this factor is neglected the results may not prove the hypothesis which the designers intended them to prove. Secondly, more intensive processing may enable the subject to use different, and probably more powerful, strategies than he could use if the processing was more superficial.

These critical remarks apply particularly to psycholinguistic experiments. Some more general comments, which nonetheless can be seen to apply also to psycholinguistics, will appear at the end of the section on memory and at the end of the last section. But one point should be made quite clear immediately. These remarks are not criticisms designed to help psychologists, in the sense that, if followed up, they would lead to the development of alternative, improved methods. Perhaps, indeed, the development of methods unassailable by such criticisms is impossible. Nonetheless, the student of AI should be able to see from the discussion here that the ability of psychology to design and carry out experiments which will give clear and indisputable results is very limited, and that their ability to provide a safe and clear insight into human language understanding is similarly very limited.

PSYCHOLOGY OF MEMORY

In the introduction it was said that (since this chapter is intended chiefly to help the reader to understand AI references to psychology) the topics chosen for review were chosen more because of their popularity in AI than because of their relative importance in psychology. This is particularly true in this section on memory. Some of the topics discussed here are considered peripheral by psychologists, and some "central" (to psychology) topics are not discussed at all. One of these peripheral topics is the reconstruction theory, which has attracted continuing interest from AI.

The Reappearance Theory Versus the Reconstruction Theory

The associationists viewed memory as a static system, roughly something like a net of associations. Within this theory recall of information from memory is made possible by means of some associative link from a given piece of information. Recall is essentially a reappearance of the information which was originally stored.

This view was radically contradicted by the reconstruction theory of Bartlett (1932), Neisser (1967) and others. They claim that it is not the product of the original construction processes (i.e. comprehension processes) which is stored in memory, but the traces of the construction processes themselves. Remembering is not simply a reactivation of old traces, as in associationist theory. Instead, the stored fragments of the construction processes are the basic pieces of information used in a new (re-)construction process.

The important organizing factor behind these construction processes is the "schema", vaguely defined by Bartlett as "an active organization of past reactions or of past experiences" (p.201). These schemata serve as a frame of reference for cognitive processing of the incoming information. So the schema plus fragments of the initial experiences together serve to reconstruct (or remember) what happened. There is a constant interaction between new incoming information and the schemata. We respond to the new incoming information by relating it to our previous "schematized" experiences, while at the same time we continually adapt the schemata to the new information. The schemata enable us to carry out the organization, but also have a negative effect in that they introduce bias and distortion into both construction and reconstruction.

In extensive studies Bartlett studied the effects of schemata on remembering stories. Some of his subjects had to recall repeatedly an Indian story, "The War of the Ghosts". He found profound changes in the reproduction: proper names, individual characteristics were lost or became more stereotyped. Often the subjects remembered no more than a vague outline of the story, but then constructed a whole new story around it. The reader may notice how near these ideas about schemata are to the frames approach (see Chapter 8). In fact, if one reads some of the paragraphs in Bartlett or Neisser and replaces some phrases by "frames" or "frame-systems", they sound very up to date. The problem with this approach within psychology was its vagueness, and the fact that there was a lack of evidence about how it could work. For this reason, the reconstruction theory never became popular within psychology. It may be that it will gain new currency under the influence of "frames" and of AI.

Since the late Fifties the amount of research on human memory has grown rapidly. In contrast to the older theories (such as the reconstruction theory) which tried to set up principles which generally govern the functioning of human memory, this later research only tried to explain what was happening within small paradigms, as, for example, the "free recall paradigm", the free reproduction of a previously learned list of items (words, syllables, numbers, etc.)

The restriction on the variety of tasks, in which the role of memory was to be explained, enabled the researchers to agree on a common methodology and therefore to argue on the basis of comparable experiments and commonly agreed interpretations of results. But as consistent as the terminology and methodology are within the paradigms, so are they equally diverse between the paradigms. The different theories are difficult to compare and to judge and they totally lack certain "sufficiency conditions" in that they cannot be easily integrated in a more encompassing theory of human memory. Our discussion of modern memory research will focus on three areas. First, the multiple store theories of memory, which have reached a remarkable position as a framework for a lot of different, often highly formalized, models, then some results and viewpoints which run under the name "organization theory", and finally the studies on semantic memory, which were initiated by Collins & Quillian (1969).

Multiple Store Theories of Memory

The multiple store models (see, e.g. Norman 1970) partition the contents of memory on a temporal basis, sometimes into two parts (short-term memory and long-term memory), sometimes into three (sensory register, STM, LTM) and sometimes even some additional store for specific information is assumed. For all these stores different mechanisms have to be provided for storage, retrieval, forgetting mechanisms, etc. In these models we have to distinguish the permanent, structural components (e.g. capacity) from the user dependent control processes (e.g. attention, rehearsal) which guide the selection and information flow (see Figure 2).

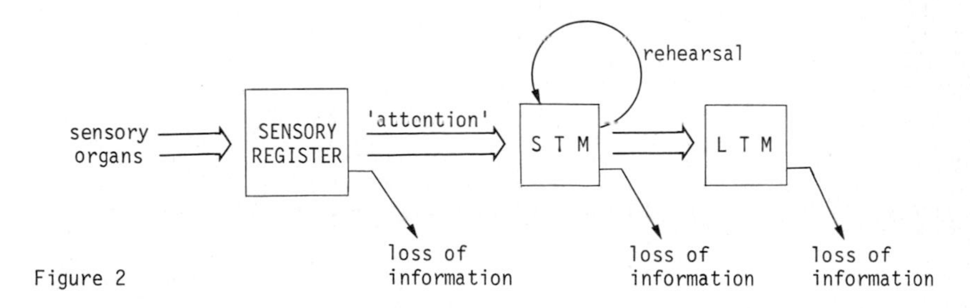

Figure 2

The following short description of some of the characteristics of these models is what one might call the brief creed about memory (version ca.1970). These characteristics were quite commonly agreed upon though the actual supporting evidence for them was quite weak. So the most recent developments in memory research have therefore been oriented toward a stepwise retreat from some of these unjustified beliefs. The reader should keep this in mind while reading the following paragraphs and is advised to read (Postman 1975) for a review of recent memory research.

The sensory register contains all the information which enters through the sense organs. The information which gains attention enters the short-term memory, the other disappears very rapidly by a pure time decay (of the order of 1/4 sec.) The short-term memory is a store of limited capacity. One could think of it as a box which can contain only a small fixed number of blocks (some believe seven), where each block may be, for example, a phoneme, a morpheme, a word, etc. A new block entering this box displaces an old one ("forgetting through displacement"). While information resides in the STM, it may be reformulated in an alternate (usually semantic) representation and transferred to LTM. Items are kept in STM through rehearsal (i.e. repetition) and if they cannot be rehearsed they quickly get lost. In contrast to the STM the LTM is of virtually unlimited capacity and the time constant associated with forgetting is fairly long and ranges from minutes to years. But even though information is permanently stored, retrieval of it may fail because the cues to find and identify an item may be incomplete or because of interference from other information.

It is not possible to discuss here all the experimental evidence for the multiple store theory, so three short examples must suffice: an intuitive everyday experience, a piece of physiological evidence, and finally the main supporting experimental paradigm from psychology.

The Telephone Number Example. The difference between STM and LTM is reflected in the difference between remembering your own telephone number and a telephone number you just looked up. Your own number is stored in the long-term memory and remains there permanently. On the other hand the number you have just looked up resides in the short-term memory and unless you rehearse it, it gets quickly lost.

Physiological Evidence. Milner (1967) reported cases of patients with brain damage, who appeared to be unable to transfer new information from STM to LTM. So one person, after having moved could not even remember the address of the new house, while he always remembered the old address. All the magazines he read over and over again were each time completely unfamiliar to him.

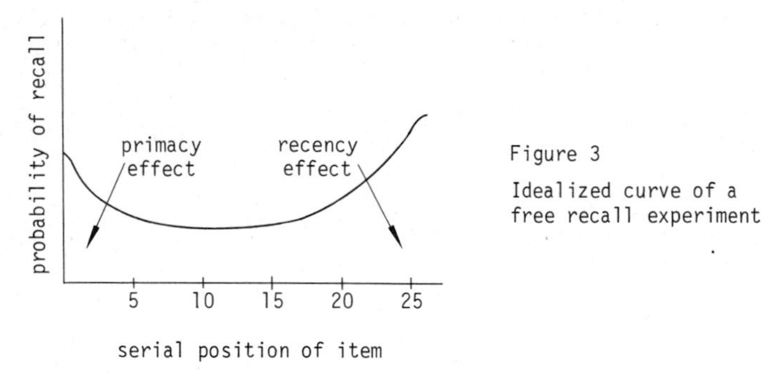

Figure 3

Idealized curve of a free recall experiment

Free Recall Experiments. In the "free recall paradigm" the subject has to learn a list of items and then has to reproduce it in any order he likes. The last items, i.e. the most recently presented, are recalled best. This is called the "recency effect" (see Figure 3). This recency effect spans over the last 7 - 8 items. It is assumed that these items are recalled from STM, whereas the previous items are recalled from LTM. To prove this, one could show that the recency effect disappears, when the subject is distracted (e.g. by counting backwards from a number) during the interval between presentation and recall, i.e. when the items in the short-term memory are replaced by numbers. The better recall of the first few items ("primacy effect") is explained in the following way: since the subject has no reason to keep pre-experimental information in STM, these items are not displaced until the STM is filled. Therefore the items stay longer in STM on the average and have a higher probability of being transferred to LTM.

Organization Theory

In the last ten years one concept in theories of memory has attracted growing interest: learning is not just a passive reception of an unordered mass of information but rather we impose some sort of organization upon the received material, based upon intrinsic properties of the items. The basic ideas of organization theory are not new, but can be traced back to the principles of perceptual organization of Gestalt psychologists, as well as to the clustering principle of Bousfield, etc. (see next paragraph). This might partially explain why organization theory is not a coherent theory, but rather a common slogan for various theoretical attempts.

One source of evidence for organizational factors in memory has been free recall experiments. Experimenters realized that people do not merely produce a list of unrelated words, but rather groups of items which share some common features (usually semantic, but also phonemic, syntactic, etc.) and that such groupings or categorizations are an essential characteristic of the subjects' organization of memory. A very old experiment by Bousfield (1953) will illustrate this. He asked his subjects to produce names of instruments and flowers and found that the subjects didn't produce them in random order, but rather in clusters of, say, four flowers, then six instruments, then five other flowers, etc. even though there was nothing in the task demands to require this.

The importance of organizational factors is also evident from a number of experiments (see overviews in Bower 1970 and in Tulving and Donaldson 1972) which showed that the learning of lists of items is facilitated by the use of grouping operations or by the use of categories. But while the effects of such categorizations seem obvious (at least to the non-psychologist) they do not provide any answer to the question of what the structure of memory might look like. One example of this sort of experiment is that of Bower et al. (1969) to show the importance of organization in learning. This experiment is impressive because of its clear-cut results. Their subjects had to learn four 28-word hierarchies amounting to 112 words in total. For half of the subjects, the words were presented as four complete hierarchical trees, like the Mineral Hierarchy tree shown in Figure 4; the control subjects learned trees of randomly intermixed words, which appeared to have no obvious structural principle. After the presentation the subjects had to recall the items in any order they wished. The subject in the "organized" condition recalled all the 112 items already by the third trial, whereas the subjects of the control group recalled less in the fourth trial than the "organized" subjects did in the first. Bower et al. concluded that hierarchy is an extremely familiar and efficient organization scaffold in human memory.

Organization theory has been popularized by contrasting it with association theory. Their proponents stressed the difference between association and organization in that association refers to relations between items which originate from contiguity of these items, while organization refers to intrinsic properties of items. But in recent research this sharp distinction has been shown not to hold since the development of organization and the establishment of associations occur simultaneously and cannot be discriminated appropriately.

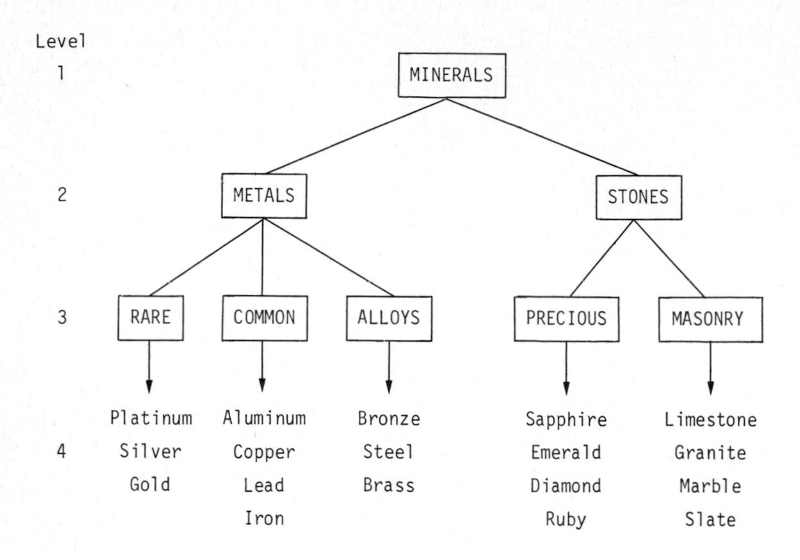

Figure 4

Example of a Conceptual Hierarchy of Words
from Bower et al. (1969)

Semantic Memory

The last paradigm to be mentioned here is the reaction time paradigm to investigate semantic memory initially used by Landauer & Freedman (1968) and by Collins & Quillian (1969). In these experiments the subjects have to decide the truth of sentences such as "A canary is a bird" or "A canary can fly" and the reaction time between presentation and judgment is measured. Collins & Quillian proposed as a model for long-term memory storage Quillian's (1967) model (see Figure 5).

Their model is based on the following two assumptions:

Hierarchy Assumption. Concepts are hierarchically organized into nested superset-chains. Thus the superset of canary is a bird and that of a bird is an animal. To decide that a canary is a bird requires one deductive step and that a canary is an animal requires two steps, namely that it is a bird and that a bird is an animal, and therefore it will take more time to decide.

Economy Assumption. Properties are attached only to the most general concept to which they apply. Thus the property "sings" is directly attached to canary, "has wings" is attached to bird and "has skin" is attached to animal. The decision that a canary has a skin needs therefore the deductive steps to bird, then to animal and from there to "has skin".

Collins & Quillian predicted that the reaction time to decide the truth of such sentences increases uniformly with the number of steps required to deduce the sentence, which seems remarkably well confirmed by their data (see Figure 6). The only exceptions are the sentences like "A canary is a canary" where they presumed that they were decided with a pattern matching process rather than by deduction.

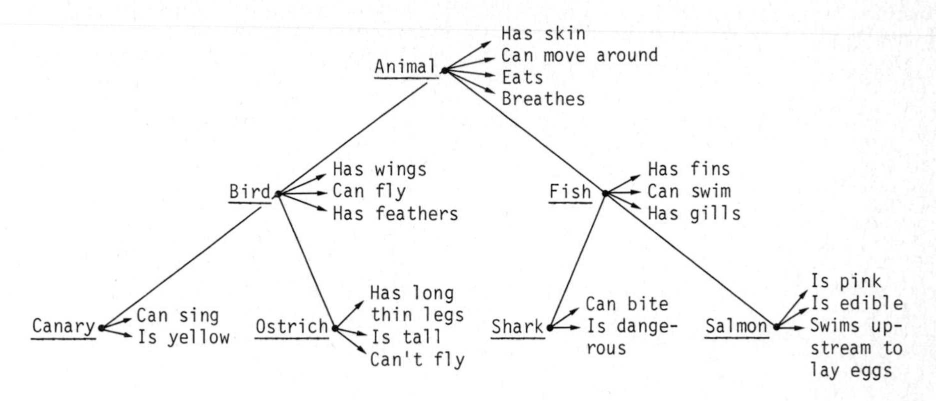

Figure 5

(Collins & Quillian 1969)

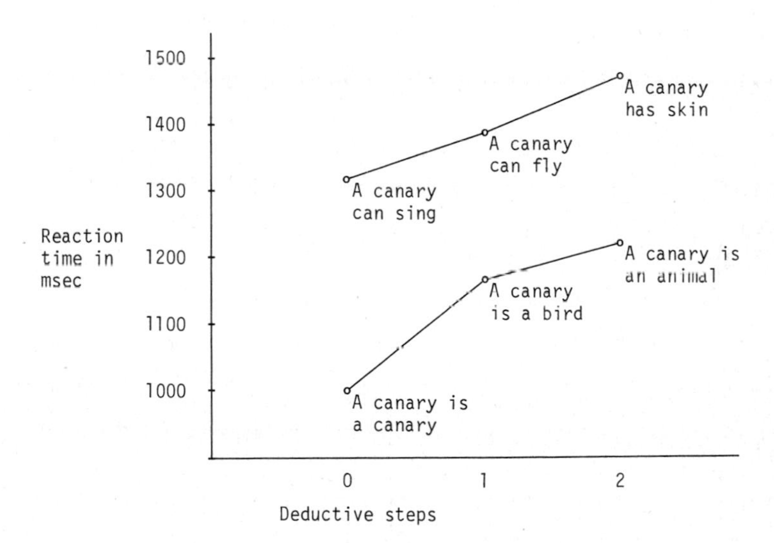

Figure 6

Average reaction time for different type of sentences adapted from (Collins & Quillian, 1969)

The Collins & Quillian paradigm has now become a standard paradigm and many experiments are performed with different variations of the material used by Collins & Quillian, such as use of quantifiers, negated sentences, sentences with nonsense concepts ("A gloop is an animal" needs more time to decide than "A gloop is a dog"), false sentences, etc. But we will only take a quick look at some of them to see the various doubts that have been cast on the Collins & Quillian model.

1) Hierarchies are not always clearly ordered, but depend on the subject's idiosyncratic interpretation. So the subjects tend to classify dog as animal though the stricter classification (of the model) would be dog - mammal - animal. Accordingly Rips et al. (1973) found that the reaction time to decide "A dog is an animal" is lower than for "A dog is a mammal".

2) The Collins & Quillian model predicts that "A robin is a bird" should require the same reaction time as "A goose is a bird" since both require one deductive step. Wilkins (1971) found that this prediction was not born out. Instead the former took less time. He found that the important factor in such cases is which is considered the more typical member of the class (as measured by the frequency with which an instance is given an exemplar).

3) Conrad (1972) replicated the Collins & Quillian experiment in a modified experiment to test the economy assumption. In a pre-experiment he asked his subjects to define the concepts like "canary", etc. He classified the produced sentences according to the frequency with which they were given into high-associative frequency and low frequency sentences and then further classified them according to their semantic distance in the Quillian-type network. With this data he replicated the experiment and found that the variability of the reaction time was totally due to the frequency of the propositions and that the semantic distance had no further influence. In re-analyzing the Collins & Quillian data he found that the high-distance propositions were of lower frequency than the low-level propositions.

The general point about all these experiments is that the structure of semantic memory is not the logical, hierarchical and economic structure proposed by Collins & Quillian. But on the other hand there is no alternative model of semantic memory which can account for all experimental findings in the reaction time paradigm, even those which are based on much more "data-sensitive" assumptions, as, for example, subject-rated semantic distance.

In all the articles on this issue one can see a clear tendency in the experiments to establish an experimental paradigm, i.e. a commonly used experimental design with only slight differences in the task used. The motivation for research in this paradigm is going to shift from the original question about the structure of human long-term memory to the question "Which model can explain all the experimental findings within the paradigm?" The paradigm is like a generator of different models based on substantially different assumptions. Future research within the Collins & Quillian paradigm may perhaps provide an answer to how humans behave in this very specific situation (which is rather rare in our everyday life), but it will not give more than some very vague hints concerning the structure of semantic memory.

AI and Experimental Psychology

In AI literature psychological questions and arguments often come up, as in the question of the psychological plausibility of a model or in references to psychological experiments. In this last section we will first try to characterize the role of psychology in AI and then discuss the use of psychological experimental findings in AI.

One important component of the relation between AI and psychology is the fact that psychology has been interested in concepts from computer science and AI since the beginnings of the latter disciplines. The interested reader is advised to read the excellent overview of Newell (1970) which discusses extensively the relationships between AI and cognitive psychology. But while that article discusses mainly the role of AI in psychology, we will concentrate here on the use of psychological findings in AI. In the computational semantics literature we can discriminate between at least three different positions towards experimental psychology. (It should be recognized, however, that this discrimination may be a subject of dispute, particularly since the role of psychology is never explicitly discussed by the different authors.)

For most researchers the findings of experimental psychology play a role similar to introspection, namely as a source of ideas for theoretical beginnings or as a first test of the plausibility of a model. This view is quite natural, because man is, after all, the only natural language understanding system that currently works, and it is hard to imagine how we could come to a theory of language understanding without observing how man does it and what he is capable of understanding. It is important to note that these researchers do not particularly consider their models psychological theories, and would not consider the theory invalidated by psychological results. Furthermore, for these researchers any scheme initially suggested by such psychological considerations must ultimately be justified on mere AI grounds (e.g. computational efficiency).

A second, basically similar, position is taken by Woods when he says:

> "In my own work, the things which have excited me and made me feel that I was discovering something important about the way people understand language, have been algorithms that are motivated by considerations of efficiency and "good engineering design" for a specific task which then turn out to have predictions which are borne out in human performance." (Woods 1975).

The difference between this and the first position is only Woods' explicit recognition of the possibility that his AI theory may (but then again may not) serve as a psychological theory.

These two positions do not lead to the problems which will be mentioned later, since the psychological experiments are not considered as binding for AI in the sense that AI theories are changed on the basis of psychological findings.

It is somewhat more difficult to judge the role of experimental psychology for those authors who consider their theories not only as AI theories, but also as psychological theories. Though their most important representatives, Schank and Norman, actually ignore most of psychological research, they still concede experimental psychology to have a potential relevance for AI. They are — in principle — inclined to adapt their theories to experimental findings. (That they do not so or do so only to a limited extent is justified by the view that the problem of modern psychology is not the lack of "good experiments" but a lack of good theories and that these theories cannot be achieved just by doing more experiments.) The important point about this position is that it has led to an increasing interest of AI people in psychological research in the last years and that psychology has in turn tried to stress its importance for AI.

But the following considerations will show that the usefulness of experimental psychology is limited and that AI is well advised not to over-estimate the importance of psychological arguments. Essentially the argument is in two parts. The first is that those who see psychology as simply lacking good theories are seriously under-estimating the internal problems of modern day psychology.

As it was shown in the previous sections and discussed in some detail with the Collins & Quillian experiments, modern psychology shows a clear trend away from theories which are designed to encompass a variety of human abilities towards theories which are designed to explain the findings within a particular experimental paradigm. These paradigms are oriented towards a particular task, for example, the free recall task, the sentence recognition task, the verification task, etc. This task-oriented theorizing can be partially understood from the inability of the methods used to discriminate between the different factors which are involved in solving a particular task (see discussion at the end of the section on language). So we find that the models which are used to explain the experimental results are often based on totally different assumptions. These models are often concurrently used to explain the experimental findings within a paradigm. First because none of these models can account for all findings; secondly, it is often extremely difficult — if not impossible — to improve a model to account for other experimental findings than those initially explained. This may be because a model becomes so complex that the testing of its underlying assumptions becomes an unmanageable experimental problem or because we just don't know how to improve the model. The result of this is that it seems impossible to build an initial model and then to extend it to a more general and less task-oriented model by comparing it with results of other paradigms.

On the other hand, researchers from outside psychology, for example from AI, are much more interested in content-oriented theories, for example, a theory of how human memory is structured. This leads to a discrepancy between what AI expects psychology to answer and what psychology is capable of answering. It would help, of course, if psychology would simply adopt one model and work on extending it to more and more phenomena, but it is not possible since the preference for one particular theory is too strong an assumption in the current state of psychology.

The trend away from old standard theories towards the task-oriented mini-models is one phenomenon in modern theorizing in psychology. But there is also a trend towards a non-theoretical and even anti-theoretical position. Many of the newer investigations could be described as "elaborated descriptions" of experimental results. They are not based on an explicit theory and their "models" consist only of a vague description of what might be an explanation of certain phenomena. It is not at all clear what value this research has since it lies in a theoretical vacuum and is based on highly specialized experimental situations. The net result of these trends is that psychology seems constitutionally incapable of producing the content-oriented theories that AI needs.

While the preceding remarks are criticisms of modern psychology itself, other arguments against the use of psychological findings in AI originate from different views AI and psychology take on language understanding systems. These arguments, in effect, say that even if psychology could produce more encompassing theories, it would be by no means clear that AI should adopt the results.

The first argument is that psychology and AI have different aims. While AI is interested in how language can be understood, psychology is interested in how humans actually do understand language. Psychological theories have to account for the constraints which are inherent in the human system while these are irrelevant to AI theories. For instance as long as we have no evidence that short-term memory is a necessary part of a language understanding system, it is not sensible to include a short-term memory mechanism in an AI theory which has no independent grounds for using one.

A second argument relates to the importance of certain phenomena for language understanding. Psychological experiments are concerned too much with activities which are non-central to language understanding (compared to what AI considers as central for language understanding) as, for example, the learning of lists of words or the reconstruction of sentences from partial information, etc. While it is undeniable that a good theory of language understanding will provide a significant part of the explanation of these phenomena, they are at this stage of research non-central issues. For they occur only in unusual situations of language use, and it is unclear how they could shed light upon the process of language understanding. At the very least it would seem ill-advised to modify AI theories on the basis of experimental findings on such seemingly non-central issues.

To summarize the preceding points in one sentence, AI researchers cannot expect experimental psychology to give them any valuable clues about whether they should prefer one model to another or about how to construct a model in the first place, simply because psychology provides no means to do the former or to do the latter.

E. Charniak and Y. Wilks (eds.), Computational Semantics

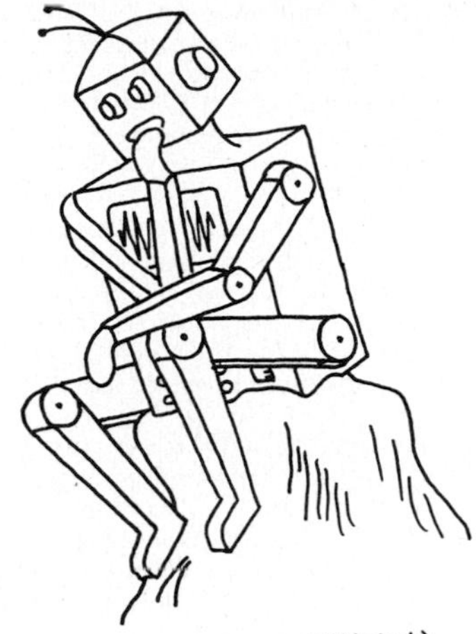

PHILOSOPHY OF LANGUAGE

Yorick Wilks

Those appalled by the generality of the title of this last chapter will be relieved to hear right away that it attempts no more than a brisk introduction followed by some detailed, though not very detailed, discussion of only two philosophers: Richard Montague and Ludwig Wittgenstein. These philosophers have been chosen not so much for their influence on our subject matter, which has been small, but because their views are diametrically opposed on the key issue of formalization: of whether, and in what ways, we should construct formalisms to express the content of natural language. I shall argue, too, that the influence of Wittgenstein has been largely beneficial while that of Montague has been largely malign. Much of what follows will be a justification of that rather sweeping judgment. It should be said that those who find even the simplified formalism of the Montague section too strenuous may turn directly to the Wittgenstein section since they are almost entirely independent of each other.

Introduction

Concentrating on two philosophers in this way means that a number of the names of the great and the good, in what is normally thought of as the philosophy of language, will not appear. To attempt to say everything is of course to say nothing. Even so, we can distinguish two very broad trends in the philosophy of language, as regards the role and importance of formalization. Broadly speaking, one group of philosophers has been for it, and for as much of it as possible, while the other group has been uncompromisingly against it. With a little stretching of the imagination one can reach back and assign even the Greek philosophers to one or other of these groups. It is clear, for example, that Aristotle was considerably more preoccupied by logic, in its conventional sense, than was Plato.

But it is with Leibniz, in the Seventeenth century, that the positive attitude to formalization we are discussing suddenly appears in full bloom. Leibniz was not only a highly original formal logician; he also believed that the formalism he proposed was the real structure of ordinary language (and, indeed, of the physical world), though without its awkward ambiguities, vaguenesses, and fallacies. In his more fantastic moments he envisaged the replacement of ordinary language by this "Universal Characteristic", to the general improvement of clarity and precision. He went further: "For once missionaries are able to introduce this universal language, then will also the true religion, which stands in intimate harmony with reason, be established, and there will be as little reason to fear any apostasy in the future as to fear the renunciation of arithmetic and geometry once they have been learnt". You will see already that the formalist attitude is not necessarily a dull and small-minded one!

By and large, the two centuries that followed saw this position sink almost without trace. The important change, for our purposes, came with the rise of formal logic at the turn of this century. It began with the definition of propositional and general logic and the investigation of their properties. The earliest account of these calculi in English is Whitehead and Russells' Principia Mathematica in which they were applied to the formalization of the notion of mathematical proof, but already Russell at least was setting out the ways in which this approach to logic was also, for him, a formalization of natural language. Like Leibniz, he wished to clear away what he thought of as the confusions of ordinary language. He was much concerned with the grammatical similarity of sentences like "Tigers are existent" and "Tigers are fierce" and how, in his view, this similarity had led philosophers into the error of thinking that tigers therefore had a property of existence as well as one of fierceness.

In the First Order Predicate Calculus, as it is now called, the first sentence might go into some form such as:

EXISTS(X) (TIGER(X))

while the second might go into some form such as:

FOR-ALL(X) (TIGER(X) IMPLIES FIERCE(X))

The important thing here (and there are many alternative forms for these sentence codings) is that in none of them is there any predicate symbol for "exists", in the way there is for tigerness or fierceness. Or, to put it another way, the assertions of existence are always in the quantifiers of the expression. There is never anything about existence in the body of the expression. And so, in the Predicate Calculus, the similarity of form between the two English sentences completely disappears.

Russell was not philosophically neutral about all this, for he believed that serious intellectual errors had followed from what he believed to be the confusion of the two logical forms caused by their having the same grammatical form. One classical argument about God's existence, for example, centered on the question as to whether a perfect being (i.e. God) had to have the property of existence if he was to be perfect. In Russell's view one could not reasonably talk about the "property of existence" at all once one had seen that the two forms of sentence above did not both translate into "property forms" in his logic.

Wittgenstein was closely associated with Russell during the period between 1910 and 1920, and was developing what is now thought of as his early philosophy. This was set out in a curious early work called the Tractatus Logico-Philosophicus, which will not be discussed in any detail here, for we shall be concentrating on his late philosophy. In that early work he proposed what is now called the "picture theory of truth", according to which sentences in ordinary language signify or mean because their structures reflect or exhibit the same relation as that which holds between the things mentioned by the sentences. Thus, a logical form of fact like "catONmat" would be true if the relation between the entity symbols "cat" and "mat", and the relational symbol "ON", reflected the relation between the appropriate entities in the world. The problems for Wittgenstein's commentators (including himself) have always been (a) about what "reflected" could mean there, which might be clear if the relational symbol had been LEFTOF, and "cat" was to the left of "mat" on the page so that the sentence would be true if the real cat was indeed to the left of the real mat and "catLEFTOFmat" would indeed be a sort of picture of the fact described. However, none of the above was so clear if the relations were more complex and realistic such as MOTHEROF. The second difficulty (b) has been about what the "entities in the world" were that the symbols referred to. It seemed clear that Wittgenstein did not mean the real objects out there in the world, like the cat and the mat themselves. He used the German word "Gegenstände" (which sometimes means "objects"), yet no one has ever been quite clear what these entities were to be. His theory of meaning at this point was more obscure than that of Russell, or Russells' predecessor, Frege.

In the late Nineteenth century Frege had proposed a "dualist" theory of meaning in which each word signified, if it did signify, in two ways: one way (Bedeutung), referred to some entity, and one (Sinn) referred to the "sense" of the word. The details of this distinction have preoccupied philosophers ever since, but the broad outline is clear. His famous example of "the Morning Star" and "the Evening Star" is still the best illustration: those phrases mean something different in that they have different SENSES; however it is also true that they refer to the same heavenly entity or REFERENT (i.e. Venus). These meaning theories need not detain us, but it should be noted that they are all in some way referential, even when they talk of "sense". For, whatever the status or nature of the thing that is "the meaning", it is an entity that is somehow pointed at by the word. In Frege's case the word points in two different ways to two quite different sorts of entity, whereas in Wittgenstein's more obscure "picture theory" there was only one kind of pointing.

Yet two ideas surfaced in Wittgenstein's early work that were to be very important in the logic of the Twenties: first the notion of significant and insignificant combination. For him the symbols for the Gegenstände (like "cat") could only be substituted into the pictorial forms of fact (like "catONmat") in certain ways and not others. That is to say "Socrates is Mortal" reflected some relation of entities in the real world, but "Mortality is Socrates" did not, and not because those entities were not in that relation, but because the symbols "Mortality" and "Socrates" could not be substituted in that particular representation of fact at all since the combination made no sense.

With his theory of "picture forms of fact" Wittgenstein was also putting forward the idea, even though hazily, that a theory of meaning required a theory of truth, because the way in which the combination of symbols reflected, or failed to reflect, a fact (i.e. was true or false) was the same thing, in some sense, as the way the statement made sense. It made sense only insofar as it reflected (was true) or failed to reflect (was false) a fact. In particular, he developed a very elementary theory of truth for the Propositional Calculus, a method called "truth tables", discovered independently at the same time by C. S. Peirce in the United States.

This notion is important for what follows, so let us just set it out quickly here: the Propositional Calculus contains variables like p, q, etc. that stand for the proposition expressed by any simple sentence such as "John is happy". These simple propositions can be made into more complex ones by means of connectives NOT, AND, OR and IMPLIES. In Chapter 1 a simple proof was given of one expression in the calculus from others: the proposition proved, ((P OR Q) IMPLIES (Q OR P)), was derived by a four-step proof. However, there is a quite different way of establishing the truth or falsity of that compound proposition, namely by the truth tables. In this method each of the connectives can be defined by a table.

P	Q	P IMPLIES Q	P OR Q	Q OR P	(P OR Q) IMPLIES (Q OR P)
T	T	T	T	T	T
T	F	F	T	T	T
F	T	T	T	T	T
F	F	T	F	F	T

The first column (to the right of the line) is the table for IMPLIES, the second and third for OR, and the last column for the expression (P OR Q) IMPLIES (Q OR P). To the left of the line we have the only four possible truth combinations of P and Q together, where truth values are expressed in terms of T for "true" and F for "false".

The column for IMPLIES defines the meaning of IMPLIES as that which is true except when its first item is T and its second F. Similarly, the second and third columns define OR as that which is always true unless both of the constituent items are false, i.e. it is always T except on the bottom line where both P and Q are F. Now we can construct the column for the complex expression on the right from the columns for the simpler ones. We already know that an IMPLIES expression is true except when the first entity in it is T and the second F. The first entity is the whole of (P OR Q) and we can see that this whole is only F when P is F and Q is F (the bottom line). But, when that is so the right hand entity in the IMPLIES pair, namely (Q OR P), is also F, hence from the first IMPLIES column we see that we must write a T at the bottom of the rightmost column and so all the items in that last column will be T. Hence the complex expression is true for all possible combinations of truth values, and that is what is meant by logically true.

Thus we have established the truth of the expression by a completely different method from that of Chapter 1, and this difference of methods is very important in what follows. Let us refer to the method of Chapter 1 as proof theoretic (it comes from the sequential relation of structures in a proof), and the second just demonstrated as semantic.

That last word "semantic" is so troublesome that it cannot be introduced into this chapter without a word of warning, because on its ambiguities rests much of the difficulty of our whole subject. But notice that, as it is used there, and will be used in the next pages, it does not mean what it does in the title of the book. This will be emphasized by writing it "L-semantic" when used in connexion with formal logic, as here.

We have introduced two of the three fundamental ideas on which the formal logic of the Twenties rests, namely, significant combination and L-semantic demonstration. That logic is the heart of the background to this chapter, because the two authors to be discussed in detail represent respectively a reaction to, and an extension of, that logic. In the hands of Tarski and Carnap the above concepts took on new names and properties: "logical syntax" (replacing "significant combination") and "L-semantic definition of truth" (replacing "L-semantic demonstration"), to which was added a third concept "meta-language".

Carnap in his "Logical Syntax of Language" developed, in a systematic way, the notion of "ill-formed expression" that we met earlier in discussing "Mortality is Socrates". Carnap distinguished, for any logic, its rules of formation and rules of transformation (those who think this is beginning to sound familiar should remember that Chomsky was many years later a student of Carnap). The rules of formation determined what were, and were not, well-formed expressions in the logical language. Thus, in the Propositional Calculus, (P IMPLIES (OR Q)) was not, while (P OR Q) was, a well-formed expression. The rules of transformation then operated on those well-formed expressions that were also true so as to produce theorems in the logic. Carnap was a formalizer in the Leibnizian sense since, to him, these distinctions applied equally well to proper formalization of natural language. Carnap constructed such a formalization in which he distinguished two types of what he called "pseudo-statement":

(1) Caesar is and

(2) Caesar is a prime number

The first was counter-syntactic in that the last word came from the wrong part-of-speech category. The second was syntactically correct but violated what he called the rules of logical syntax. In his system he also made use of a distinction between an object-language and a meta-language. So, (1) above is in the object-language (what Carnap called Language I) and

Sentence (1) is syntactically incorrect

and

In sentence (1) "Caesar" occurs immediately before "is"

are both statements in the metalanguage, or Language II. Carnap was far from dispassionate in all this, in that his purpose was what Russell's had been, namely to do away with certain kinds of sentence, and particularly those that arose in certain kinds of philosophical writing, by showing that they violated the rules of logical syntax.

The distinction of language and meta-language did not arise from any considerations about the structure of natural language, however, but was due to Tarski who proposed it to solve an apparently intractable problem of logic that he had inherited from Russell, who had discovered certain logical paradoxes. Tarski's statement of the problem of the paradoxes was usually in terms of the example:

THE SENTENCE IN THIS RECTANGLE IS FALSE

where any attempts to assign a truth-value to the sentence led to trouble. Tarski thought that this problem would be solved if we only used "true" in a meta-language and never in an object-language. Thus "That John is happy is true" would be a sentence with level confusion, for the proper form would be the meta-language sentence "'John is happy' is true", where the sentence "John is happy" is mentioned in the meta-language sentence but not used in it.

Tarski's fundamental achievement was a theory of truth and logical consequence for formalized languages, or what, using our convention, we are calling a L-semantic theory.

Like many apparently revolutionary theories, Tarski's is in fact a systematization of ideas that had existed for a long time. It used to be conventional to say that classical logic did not have a theory of truth, that it was wholly syntactic, or proof-theoretic. That is to say that Aristotle's forms of proof, (called syllogisms) such as:

All men are mortal
Socrates is a man
therefore
Socrates is mortal

were no more than forms of inference, such that one line was derivable from two others by a rule just as in the derivation given in Chapter 1 for ((P OR Q) IMPLIES (Q OR P)). There was, on this view of the syllogism, nothing analogous here to the truth table method of proof that we saw a little earlier for the Propositional Calculus, in which actual substitution values were given to items.

But now consider a slightly different "syllogism":

Some Panthers are not Mammals
Some Mammals are not Swans
therefore
Some Panthers are not Swans

On that view, that syllogisms were purely proof theoretic, logical derivability is independent of meaning, in that it is of no importance what is put in place of the words "Panther", "Swan" and "Mammal".

However, that view is not correct, for it was known in ancient times that the last line above did not follow from the other two, and for the following reason: suppose we replace "Panther", "Swan" and "Mammal" by "Pig", "Swine" and "Mammoth" respectively. Then we get the following inference form:

Some Pigs are not Mammoths
Some Mammoths are not Swine
therefore
Some Pigs are not Swine

Here the premises are true and the consequence clearly false, so the new conclusion cannot follow from the new premises, and so the old conclusion does not follow from the old premises. This fact was known in ancient times, and by this totally non-proof theoretic method: one in which the meanings of "Pig", "Swine" and "Mammoth" were essential to the demonstration, that is to say, an L-semantic method.

One might say, at the risk of enormous simplification, that Tarski's theory of consequence and truth is a systematic generalization of this method of replacement of Leibniz's slogan "Logical truth is truth in all possible worlds" and of the truth-table notion that the logical truth of compound expressions is to be settled in terms, and only in terms, of the truth-conditions of the simpler propositions of which they are constructed. "Possible world" is not meant technically in that slogan, and its more modern, technical, meaning will be explained later.

One could say that the heart of Tarski's L-semantics is his very general definition of logical consequence, and his very general definition of logical truth as a special case of consequence. The questions that then arise for technical logicians are how far this definition of consequence is the same as the proof-theoretic one.

Let us begin with two important Tarskian notions: those of truth definition and truth condition. The truth conditions of a sentence are, unsurprisingly, the conditions under which it is true, and the truth definition of a sentence is the specification of its truth conditions. The usual illustrative statement of a truth definition is:

> "Snow is white" is true if and only if snow is white.

This is a sentence, in a meta-language, which states the truth condition of a sentence in an object-language. It is not quite as trivial as it might appear at first sight, as can be seen by putting a German sentence in the quoted sentence space:

> "Schnee ist weiss" is true if and only if snow is white.

This can now be seen to be an empirical truth about a German sentence, one that might easily have been false. Moreover, this definition cannot be generalized trivially as:

> "X" is true if and only if X

because the whole point of the quotation convention is that the first object in that sentence (i.e. "X") means: the symbol X. It does not, and cannot, mean: any symbol(s) we care to put here for X. So the truth-definition cannot be generalized in that way.

In an ideal Tarskian "theory of truth" truth-definition sentences like the one above:

> "Snow is white" is true if and only if snow is white

would appear as ultimate consequences: the final deductions from a set of truth axioms. On the way there would be more substantial looking truth conditions such as (to adapt an example Davidson gave for a famous tricky sentence of Bar-Hillel's):

> '"The box was in the pen" is true for an English speaker, at time t if and only if either the box was in the playpen before t and the surrounding circumstances at t meet some condition C, OR the box was in the writing pen before t and the surrounding circumstances at t meet condition C'.

The above definition of the truth conditions of the sentence "Snow is white" is not to be considered a definition of the concept truth itself, though it would lead to one in principle if such meta-statements could be set out for all possible object sentences. That would be what might be called a definition of truth itself by extension, or by complete listing, as we might say. However, it would still be open to the charge of triviality, in that it lacks recursiveness, or interesting calculability.

It is difficult to give a simplified and brief account of how Tarski constructed a recursive definition of truth for formal languages; one from which the truth definitions of individual sentences could be calculated, rather than being simply listed in advance.

The key feature of such a definition, though, is that it has the form:

DEF: "A sentence is true if and only if it has property X"

where X is some complicated property (in fact involving a technical notion of "satisfaction by all sequences of objects") that can be calculated. The last phrase is the key point, because it would allow us to reach such statements as:

"Snow is white" is true if and only if snow is white

as results of calculation.

But it would be gratuitous to attempt a full account of DEF here, because Montague's work, to which we shall shortly turn, is itself intended to yield such recursive truth definitions for the sentences of a natural language: a system in which the truth conditions of complex statements could be seen to be composed from the truth conditions of simple ones in just the sort of way that we saw the truth-table settling the truth of statements like (P IMPLIES Q) OR (Q IMPLIES P) in terms of the truth or falsehood of P and Q.

Montague's work is thus making even stronger claims than Tarski's, because Tarski did not think that such a theory could be constructed for a natural, non-formal, language. But it is important to note that if applied to natural language, a theory of this sort should be testable, because it should be possible to see if the truth definitions (like the box and pen one above) that result from the theory are acceptable or not.

One reason why Tarski did not think such a theory applicable to any single natural language was because that would mean having the same language inside and outside the quotation marks in sentences like:

"Snow is white" is true if and only if snow is white

or, to put it another way, it would mean that in the case of a natural language the object-language and meta-language would be the same, and Tarski thought that was bound to lead to trouble: the trouble that the meta/object distinction had been invented to cure, namely of having "true" in the object-language. This was what led to the difficulty of interpreting the sentence in the rectangle given earlier, and of sentences like:

"Is not true of itself" is not true of itself.

One assumption behind all of this work is that the stating of truth conditions is explaining the meaning of a sentence. This is an assumption not shared by much of the semantic work discussed in earlier chapters; very little of it explained meaning (whether in primitives or otherwise) as what would be true if such and such a sentence was true. Those in the Tarskian tradition are highly critical of much work in linguistics and AI because meanings are not stated in that way, and it is an interesting open question whether AI work on natural language could be so stated in general.

This "truth-condition" approach following Tarski should not be confused with the claims of a movement contemporary with Tarski, that of the logical positivists. They also had a thesis about the dependence of meaning on truth and it is easy to confuse it with the truth condition approach. Their principle was called the Principle of Verification, and it said "The meaning of a statement is the procedures we would carry out to establish its truth or falsehood". This principle will surface again later during the discussion of Montague where it will be claimed that, however wrong this principle might be (and it is wrong), it was at least serious, in a way that the modern truth condition approach is not.

Although Montague is the best known logician seeking to apply these general notions to natural language in detail, there is a school of logicians sharing general principles concerning the applicability of Tarski-like theories to natural language, of whom the most readable is Davidson. The thesis they share is that of the "truth theory of meaning": namely that the meaning of a sentence is determined by its truth conditions, in the Tarskian sense of that phrase. It would be quite possible to reject Montague's detailed "Semantics for Natural Language" and still accept the general tenets of this school about meaning and truth, namely that truth conditions determine the meaning of the sentences of natural language in just the way that they can be said to do so, in Tarski's theories, for the sentences of logic and mathematics.

One point where Montague diverges from Tarski is a highly technical, but important, one. The Tarskian notion "true", as given by a "definition of truth" like DEF above, is rather like the notion logically true in the Proposition Calculus: in the sense in which (A OR B) IMPLIES (B OR A) was shown to be logically true. The notion of truth defined in DEF above is normally called absolute truth by Tarskians.

There is something very odd about this notion of Tarski's, in particular because it does not seem to draw the common-sense distinction between something that just happens to be true in our world like "Snow is white" or "Lugano is in Switzerland", and something that has to be true (in all possible worlds, as we put it) like the Propositional Calculus statement above. We haven't yet come to a technical definition of "possible world" but it should be fairly easy to see that a DEF, stated in terms of "all sequences of objects", would assign exactly the same sort of truth to "Lugano is in Switzerland" and to a logical truth like ((A OR B) IMPLIES (B OR A)).

This difficulty has caused writers like Montague to shift to the notion of "truth relative to a model" interpretation or possible world as the standard sense of "true", and not that of "true" as defined in DEF above. This involves giving up what Tarski called "Convention T", roughly that there was a basic sense of truth independent of particular models or interpretations, and sticking only to the notion of "truth within a model" or interpretation, or what is usually called a relativistic notion of truth. The notion of truth relative to an interpretation is quite easy to grasp: for example:

$$2 * 3 = 6$$

is true under an interpretation in which "*" means "times", but false under one where "*" means "plus" (provided the other symbols all have their normal interpretations throughout).

A word of warning is appropriate here before going into the details of Montague's work. Thus far, the chapter has discussed formalist approaches to language in general, and it will go on to criticize Montague's approach, and then to some extent recommend the views of Wittgenstein. However, the reader should not get the impression that the formal analysis of natural language is being criticized as such. That would be absurd in the context of this book. What is being opposed is pointless formalizations of natural language, and it is suggested that Wittgenstein is one of the few philosophers who can provide insights into what a fruitful approach to natural language might be like.

We must tread carefully here because Wittgenstein was a foe of all attempts to apply formal logic to the analysis and understanding of natural language. Moreover, the philosopher Dreyfus, a full-time opponent of the very possibility of artificial intelligence, has made much use of Wittgenstein's arguments against formal logic in his own arguments against AI. However, the general position of this chapter is that AI has real philosophical importance because it has completely changed the old debate between formalists and anti-formalists. For, to handle language "formally" on a computer, it is in no way necessary to accept the tenets of Tarski, Montague or any other approach based on formal logic. On the contrary, and as has been argued in earlier chapters, the most fruitful approaches to understanding language are precisely those not subservient to a powerful logical or L-semantic theory.

Thus it is that AI has provided a sense to the notion of the precise manipulation of language (and anything computable must be precise of course) that is not necessarily open to the attacks of the anti-formalists like Wittgenstein. And a large part of the credit for breaking the old formalist/anti-formalist opposition in a new way must go to Chomsky.

Chomsky's theory of transformational grammar (Chapter 2), whatever its drawbacks, is certainly a precise theory of language: it also has the form of a logic, but, and here was the key originality, not the content. One way of describing transformational grammar (a non-standard but revealing way) is to say that Chomsky took the structure of proof-theoretic logic (what Carnap, you will remember, called transformation rules), namely the repeated derivation of structures from other structures by means of rules of inference, but he let its content be no more than what Carnap had meant by Formation Rules, namely the separation of the well-formed from the ill-formed. Thus, in transformational grammar the inference (= transformational) rules were to apply to axioms and theorems (= kernels, etc.), but to produce not new theorems but well-formed English sentences.

Thus, Chomsky had a precise system of handling language to propose, but one which had no semantic definition of truth, and not even a syntactic, proof-theoretic, one either. For the notion of truth never came into the matter at all. Thus, Chomsky's was the first concrete proposal to breach the wall between formal and anti-formal approaches, where "formal" refers to truth and not to precision. AI has gone considerably further in all this, and indeed Chomsky's paradigm still shares many of the obvious drawbacks to formal approaches discussed here: in particular the rigid "derivational" structure common to logical proofs and to Chomskyan transformational derivations.

Montague

It was argued just now that Chomsky's transformational grammar could be seen as a move to preserve the advantages of formalization, but without its "logicism". Montague saw his task, quite explicitly, as reversing that move: he began papers by saying that he intended to tackle the formalization of natural language in a way more serious than what he called "the developments emanating from MIT", by which he intended Chomsky.

There is an initial expositional problem with Montague's work: most people who read it find it incomprehensible. For this reason it is far simpler to follow one of the more lucid expositions of his work, due to Barbara Partee, or to Dov Gabbay, and this chapter will make use of the latter.

The account of Montague grammar that follows is unfair to it, and it could not be sketched adequately in the space available here. All that can be given is some inkling of the basic mechanism that drives it, and motivates its practitioners. The best way is to follow out the analysis of a sentence of Montague's, one that he claimed was not adequately treated by transformational grammar, and indeed could not be so treated. He meant sentences like "Every man loves some woman" which, to a logician have two quite different readings, and corresponding to each is a different truth condition. The "readings" of the sentence are taken to be (see Chapter 6):

(i) for every man there is some woman that he loves.

(ii) there is some woman such that every man loves her.

Let us leave aside here the question as to whether or not such a sentence is really ambiguous to a normal speaker of the language. One might argue that a speaker has to have some acquaintance with the notions of formal logic in order to see that there is a reading (ii) at all. Let us also leave aside the question as to whether recent work in Generative Semantics (see Chapter 4) has brought such logical ambiguities within the compass of a generative linguistics.

Montague's own system is set up on the basis of a categorial grammar (which need not concern us here) whereas Gabbay's is based on the more familiar (see Chapter 7), but formally equivalent, notion of a phrase structure grammar, and we shall follow Gabbay. With each word category is associated both a syntactic type, that enables a phrase structure tree to be set up in a more-or-less conventional way, and a L-semantic type. The essential process consists in combining semantic types node-by-node up the syntactic tree so as to reach a single L-semantic item at the top. This item is then an expression of the truth-conditions of the whole sentence.

Let us start with the syntactic categories, and take only those we need for the example sentences (i) and (ii).

S = sentence

VI and IV = intransitive verb = (run, etc.)

TV = transitive verb = (love, etc.)

CN = common noun = (man, woman, ...)

Q1 = universal quantifier = (every)

Q2 = existential quantifier = (some)

NP = noun phrase

The rules of the phrase structure grammar for our purposes are simply:

$$S \rightarrow NP + IV$$

$$IV \rightarrow TV + NP$$

$$S \rightarrow VI + NP$$

$$VI \rightarrow NP + TV$$

$$NP \rightarrow Q1 + CN$$

$$NP \rightarrow Q2 + CN$$

This primitive grammar can now assign the sentence "Every man loves some woman" two different structures corresponding to (i) and (ii). The odd feature is that the "intransitive verb" categories IV and VI are taken more widely than normal:

VI is taken to cover "verb plus subject" phrases like "Every man loves" while IV covers "verb plus object" phrases like "loves some woman".

The two tree structures derived here are:

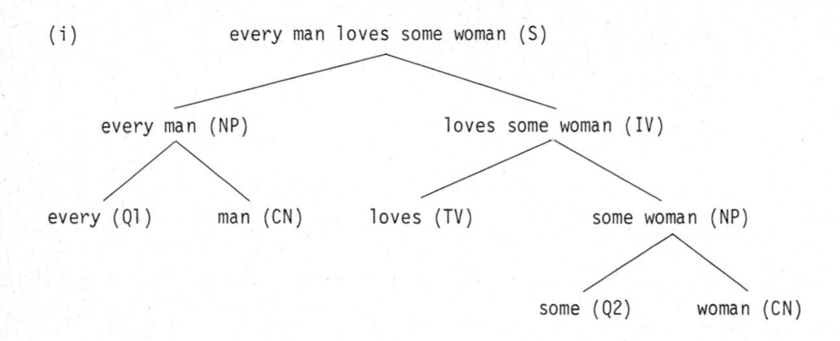

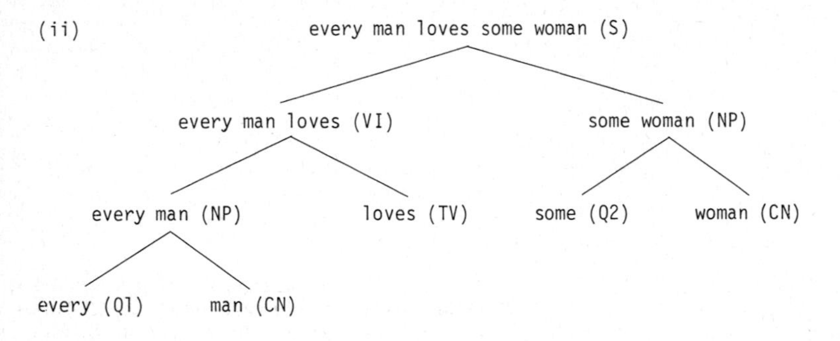

Anyone having difficulty in seeing how the two trees were obtained should realize that the first comes from taking, in order, the rules

$$S \rightarrow NP + IV$$
$$IV \rightarrow TV + NP$$
etc.

and the second from

$$S \rightarrow VI + NP$$
$$VI \rightarrow NP + TV$$
etc.

Now we turn to the semantic part, which requires the notion of I, a set of possible worlds or interpretations, and if J is the number of instants of time, we have a set IXJ states of affairs in all, each labelled by an ordered pair of variables (i,j). ("X" denotes the cross-product of two sets. If we have sets (i, i_2, i_r, i_n) and (j, j_2, j_s, j_m) then the cross-product is the set of all possible pairs like $<i_r, j_s>$. If one set has n things and the other has m, then there will be n X m pairs in the cross-product, where "X" means multiplied by.) "Possible world" simply expresses the idea that we can imagine worlds in which any combinations of ordinary propositions are true. "John Kennedy is dead" is true in our world, but we can imagine worlds, very like our own in other ways, in which it is false and in which Kennedy is still President. Logical truths, however, are considered to be true in all possible worlds. To put it simply, one could say that anyone who makes contingency plans is envisaging a set of possible worlds.

We shall use the convention of calling a state of affairs (a world at an instant of time) a world and labelling it (i,j). D is the domain of individuals living in these worlds. Let us think of them as people, for this sentence, and as the same people in all the worlds. With each word of the sentence, whose syntactic category was given earlier, we shall now associate an L-semantic category giving its "meaning", which will be written as vertical bars round its word(s). Thus "John" is the name of a person, and with it we associate an element in the domain called || John ||. We shall actually treat || John || as a set containing just John, so as to make || John || of the same type as || John and Mary || . This is far simpler than Montague, who treats John as a set of his properties, but the formal points will remain the same. "Running" will be a property of people and || run || will be a function that gives for each state of affairs (i,j) the set of those who run, i.e. $\| run \|_{i,j} \subseteq D$. Similarly $\| love \|_{i,j} \subseteq DXD$ and is a list of who loves whom in state of affairs (i,j), i.e. a list of ordered pairs, where $\subseteq$ denotes set inclusions, i.e. $\| run \|_{i,j} \subseteq D$ simply means that the set of those who run is a subset of the domain of people D.

There are two more sorts of rules: the first defines the properties of $\|\cap\|$ by showing the correspondence between the syntactic and semantic assignments. In these rules $\in$ is to be read "is a member of", $\subseteq$ is again to be read "is contained in", and {|} is to be read "the set such that", and $\Rightarrow$ as "implies". In each of the illustrative rules that follow some syntactic category appears on the left hand side (in order the categories are IV, CN, Q1 and Q2), while on the right a corresponding semantic category is defined in terms of $\|\cap\|$.

(i) $x \in IV \Rightarrow \| x \|_{i,j} \subseteq D$

(i.e. if some x is a member of the things classified under the category intransitive verb, — which includes, you remember, things that love some woman, for example, — then the set of x - ing things in the world (i,j) is contained in the domain of individuals D).

(ii) $x \in CN \Rightarrow \| x \|_{i,j} \subseteq D$

(if x is a member of the things classified as common nouns, then again the set of x - like things is in D).

The function $\|\cap\|$ is usually described as giving values — the L-semantical objects which you can recognize by the $\|\cap\|$ sign — to each element x of a world (i,j). For the third and fourth rules we need a definition of || every ||, and || some ||.

|| every || operates on any sub-domain D_0 that is within D, to produce a set E

containing D_o. That is

$$\|\text{every}\|(D_o) = \{E \mid E \supseteq D_o\}$$

Thus the universal quantifier Q1 is tied to this explanation by the rule:

(iii) $Q1 \Rightarrow \|\text{every}\|(D_o) = \{E \mid E \supseteq D_o\}$

Similarly, $\|\text{some}\|$ is an operator on a subdomain D_o (of D) that produces a set which has an intersection (written $\cap$) with D_o which has at least one element in it. That it, the intersection does not equal the empty set ($\emptyset$).

(iv) $Q2 \Rightarrow \|\text{some}\|(D_o) = \{E \mid E \cap D_o \neq \emptyset\}$

Now we turn to the second, and last, type of rule required. These are rules in one-to-one correspondence with the syntax rules given earlier, such as $NP \rightarrow Q1 + CN$. Just as the last rules (i) - (iv) yielded L-semantic analogues to syntactic categories, so these new rules are L-semantic analogues to syntax rules. You will remember from Chapter 7 that phrase structure rules correspond to hierarchically ordered nodes on a tree. Application of the rule just mentioned could be written:

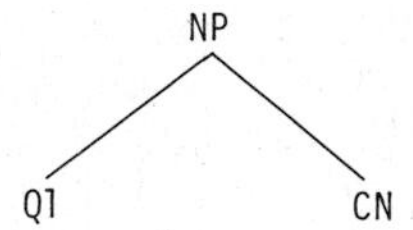

What Montague wants at this point is a rule that will combine L-semantic items at the lower nodes to produce an L-semantic item at the upper node, in just the way that $NP \rightarrow Q1 + CN$ does so for syntactic categories.

If we label that tree thus:

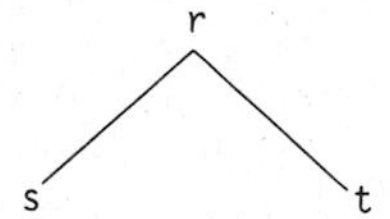

and write L-semantic items at those nodes as K_r, K_s, K_t respectively, then these last rules will construct the semantical object K_r at r from the objects at K_t at t and K_s at s. These combination rules correspond one-to-one with the syntactic rules, and this correspondence is simply given (i.e. not itself constructed by a higher rule). So, we could set out two example syntactic rules that we have already encountered alongside the corresponding semantic combination rules, where, in each case, the left hand side of the syntactic rule refers to the syntactic category at the upper node r, and the two syntactic categories on the right hand side refer in order to the categories at s and t respectively.

(v) $NP \rightarrow Q1 + CN$ $\qquad$ $K[NP] = K[Q1](K[CN])$

where K [NP] means the L-semantic item at the node whose syntactic category is NP. The notation on the right of the equality means "the L-semantic object at the Q1 node applied to the L-semantic object at the CN node".

(vi) $S \rightarrow NP + IV$ For each (i,j) world. K[S] is true if and only if (K[IV] $\in$ K[NP]) otherwise false.

The usage here of putting the syntactic categories in the L-semantic rules on the right does not imply that those rules have anything at all to do with syntactic categories, only that we are using a naming device to pick out the same nodes on the tree, i.e. K[NP] is the L-semantic object that is at the node that happens also to have syntactic category NP.

Now let us put L-semantic labels on the tree of figure (i) given earlier:

at "every(Q1)" : we have the function $\|every\|$ of rule (iii).

at "man(CN)" : we have $\|man\| \subseteq D$ by rule (ii).

at "every man(NP)" : we have the set $\|every\ man\|$ which is worked out by rule (v) which tells us to apply the function at the "Q1" node to what is at the "CN" node. At "Q1" node we have $\|every\| = \{E \mid E \supseteq D_o\}$ where D_o is the subdomain in question, men in this case. So at this node we have $\{E \mid E \supseteq \|man\|\}$, or all sets E containing at least all men.

at "some(Q2)" : we have the function $\|some\| = \{E \mid E \cap D_o \neq \emptyset\}$.

at "woman(CN)" : we have $\|woman\| \subseteq D$ by rule (ii).

at "some woman(NP)" : we have a rule just like (v) (for $\|some\|$ rather than $\|every\|$) and therefore get $\|some\ woman\| = \{E \mid E \cap \|woman\| \neq \emptyset\}$ that is, all sets that contain some woman. Notice here that $\|some\ woman\|$ is a set of sets of women. The semantic rule for Q2 here is identical with (v) for Q1.

at "loves(TV)" : we have not given the L-semantic item for a transitive verb yet. It is a set of pairs of loves and loved, so $\|loves\|$ is a set of pairs contained in the i,j cross product of the domain with itself D X D.

at "loves some woman(IV)" : we have an object $\|loves\ some\ woman\|$ constructed by a rule parallel to the syntax rule $IV \rightarrow TV + NP$ and which is $K[IV] = \{a \in D \mid \{r \mid (a,r) \in K[TV]\} \in K[NP]\}$ Now K[TV] is $\|loves\|$ as we already know, and K[NP], we also know, is $\|some\ woman\|$. So, the L-semantic object we want is going to be (substituting in K [IV] above): $\{a \mid \{r \mid (a,r) \in \|loves\|\} \in \|some\ woman\|\}$. Here r is the set such that, for any a, $(a,r) \in \|loves\|$. That is, r is the set of all the things a loves. Therefore, K[IV] is a, the set such that the set of things an a loves is a member of the set $\|some\ woman\|$. Or, in other words

		a, the object $\|\text{loves some woman}\|$ is the set of things that loves some woman.
at "every man loves some woman" (S)	:	we have rule (vi) the L-semantic analogue of $S \rightarrow NP + IV$ to tell us that the sentential L-semantic object $\|\text{every man loves some woman}\|$ is true if and only if $\|\text{loves some woman}\| \in \|\text{every man}\|$. That is, if the set a defined above is a member of the set E containing all sets of at least all men. Which is to say the sentence is true if and only if for every a-like entity that defines some woman-like thing that it loves, that a-like thing is in the set of (at least) all men. Or, for every man there is some woman that he loves.

It is an exercise for the reader to attach similar labels to the tree of the other figure, (ii), via a set $\|\text{every man loves}\|$ which is:

$$\{a \mid \{r \mid (r,a) \in \|\text{loves}\|\} \in \|\text{every man}\|\}$$

the set of a-like things that are loved by every r-like thing, where r-like things are all men. This expression defines a female entity loved by every man.

There is really no more to the basic idea than that: namely the construction of an L-semantical object that states what it is, in set-theoretic terms, for the corresponding reading of some sentence to be true. And the production of the whole statement "Every man loves some woman" is true if and only if ...(the L-semantic object's content) is precisely the Tarskian goal that Montague set out to reach for a natural language: that is, a whole theory, functioning as a Tarskian definition of truth (DEF above), that produces, as non-trivial consequences the truth-definitions of individual sentences of the language.

The advantage of Gabbay's L-semantics (which we have followed) over the one Montague actually presents is not just its theoretical simplicity, but that it gets over one major fault of the Montague system: that all "logically false" sentences have the same representation. This is very counter-intuitive, for we feel fairly sure that, whatever "I have proved the completability of arithmetic" and "This is a round triangle" mean, they certainly don't mean the same. In the Gabbay system, the "meaning" of a sentence can be identified, not just with the L-semantical object found, but with the constructive process of placing it at a node on the syntactic tree. In that way Gabbay claims, two "logically false" sentences with the same L-semantic object at the top of the tree can be said to "mean something different" because of the two tree-construction processes that gave rise to them.

What can one say in general about an L-semantics of this sort?

1) One could argue that the syntax is arbitrary and unmotivated. There are indeed two syntactic readings for the sentence, <u>which is what was wanted</u>, but no one given two tree diagrams could easily guess <u>which corresponded to which</u>! There will also, of course, be two readings for "Every man loves ice cream", and to no particular logical purpose.

2) The L-semantics is entirely a reflexion of the syntax and the two could not in principle diverge. This seems extraordinary, and very implausible. Consider what will happen with Chomsky's examples "John is easy to please" and "John is eager to please" where the surface syntax (of the sort expressed in phrase-struc-

ture grammars as used by Montague) is the same, but where a reader will see on reflexion that their meaning structure is quite different. Montague might well have wanted to introduce transformations to get over the problems of surface syntax, but then the nice one-to-one correspondence of syntax rules and L-semantic rules would be lost

3) The assumption at every stage is that there is a molecular confrontation between language and the world. This seems plausible enough perhaps for "John loves Mary" but wildly improbable for sentences whose meaning is explained by their inferential structure to other sentences. Consider how far Montague's assumption is from any AI, or "frames", view of meaning, on which we cannot talk about meaning independently of large structures of knowledge existing, as it were, outside the sentence examined. There is no place for that in Montague's system because meaning is to be built up only from very simple L-semantical objects, attached to the items of the sentence directly.

4) We can contrast the triviality of the L-semantic view with the seriousness of what was earlier called the logical positivist view of meaning, that what a sentence means is the procedures we would carry out to see if it was true. A logical positivist, faced with a difficult sentence like "God is good" might talk about what conceivable observations would be relevant to checking up on, and so giving meaning to it. But on an L-semantic view the meaning comes down in the end to some structure like (True if and only if "God" is in the class of "Good things"), indicating that truth conditions are trivialization of a serious empirical notion.

5) Is the notion of "truth-condition" computable? In a clear sense it is not, in that there is a possible world corresponding to every real fraction of an inch by which Wellington was taller than Napoleon, say, and so there is at least a non-denumerable infinity of possible worlds in which "Wellington is taller than Napolean" is true. Computing over them would clearly be no joke. Even were some contraction possible it is hard to see that the notion of a "class of things that run at a given time t" is a useful form of manipulable information about the world. Again, procedures have to be represented by static sets in L-semantics. Consider "8 is greater than 5". To establish the truth of that with computer we would do a calculation. In L-semantics we would have to search the set greaterthan which contains all possible pairs such that one member is greater than the other. Some set, some computation! And notice that these sets cannot be simply replaced with an algorithm to work out greaterthan sums without radically changing the theory.

A cynic might say that, whatever the value of L-semantics as a subsequent axiomatization, or reconstruction, of linguistic computations, it could never be a research tool; one in which important contentful linguistic rules were established initially. In the same way, science is never done by thinking about the axioms of formal scientific systems. The notions of L-semantics are all mathematical notions and belong there. In the world of natural language, they are, in Ryle's phrase, "on holiday" and cannot be expected to earn their keep.

Wittgenstein

Wittgenstein shares the feature with Montague of being a "difficult" writer. All that can be done here, by way of introducing his work, is to take a number of loosely connected topics, and give under each a few basic quotations followed by some exposition and remarks on their relevance to the present situation in AI, or as to how they clash, where they do, with the views of the formalist school just described in some detail. This will do no sort of justice to Wittgenstein: each of the following topics has already been the subject of many articles and books.

The idea is simply to give a flavor, to those unfamiliar with him, of what Wittgenstein has to offer.

When reading Wittgenstein, a number of unmentioned presences have to be kept in mind at all times. The principal one is Wittgenstein's early self, and his "picture theory of truth" mentioned earlier. Much of the motivation of the Philosophical Investigations was to set out why that view and its associated doctrines were wrong. Also in the background are Tarski and Carnap, who still advocated formalist views long after Wittgenstein had given them up. Most of the views attacked in Philosophical Investigations were held in one form or another by Tarski. The change in Wittgenstein was that he ceased to believe that words in natural language had meaning chiefly because they pointed at objects in the world, and that sentences were true because they matched up to the world in some direct one-to-one way. He became more and more convinced that what was important about language was its "deep grammatical forms", and it was from here that the metaphor of "depth" in modern linguistics took off. Wittgenstein always resisted any attempt to formalize a theory of these deep forms, and there is no point in imagining that he would have been deliriously happy had he lived to see modern linguistics and AI as alternatives to the logical paradigm.

But I shall try to show that many of the concerns of modern AI are already there in his work, and that his line of thinking is a powerful antidote to the naive errors with which the subject is still riddled, and hence that a leading practitioner of AI was quite wrong in his judgment that "Wittgenstein set philosophy back 50 years."

Wittgenstein also had a peculiar style: his work, early and late, takes the form of a series of numbered remarks. Some of these were arranged in their present order after his death, in the early Fifties, by editors. The remarks are not themselves arranged neatly under headings, and reading Wittgenstein therefore takes the form of tracing connexions through the remarks for oneself. The quotations that follow are mostly from his Philosophical Investigations and occasionally from his Philosophical Remarks (written PR). Both are available in German-English parallel texts. The dollar sign $ will indicate paragraph numbers, and p, as is normal, page numbers. Each section that follows consists of an attempt to state a thesis, then one or more quotations, followed by comment.

Here is an epigraphic quote for all that follows:

> $ 122. A main source of our failure to understand is that we do not command a clear view of the use of our words — our grammar is lacking in this sort of perspicuity. A perspicuous representation produces just that understanding which consists in "seeing connexions". Hence the importance of finding and inventing intermediate cases.
>
> The concept of a perspicuous representation is of fundamental significance for us. It earmarks the form of account we give, the way we look at things.

(i) Reference

Thesis: words do not in general have meaning in virtue of pointing at objects in the real world (or "conceptual objects" either).

> $ 2. That philosophical concept of meaning [i.e. of meaning as pointing] has its place in a primitive idea of the way language functions. But one can also say that it is the idea of a

language more primitive than ours.

$ 13. When we say: Every word in language signifies something" we have so far said nothing whatever; unless we have explained exactly what distinction we wish to make. (It might be, of course, that we wanted to distinguish the words of [some] language from words "without meaning" such as occur in Lewis Carroll's poems, or words like "Lilliburlero" in songs.

$ 30. So one might say: the ostensive [i.e. pointing to] definition explains the use — the meaning — of the word when the overall role of the word in language is clear. Thus if I know that someone means to explain a color-word to me the ostensive definition "That is called 'sepia'" will help me to understand the word.

$ 35. There are, of course, what can be called "characteristic experiences" of pointing to (e.g.) the shape. For example, following the outline with one's finger or with one's eyes as one points. But this does not happen in all cases in which I "mean the shape" and no more does any other one characteristic process occur in all these cases. Besides, even if something of the sort did recur in all cases, it would still depend on the circumstances — that is, on what happened before and after the pointing — whether we should say "he pointed to the shape and not to the color".

Comment: Wittgenstein is arguing that pointing or referring is <u>in principle</u> a vague activity. It can only be made clear by explaining from within the language <u>what</u> we are pointing at — i.e. pointing already assumes the whole language. <u>Hence</u> it is not that pointing <u>explains</u> how we mean, as the formalists thought when they defined the denotations of their symbols as objects, or sets of objects, because, argues Wittgenstein, the pointing presumes upon the language rather than explains it.

Wittgenstein says we <u>could</u> have a language based on the referential notion ($2), but it would be a language more primitive than what we call natural language. The relation of this point to the referential assumption of both Montague and many AI workers should be obvious.

(ii) <u>Mini languages and language games</u>

Thesis: we can construct mini-languages obeying any rules we like, and we can think of them as <u>games</u>. The important question is whether these games are sufficiently like the "whole game" of natural language. This question does not have a <u>definite</u> answer any more than this question: "Can one play chess without the Queen?"

Wittgenstein attributes the ostensive or "pointing" view of meaning to St. Augustine and then proceeds to construct a mini-language of commands and objects like "block", "slab", and colors like "red", etc.

$ 2. Let us imagine a language for which the description given by Augustine is right. The language is meant to serve for communication between a builder A and an assistant B. A is building with building-stones: there are blocks, pillars, slabs and beams. B has to pass the stones, and that in the order in which A needs them. For this purpose they use a language consisting of the words "block", "pillar", "slab", "beam". A calls them out; B brings the stone which he has learnt to bring at such-and-such a call. Conceive this as a complete primitive language.

$ 3. Augustine, we might say, does describe a system of communication; only not everything that we call language is this system. And one has to say this in many cases where the question arises "Is this an appropriate description or not?" The answer is: "Yes, it is appropriate, but only for this narrowly circumscribed region, not for the whole of what you were claiming to describe".

It is as if someone were to say: "A game consists in moving objects about on a surface according to certain rules ..." — and we replied: You seem to be thinking of board games, but there are others. You can make your definition correct by expressly restricting it to those games.

Comment: This mini-language that Wittgenstein constructs with "block", "slab" and commands may remind readers of Winograd's mini-language (Chapter 7). The parallel is a fair one in many ways, and Wittgenstein can be seen as presenting the dangers of taking a mini-language with certain properties (definite reference to objects, for example) and assuming that they are properties of the whole natural language. One could say that it is not clear how, or whether, a Winogradian system could function in a world without definite locatable objects, such as the world of newspaper articles or of this book.

One could argue similarly that the languages of semantic primitives in Schank's or Wilks' systems (Chapter 9) are also mini-languages, or language games, in a wide sense, and that there would be similar problems if they started to postulate "conceptual objects" to which the primitives refer, and Schank has in fact sometimes suggested that his primitives "really" refer to entities in the mind or brain. If a language of primitives is given <u>that</u> property then it <u>loses</u> one essential feature of a full natural language, and begins to look more like a "blocks world" mini-language.

However, it should not be thought that Wittgenstein is a defender of linguistic primitives, or primitives of any sort. Indeed, one of the attractions to him of his "truth-table" method of presenting the Propositional Calculus was that it avoided the more conventional form in terms of primitive formulas, like P IMPLIES (Q OR NOT-Q) from which all other true formulas could be derived. Yet, one could argue that a large part of what Wittgenstein found objectionable about the notion of "primitive" in logic was the idea that there is a <u>right set</u> of them, if only we could discover it, to provide an infallible starting <u>point</u>. But in the case of semantic primitives, it is still possible to use them, as Wilks does, without claiming that there is <u>a</u> single right set of them, as Schank does.

(iii) <u>Family resemblances and boundaries</u>

Thesis: the conventional notion of <u>a concept</u> is wrong: namely the view that a concept relates in some way to the qualities or characteristics that <u>all things falling under the concept have</u>. As, for example, one might claim in a <u>simple-minded way that everything that</u> is an <u>arch</u> has such-and-such properties. Wittgenstein takes the concept of a <u>game</u> and <u>argues</u> that one could not define a game by necessary and sufficient qualities. For any proposed necessary characteristic of being a game, Wittgenstein claims he can think of a game that does not have the characteristic. Patience (Solitaire), for example, is not <u>competetive</u>, and so on. Along these lines it has been argued that entities under a concept form a something more like a family, for some members of a family share the characteristic "long nose", while some share the characteristic "tiny feet", but there need be no characteristic they <u>all</u> share for them to have a "family resemblance". The moral is that there are not firm boundaries to concepts, nor are there to linguistic usage, nor to the application of linguistic rules.

$ 69. How should we explain to someone what a game is? I imagine that we should describe games to him, and we might add: "This and similar things are called 'games'". And do we know any more about it ourselves? Is it only other people whom we cannot tell exactly what a game is? — But this is not ignorance. We do not know the boundaries because none have been drawn. To repeat, we can draw a boundary — for a special purpose. Does it take that to make the concept usable? Not at all! (Except for that special purpose.) No more than it took the definition: 1 pace = 75 cm. to make the measure of length 'one pace' usable. And if you want to say "But still, before that it wasn't an exact measure", then I reply: Very well, it was an inexact one. — Though you still owe me a definition of exactness.

$ 70. "But if the concept 'game' is uncircumscribed like that, you don't really know what you mean by a 'game'". — When I give the description: "The ground was quite covered with plants" — do you want to say I don't know what I am talking about until I can give a definition of a plant?

$ 71. One might say that the concept game is a concept with blurred edges. — "But is a blurred concept a concept at all?" — Is an indistinct photograph a picture of a person at all? Is it even always an advantage to replace an indistinct picture by a sharp one? Isn't the indistinct one often exactly what we need?

$ 76. If someone were to draw a sharp boundary I could not acknowledge it as the one that I too always wanted to draw, or had drawn in my mind. For I did not want to draw one at all. His concept can then be said to be not the same as mine, but akin to it. The kinship is that of two pictures, one of which consists of color patches with vague contours, and the other of patches similarly shaped and distributed, but with clear contours. The kinship is just as undeniable as the difference.

$ 84. I said that the application of a word is not everywhere bounded by rules. But what does a game look like that is everywhere bounded by rules? whose rules never let a doubt creep in, but stop up all the cracks where it might? — Can't we imagine a rule determining the application of a rule, and a doubt which it removes — and so on?

$ 80. I say "There is a chair". What if I go up to it, meaning to fetch it, and it suddenly disappears from sight? — "So it wasn't a chair, but some kind of illusion". But in a few moments we see it again and are able to touch it and so on. — "So the chair was there after all and its disappearance was some kind of illusion". — But suppose that after a time it disappears again — or seems to disappear. What are we to say now? Have you rules ready for such cases — rules saying whether one may use the word "chair" to include this kind of thing? But do we miss them when we use the word "chair"; and are we to say that we do not really attach any meaning to this word, because we are not equipped with rules for every possible application of it?

§ 88. If I tell someone "Stand roughly here" — may not this explanation work perfectly? And cannot every other one fail too? <u>But isn't it an inexact explanation? — Yes; why shouldn't we call it "inexact"? Only let us understand what "inexact" means. For it does not mean "unusable"</u>. And let us consider what we call "inexact".

§ 99. The sense of a sentence — one would like to say — may, of course, leave this or that open, but the sentence must nevertheless have a definite sense. An indefinite sense — that would really not be a sense at all. — This is like: <u>An indefinite boundary is not really a boundary at all</u>. Here one thinks perhaps: if I say "I have locked the man up fast in the room — there is only one door left open" — then I simply haven't locked him in at all; his being locked in is a sham. One would be inclined to say here: "You haven't done anything at all". An enclosure with a hole in it is as good as none. — But is that true?

§ 100. "But still, it isn't a game, if there is some vagueness in the rules". — But does this prevent its being a game? — "Perhaps you'll call it a game, but at any rate it certainly isn't a perfect game." This means: it has impurities, and what I am interested in at present is the pure article.— But I want to say: we misunderstand the role of the ideal in our language. That is to say: we too should call it a game, only we are dazzled by the ideal and therefore fail to see the actual use of the word "game" clearly.

§ 133. It is not our aim to refine or complete the system of rules for the use of our words in unheard-of ways.

Comment: There are many large issues touched on in these quotations, and the other paragraphs that surround them in the original. The central theme here is that natural language has an essential vagueness in its everyday employment, one that does no harm, and which in no way interferes with our understanding each other. It is, however, a feature that no one at the moment has any idea how to put into a computational system. On the contrary, all the systems you have encountered in this book assume that there is a correct formal interpretation to any piece of language use, and that we can decide by fairly simple rules what that interpretation is. The considerations Wittgenstein brings forward in these quotations suggest that in real life it is not so simple.

It is certainly not true, as is often assumed by AI workers, that language is at bottom a mechanism by which experts in various fields convey back to each other. If that assumption was true then 99% of all actual human communication would be in some way inadequate — and we just <u>know</u> that cannot be so.

The quotations suggest that a feature a <u>satisfactory</u> language system would have to embody is the ability to redraw its own boundaries, and to be as vague or specific as necessary, in the way that we can.

To widen our scope slightly, these considerations might suggest that a theory of language can <u>never</u> be, <u>in a straightforward way</u>, a scientific theory, that is to say a body of rules that decides, rightly or wrongly, of any utterance, what its correct structure is. But that is another and very difficult discussion in its own right.

A fuller discussion of $ 133 might lead us to question the whole possibility and usefulness of "ingenious knockdown counter-examples" to theories of language.

(iv) The linguistic whole and confronting the world

Thesis: a language is a whole and does not confront the world sentence by sentence for the testing of the truth or falsity of each individual part.

$ 199. To understand a sentence means to understand a language.

Comment: This thesis is clearly incompatible both with Wittgenstein's own early "picture theory of truth", and with any theory like Montague's, where the assumption is precisely that each sentence of a language has its truth (and its meaning) tested individually and in isolation. One could argue that Wittgenstein's view is not at all inconsistent with a standard view of scientific truth, where sentences such as "This particle has spin 1/2" or "Rats are carriers of plague" are not tested directly but belong only within large systems of inference that must be tested indirectly if at all. That is to say that sentences like those two can only be understood within a wider theory which, in its turn, explains complex notions like "spin", "particle" and "carried by".

It should be clear that the more interesting AI systems that understand language, described in part III, are also of this type in that they envisage sentences as being understood by means of a complex knowledge structure and not by being checked-off one-to-one against the facts of the world.

The notion that we can only understand on the basis of a whole language is clearly more attractive than the distant alternative of understanding within "block" and "slab" micro-worlds. But it, too, has its dangers: if taken far enough, it can lead to the view that there can be no significant generalizations about language at all, because each use of each sentence has a special relation to the language as a whole. And Wittgenstein has sometimes been accused of holding this view.

What seems more likely to have been his position was an intermediate one; namely, that there are islands of discourse each with its own criteria of inference, truth and so on, and it is with respect to these (rather than to a micro-world or to the whole language) that utterances are to be understood. The notion of an "island of discourse" is not a self-explanatory one but, roughly speaking, it means an area defined by subject matter (say, history, or quantum physics), but still wide enough to have all the features of a full natural language (in a way that a "slab" and "block" micro-world does not).

One could argue that the "frames" view in AI is moving towards a position compatible with this intermediate "island of discourse" one.

(v) Logicians have a false picture of how language is

Thesis: logicians think that language is like their favorite calculus, but they are quite wrong. Moreover, it is language itself and its use that is the standard for testing disputes that arise, not what logicians dictate.

$ 81. F. P. Ramsey once emphasized in conversation with me that logic was a "normative science". I do not know exactly what he had in mind, but it was doubtless closely related to what only dawned on me later: namely, that in philosophy we often compare the use of words with games and calculi which have fixed rules, but cannot say that someone who is using language must be playing such a game. — But if you say that our languages only approximate to such calculi you are standing on the very brink of a misunderstanding. For then it may look as if what we are talking about is an ideal language. As if our logic were, so to speak, a logic for a vacuum. — Whereas logic does not treat of language — or of thought — in the sense in which a natural science treats a natural phenomenon, and the most that can be said is that we construct ideal languages. But here the word "ideal" is liable to mislead, for it sounds as if these languages were better, more perfect, than our everyday language; and as if it took the logician to shew people at last what a proper sentence looked like.

All this, however, can only appear in the right light when one has attained greater clarity about the concepts of understanding, meaning, and thinking. For it will then also become clear what can lead us (and did lead me) to think that if anyone utters a sentence and means or understands it he is operating a calculus according to definite rules.

$ 91. But now it may come to look as if there were something like a final analysis of our forms of language, and so a single completely resolved form of every expression. That is, as if our usual forms of expression were, essentially, unanalyzed; as if there were something hidden in them that had to be brought to light. When this is done the expression is completely clarified and our problem is solved.

It can also be put like this: we eliminate misunderstandings by making our expressions more exact; but now it may look as if we were moving towards a particular state, a state of complete exactness; and as if this were the real goal of our investigation.

$ 101. We want to say that there can't be any vagueness in logic. The idea now absorbs us, that the ideal "must" be found in reality. Meanwhile we do not as yet see how it occurs there, nor do we understand the nature of this "must". We think it must be in reality; for we think we already see it there.

$ 115. A picture held us captive. And we could not get outside it, for it lay in our language and language seemed to repeat it to us inexorably.

Comment: This thesis clearly clashes head on, not only with Montague, but also with those logicians who believe in the applicability of the Predicate Calculus to language. Notice that Wittgenstein is not claiming that the logicians are being <u>inconsistent</u>, as between their beliefs and the way they talk every day of their lives, any more than Phlogiston theorists in the Eighteenth century were being inconsistent when they speculated on the phlogistic process (the <u>reverse</u> of chemical oxidation) while their lungs actually kept them alive by oxidation processes. They were simply describing phenomena they had not <u>examined</u>.

(vi) Understanding is not a feeling

Thesis: we have the idea that "understanding" something involves, or is associated with, a special feeling of being right. But the tests of our being right are quite different from the feeling.

P. 59. (a) "Understanding a word": a state. But a mental state? — Depression, excitement, pain, are called mental states. Carry out a grammatical investigation as follows: we say:
"He was depressed the whole day."
"He was in great excitement the whole day."
"He has been in continuous pain since yesterday." —
We also say "Since yesterday I have understood this word." "Continuously", though? — To be sure, one can speak of an interruption of understanding. But in what cases? Compare: "When did your pains get less?" and "When did you stop understanding that word?"

$ 122. A perspicuous representation produces just that understanding which consists in "seeing connexions".

$ 139. When someone says the word "cube" to me, for example, I know what it means. But can the whole use of the word come before my mind, when I understand it in this way?

Well, but on the other hand isn't the meaning of the word also determined by this use? And can these ways of determining meaning conflict? Can what we grasp in a flash accord with a use, fit or fail to fit it? And how can what is present to us in an instant, what comes before our mind in an instant, fit a use?

What really comes before our mind when we understand a word? — Isn't it something like a picture? Can't it be a picture?

Well, suppose that a picture does come before your mind when you hear the word "cube", say the drawing of a cube. In what sense can this picture fit or fail to fit a use of the word "cube"? — Perhaps you say: "It's quite simple; — if that picture occurs to me and I point to a triangular prism for instance, and say it is a cube, then this use of the word doesn't fit the picture." — But doesn't it fit? I have purposely so chosen the example that it is quite easy to imagine a method of projection according to which the picture does fit after all.

The picture of the cube did indeed suggest a certain use to us, but it was possible for me to use it differently.

$ 151. But there is also this use of the word "to know": we say "Now I know!" — and similarly "Now I can do it!" and "Now I understand!"

Let us imagine the following example: A writes series of numbers down: B watches him and tries to find a law for the sequence of numbers. If he succeeds he exclaims: "Now I can go on!" — So this capacity, this understanding, is something that makes its appearance in a moment. So let us try and see what it is that makes its appearance here. — A has written down the numbers 1, 5, 11, 19, 29; at this point B says he knows how to go on. What happened here? Various things may have happened: for example, while A was slowly putting one number after another, B was occupied with trying various algebraic formulae on the numbers which had been written down. After A had written the number 19 B tried the formula $a_n = n^2 + n - 1$; and the next number confirmed his hypothesis.

$ 155. Thus what I wanted to say was: when he suddenly knew how to go on, when he understood the principle, then possibly he had a special experience — and if he is asked: "What was it? What took place when you suddenly grasped the principle?" perhaps he will describe it much as we described it above — but for us it is the circumstances under which he had such an experience that justify him in saying in such a case that he understands, that he knows how to go on.

Part II, p.181. Even if someone had a particular capacity only when, and only as long as he had a particular feeling, the feeling would not be the capacity.

The meaning of a word is not the experience one has in hearing or saying it, and the sense of a sentence is not a complex of such experiences. — (How do the meanings of the individual words make up the sense of the sentence "I still haven't seen him yet"?) The sentence is composed of the words, and that is enough.

Comment: First Wittgenstein is making the point that it is dangerous to assess understanding other than in terms of actual and possible performances, and, if we take that to mean "performances with language" we will see that it argues against one sort of criticism that AI workers have some times made of each other's systems: that they only "appeared to understand" but "didn't really do so". The reader should refer back to the discussion of Colby in Chapter 9 for an example of that. Those who employ that sort of criticism are, in Wittgenstein's terms, acting as if understanding is a special feeling. $ 122, and its surroundings, are relevant here and could support the view that the purpose of our representations are to establish connexions, and not to produce some non-performative sort of "understanding".

Secondly, there is a very general theme running through Wittgenstein's work about the relation of knowledge and understanding to performance and to what he calls the ability to "go on", "to continue" ($ 151). This theme could be held to support those AI workers who go beyond the assertion that our understanding of words depends on our ability to use them, to perform with them, to the much stronger and less plausible claim that our understanding of language about physical processes (say, tying our shoelaces, or stacking blocks) is closely connected with (and may even require) our ability to carry out the corresponding task. That would mean that a computer could not understand language about, say, dining in a restaurant, unless it could itself dine in a restaurant. This is a complex issue and one where Wittgenstein's explorations are essential background.

Thirdly, there is often confusion between (1) what the processes actually are in our heads in carrying out a task, (2) how we feel about what they are, and (3) what an automaton or computer should do in its program to carry out the same task. These are three quite separate things and arguments to connect them are dangerous: Wittgenstein warns us in the underlined part of $ 139. Consider the following argument of Dreyfus and its similarity to Schank's position that a proper analysis system never follows a wrong path <u>because we ourselves</u> unhesitatingly go for the correct interpretation of an utterance:

> Of course [this human process] only looks like "narrowing down" or "dis-ambiguation" to someone who approaches the problem from the computer's point of view. We shall see later that for a human being the situation is structured in terms of interrelated meanings so that the other possible meanings of a word or utterance never even have to be eliminated. They simply do not arise.

Are these positions not very similar to the one Wittgenstein describes and implicitly criticises in relation to "the whole use of a word coming before the mind"? ($ 139) Wittgenstein is suggesting there that what does, or does not, "come before the mind" is not essentially connected with our abilities to perform with, that is to use, a word correctly. One might argue that, similarly, how we think we function (what, that is, comes before our minds about ourselves) is no sure guide to how we do function, or to how a computer program simulating us should function.

Dreyfus has argued that AI is impossible because, to be intelligent, a computer would have to be exactly like us: bodies, feelings and all. He has often quoted Wittgenstein in support of his own position, but it can equally well be argued that Wittgenstein's clear distinction between understanding-as-performance (which AI workers believe a machine can have) and understanding-as-feeling (which no doubt only we have) supports exactly the opposite position.

(vii) Application justifies our structures

Thesis: the significance of a representational structure cannot be divorced from the process of its application to actual language.

> $ 43-5. We cannot compare a picture with reality if we cannot lay it against reality as a measuring rod.
>
> (PR., p. 308) The rod must be in the same space as the object to be measured.

Comment: These two tiny quotes only hint at Wittgenstein's discussion of an issue raised in point (iv): how do our representational structures actually function if they cannot be "laid direct against the world they represent". They cannot be laid on direct because they are not "in the same space", that is to say the representation is in symbols and the world is the chairs, tables, ocean and government buildings out there. Those who advocate Montague-type systems do seem to believe that in some way their representations are "laid against the world" directly via the L-semantic notions of "set" and "function".

One might argue that, on the contrary, the application of such a system, is only, and can only be, the contact of two symbolisms. The same goes for AI representations and natural language (though AI workers do not normally claim to be laying representations directly onto the world — and the fact that all our AI processes are symbol manipulations in a computer helps keep this point clear). However, it follows that, to be in the "same space" as what they measure, AI representations for language must preserve the essential features of natural languages.

This view is then supplemented by one to the effect that the measuring rod (i.e. the representation) only has sense — is only understandable — via its function of being laid onto what it measures. We can only explain the markings on a ruler to someone by measuring something. Similarly, with our semantic or other representations in AI: they may mean nothing until we give procedures for applying them to the natural language they "measure".

(viii) Real world knowledge and forms of life

Thesis: language understanding is not independent of very general inductive truths about our human experience.

> §142. It is only in normal cases that the use of a word is clearly prescribed; we know, are in no doubt, what to say in this or that case. The more abnormal the case, the more doubtful it becomes what we are to say. And if things were quite different from what they actually are — if there were for instance no characteristic expression of pain, of fear, of joy; if rule became exception and exception rule; or if both became phenomena of roughly equal frequency — this would make our normal language-games lose their point. — The procedure of putting a lump of cheese on a balance and fixing the price by the turn of the scale would lose its point if it frequently happened for such lumps to suddenly grow or shrink for no obvious reason. This remark will become clearer when we discuss such things as the relation of expression to feeling, and similar topics.

> II. xii. If the formation of concepts can be explained by facts of nature, should we not be interested, not in grammar, so much as in nature which forms the basis of grammar? — Our interest certainly includes the way concepts answer to very general facts of nature. (Such facts as usually do not strike us because of their generality.) But our interest does not revert to these possible causes of concept-formation: we're not doing natural science, nor even natural history — since we can indeed construct fictitious natural history for our purposes.

Comment: The whole thrust of this book has been a defense of the role of knowledge of the world in our understanding of language, largely ignored by linguists, and reasserted recently by AI work. It is nevertheless useful to follow Wittgenstein's exploration of this theme forty years ago.

There are hints in his work that the thesis could also be turned on its head. In Chapter 9, while comparing a number of AI systems, it was argued that some emphasize very general knowledge of the world, like that of human wishes and desires, while others emphasize the role in understanding of very particular knowledge, such as that of birthday parties. But it could be argued that if this knowledge of, say, human desires is essential to our understanding of our language (as Wittgenstein suggests in §142) then that knowledge may in a sense be knowledge of our language and not knowledge of the physical world at all. That is to say that, on this view, "Humans try to get what they want" is not really a descriptive fact about people, but is a disguised way of stating what we mean by "get" and "want", in that we would not admit that someone really wanted something unless he tried to get it.

This is a large and difficult issue, but worth bearing in mind if, as seems to be the case, "frames" get more and more like what were called Wittgenstein's "islands of discourse" which have as much emphasis on how we talk about a topic as on the real structure of the topic.

In conclusion, it must be admitted that Wittgenstein is a frustrating author: at times he writes so that he can be taken both ways on important questions. The value of his view of language, as Max Black put it, is that it contains the means for its own supplementation.

The contrast between Montague and Wittgenstein, and their importance for present day discussion of AI and natural language, comes down to two issues: is there a hidden structure to natural language and is natural language itself, and its use, to be the final court of appeal. Montague gives a yes to the first and proffers a simple logic as the hidden structure; as to the second, his choice of examples, far from the concerns of ordinary speakers, such as "Every man loves some woman" suggests that his answer is no. Wittgenstein's answer to the first is complex: his use of "deep grammatical structures" suggests that he thought there was structure but not one to be revealed by simple techniques, like logic, whose interests were really always somewhere else. It is, after all, the different structures of "Every man etc." as they can participate in proofs in the Predicate Calculus that interest the logician, and the ordinary speaker rarely, if ever, sees that there is a "second interpretation" of the sentence. Considerations like this last suggest that Wittgenstein's answer to the second question is a firm yes.

E. Charniak and Y. Wilks (eds.), Computational Semantics

AN INTRODUCTION TO PROGRAMMING IN LISP

Margaret King and Philip Hayes

INTRODUCTION

A chapter on programming clearly has a place in a textbook on computational semantics. If one claims to be constructing theories of natural language comprehension sufficiently precise to be implementable on a computer, one must surely know how to program in order to know what degree of precision is thereby entailed. But the choice of LISP as the specific programming language discussed needs more justification.

LISP is probably the most widely used computer language in the area of Artificial Intelligence in general and Natural Language Processing in particular. It owes this pre-eminence partly to historical factors, but mainly to its suitability for symbol manipulation. LISP is oriented towards symbols in the way that most other languages are oriented towards numbers. In addition, the sort of objects it deals with are well suited to the representation of data whose structure cannot be specified completely in advance, as is often found to be the case in natural language work. LISP allows intermediate structures to be built and discarded without causing the programmer any worries about how to find and later reuse the space necessary for their storage. The syntax of LISP is simply and elegantly defined (although this same simplicity can cause problems in practical programming as will become clear later). The natural way of building programs in LISP viz. by function composition, encourages good programming style and facilitates modular programming. In short it is no accident that LISP is the most widely used language in the field of natural language processing. It is one of the most suitable.

This same ubiquity of LISP provides a secondary reason to teach it. Many papers in the field quote parts of programs written in LISP or in a language whose syntax closely resembles that of LISP (CONNIVER and the various brands of PLANNER are examples of these, being extensions of LISP with more sophisticated control and data structures). A reader familiar with LISP will thus understand such papers so much the better.

One of the chief problems in writing an introduction to LISP is that there are many versions of LISP, all varying in different ways. The LISP described here is therefore unlikely to match exactly the LISP to which, we hope, the reader has access. Some of the differences will be small, some much more important. The reader would therefore be well advised to check against a manual for his own LISP system as he goes through this chapter. We believe that it is very unlikely that the differences between systems are wide enough to invalidate this exposition.

Also, the exposition of LISP which follows is non-standard. It fails to describe some basic features of LISP (most notably dotted pairs) and deviates from the norm on other important points (notably conditionals, function definitions and variable bindings). All omissions and irregularities occur for the sake of expositional clarity and no apology is made for them. A more complete version of LISP can be found in either of the standard introductions "LISP 1.5 Programmer's Manual" (McCarthy J. et al., Cambridge Massachusetts: MIT Press, 1962) or "LISP 1.5 Primer" (Weissman C., Belmont, California: Dickenson, 1967). The picture of LISP painted by these notes is however more in line with most modern LISP systems than either of these now rather dated manuals. A complete though voluminous description of a modern LISP system can be found in the "Interlisp Reference Manual" (Teitelman W., Xerox Corporation, 1974).

There is a further aspect in which the exposition varies from that of a standard textbook. It aims to give both informal explanation which can be understood even by someone who has never programmed before as well as sufficient formal explanation to enable the experienced programmer to concentrate on essential points. The more technical sections are marked by being enclosed in square brackets. They can be skipped with safety by those who simply want a beginner's introduction to programming in general but based on LISP, and should also serve as signposts for the more experienced who need only condensed explanation.

A final note to the reader; it is as impossible to learn to program by reading about programming and omitting the programming exercises as it is to learn to drive a car by reading a manual only. Exercises have been included, with solutions, at several points. These should, in every case, be attempted before the reader goes on to the next section. Clearly, if access to a LISP system is possible, the best way to do the exercises is on the computer. However, should the reader not have access to a LISP system, much can be gained from solving the exercises on paper.

AN INFORMAL INTRODUCTION TO THE BASIC IDEA OF PROGRAMMING

This is a chapter about programming: that is about how to get a computer to do what you want it to do. To get a computer to perform a specified task, you must give it a set of instructions which constitute a description of the method by which the task can be performed (this description is technically known as an "algorithm"). The instructions have to be written in a programming language, in our case LISP. Each programming language specifies in its description a number of primitive operations which the computer already knows how to perform and also specifies what you must write so as to make it perform these primitive operations.

Your description must be built up entirely of primitive operations - you cannot assume that the computer itself will be able to break down a complicated task into the primitive operations which make it up, even though to you the resolution may seem obvious. (Exactly what primitive operations are available varies from one computer language to another. You will begin to become acquainted with LISP's repertoire as we procede.)

An Analogy

In order to clarify this point, let us forget about LISP for a moment and imagine a human-like robot, which only knows how to perform the following simple tasks:

1. It can read a line of writing and distinguish between items on a line, i.e. it assumes that one or more spaces appearing after a sequence of characters delimits an item. Thus a line

   THIS IS A LINE OF PRINT

   contains six items.

2. It can count.

3. It can maintain a number of lists, and can manipulate lists to the extent of adding or deleting an item.

4. It knows what "if" means, and can transfer its attention from one task to another when commanded to do so.

5. When told to stop work it will do so.

Now let us assume that, for some obscure reason, we want to discover how many people in a specific collection of people have only one forename, and we want our robot to perform the mechanical task of collecting into a list the names of all such people.

First we must get our initial information (our data) into a form which can be manipulated by the robot. So, in this case, we might write each person's full name on a separate line:

e.g. JOHN HIGGINBOTTOM SMITH
MARY JONES
DIETMAR HANS KRIEGER
COLLETTE MEUNIER

- etc -

Now we must specify an algorithm for the robot:

0. Set up a list to contain the names which have only one forename. This list will initially be empty (i.e. will contain no names).

1. Check if there are lines to be read. If there are not, give back the list of names which have only one forename and stop work. (Note that if there are no lines at all to be read, this means give back a list with nothing in it.)

2. Count how many items there are on the next line of data.

3. If there are only two items, add this line of writing to the list of names with only one forename. If there are more than two, go on to the next instruction.

4. Delete this line of data and return to instruction 1.

There are several points worth noticing in this. First, the robot does not know, and does not need to know, that he is dealing with the names of people, or even names at all. We have arranged the data in a form whereby it conforms to a construct ("a line of writing") which the robot knows about. What this line represents is irrelevant to the robot. The same situation obtains with the computer. Via a programming language it knows about certain sorts of constructs, and what these constructs relate to in the world outside is irrelevant to it.

Secondly, deciding on the set of instructions is an arduous task. It is difficult to be sure of the logic, to be sure that everything which has to be done is done, that nothing which should not be done is done, that the robot knows when to stop. This is true also of programming. Finding a correct algorithm is the most difficult part of the job, and the part that merits most attention. Once an algorithm is found, describing it in the correct syntactic form for a particular language is a secondary, although sometimes frustrating, task.

A LISP Program

Just so that the reader can see what LISP looks like, what follows is a translation into LISP of the steps detailed above. Although he obviously cannot, and should not try, to understand in detail how this program works, some parts of it are intuitively clear. It consists of the definition in LISP of a function called NAMES, which will return as its value the list of people with only one forename. This list is built up in the next to the last line of the function.

```
(DE NAMES (NAMESLIST)
          (COND ((NULL NAMESLIST) NIL)
                ((EQUAL (LENGTH (CAR NAMESLIST)) 2)
                 (CONS (CAR NAMESLIST) (NAMES (CDR NAMESLIST))))
                (T (NAMES (CDR NAMESLIST)))))
```

To try out this program a specific list of names must be set up and the computer instructed to apply to that list the function, NAMES, as defined above. (We shall return to this notion of a function and its application later.) This is done by using the function name to call the function, and giving it a specific list as its argument:

```
e.g.    (NAMES (QUOTE ((JAMES SMITH)          }
          ↑             (MARY ANN ROGERS)      }
                                               }  argument
     function name      (PETER WILLIAMS)       }
                        (JOHN ALBERT GOOD))))  }
```

We shall return to this example later to illustrate various points.

The Primitives of LISP

The objects that LISP deals with are very simple, consisting only of "atoms" or "lists". In LISP these are called S-expressions, an abbreviation for symbolic expressions.

Atoms

Atoms are of two sorts, literal and numeric.

Literal Atoms. A literal atom is, roughly, a string of capital letters and decimal digits.

e.g. A
APPLE
A2

are all atoms. Literal atoms are used as names: in our example program, one, NAMESLIST, was used as the name of a list, and another, NAMES, as the name of a function. Sometimes the value assigned to a particular name is changed during the course of execution of the program, as happens with NAMESLIST in the example program. Names whose value changes are technically known as variables.

When the LISP system tries to find the value of a literal atom (i.e. to evaluate it), the result is the value assigned to that atom.

[Literal atoms are analogous to identifiers in other languages. As we have seen, they may have values and refer to functions. In fact, as we shall see later, they may also have objects associated with them in other ways. But, unlike identifiers in other languages, LISP atoms are not just names, but are program manipulable objects that have names. They are the primitive symbols on which the symbolic processing ability of LISP is founded. Also the names of literal atoms are subject to fewer restrictions than the identifiers of other languages. They may be any sequence of letters, digits or other characters (excluding parentheses, commas, periods and blanks, which all serve as delimiters) that cannot be interpreted as a number.]

Numeric Atoms. A numeric atom is simply a number, and means what it intuitively ought to mean.

e.g. 2
-10
357

are all numeric atoms.

When a numeric atom is evaluated the result is the number itself.

Real numbers too can be numeric atoms. We shall not use them in the examples of this chapter.

Lists

The other primitive construct of LISP is the "list". LISP lists have to be given in a linear form since LISP ignores how the program is laid out and therefore no use can be made of new lines, end of lines as indicators of structure. So, in the example program in the first section, the original list of names when it appears in the argument of the function call is one long list enclosing a number of shorter lists, where each of the shorter lists is the name of one person.

The structure of a list is shown by bracketing. A list is always enclosed in brackets, so all the following are lists:

(A B C)	is a list of three elements, each of which is an atom.
(A)	is a list of one element, which is an atom.
( )	is a list of no elements (the empty list). (Also written NIL)
((A B) (C D))	is a list of two elements, each of which is also a list. Each of these two sub-lists is a list of two elements, each of which is an atom.

A careful distinction must be made between the list (A) which is a list containing just one element A, and A (without brackets) which is an atom.

Some LISP Functions

With these two primitives defined we can make a start in learning LISP.

LISP is often said to be a functional language, in that its instructions consist of instructions to apply some function to some argument(s). Most people are familiar with the function notation of mathematics, where, for example, f(x) means that f (not here specifically defined) is a function which is to be applied to some argument x. LISP works the same way, the functions being defined either within the system itself or by the user. We shall first consider some system defined functions and return to user defined functions later.

The arithmetic functions are intuitively obvious.

1. (TIMES 2 3)

fairly obviously requires the computer to multiply 2 and 3 together to get the answer 6. The result of typing this expression into the system will be that 6 is printed out as the result of the function.

One thing that may seem a little odd to some people is that the function name TIMES appears before the arguments rather than between them. This follows the function notation of mathematics and is modelled on it, except that the function name appears inside rather than outside the opening bracket.

Before we continue with the arithmetic functions it is worth pointing out that when the user is communicating with the LISP system, the system always expects him to type in an expression to be evaluated. This expression may be a list or an atom. As we noticed earlier, the result of evaluating a literal atom is the value assigned to that atom, and the result of evaluating a numeric atom is the number itself. When the expression typed in is a list, the system expects that list to consist of the name of the function to be applied, TIMES in example (1) above, followed by the arguments to which the function is to be applied, 2 3 in example (1). Sometimes the arguments themselves are calls on functions so that they too consist of a list structured in the same way:

(<function name> <argument(s)>).

In this way quite complicated instructions can be built up.

To return to the arithmetic functions:

TIMES has already been mentioned. It may have any number of arguments and will return their product.

(TIMES 3 3 3) will return 3 x 3 x 3, i.e. 27.

PLUS also may have any number of arguments and will return their sum.

(PLUS 3 3 3) will return 3 + 3 + 3, i.e. 9.

To illustrate the point about arguments sometimes being function calls themselves, consider what happens if the expression

(TIMES (PLUS 2 2) 3)

is given to the LISP system for evaluation. The first element of the list which forms the expression is the name of the function to be applied, TIMES. The second element is itself a list, so the system expects to find an instruction to evaluate a function here, and then use the result as an argument to the first function. So it will evaluate

(PLUS 2 2)

PLUS, which is a call of the function which performs addition, together with its arguments, 2 2, to which the function is to be applied. This intermediate result, of course, is 4, although, since it is an intermediate result, the 4 will not be printed out by the system. This result can now be used as an argument of TIMES, so TIMES has the arguments 4 3. The result of evaluating TIMES then is 12, and this final value of the expression will be printed out. The process of including function calls as arguments may go on as far as the user wishes: the following is valid LISP, and the reader may find it instructive to evaluate it himself:

```
(TIMES (PLUS (TIMES (PLUS 2 2) 3) (TIMES 2 (PLUS 3 4)) 5) (TIMES (PLUS
(TIMES 2 4) (TIMES 3 6) 6) (PLUS 2 3)))
```

Here, briefly, is a list of some other arithmetic functions and what they do:

(ADD1 arg)	adds 1 to the argument, which may be either a number or an expression which evaluates to a number.
(SUB1 arg)	subtracts 1 from the argument, with the same constraints on the argument as in ADD1.
(DIFFERENCE arg1 arg2)	subtracts the second argument from the first. (Same constraints on arguments as above.)
(QUOTIENT arg1 arg2)	divides the first argument by the second, giving as its result the integer part of the actual answer, i.e. (QUOTIENT 6 2) is 3, but (QUOTIENT 6 4) is 1, since the fractional part of the answer is discarded. (Same constraints on arguments as above.)

EXERCISES 1

What would you have to type in to get the computer to perform the following calculations?

1. $3+7$
2. $7-3$
3. $8/3$
4. 8^2
5. $10+1$
6. $10-1$
7. $(3+7) \times 10$
8. $(5+1)/2$
9. $((3+7)/5) \times 10$
10. $((5+1)/(4-1)) \times ((7+3)/(7-2))$
11. 3^7
12. The remainder when 538 is divided by 3.

(Use QUOTIENT for division, and ignore the remainder except in 12.)

A CLOSER LOOK AT EVALUATION

Earlier we talked very briefly about the evaluation by the system of atoms and lists. Let us here briefly backtrack and consider evaluation in more detail. S-expressions (atoms and lists) as described in the section on LISP primitives are the only things LISP deals with. They suffice to represent both program *and* data. The common distinction between program and data, thus, does not exist in *LISP*.

A LISP program consists of one or more S-expressions which are to be evaluated.

Interactive LISP systems (the most common) are typically based on a read-evaluate loop. With such a system, the user, sitting at a computer terminal, types an S-expression, and the system responds by evaluating it and printing its value. After the value has been printed, the system restarts the cycle by waiting for the user to type another S-expression for evaluation. As will be clear later, the evaluation of a single S-expression can cause the execution of an entire program.

We have already informally discussed the evaluation of atoms and lists, but since this topic is so important it is worthwhile to give a brief recapitulation here:

Evaluating a numeric atom not surprisingly yields the same numeric atom (all this means is that numbers behave as one would expect them to).

Evaluating a literal atom is analogous to finding the value of a variable in other languages. It yields the value of the atom if one has been assigned, or an error if no value has been assigned.

Evaluating a list is analogous to calling a function (or procedure or subroutine) in other languages. The first element of the list specifies which function is being called and the remaining elements specify the arguments of the function. The specified function is called with the specified arguments, and the value it returns provides the value of the list. (Every LISP function returns exactly one value.)

Unless the function is one of a small class of functions called "*special forms*" the arguments are themselves evaluated before being passed to the function. The number of arguments taken by a function varies from function to function and can even be zero. When a function is called it is said to be *applied* to its arguments.

There are thus only two sorts of computation possible in LISP, finding the values of variables and calling functions. LISP "programs" therefore usually consist of collections of user defined functions built up in a hierarchical calling structure until the entire "program" can be run by a call of one function. LISP provides a large number of pre-defined or system functions (over 100 in a typical system) to give the user building blocks out of which his own functions can be constructed. In particular, all the operations for which other programming languages typically provide special syntactic constructs, such as assignment and conditional branching, are necessarily handled in LISP by calls of system functions.

Understanding this process of evaluation is indispensable for a proper understanding of LISP.

PRIMITIVE LIST MANIPULATING FUNCTIONS

So far we have introduced the idea of LISP as a functional language, saying that all instructions in LISP, except when an atom is being evaluated, were instructions to apply a function to one or more arguments. We then looked briefly at the arithmetic functions as an illustration of this. But LISP is not designed as a programming language in which to do arithmetic: it is designed as a language to do symbol manipulation. Hence its prevalence in AI work. We shall therefore now begin to investigate LISP's symbol manipulation facilities by considering first its ability to manipulate lists.

The reader should remember that a list may have other lists among its elements, that these other lists may themselves have sublists, and that this sort of nesting may go to any depth.

CAR

CAR is a function which takes one argument. This argument is always evaluated and should evaluate to a list. (An attempt to find CAR of an atom will cause an error.) The value CAR returns will be the first, i.e. leftmost, element of the list to which its argument evaluates. Thus

2. (CAR (QUOTE (A B C D)))

will return A as its value.

A further function QUOTE has crept into example (2). It is needed because, as we said in the paragraph introducing CAR, the argument of CAR is always evaluated. Now, the reader will remember from the earlier sections that when the system evaluates a list, it expects to find a function name as the first element of the list and to be able to interpret the remaining elements of the list as arguments of that function. Thus the value of (A B C D) is <u>not</u> (A B C D). In fact, unless a function called A has been defined, it has no value, and an attempt to evaluate it will cause an error message to be printed out. If what we want to do is to find the first element of (A B C D) we must therefore find some way of suppressing evaluation of the list. This is precisely what the function QUOTE does. Its value is simply its argument, unevaluated.

```
(QUOTE (A B C D))
```

has the value (A B C D), and example (2) will work correctly.

If the list (A B C D) was to be used frequently, it would soon become tiresome to have to write (QUOTE (A B C D)) every time we wanted to perform an operation on the list. It would be easier to assign the value (A B C D) to a variable and use the variable instead. This can be done by using the SETQ function. SETQ takes two arguments: the first is the variable to which the value is to be assigned, the second the value itself. Only the second argument is evaluated, i.e. SETQ quotes its first argument - the Q is there to remind you of this. Thus

```
(SETQ D1 (QUOTE (A B C D)))
```

gives the value (A B C D) to the variable D1, and a later function call

```
(CAR D1)
```

will have the value A, since the result of evaluation of a literal atom is the value which has been assigned to that atom.

QUOTE need not be used with numeric atoms, since they evaluate to the number itself.

```
(SETQ B1 4)
```

will assign the value 4 to the literal atom (variable) B1.

Calls to other functions can of course appear in the second argument of SETQ. For example,

```
(SETQ NUMBER (PLUS 2 3))
```

This assigns the value 5 to the literal atom (variable) NUMBER.

[A note on the special forms QUOTE and SETQ. QUOTE and SETQ are special forms. The arguments of special forms are not evaluated automatically. With special forms argument evaluation is under control of the function itself; a special form may "please itself" which of its arguments it evaluates. QUOTE is the simplest of the special forms since essentially it does nothing. It takes one argument and returns it unevaluated. SETQ is the equivalent of the Fortran or Algol assignment statement, in that it makes its second argument the value of its first. It also returns its second argument as its own value.

SETQ is our first example of a function which besides returning a value has side effects which may affect later computation. Such functions are sometimes called "pseudofunctions". This name is used to distinguish functions with side effects from pure functions which can only influence later computation through the values they return. In other languages in which it is possible to write functions which have side effects, the practice is often discouraged as bad programming style. With LISP, however, functions with side effects are unavoidable, since essentially everything has to be done via function calls. Used with care, functions with side effects cause no problems. Functions with unnecessarily obscure side effects should, however, be avoided since they can cause debugging problems. The value of a pseudofunction is typically of secondary importance to its side effects. The value of SETQ nevertheless comes in handy if one wishes to give several atoms the same value.

(SETQ X3 (SETQ X2 (SETQ X1 (QUOTE (LIKE AN ARROW))))) evaluates to (LIKE AN ARROW)

As a side effect all three of the atoms X1, X2, X3 are given this same value.]

To recapitulate: CAR returns as its value the first element of the list to which its argument evaluates. This first element may of course be either an atom or a list.

CDR

CDR, like CAR, takes one argument, which again should evaluate to a list. It returns as its value a list of the items remaining when the first element of the list has been deleted. Thus:

    (CDR (QUOTE (A B C D)))

returns as its value (B C D) and

    (CDR (QUOTE ((A B) C D)))

returns as its value (C D).

The relationship between CAR and CDR should be quite clear.

Combining CAR and CDR

CAR's and CDR's may be combined, as you would expect. For example, say we have a list (THIS IS A LIST) and we want to get at the A. In order to achieve this we can evaluate

3. (CAR (CDR (CDR (QUOTE (THIS IS A LIST)))))

One of LISP's chief characteristics is function composition (i.e. allowing function calls to appear as arguments to functions, as in the earlier examples and as in example (3) here). Since the composition of CAR's and CDR's is very frequent in most LISP programs, special functions have been defined which serve as a shorthand. C always begins the function name, R always ends it. In between the C and the R may come up to 8 (in the system described here) A's and/or D's: each A stands for a CAR, each D for a CDR. The order of A's or D's follows the order in which the expressions would come if written out in full. Thus the expression in example (3) may be re-written:

    (CADDR (QUOTE (THIS IS A LIST)))

CONS

CAR and CDR take lists apart. CONS provides a way of building lists up. CONS is a function which takes two arguments; the first may be any expression (i.e. a literal atom, a numeric atom, or a list), but the second must evaluate to a list. Both arguments are evaluated. The value of CONS is the new list formed by adding the value of the first argument to the beginning of the value of the second. Thus:

    (CONS (QUOTE THE) (QUOTE (GIRL IS GERMAN)))

will return as its value (THE GIRL IS GERMAN).

If the first argument of CONS is a list, the new list formed will have the first argument as its first element - the lists will not be joined together. Thus:

    (CONS (QUOTE (THE PRETTY)) (QUOTE (GIRL IS GERMAN)))

will return as its value ((THE PRETTY) GIRL IS GERMAN).

Using CONS with an atom as its first argument and the empty list, NIL, as its second, will, as you would expect, form a new list which has the atom as its only member. Thus:

    (CONS (QUOTE THE) NIL)

will return (THE).

If the first argument is a list and the second the empty list the new list will, similarly, be a list of only one member, but that one member will itself be a list. Thus:

```
(CONS (QUOTE (A LIST)) NIL)
```

will return ((A LIST)).

CAR, CONS and CDR are logically related. The reader should convince himself of the relationship by working out the values of the following, assuming that A has the value (FIRST PART) and B has the value (SECOND PART).

a. (CAR (CONS A B))

b. (CDR (CONS A B))

c. (CONS (CAR A) (CDR A))

CAR, CDR and CONS are the three primitive list manipulation functions.

EXERCISES 2

1. Evaluate the following expressions:

   a) (CAR (QUOTE (A B C)))

   b) (CAR (QUOTE ((A B C))))

   c) (CAR (QUOTE ((A) B C)))

   d) (CDR (QUOTE (A B C)))

   e) (CDR (QUOTE ((A B C))))

   f) (CDR (QUOTE (A (B C))))

   g) (CADR (QUOTE (A (B C))))

   h) (CDAR (QUOTE ((A B) C)))

   i) (CADADR (QUOTE (A (B (C (D))))))

   j) (CAADR (QUOTE (A (B (C (D))))))

   k) (CAADAADDR (QUOTE ((A (B C)) D((E (F))))))

   l) (CONS (QUOTE A) (QUOTE (B C)))

   m) (CONS (QUOTE (A)) (QUOTE ((B C))))

   n) (CONS (CONS (QUOTE (A)) (QUOTE (B C)) NIL))

   o) (CONS (QUOTE A) (CONS (QUOTE B) (CONS (QUOTE C NIL))))

   p) (CONS (CDR (QUOTE (A))) (CAR (QUOTE ((A B C)))))

2. For each of the following expressions, give a function which when applied to the expression would evaluate to the atom, X.

   a) (X MARKS THE SPOT)

   b) ((X MARKS THE SPOT))

   c) (MARKS THE SPOT (X))

   d) ((MARKS THE SPOT X))

   e) (MARKS (THE (SPOT (X))))

   f) ((AS (EASY) (AS (X Y Z))))

   g) ((AS (EASY (AS) ((X (B C))))))

3. Suppose the atoms U, V initially both have the value NIL. What are the successive values of U, V after the evaluation of each of the following expressions.

   a) (SETQ U (QUOTE (A B C)))

   b) (SETQ U (CONS (QUOTE X) U))

   c) (SETQ U (CDR (SETQ V U)))

   d) (CONS (SETQ U V) (SETQ V (CDDR U)))

   e) (SETQ U (SETQ V (CDR (SETQ V (CDR V)))))

The COND function

A program rarely consists of instructions which must all be obeyed under all circumstances. An instruction is needed which allows some instructions sometimes not to be obeyed (as in the example in the introduction where we didn't want the robot to add the new name to the list of names with only one forename if in fact that name had more than one forename). LISP provides this facility in the COND function:

Its general form is this:

```
(COND ((if this expression is true) (evaluate these expressions))
      ((otherwise, if this expression is true) (evaluate these expressions))
                         .
                         .
                         .
      ((otherwise, if this expression is true) (evaluate these expressions)) )
```

As you can see, COND may have any number of arguments, each argument consisting of a list, the first element of which is a test condition the result of whose evaluation is either true or false, the second a list of one or more expressions which are to be evaluated if the value of the test condition is true. COND procedes through its argument list until it finds a test condition which is true. Then it evaluates the instructions associated with that test condition and stops. It does not carry on through the remaining arguments.

The most obvious question raised by this account of COND is how a test condition can be formulated. A number of LISP functions act specifically as predicate functions, i.e. they return the values true or false. A list of some of the most useful predicate expressions follows:

Predicate Expressions

1. Functions which compare atoms or expressions.
   a. (EQUAL arg1 arg2) compares two expressions. It returns the value true (usually T) if they evaluate to the same expression, false (NIL) otherwise.

2. Functions associated with arithmetic predicates.
   a. (NUMBERP arg) returns true if its argument is a number, false otherwise.
   b. (ZEROP arg) returns true if its argument is zero, false otherwise.
   c. (LESSP arg1 arg2) returns true if its first argument is less than the second, false otherwise.
   d. (GREATERP arg1 arg2) returns true if its first argument is greater than the second, false otherwise.

3. Functions associated with logical predicates.
   a. (AND arg1 arg2 arg3 ..... argn) AND evaluates each of its arguments in turn starting with the first. If it finds an argument which evaluates to false, it returns false as its own value and does not evaluate the remaining arguments. If all its arguments evaluate to true it returns true.
   b. (OR arg1 arg2 arg3 ..... argn) OR evaluates each of its arguments in turn. If it finds an argument which evaluates to true, it returns true

as its own value and does not evaluate the remaining arguments. If all its arguments evaluate to false it returns false as its own value.

c. (NULL arg1) or (NOT arg1). These are equivalent ways of writing the same function. It returns true if its argument is false, i.e. NIL. Otherwise if its argument is true it returns false. It is the logical negation operator. (Remember that an empty list is represented by NIL - this makes this particular predicate very useful.)

To understand COND thoroughly, we should know more exactly how true and false are represented in LISP. It is very simple - false is represented by the hard-working atom NIL and true by any other S-expression. Every S-expression can thus be viewed as representing either true or false, and any LISP function (system or user defined) can be used as a predicate (a function whose value is a truth value).

An example of COND may be useful at this point:

```
(COND ((NULL L1) 0)
      ((NULL (CDR L1)) (SETQ LASTEL (CAR L1)) 1)
      ((NULL (CDDR L1)) (SETQ LASTEL (CADR L1)) 2)
      (T (QUOTE (I CANT COUNT PAST TWO))
     )
```

Evaluating the above expression tests the length of the list which is assumed to be the value of L1. If the length of the list is two or less, the expression evaluates to that length. If the length is greater than two, the expression evaluates to the list (I CANT COUNT PAST TWO). In the cases in which the list is of length 1 or 2, the atom LASTEL is given the last element of the list as its value. Note the use of T in the last clause to provide an expression which always evaluates to true and so makes the last clause into a catch-all which applies to all lists of length greater than two. The reader should evaluate the above expression supposing in turn that L1 has the values NIL, (GREEN), (GREEN IDEAS), (GREEN IDEAS SLEEP), (GREEN IDEAS SLEEP FURIOUSLY).

Example Program

If we now look again at the very first example program, we find that it has become a great deal more comprehensible. It is reproduced for convenience here.

```
(DE NAMES (NAMESLIST)
          (COND ((NULL NAMESLIST) NIL)
                ((EQUAL (LENGTH (CAR NAMESLIST)) 2)
                 (CONS (CAR NAMESLIST) (NAMES (CDR NAMESLIST))))
                (T (NAMES (CDR NAMESLIST)))))
```

A function LENGTH is used which has not so far been mentioned. It takes one argument, a list, and returns the number of items in the list. The last argument of the COND, as in the previous example, has a test condition which is simply T. This makes certain, as before, that if all the other tests have failed, this one won't and the instructions associated with it will be executed.

EXERCISES 3

Write a COND expression which will set a variable B to the list (VALUE IS ZERO) if another variable A is equal to zero, and to the list (VALUE IS NOT ZERO) if it is not. Give A a value <u>before</u> typing in the COND expression. (You will be able to tell whether your COND expression has worked correctly by the value it prints out. COND always returns as its value the value of the last expression evaluated within the COND.)

DEFINING FUNCTIONS

To understand the example program completely now, it is only necessary to understand the DE function which starts it off, and which is indeed the function of which all the rest are arguments. It is the function which allows the user to define functions for himself, in addition to the predefined system functions. Its first argument is the name by which the function being defined is to be known - in the example NAMES. Its second argument is a list of variable names. When the function is actually used, the arguments given it in the call are evaluated. The value of each argument in the call is attached to the corresponding variable in the function definition. The correspondence is positional - the value of the first argument in the call is attached to the first variable in the list of variables in the function definition, the second to the second and so on. For example if the function NAMES reproduced above is called by the following:

```
(NAMES (QUOTE ((MARY SMITH) (JOHN BROWN))))
```

the argument (QUOTE ((MARY SMITH) (JOHN BROWN)))

is evaluated giving ((MARY SMITH) (JOHN BROWN))

and this becomes the value of NAMESLIST.

The remaining argument of DE is the expression (which may be quite complicated) which is to be evaluated when the function is called.

An Example

To elucidate this a little further let us define a function ATOMIC which will return the message (ATOMS ONLY) if the list which is its argument contains only atoms, and the message (NOT ALL ATOMS) if any of the elements in the list are not atoms. Thus if LISTA has the value (A B C D) then (ATOMIC LISTA) should produce the message (ATOMS ONLY), whilst if LISTB has the value ((A B) C D) (ATOMIC LISTB) should produce the message (NOT ALL ATOMS).

First we must define an algorithm for the task, that is we must find a general recipe by which it can always be decided whether a list contains only atoms.

This is relatively easy, since it is clear that we must look at each element in turn and test to see whether it is an atom or not, and LISP provides a predicate function (ATOM arg) which returns <u>true</u> if its argument is an atom (literal or numeric) and <u>false</u> otherwise. But <u>how</u> do we look at each member of a list? CAR will get us the first element of the list, CDR will get what remains of it when the first element has been deleted. So if we test CAR of the list to see if it is an atom, we can stop with the appropriate message if it is not (there is no point in continuing to look at the remaining elements of the list) and, if it is an atom, we can replace the list by CDR of the list and repeat this operation. We can summarize the decisions taken so far thus:

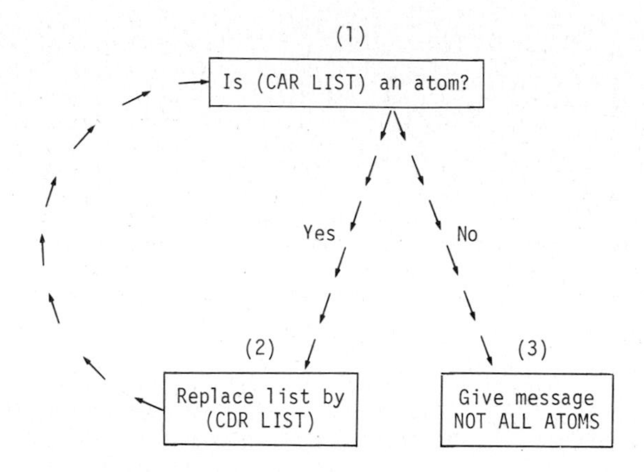

This looks satisfactorily tidy, except that there is no way of getting out of the loop which results from answering "yes" to the question in box (1), i.e. we have no way of knowing when every element of the list has been checked. But successive CDR's of the list will eventually, after all the elements have been eliminated, produce the empty list. If we get to the empty list without having found a non-atomic element, then obviously all the elements are atoms and we should produce the message "ATOMS ONLY". So a test for the empty list must be included somewhere in the loop. It would be sensible to put it before the test to see if CAR of the list is an atom for two reasons: first, someone may call the function with an empty list as its argument - so this should be tested first; secondly, the empty list is simply the atom NIL, and an attempt to find CAR of an atom will cause an error, as we noted earlier.

With these modifications in mind the algorithm can be completed.

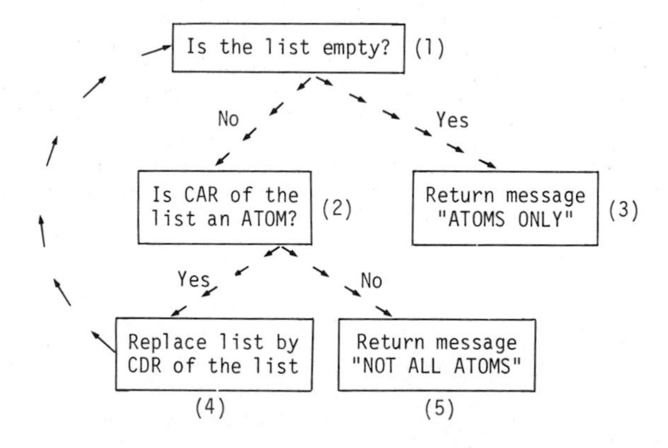

Note that both these diagrams are only an approximation of the process involved. The process described as "replace list by CDR of list" in box (4) could more accurately be described as "re-enter the whole process which this diagram defines only now using the CDR of the list". When this is translated into LISP terms, since the process will be defined as a function and will therefore have a name by which it can be called, it comes out as "call this same function with CDR of the list as argument". Any reader who is interested in a fuller account of this technique of calling a function from within its own definition (technically known as recursion) will find such an account in the next section.

The function ATOMIC can now be defined as follows:

```
(DE ATOMIC (L)
        (COND ((NULL L) (QUOTE (ATOMS ONLY)))
              ((ATOM (CAR L)) (ATOMIC (CDR L)))
              (T (QUOTE (NOT ALL ATOMS)))))
```

Once the programmer knows how to define functions himself it becomes possible to produce quite complicated programs.

EXERCISES 4

1. For each of the following conditions define a function of one argument L which has value <u>true</u> if the condition is satisfied and NIL otherwise.

   a) The first element of L is a literal atom.

   b) The first element of L is 12.

   c) L has at most four elements (either atoms or lists)

   d) The second element of L is greater than the fourth.
   (Assume that L is a four element list where each element is a numeric atom.)

2. Paraphrase the following conditional expression in English:

```
(COND ((ATOM EXP) (SETQ RES EXP) T)
      ((ATOM (CAR EXP)) (SETQ RES (CAR EXP)) T)
      ((NULL (CDR EXP)) NIL)
      (T (SETQ RES (CAAR EXP)) (CDR EXP))
)
```

3. Define a function, SECOND, that takes one argument which must be a list and returns the second element of the list. If the list has less than two elements SECOND should return NIL.

A Closer Look at Recursion

In order to examine recursion more closely let us try to define another function. This time we will define a predicate function, called MEMBER, which determines if a given S-expression is an element of a given list. Thus we want:

(MEMBER (QUOTE MALE) (QUOTE (YOUNG MALE HUMAN))) to evaluate to T.

(MEMBER (QUOTE FEMALE) (QUOTE (YOUNG MALE HUMAN))) to evaluate to NIL

(MEMBER (QUOTE (MALE HUMAN)) (QUOTE (YOUNG MALE HUMAN))) to evaluate to NIL

and (MEMBER (QUOTE MALE) (QUOTE HUMAN)) to give an error.

Obviously we shall again use the system function DE. To recapitulate briefly, DE is a special form which takes three arguments, none of which are evaluated. The first is an atom (the name of the function being defined), the second is a list of atoms (the variable list) and the third is an S-expression (analogous to the body of an Algol procedure or Fortran subroutine), which will provide the value of the new function each time it is called. Thus evaluating

```
(DE MEMBER (EL LST)
   (COND ((NULL LST) NIL)
         ((EQUAL EL (CAR LST)) T)
         (T (MEMBER EL (CDR LST)))
   )
)
```

results in the definition of a new function called MEMBER which takes two arguments (the two variable names being EL and LST). The variables, as before, are atoms whose values are temporarily set to the arguments of a function, whenever the function is called. Thus, each time MEMBER is called, the values of its two arguments are temporarily made the values of EL and LST. The value to be returned by a call of MEMBER is found by evaluating the COND expression which is the third argument of the call of DE above. The value of this conditional expression (which will often be referred to below simply as the COND) depends on the values of EL and LST, which in turn depend on the arguments to which MEMBER is applied. It should not be too hard to see how the COND does indeed produce the correct values for MEMBER. If LST (really we mean the value of LST, but, in talking about variables we can take the liberty of referring simply to the atom when really its value is meant) is NULL then EL clearly cannot be a member of it, and so the value of the COND is NIL. If EL is equal to the first element of LST, then it certainly is a member of LST, and so the value of the COND is T. Otherwise, EL is a member of LST if and only if it is a member of the CDR of LST, i.e. LST without its first element. In this last conditional clause, MEMBER thus makes a call of itself. Functions that call themselves in this way, as we said earlier, are known as recursive functions.

[Many people find the idea of recursive definition of functions very disturbing. They ask three main questions:

1. Is it not cheating in some sense to use something you have not already defined in its own definition? Does it not confuse the LISP system?

2. What happens to the parameters of a recursive function? Do their values not get mixed up if there are several recursive calls?

3. Why does the recursion ever stop? Why does the function not go on calling itself in an infinite cycle?

These questions can be answered more or less satisfactorily as follows:

1. Just think of the recursive definition as a self-referential sentence. For example, this sentence is six words long. Just as the human reader has no difficulty in finding the referent of "this sentence", so the LISP system has no difficulty in finding the "referent" of MEMBER within the definition of MEMBER. A recursive function call is no different from any other as far as LISP is concerned.
2. During every LISP function call (whether recursive or not), after the arguments are evaluated, but before their values are assigned to the parameters, the current values of the parameters are saved in a special type of store called a push-down stack. At the end of the function call, i.e. when the body of the function has been evaluated, the old values of the parameters are retrieved from the push-down stack. A push-down stack (which will be abbreviated to p.d.s. or referred to simply as a stack) is a store from which only the last element put in may be retrieved. A good analogy might be a pile of concrete slabs, so heavy that only one could be lifted at once, so rough that one could not slide against another, and so wide that the pile could not be pushed over. A moment's thought makes it clear that this sort of store is eminently suitable for LISP parameters, for, if a second function is called during the evaluation of a first, then the second must finish before the first can.
3. Of course, it is possible to write functions that do recurse infinitely (what they actually do is overflow the p.d.s.) With well defined recursive functions, however, there is always at least one condition on the arguments for which the function behaves non-recursively (in MEMBER there are two: LST being NIL and EL being equal to CAR of LST). In addition the recursive call of a good recursive function will always be made with arguments which are "closer" than the original arguments to fulfilling one of these conditions. In MEMBER the call is made with a list one element shorter than LST, and thus closer to fulfilling the condition of being NIL. In this way, one call will eventually return a value without needing to recurse, thus breaking the recursive cycle. The condition of a list being NIL is by far the most common condition used to terminate a recursion in LISP.

To see how all this works let us follow MEMBER through a couple of examples. Consider first the evaluation of:

```
(MEMBER (QUOTE MALE) (QUOTE (YOUNG MALE HUMAN)))
```

At the start of this evaluation we will suppose that the stack is empty and that the atoms EL and LST have no value.

p.d.s.		atom values
empty	EL	undefined value
	LST	undefined value

The arguments of the above function call evaluate to MALE and (YOUNG MALE HUMAN). Before evaluating the condition expression to find the value of the call of MEMBER, the old "values" of EL and LST are therefore saved on the p.d.s. (that these "values" are "undefined" is of no concern to LISP). The argument values are then substituted, so the diagram becomes:

p.d.s.		atom values	
LST	undefined value	EL	MALE
EL	undefined value	LST	(YOUNG MALE HUMAN)

The evaluation of the body of MEMBER proceeds, and, since LST is not NIL and MALE is not equal to YOUNG, the value of the COND is given by its third clause, i.e. the value of

(MEMBER EL (CDR LST)).

The value of this list is found by a call of MEMBER, the fact that this is a recursive call being of no particular significance to the LISP function calling mechanism. The arguments of this call evaluate to MALE and (MALE HUMAN) respectively. Before the COND is evaluated for this second call of MEMBER the diagram will, therefore, look like:

p.d.s.			atom values	
LST	(YOUNG MALE HUMAN)	saved by 2nd call of MEMBER		
EL	MALE		EL	MALE
LST	undefined value	saved by 1st call of MEMBER	LST	(MALE HUMAN)
EL	undefined value			

On this second call of MEMBER, the value of the COND and hence of the entire call will be provided by the second clause since this time EL is equal to the first element of LST. The value of the second application of MEMBER is thus T. After this application of MEMBER has finished the values of its parameters are overwritten by the values saved when it began, and these values removed from the p.d.s., so the diagram now becomes:

p.d.s.		atom values	
LST	undefined value	EL	MALE
EL	undefined value	LST	(YOUNG MALE HUMAN)

The reason that the second call of MEMBER was originally made was to provide the value of the COND in the first call. Nothing now remains to be evaluated to complete the first call, and so the value of the first call is the value of the COND in the first call, which is T. Saved values of LST and EL are once again "popped" off the top of the stack and the diagram returns to its original condition:

p.d.s.		atom values
empty	EL	undefined value
	LST	undefined value

To make this important process crystal clear in the reader's mind, let us consider a second example, the evaluation of:

```
(MEMBER (QUOTE FEMALE) (QUOTE (YOUNG MALE HUMAN)))
```

Events follow much the same course as in the last example until the evaluation of the COND in the second call of MEMBER at which point the diagram looks like:

p.d.s. — atom values

	p.d.s.			atom values
LST	(YOUNG MALE HUMAN)	saved by 2nd call		
EL	FEMALE		EL	FEMALE
LST	undefined value	saved by 1st call	LST	(MALE HUMAN)
EL	undefined value			

This time EL is not equal to the first element of LST and so the third conditional clause again provides the value and entails another recursive call. In fact two more calls on MEMBER are needed. At the start of the fourth call the reader should convince himself that the diagram will be:

	p.d.s.			atom values
LST	(HUMAN)	saved by 4th call		
EL	FEMALE			
LST	(MALE HUMAN)	saved by 3rd call		
EL	FEMALE		EL	FEMALE
LST	(YOUNG MALE HUMAN)	saved by 2nd call	LST	NIL
EL	FEMALE			
LST	undefined value	saved by 1st call		
EL	undefined value			

On this call, LST is NIL and so the first COND clause supplies NIL as the value of the call. In just the same way as the value of the second call became the value of the first in the previous example, so the value of this fourth call becomes the value of the third, the value of the third becomes the value of the second, and the value of the second becomes the value of the first. The stack gives up one of the values for EL and for LST each time a value is passed back in this way, finally leaving the diagram in its original state. The value of

```
(MEMBER (QUOTE FEMALE) (QUOTE (YOUNG MALE HUMAN)))
```

thus turns out to be NIL as we intended.

In the case of MEMBER, there was little point in saving all the values of the parameters for each call, since once the parameters had been used in making the recursive call, they were never used again, only the value of the recursive call was of interest. Here is a definition of a function which does need to save its parameters:

```
(DE OUREQUAL (EXP1 EXP2)
   (COND ((ATOM EXP1) (EQ EXP1 EXP2))
         ((ATOM EXP2) NIL)
         (T (AND (OUREQUAL (CAR EXP1) (CAR EXP2))
                 (OUREQUAL (CDR EXP1) (CDR EXP2))
            )
         )
   )
)
```

Evaluating the above expression defines a function called OUREQUAL which is a home-made version of the system function EQUAL we used in the definition of MEMBER. It uses two system functions: EQ takes two arguments and returns true if they are the same atom and NIL in all other cases. AND (a special form) performs a logical and on its arguments, of which there may be an arbitrary number, i.e. it returns true if all its arguments evaluate to true and false otherwise. It does this by evaluating its arguments from left to right, until it finds a false one or reaches the last, and then returning the last value it obtained. The reader should convince himself that OUREQUAL really behaves the same was as EQUAL, by working through a few examples, using the method we adopted above for MEMBER.]

EXERCISES 5

1. Define a function, LAST, which takes one argument which must be a list and returns the last element. Adopt the convention that the last element of an empty list is NIL.

[2. Define a function, INTERSECTION, which takes two lists as arguments and returns a list of all S-expressions which are members of both lists. (Hint: use MEMBER as a subfunction.)

3. Define a function, UNION, which takes two lists as arguments and returns a non-repetitious list of all S-expressions which are members of at least one of the argument lists (assume these lists are non-repetitious). (Hint: MEMBER is useful here too.)

4. The Tower of Hanoi puzzle can be described as follows:

A certain number of discs with holes in the middle are placed one on top of each other on a post (i.e. the post passes through the hole in each disc). The discs are all of different sizes and are stacked in order of size, with the largest at the bottom. The problem is to move all the discs to a second post, using a third post. The movement of discs is regulated by the rules that no larger disc may ever be placed on a smaller one, and that there may be only one disc not on a post at any one time. (Each post is a p.d.s.) The starting and finishing states for the puzzle with three discs may be diagrammed as follows:

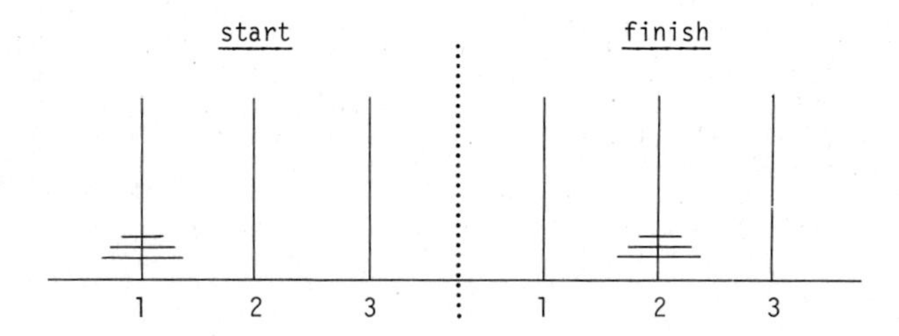

and the moves of the solution may be written as follows: (1 TO 2), (1 TO 3), (2 TO 3), (1 TO 2), (3 TO 1), (3 TO 2), (1 TO 2) where (x TO y) means move the top disc from post x to post y. Define a function HANOI with one argument N, (an integer), which prints the moves for moving N discs from post 1 to post 2. The system function PRINT takes one argument which may be any S-expression, and prints it on a new line. Thus a useful sub-function to define would be:

```
(DE MAKEMOVE (POSTA POSTB)
   (PRINT (CONS POSTA (CONS (QUOTE TO) (CONS POSTB NIL))))
)
```

(Hint: another subfunction you might find useful is one of four arguments M, PA, PB, PC which prints the moves for moving M discs from post PA to post PB using post PC.)]

ITERATION

In the two last sections we discussed recursion. The basic pattern of the functions defined there was: "If the list is not empty, do something to the first element of the list. Substitute the remaining elements of the list for the original list and repeat the whole operation on the list thus obtained. It was convenient to be able to define ATOMIC and MEMBER as functions and then to be able to re-call the same function from within the function definition. Many operations upon lists follow the same basic pattern, so the recursion technique is very useful. But some operations are not recursive in character, and it sometimes happens that for efficiency's sake it is preferable to write even inherently recursive functions non-recursively. In this section we shall discuss how that can be done.

If we want to be able to write non-recursive functions we need to be able to execute instructions sequentially, so that we can write loops. To see how this works, let us first look at a recursive definition of the function FACTORIAL, and then compare with it its non-recursive version.

Mathematically, the function factorial (n) can be defined by:

factorial (o) = 1

factorial (n) = n x factorial (n-1)

This can be paraphrased in English by saying: "The factorial of any number is that number multiplied by the factorial of that number minus one, except in the case of zero, whose factorial is one".

```
Thus factorial (0) = 1

     factorial (1) = 1 x factorial (0)
                   = 1 x 1
                   = 1

     factorial (2) = 2 x factorial (1)
                   = 2 x 1 x factorial (0)
                   = 2 x 1 x 1
                   - 2

     factorial (3) = 3 x factorial (2)
                   = 3 x 2 x factorial (1)
                   = 3 x 2 x 1 x factorial (0)
                   = 3 x 2 x 1 x 1
                   = 6
```

and so on.

It was said earlier that LISP was not intended as a language in which to do mathematics, so it may seem a little strange to use a mathematical example here. Nonetheless, factorial is one of the most intuitively obvious recursive functions which can be programmed in only a few lines, so it makes a good example.

Its recursive definition in LISP is:

```
(DE FACTORIAL (N)
      (COND ((ZEROP N) 1)
            (T (TIMES N (FACTORIAL (SUB1 N))))))
```

A non-recursive version needs a loop, as in the diagram below.

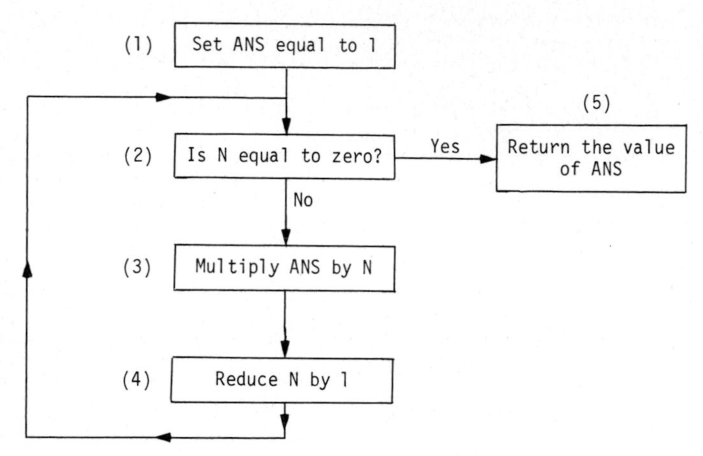

(Actually this could be made slightly more efficient by testing to see if N is 1 rather than zero. But we will leave it like this so that it matches the earlier definition of factorial.)

An inspection of the diagram should convince the reader that he knows how to deal with boxes (1) to (4): their LISP equivalents can easily be stated in terms of SETQ, COND, TIMES and SUB1. But as yet we have no way of dealing with (5) or of constructing a LISP equivalent of the line which shows what must be executed after the instruction equivalent to box (4) has been executed.

Both these difficulties are overcome by use of the function PROG. A call of PROG has a general form thus:

```
(PROG (list of variables)
      (1st instruction)
      (2nd instruction)
            .
            .
            .
      (nth instruction)
```

It allows iteration ("jumping back") because the sequence of instructions may contain GO and/or RETURN instructions.

A GO instruction has the form (GO label) where the label is a literal atom which must appear before some instruction within the PROG sequence. When the GO is executed, control is transferred to the instruction preceded by the label specified. This can be shown by altering our earlier diagram slightly:

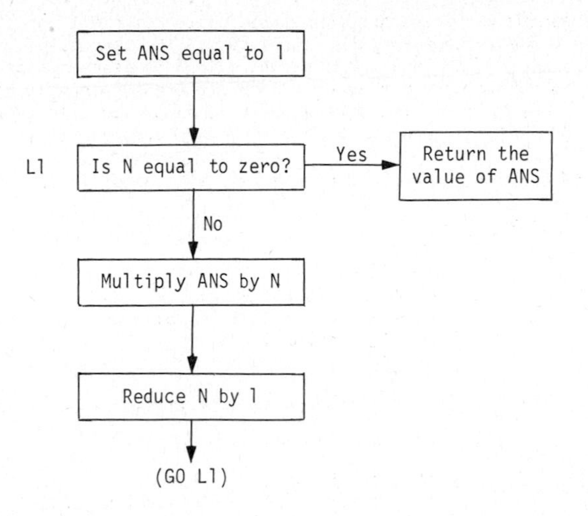

The RETURN instruction allows execution to leave the PROG sequence at any point. It has the form (RETURN expression). When the RETURN instruction is reached, the expression which forms its argument is evaluated and becomes the value of the whole PROG. So we can incorporate it into our diagram:

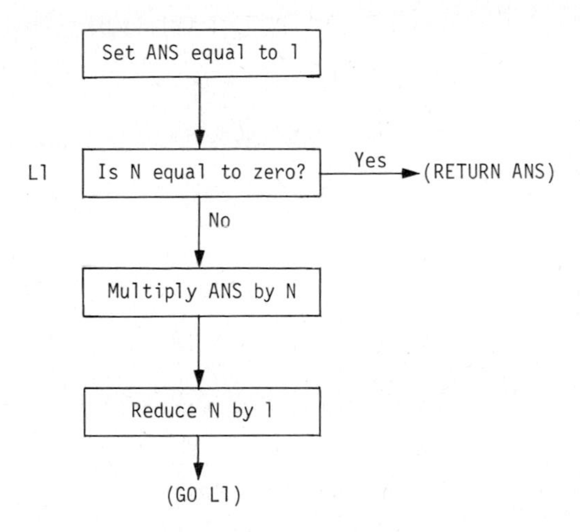

If the last instruction in a PROG sequence is executed and it is not a call on either of the functions GO or RETURN, PROG returns NIL. Execution has "dropped out of the bottom" as it were.

The only other new feature of the PROG is the list of variables which appears as its first argument. These variables serve as temporary variables within the

PROG. They are initially set to NIL and cannot be accessed from outside the PROG. Even if no temporary variables are used, this list must still appear. In the case where there are no temporary variables it will be the empty list, ( ). In the factorial example, ANS is a variable which is only used within the PROG: it can therefore be a temporary variable. N is different, since it carries a value into the PROG sequence. It must therefore be a dummy variable (an argument) in the function definition of which the PROG sequence forms the body.

We can now translate the whole of this sequence into LISP.

```
(DE FACTORIAL (N)
              (PROG (ANS)
                    (SETQ ANS 1)
                 L1 (COND ((ZEROP N) (RETURN ANS)))
                    (SETQ ANS (TIMES ANS N))
                    (SETQ N (SUB1 N))
                    (GO L1)))
```

It is worth comparing this with the recursive definition of the same function:

```
(DE FACTORIAL (N)
              (COND ((ZEROP N) 1)
                    (T (TIMES (FACTORIAL (SUB1 N)) N))))
```

In this case it is clear that the recursive version is simpler and easier to follow. Although the exercises attached to this section ask that the same function should be defined both iteratively and recursively, the programmer should in real life take some care about which version he chooses, using clarity and simplicity as guides in making his choice.

EXERCISES 6

Define each of the following functions first recursively and then iteratively:

1. A function LONG which counts how many top level elements there are in a list.

   e.g. (LONG (QUOTE ((A B) C))) is 2

   (LONG (QUOTE (A B C))) is 3

   This is the function LENGTH which was used in the example program preceding EXERCISES 3. But don't use that name for it or you will re-define the system function.

2. A function ZEROES which returns the number of zeroes in a list.

3. A function LAST which returns the last element in a list.

PROPERTY LISTS

So far we have discussed literal atoms as symbols which can have values and can name functions. As was mentioned earlier they can also have other things associated with them. Thus an atom is able to refer to many different pieces of information through its "property list". We saw in Chapter 1 how Raphael's SIR would represent the facts that girls are persons and persons have hearts by putting the following on the property list of PERSON:

```
(SUBSET (GIRL) SUBPART (HEART))
```

More generally for each piece of information included in the list there is a corresponding indicator, a literal atom used to name the property. The form of a property list is:

$(ind_1\ prop_1\ ind_2\ prop_2\ .....)$

where each prop is a piece of information (or property) which is named by the corresponding ind. One says that an atom has a property under an indicator. So, in our example, the atom PERSON has the properties (GIRL) and (HEART) under the indicators SUBSET and SUBPART respectively.

Some indicators are known to and their corresponding values used by the LISP system. Among these are PNAME (print name) and EXPR (function definition). The property list of the function MEMBER discussed in the detailed section on recursion would thus be:

```
(EXPR (LAMBDA (EL LST)
         (COND ((NULL LST) NIL)
               ((EQUAL EL (CAR LST)) T)
               (T (MEMBER EL (CDR LST)))
         )
      )
 PNAME <M,E,M,B,E,R>)
```

Looking at the property list for MEMBER given above brings to our attention several aspects of LISP which have not been previously encountered, namely EXPR, LAMBDA and PNAME.

EXPR and LAMBDA will be discussed in detail in the next section. PNAME simply gives the PrintNAME of the atom, so that LISP knows what to print out. In our example <M,E,M,B,E,R> (the property under the indicator PNAME) represents the internal computer codes for the letters M,E,M,B,E,R. (This notation will be used for all print names.) Property lists thus differ from ordinary lists in that they can contain things which are not atoms or lists. The user should, as a general rule, only manipulate property lists by use of the system functions PUT and GET.

(PUT atm ind prop)	evaluates to atm, but also puts prop on the property list of atm under the indicator ind. If there already is a property under that indicator, it is overwritten.
(GET atm ind)	returns the property stored under the indicator ind on the property list of atm, (or NIL if there is no such property).

Thus evaluating

```
(PUT (QUOTE MEMBER) (QUOTE SPEECHPART) (QUOTE NOUN))
```

would transform the property list of MEMBER into

    (SPEECHPART NOUN EXPR (LAMBDA etc) PNAME <M,E,M,B,E,R>)

and subsequently

    (GET (QUOTE MEMBER) (QUOTE SPEECHPART))

would evaluate to

    NOUN

At this stage it should not be hard to see that property lists provide a straightforward way to implement semantic nets such as those discussed in Chapter 7. Thus

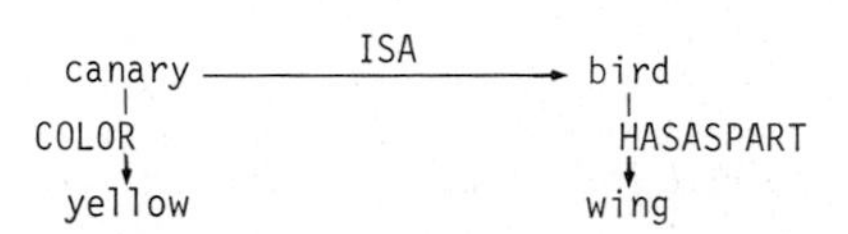

could be represented using property lists as follows:

Atom	Property List
CANARY	(COLOR YELLOW ISA BIRD PNAME <C,A,N,A,R,Y>)
BIRD	(HASASPART WING PNAME <B,I,R,D>)

LISP also provides a function, GENSYM, to generate atoms for which the user has no particular name. Each call of GENSYM produces a unique new atom, with a correspondingly unique print name (typically of the form: a letter followed by a number of digits, e.g. G000036). Such a function is extremely useful for representing new entities introduced into such a semantic net through natural language input. Thus, in response to "a boy", there might be produced a gensymed atom, G00057, whose property list was:

    (AGE YOUNG SEX MALE ISA HUMAN PNAME <G,0,0,0,5,7>)

The reader should convince himself that such an atom would be the result of evaluating

```
(PUT (PUT (PUT (GENSYM)(QUOTE ISA)(QUOTE HUMAN))(QUOTE SEX)(QUOTE MALE))
                                        (QUOTE AGE)(QUOTE YOUNG))
```

[MORE ABOUT FUNCTIONS

We saw in the last section how function definitions were stored on the function name's property list, under the indicator EXPR. EXPR tells LISP two things: first that what follows is a function definition and secondly that the function is a "normal function" as opposed to the "special form" functions we have encountered earlier. (Special forms are indicated by FEXPR instead of EXPR.)

Looking beyond EXPR to the actual function definition we see that the internal representation of a user defined function is:

    (LAMBDA local variable list function body)

All DE does, in fact, is to construct a list with three elements - LAMBDA followed by its unevaluated second and third arguments - and put that list on the property list of its first argument under the indicator EXPR. Such lists are known as lambda expressions, and are the only things that LISP uses to represent user-defined functions.

Instead of naming a function, it is always possible to use the corresponding lambda expression directly. Thus,

```
((LAMBDA (EL LST) body of MEMBER) (QUOTE MALE) (QUOTE (YOUNG
                                                MALE HUMAN)))
```

evaluates to

```
T
```

just like

```
(MEMBER (QUOTE MALE) (QUOTE (YOUNG MALE HUMAN)))
```

One can be even freer than that, since, if LISP tries to evaluate a list the first element of which is neither a lambda expression nor an atom which is the name of a function, that first element will itself be evaluated.

Thus, after evaluating

```
(SETQ MEM (QUOTE MEMBER)),
(MEM (QUOTE MALE) (QUOTE (YOUNG MALE HUMAN)))
```

will evaluate to

```
T
```

as will

```
((CAR (QUOTE (MEMBER))) (QUOTE MALE) (QUOTE (YOUNG MALE HUMAN)))
```

Because of this last feature, it is possible to define functions which take functions as arguments and then call these arguments. For example, after evaluating

```
(DE COMP (FN1 FN2 ARG) (FN1 (FN2 ARG))),
 (COMP (QUOTE ATOM) (QUOTE CAR) (QUOTE (LIKE AN ARROW)))
```

will evaluate to

```
T, i.e. the value of (ATOM (CAR (QUOTE (LIKE AN ARROW))))
```

The system function, MAPCAR, also takes a functional argument and is rather more useful. In fact, it takes two arguments, a list and a function of one argument. It applies its second argument to each element of its first argument in turn and returns a list of the values thus obtained (in the order of the original list). Thus,

```
(MAPCAR (QUOTE (TIME (FLIES LIKE) AN (ARROW))) (QUOTE ATOM))
```

evaluates to

```
(T NIL T NIL)
```

There is a corresponding function MAPC which does exactly the same thing as MAPCAR, but ignores the values it obtains and returns NIL. MAPC can be used to define a function PUTLIST which puts the same value, VAL, under the same indicator, IND, on the property list of each of a list of atoms, ATS.

```
(DE PUTLIST (ATS IND VAL)
     (MAPC ATS (QUOTE (LAMBDA (ATM) (PUT ATM IND VAL))))
)
```

```
(PUTLIST (QUOTE (DOG CAT MAT)) (QUOTE SPEECHPART) (QUOTE NOUN))
```

would thus evaluate to

```
NIL
```

but result in each of the three atoms DOG, CAT and MAT receiving NOUN as their SPEECHPART property.

In addition to ordinary functions, the user may also define special forms. The system function DF, itself a special form, is provided for this purpose. It treats its arguments just like DE, except that the indicator on the function name's property list will be FEXPR instead of EXPR.

```
(DF OURDE (ARGS)
     (PUT (CAR ARGS) (QUOTE EXPR) (CONS (QUOTE LAMBDA) (CDR ARGS)))
)
```

Evaluating the above expression defines a function OURDE, which is equivalent to the system function, DE. To understand how OURDE works, only one extra piece of knowledge is required, viz. that all special forms have exactly one argument which, when the special form is called, is instantiated to the CDR of the list whose evaluation causes the call. Thus evaluating

```
(OURDE INSULT (X) (CONS X (QUOTE (IS A FOOL))))
```

causes ARGS to receive the value

```
(INSULT (X) (CONS X (QUOTE (IS A FOOL))))
```

The reader should now be able to convince himself that OURDE behaves just like DE.

Some special forms, unlike OURDE, require some or all of their arguments to be evaluated. The system function, EVAL, which returns the value of its single argument can be used in such cases. Since EVAL is not itself a special form, its argument is evaluated twice, once by the normal function calling mechanism, and once by EVAL itself.

```
(DF OURAND (ARGS)
    (PROG ( )
  LOOP (COND ((NULL ARGS) (RETURN T))
             ((NOT (EVAL (CAR ARGS))) (RETURN NIL))
       )
       (SETQ ARGS (CDR ARGS))
       (GO LOOP)
    )
)
```

The definition of OURAND above (which behaves in the same way as the system function AND described earlier) illustrates the use of EVAL.]

In conclusion, some of the more important system functions not so far mentioned are described below. All special forms are explicitly described as such.

(LIST exp1 ..... expn)

LIST is a special form which takes an arbitrary number of arguments and returns a list of their values.

E.g. (LIST (QUOTE A) (CAR (QUOTE (B D))) (QUOTE (X Y))) evaluates to (A B (X Y))

(APPEND lst1 lst2)

APPEND takes two arguments, both of which must be lists, and joins them together.

E.g. (APPEND (QUOTE (A (B))) (QUOTE (D (E F)))) evaluates to (A (B) D (E F))

(REVERSE lst)

REVERSE takes one argument which must be a list. It returns a list whose elements are the same as those of the argument, but which are in the opposite order. Sublists of the argument are not reversed.

E.g. (REVERSE (QUOTE (A (B C) D (E (F G))))) evaluates to ((E (F G)) D (B C) A)

(PROG2 exp exp)

PROG2 returns the value of its second argument.

(PROGN exp ..... exp)

PROGN is a special form which takes an arbitrary number of arguments, evaluates them all and returns the value of the last.

PROG2 and PROGN are similar to PROG in that they allow the sequential evaluation of a number of S-expressions, but differ from PROG in that they can be used to provide neither local variables nor jumps.

EXERCISES 7

1. Just try to write an iterative version of HANOI, but do not waste too much time on it.

2. Define a function (using MAPCAR) which takes a list of atoms and returns a corresponding list of their ISA properties.

3. Evaluate:

```
((LAMBDA (LST) (MAPCAR LST (QUOTE (LAMBDA (EL) (CONS EL NIL)
    )))) (QUOTE (CAN I CONFUSE YOU)))
```

4. All participants in some conference are represented in a computer by LISP atoms. Each atom carries personal data about the participant on its property list under indicators which include: SURNAME, FORENAMES (always has a list as corresponding value even if participant has only one forename), NATIONALITY, PROFESSION, SEX, and so on. An atom representing a typical participant might thus be:

```
(SURNAME BLOGGS FORENAMES (JOSEPH FRED) NATIONALITY FRENCH etc.)
```

   a) Write a function, PRINTNAMES, which takes one argument, a list of atoms representing participants, and which prints out (using PRINT) the full name of each participant represented on that list.

   b) Suppose the atom, PARTICIPANTS, has as its value a list of all atoms representing participants. Write a function, PRINTALL, which is a special form taking an indefinite number of arguments which are alternately property indicators and property values. PRINTALL should print out the full names of all participants who have all the properties indicated by the arguments. Thus evaluating

```
(PRINTALL NATIONALITY GERMAN PROFESSION LINGUIST)
```

   should cause the names of all participants who are German linguists to be printed.

   c) Change PRINTALL so that it would only require property values and not the corresponding indicators as its arguments, e.g. so that evaluating

```
(PRINTALL GERMAN LINGUIST)
```

   would print out the names of all participating German linguists. Do you need to assume anything?

5. The function LIT can be defined as follows:

```
(DE LIT (LST TERMIN FN)
    (COND ((NULL LST) TERMIN)
          (T (FN (CAR LST) (LIT (CDR LST) TERMIN FN))
    )
)
```

   Evaluate:

   a) (LIT (QUOTE (LIKE AN ARROW)) NIL (QUOTE CONS))

   b) (LIT (QUOTE (1 2 3 4)) 0 (QUOTE PLUS))

[6. Using only LIT (no recursion or iteration) define a function CARTPROD that takes one argument, a list of lists and returns the cartesian product of the elements of that list.

E.g. (CARTPROD (QUOTE ((A B) (U V) (X Y)))) evaluates to
((A U X) (A U Y) (A V X) (A V Y) (B U X) (B U Y) (B V X) (B V Y))]

SOLUTIONS TO EXERCISES 1

1. (PLUS 3 7)
2. (DIFFERENCE 7 3)
3. (QUOTIENT 8 3)
4. (TIMES 8 8)
5. (ADD1 10)
6. (SUB1 10)
7. (TIMES (PLUS 3 7) 10)
8. (QUOTIENT (ADD1 5) 2)
9. (TIMES (QUOTIENT (PLUS 3 7) 5) 10)
10. (TIMES (QUOTIENT (ADD1 5) (SUB1 4)) (QUOTIENT (PLUS 7 3) (DIFFERENCE 7 2)))
11. (TIMES 3 3 3 3 3 3 3)
12. (DIFFERENCE 538 (TIMES (QUOTIENT 538 3) 3))

SOLUTIONS TO EXERCISES 2

1. a) A b) (A B C) c) (A)
   d) (B C) e) NIL f) ((B C))
   g) (B C) h) (B) i) (C (D))
   j) B k) F l) (A B C)
   m) ((A) (B C)) n) (((A) B C)) o) (A B C)
   p) (NIL A B C)

2. a) CAR b) CAAR c) CAADDDR
   d) CADDDAR e) CAADADADR f) CAADADDAR
   g) CAAADDADAR

3. a) (A B C), NIL b) (X A B C), NIL c) (A B C), (X A B C)
   d) (X A B C), (B C) e) NIL, NIL

SOLUTION TO EXERCISE 3

```
(SETQ A..........)
(COND ((ZEROP A) (SETQ B (QUOTE (VALUE IS ZERO))))
     (T (SETQ B (QUOTE (VALUE IS NOT ZERO)))))
```

SOLUTIONS TO EXERCISES 4

1\. a)
```
(DE F1 (L)
       (AND (ATOM (CAR L)) (NOT(NUMBERP (CAR L)))))
```

b)
```
(DE F2 (L)
       (AND (NUMBERP (CAR L)) (EQUAL (CAR L) 12)))
```

c)
```
(DE F3 (L)
       (NOT (GREATERP 4 (LENGTH L))))
```

d)
```
(DE F4 (L)
       (GREATERP (CADR L) (CADDDR L)))
```

2\.

	value of conditional	value of RES
If EXP atomic	T	same as EXP
Otherwise, if first element of EXP is atomic	T	first element of EXP
Otherwise, if EXP has only one element	NIL	same as before evaluation of conditional
In all other cases	CDR of EXP	first element of first element of EXP

3\.
```
(DE SECOND (LST)
   (COND ((NULL LST) NIL)
         ((NULL (CDR LST)) NIL)
         (T (CADR LST))
   )
)
```

SOLUTIONS TO EXERCISES 5

1.
```
(DE LAST (LST)
   (COND ((NULL LST) NIL)
         ((NULL (CDR LST))(CAR LST))
         (T (LAST (CDR LST)))
   )
)
```

2.
```
(DE INTERSECTION (LST1 LST2)
   (COND ((NULL LST1) NIL)
         ((MEMBER (CAR LST1) LST2)
         (CONS (CAR LST1) (INTERSECTION (CDR LST1) LST2)))
         (T (INTERSECTION (CDR LST1) LST2))
   )
)
```

3.
```
(DE UNION (LST1 LST2)
   (COND ((NULL LST1) LST2)
         ((MEMBER (CAR LST1) LST2)
          (UNION (CDR LST1) LST2))
          (T (CONS (CAR LST1) (UNION (CDR LST1) LST2)))
   )
)
```

4.
```
(DE MAKEMOVE (POSTA POSTB)
   (PRINT (CONS POSTA (CONS (QUOTE TO) (CONS POSTB NIL))))
)
(DE HAN (M PA PB PC)
   (COND ((EQUAL M 0) NIL)
         (T (HAN (DIFFERENCE M 1) PA PC PB)
            (MAKEMOVE PA PB)
            (HAN (DIFFERENCE M 1) PC PB PA)
         )
   )
)
(DE HANOI (N)
   (HAN N (QUOTE POST1) (QUOTE POST2) (QUOTE POST3))
)
```

SOLUTIONS TO EXERCISES 6

1. a)
```
(DE LONG (L)
         (COND ((NULL L) 0)
               (T (ADD1 (LONG (CDR L))))))
```

b)
```
(DE LONG (L)
   (PROG (X)
         (SETQ X 0)
    BACK (COND ((NULL L) (RETURN X)))
         (SETQ X (ADD1 X))
         (SETQ L (CDR L))
         (GO BACK)))
```

2. a)
```
(DE ZEROS (L)
          (COND ((NULL L) 0)
                ((AND (NUMBERP (CAR L)) (ZEROP (CAR L)))
                      (ADD1 (ZEROS (CDR L))))
                (T (ZEROS (CDR L)))))
```

b)
```
(DE ZEROS (L)
    (PROG (SUM)
          (SETQ SUM 0)
     BACK (COND ((NULL L) (RETURN SUM))
          ((AND (NUMBERP (CAR L) (ZEROP (CAR L)))
          (SETQ SUM (ADD1 SUM))))
          (SETQ L (CDR L))
          (GO BACK)
                  ))
```

3. a)
```
(DE LAST (L)
         (COND ((NULL (CDR L)) (CAR L))
               (T (LAST (CDR L)))))
```

b)
```
(DE LAST (L)
   (PROG ( )
    BACK (COND ((NULL (CDR L)) (RETURN (CAR L))))
         (SETQ L (CDR L))
         (GO BACK)))
```

n.b. This solution will not work if LAST is called with the empty list as its argument. Why not? Can you alter it so that it will work even under this condition?

SOLUTIONS TO EXERCISES 7

1. As for the recursive case, except that the recursive function HAN is replaced by the following two functions.

```
(DE STACK (LAB)
   (PROG2 (SETQ PDS (CONS (LIST LAB PA PB PC) PDS))
          (SETQ M (SUB1 M))
   )
)
(DE HAN (M PA PB PC)
   (PROG (PDS TEMP)
    BEFORE (COND ((EQUAL M 0) (GO AFTER)))
           (STACK (QUOTE MOVE))
           (SETQ TEMP PB)
           (SETQ PB PC)
           (SETQ PC TEMP)
           (GO BEFORE)
      MOVE (MAKEMOVE PA PB)
           (STACK (QUOTE AFTER))
           (SETQ TEMP PC)
           (SETQ PC PA)
           (SETQ PA TEMP)
           (GO BEFORE)
     AFTER (COND ((NULL PDS) (RETURN NIL)))
           (SETQ PA (CADR (SETQ TEMP (CAR PDS))))
           (SETQ PB (CADDR TEMP))
           (SETQ PC (CADDDR TEMP))
           (SETQ PDS (CDR PDS))
           (SETQ M (ADD1 M))
           (GO (CAR TEMP))
   )
)
```

2.
```
(DE ISAS (LST)
   (MAPCAR LST (QUOTE (LAMBDA (EL) (GET EL (QUOTE ISA)))))
)
```

3.
```
((CAN) (I) (CONFUSE) (YOU))
```

4. a)
```
(DE PRINTNAMES (LST)
   (MAPC LST (QUOTE (LAMBDA (ATM)
      (PRINT (APPEND (GET ATM (QUOTE FORENAMES))
                     (CONS (GET ATM (QUOTE SURNAME)) NIL)
             )
      )
                     )
             )
   )
)
```

b)
```
(DF PRINTALL (CHARS)
   (PRINTNAMES (FINDALL PARTICIPANTS CHARS))
)
(DE FINDALL (LST CHARS)
   (COND ((NULL CHARS)LST)
         (T (FINDALL (FINDALL1 LST (CAR CHARS) (CADR CHARS))
                     (CDDR CHARS)))
   )
)
(DE FINDALL1 (LST IND VAL)
   (PROG (RES TEMP)
   LOOP (COND ((NULL LST) (RETURN (REVERSE RES)))
              ((EQUAL (GET (SETQ TEMP (CAR LST)) IND)
                      VAL)
               (SETQ RES (CONS TEMP RES)))
        )
        (SETQ LST (CDR LST))
        (GO LOOP)
   )
)
```

c) It is possible if we make the restriction that all property values to be used as arguments of PRINTALL are atoms which have on their property list under the indicator TYPE, the indicator under which they appear on the property lists of participants atoms, (so that GERMAN would have the property NATIONALITY, under the indicator TYPE). Then redefining FINDALL as follows would make PRINTALL behave in the desired way.

```
(DE FINDALL (LST CHARS)
   (COND ((NULL CHARS) LST)
         (T (FINDALL (FINDALL1 LST (GET (CAR CHARS) (QUOTE TYPE))
                                        (CAR CHARS))
                     (CDR CHARS))))
)
```

This restriction would, of course, not be practical if we wanted PRINTALL to work for names.

5. a) (LIKE AN ARROW)

   b) 10 (= 1 + 2 + 3 + 4)

6.

```
(DE CARTPROD (LSTLST)
   (LIT LSTLST (QUOTE (NIL))
      (QUOTE (LAMBDA (LST LSTLST2)
               (LIT LST NIL
                  (QUOTE (LAMBDA (EL LSTLST3)
                           (LIT LSTLST2 LSTLST3
                              (QUOTE (LAMBDA (LST2 LSTLST4)
                                 (CONS (CONS EL LST2) LSTLST4)
                                    )
                              )
                           )
                        )
                     )
                  )
               )
            )
         )
   )
)
```

BIBLIOGRAPHY

In order to compress the Bibliography, the following abbreviations have been used. Some refer to books which collect numerous well known articles, while other abbreviations are for series of individual publications. The student who wants to read further in this subject would be well advised to start with one or more of the collections.

IJCAI3 Advanced papers for the Third International Joint Conference in Artificial Intelligence, Stanford, USA, 1973. (SRI, Menlo Park, 1973.)

IJCAI4 Advanced papers for the Fourth International Joint Conference in Artificial Intelligence, Tbilisi, USSR, 1975. (MIT, Cambridge, Mass., 1975.)

AISB Proceedings of the Summer Conference of the Society for Artificial Intelligence and Simulation of Behavior, University of Sussex, UK, 1974.

TEDD Proceedings of the First International Conference on Machine Translation, National Physical Laboratory, Teddington, UK, 1961. (HMSO, London, 1961.)

ACL Proceedings of the Conference of the Association for Computational Linguistics, Amherst, Mass., 1974.

ISSCO Memoranda from the Istituto per gli Studi Semantici e Cognitivi, Castagnola, Switzerland.

MITAI Memoranda from the Artificial Intelligence Laboratory, Massachusetts Institute of Technology.

SUAIM Memoranda from the Artificial Intelligence Laboratory, Stanford University, Stanford, California.

SRITN Technical notes from the Stanford Research Institute, Menlo Park, California.

SAC Papers in *Computer Models of Thought and Language*, ed. by Schank and Colby, (Freeman, San Francisco, 1973).

TINLAP Position papers for the Workshop on Theoretical Issues in Natural Language Processing, Massachusetts Institute of Technology, 1975. (BBN, Cambridge, Mass., 1975.)

KEEN *Formal Semantics of Natural Language*, ed. by E. Keenan, (Cambridge U.P., 1975).

Abelson, R. P. (1973) The Structure of Belief Systems, in SAC.

Abelson, R. P. (1974) Discourse Headers, Second draft of paper for presentation at the Carbonell Memorial Conference, Pajaro Dunes, Calif.

Anderson, J. R. & Bower, G. H. (1973) Human Associative Memory, (Winston, Washington).

Bach, E. (1968) Nouns and Noun Phrases, in Bach & Harms (eds.) Universals in Linguistic Theory, (Holt, Rinehart & Winston, New York) 91-122.

Bartlett, F. C. (1932) Remembering, (Cambridge, U.P.)

Berkeley, E. C. & Bobrow, D. G. (1966) The Programming Language LISP: Its Operation and Applications, (MIT Press, Cambridge, Mass.)

Bever, T. G., Lackner, J. & Kirk, R. (1969) The Underlying Structures of Sentences are the Primary Units of Immediate Speech Processing, Perception and Psychophysics, 5, 225-234.

Bever, T. G. (1970) The Cognitive Basis for Linguistic Structures, in Hayes (ed.) Cognition and the Development of Language, (Wiley, New York) 279-352.

Bolinger, D. (1965) The Atomization of Meaning, Language, 41, 555-573.

Bousfield, W. A. (1953) The Occurrence of Clustering in the Recall of Randomly Arranged Associates, Journal of Genetic Psychology, 49, 229-240.

Bower, G. H., Clark, M., Winzenz, D. & Lesgold, A. (1969) Hierarchical Retrieval Schemes in Recall of Categorized Lists, Journal of Verbal Learning and Verbal Behavior, 8, 323-343.

Bower, G. H. (1970) Organizational Factors in Memory, Cognitive Psychology, 1, 18-46.

Bransford, J. D. & Franks, J. J. (1971) The Abstraction of Linguistic Ideas, Cognitive Psychology, 2, 331-350.

Bransford, J. D. & Johnson, M. K. (1972) Contextual Prerequisites for Understanding: Some Investigations of Comprehension and Recall, Journal of Verbal Learning and Verbal Behavior, 11, 717-726.

Carnap, R. (1937) The Logical Syntax of Language, (Harcourt Brace, New York).

Carnap, R. (1942) Introduction to Semantics, (Harvard U.P., Cambridge, Mass.)

Charniak, E. (1972) Toward a Model of Children's Story Comprehension, MITAI TR266.

Charniak, E. (1974) He will make you take it back: A study in the Pragmatics of Language, ISSCO 3.

Charniak, E. (1975a) A Partial Taxonomy of Knowledge about Actions, IJCAI4.

Charniak, E. (1975b) Organization and Inference in a Frame-like System of Common Sense Knowledge, TINLAP.

Chomsky, N. (1957) Syntactic Structures, (Mouton & Co., The Hague).

Chomsky, N. (1959) Review of Verbal Behavior by B. F. Skinner, Language, 35, 26-58.

Chomsky, N. (1965) Aspects of the Theory of Syntax, (MIT Press, Cambridge, Mass.)

Chomsky, N. (1966) Topics in the Theory of Generative Grammar, in Sebeok (ed.) Current Trends in Linguistics III, (Mouton & Co., The Hague, Paris) 1-58.

Chomsky, N. (1972) Deep Structure, Surface Structure, and Semantic Interpretation, in Steinberg and Jakobvits (eds.) Semantics: An Interdisciplinary Reader, (Cambridge U.P.) 183-216.

Clark, H. (1975) On Bridging, TINLAP.

Colby, K. M. & Parkinson, R. C. (1974) Pattern-Matching Rules for the Recognition of Natural Language Dialogue Expressions, American Journal of Computational Linguistics, 1, 1-70.

Colby, K. M. & Hilf, F. D. (1973) Multidimensional Analysis in Evaluating a Simulation of Paranoid Thought, SUAIM 194.

Colby, K. M. et al.(1971) Artificial Paranoia, Artificial Intelligence, 2, 1-25.

Collins, A. M. & Quillian, M. R. (1969) Retrieval Time from Semantic Memory, Journal of Verbal Learning and Verbal Behavior, 8, 240-247.

Conrad, C. (1972) Cognitive Economy in Semantic Memory, Journal of Experimental Psychology, 92, 149-154.

Davidson, D. (1967) Truth and Meaning, Synthese, 17, 304-323.

Davidson, D. (1970) Semantics for Natural Languages, in Visentini et al.(eds.) Linguaggi nella Tecnica e nella Societa, (Olivetti, Milan), 177-188.

Dreyfus, H. (1972) What Computers Can't Do, (Harper & Row, New York).

Dummett, M. (1973) The Justification of Deduction, (British Academy, London).

Enea, H. & Colby, K. M. (1973) Idiolectic Language Analysis for Understanding Doctor-Patient Dialogues, IJCAI3.

Eisenstadt, M. & Kareev, Y. (1973) Towards a Model of Human Game Playing, CHIP Report, 33, (Center for Human Information Processing, University of California, San Diego).

Fikes, E. E. (1971) Monitored Execution of Robot Plans produced by STRIPS, (International Federation of Information Processing Societies Proceedings, Ljubljana, Yugoslavia).

Fillenbaum, S. (1971) Psycholinguistics, Annual Review of Psychology, 251-308.

Fillmore, C. (1968) The Case for Case, in Bach & Harms (eds.) Universals in Linguistics Theory, (Holt, Rinehart & Winston, New York), 1-90.

Fillmore, C. (1968) Lexical Entries for Verbs, Foundations of Language 4, 373-393.

Fillmore, C. (1969) Types of Lexical Information in Kiefer (ed.) Studies in Syntax and Semantics, (Reidel, Dordrecht), 109-137.

Fillmore, C. (1970) The Grammar of Hitting and Breaking, in Jacobs & Rosenbaum (eds.) Readings in Transformational Grammar, (Ginn & Co., Waltham, Mass.) 120-133.

Fillmore, C. (1970) Subjects, Speakers and Roles, Synthese, 21, 251-275.

Fillmore, C. (1971) Some Problems for Case Grammar, in O'Brien (ed.) Report of the 22nd Annual Round-Table Meeting on Linguistics and Language Studies, (Georgetown U.P., Washington D.C.), 35-56.

Fillmore, C. (1971) Verbs of Judging, an Exercise in Semantic Description, in Fillmore & Langendoen (eds.) Studies in Linguistic Semantics, (Holt, Rinehart & Winston, New York), 273-290.

Fillmore, C. (1974) Summer School Lectures, University of Pisa, Italy.

Finke, P. (1974) Theoretische Probleme der Kasusgrammatik, Vol. 9 of Scripten Linguistik und Kommunikationswissenschaft (Scriptor Verlag, Kronberg/Ts).

Francis, D. (1975) Blood Sport, (Pocket Books, New York).

Frederiksen, C. H. (1975) Acquisition of Semantic Information from Discourse: Effects of Repeated Exposures, Journal of Verbal Learning and Verbal Behavior 14, 158-169.

Gabbay, D. (1973) Representation of the Montague Semantics as a Form of the Suppes Semantics, in Hintikka, Moravcsik & Suppes (eds.) Approaches to Natural Language, (Reidel, Dordrecht),395-412.

Gabbay, D. & Moravcsik, J. (1974) Branching Quantifiers, English & Montague Grammar, Theoretical Linguistics, 1, 139-157.

Goldman, N. M. (1974) Computer Generation of Natural Language from a Deep Conceptual Base, ISSCO, 2.

Goldman, N. M. & Hayes, P. (1975) LISP Users Manual, ISSCO.

Green, C. C. (1969) Application of Theorem Proving to Problem Solving, in Walker & Norton (eds.) Proceedings of the International Joint Conference on Artificial Intelligence, 219-240.

Halliday, M. A. K. (1970) Functional Diversity in Language, Foundations of Language, 6, 322-361.

Hayes, P. J. (1971) The Frame Problem and Related Problems in Artificial Intelligence, SUAIM 53.

Hayes, P. J. (1974) Some Problems and Non-Problems in Representation Theory, AISB.

Hays, D. (1964) Dependency Theory: A Formalism and Some Observation, Language, 40 511-525.

Herriot, P. (1969) The Comprehension of Active and Passive Sentences as a Function of Pragmatic Expectations, Journal of Verbal Learning and Verbal Behavior, 8, 166-169.

Herriot, P. (1970) An Introduction to the Psychology of Language (Methuen, London).

Herskovits, A. (1973) The Generation of French from a Semantic Representation, SUAIM 212.

Hewitt, C. (1969) Planner: A Language for Proving Theorems in Robots, Walker & Norton (eds.) Proceedings of the International Joint Conference on Artificial Intelligence, 295-301.

Jardine, N. & Jardine, C. (1975) Model Theoretic Semantics and Natural Language, in KEEN.

Johnson, N. F. (1965) Linguistic Models and Functional Units of Language Behavior, in Rosenberg S. (ed.) Directions in Psycholinguistics, (McMillan, London) 29-65.

Johnson, M. K., Bransford, J. D. & Solomon, S. K. (1973) Memory for Tacit Implications of Sentences, Journal of Experimental Psychology, 98, 203-205.

Johnson-Laird, P. (1974) Memory for Words, Nature, 251, 104-105.

Katz, J. & Fodor, J. A. (1963) The Structure of a Semantic Theory, Language, 39, 170-210.

Katz, J. & Postal, P. M. (1964) An Intergrated Theory of Linguistic Descriptions, (MIT Press, Cambridge, Mass.)

Katz, J. (1967) Recent Issues in Semantic Theory, Foundations of Language, 3, 124-194.

Katz, J. (1970) Interpretive Semantics vs. Generative Semantics, Foundations of Language, 6, 220-259.

Kenney, A. J. (1975) Wittgenstein, (Penguin Books, London).

Lakoff, G. (1965) On the Nature of Syntactic Irregularity (Indiana University Dissertation) published (1970) under the title Syntactic Irregularity, (Holt, Rinehart & Winston, New York).

Lakoff, G. (1970) Linguistics and Natural Logic, in Davidson & Harman (eds.) Semantics of Natural Language, (Reidel, Dordrecht) 545-665.

Lakoff, G. (1974) What is the Way to do Linguistics Today, (to appear).

Landauer, T. K. & Freeman, J. L. (1968) Information Retrieval from Long-Term Memory: Category Size and Recognition Time, Journal of Verbal Learning and Verbal Behavior, 7, 291-295.

McCarthy, J., Abrahams, P. W., Edwards, D. J., Hart, P. & Levin, M. I. (1962) LISP 1.5 Programmer's Manual, (MIT Press, Cambridge, Mass.)

McCawley, J. (1968) The Role of Semantics in a Grammar, in Bach & Harms (eds.) Universals in Linguistic Theory, (Holt, Rinehart & Winston, New York) 124-169.

McCawley, J. (——) Meaning and the Description of Language, unpublished manuscript.

McCawley, J. (1970) Where do Noun Phrases Come From? in Jacobs & Rosenbaum (eds.) Readings in English Transformational Grammar, (Ginn & Co., Waltham, Mass.) 166-183.

McCawley, J. (1972) Syntactic and Logical Arguments for Semantic Structures (Indiana University Linguistics Club).

McCawley, J. (1971) Interpretive Semantics meets Frankenstein, in Foundations of Language, 7, 285-296.

McDermott, D. V. (1974) Assimilation of New Information by a Natural Language Understanding System, MITAI TR-291.

McKean, K., Slobin, D. & Miller, G. A., (1962) cited in Miller, G. A., Some Psychological Studies of Grammar, American Psychologist, 17, 748-762.

Mehler, J. (1963) Some Effects of Grammatical Transformations on the Recall of English Sentences, Journal of Verbal Learning and Verbal Behavior, 2, 346-351.

Milner, B. (1967) Amnesia Following Operation on the Temporal Lobes, in Zangwill & Whitty (eds.) Amnesia, (Butterworth, London).

Minsky, M. (1975) A Framework for Representing Knowledge, in Winston (ed.) The Psychology of Computer Vision, (McGraw-Hill, New York) 211-277.

Montague, R. (1970) English as a Formal Language, in Visentini et al. (eds.) Linguaggi nella Tecnica e nella Societa (Olivetti, Milan), 189-224.

Montague, R. (1972) The Proper Treatment of Quantification in Ordinary English, in Hintikka, Moravcsik & Suppes (eds.) Approaches to Natural Language, (Reidel, Dordrecht) 221-242.

Montague, R. (1974) Formal Philosophy (ed. R. Thomason), (Yale U.P., New Haven).

Neisser, U. (1967) Cognitive Psychology (Prentice-Hall, Englewood Cliffs, New Jersey).

Newell, A. (1970) Remarks on the Relationship Between Artificial Intelligence and Cognitive Psychology, in Banerji & Mesarovich (eds.) Theoretical Approaches to Non-Numerical Problem Solving, (Springer, Berlin) 363-400.

Norman, D. A. (1970) (ed.) Models of Human Memory, (Academic Press, New York).

Norman, D. A. (1973) Memory, Knowledge and the Answering of Questions, in Solso (ed.) Contemporary Issues in Cognitive Psychology: The Loyola Symposium, (Winston, Washington).

Norman, D. A., Rumelhart, D. E. & The LNR Research Group (1975) Explorations in Cognition, (Freeman, San Francisco).

Palme, J. (1973) The SQAP data base for natural language information, (Report No. C8376-M3 (E5), (Research Institute of National Defense, Stockholm).

Partee, B. (1973) Some Transformational Extensions of Montague Grammar, Journal of Philosophical Logic, 2, 509-534.

Partee, B. (1975) Montague Grammar and Transformational Grammar, Linguistic Inquiry, 6, 203-300.

Partee, B. (Forthcoming) (ed.) Montague Grammar, (Academic Press, New York).

Postal, P. (1971) On the Surface Verb 'remind', in Fillmore & Langendoen (eds.) Studies in Linguistic Semantics, (Holt, Rinehart & Winston, New York), 181-270.

Postal, P. (1972) The Best Theory, in Peters (ed.) Goals of Linguistic Theory, (Prentice-Hall, Englewood Cliffs, New Jersey), 131-171.

Postman, L. (1975) Verbal Learning and Memory, Annual Review of Psychology, 291-335.

Potts, T. (1975) Montague's Semiotic: A Syllabus of Errors, in KEEN.

Quillian, M. R. (1968) Semantic Memory, in Minsky (ed.) Semantic Information Processing, (MIT Press, Cambridge, Mass.) 227-270.

Quillian, M. R. (1967) Word Concepts: A Theory and Simulation of Some Basic Semantic Capabilities, Behavioral Science, 12, 410-430.

Raphael, B. (1968) SIR: A Computer Program for Semantic Information Retrieval, in Minsky (ed.) Semantic Information Processing, (MIT Press, Cambridge, Mass.) 33-145.

Rieger, C. (1974) Conceptual Memory, (Unpublished Ph.D. Thesis, Stanford University).

Rieger, C. (1975) The Common-Sense Algorithm, TINLAP.

Riesbeck, C. K. (1974) Computational Understanding: Analysis Sentences & Context ISSCO 4.

Rips, L. R., Shoben, E. J. & Smith, E. E. (1973) Semantic Distance and the Verification of Semantic Relations, Journal of Verbal Learning and Verbal Behavior 12, 1-20.

Rodman, R. (1972) (ed.) Papers in Montague Grammar, Occasional Papers in Linguistics, 2, (University of California, Los Angeles).

Rosenbaum, P. (1965) The Grammar of English Predicate Complement Constructions, (Unpublished MIT Dissertation).

Rumelhart, D. E., Lindsay, P. H. & Norman, D. A. (1972) A Process Model for Long-Term Memory, in Tulving & Donaldson (eds.) Organization of Memory, (Academic Press, New York) 198-246.

Rumelhart, D. E. & Norman, D. A. (1973) Active Semantic Networks as a Model of Human Memory, CHIP report 33, (Center for Human Information Processing, San Diego).

Sandewall, E. (1970) Formal Methods in the Design of Question-Answering Systems, Report 28, (Department of Computer Sciences, Uppsala University).

Savin, H. & Perchonok, E. (1965) Grammatical Structure and the Immediate Recall of English Sentences, Journal of Verbal Learning and Verbal Behavior, 4, 348-353.

Searle, J. (1969) Speech Acts, (Cambridge U.P.)

Schank, R. (1971) Intention, Memory and Computer Understanding, SUAIM 140.

Schank, R. (1972) Conceptual Dependency: A Theory of Natural Language Understanding, Cognitive Psychology, 3, 552-631.

Schank, R. (1973a) Causality and Reasoning, ISSCO 1.

Schank, R. (1973b) Identification of Conceptualizations Underlying Natural Language, SAC.

Schank, R. (1973c) The Fourteen Primitive Actions and their Inferences, SUAIM 183.

Schank, R. (1974a) Adverbs and Belief, Lingua 33, 45-67.

Schank, R. (1974b) Is there a Semantic Memory? ISSCO 3.

Schank, R. (1975a) Using Knowledge to Understand, TINLAP.

Schank, R. (1975b) (ed.) Conceptual Informational Processing (North Holland, Amsterdam).

Schank, R., Goldman, C. & Riesbeck, C. (1972) Primitive Concepts Underlying Verbs of Thought, SUAIM 162.

Schank, R., Goldman, N., Rieger, C. & Riesbeck, R. (1973) MARGIE: Memory, Analysis, Response, Generation and Inference on English, IJCAI3.

Schank, R. & Wilks, Y. (1974) The Goals of Linguistic Theory Revisited, Lingua, 34 301-326.

Schank, R. & Abelson, R. (1975) Scripts, Plans and Knowledge, IJCAI4.

Schlesinger, I. M. (1966) The Influence of Sentence Structure on Reading Process, U.S. Office of Naval Research Technical Report 24.

Schubert, L. K. (1975) Extending the Expressive Power of Semantic Networks, IJCAI4.

Schwarcz, R. M., Burger, J. F. & Simmons, R. F. (1970) A Deductive Question-Answerer for Natural Language Inference, Comm. ACM, 13, 167-183.

Scragg, G. W. (1973) LUIGI: An English Question Answering Program, (internal manuscript , Center for Human Information Processing, San Diego, California).

Scragg, G. W. (1974) Answering Questions About Processes, (U. of California Thesis), reproduced in part in Norman, Rumelhart et al., Explorations in Cognition, (Freeman, San Francisco), 349-375.

Scragg, G. W. (1975) A Structure for Actions, ISSCO.

Simmons, R. F. (1970) Natural Language Question Answering Systems: 1969, Comm. ACM, 13, 15-30.

Simmons, R. F. (1972) Some Semantic Structures for Representing English Meanings, Tech. Rept., NL-1, (Computer Science Dept., U. of Texas, Austin).

Simmons, R. F. (1973) Semantic Networks: Their Computation and Use for Understanding English Sentences, SAC.

Simmons, R. and Slocum, J. (1972) Generating English Discourse from Semantic Nets, Comm. ACM, 15, 891-905.

Slobin, D. I. (1966) Grammatical Transformations and Sentence Comprehension in Childhood and Adulthood, Journal of Verbal Learning and Verbal Behavior, 5, 219-227.

Strawson, P. F. (1952) Introduction to Logical Theory, (Methuen, London).

Strawson, P. F. (1971) Meaning and Truth, (Oxford U.P.)

Sussman, G., Winograd, T. & Charniak, E. (1971) Micro-Planner Reference Manual, MITAI 203A.

Tarski, A. (1935) On the Concept of Logical Consequence, in Logic, Semantics and Mathematics, (Oxford U.P., 1956), 409-420.

Tarski, A. (1944) The Semantic Conception of Truth, in Linsky, (ed.) Semantics and the Philosophy of Language, (U. of Illinois Press, 1952).

Teitelman, W. (1974) Interlisp Reference Manual, Xerox Corporation.

Tulving, E. & Donaldson, W. (1972) (eds.) Organization of Memory, (Academic Press, New York).

Turing, A. (1951) Computing Machinery and Intelligence, Mind, 1-17.

Weber, S. (1972) Semantic Categories of Nominals for Conceptual Dependency Analysis of Natural Language, SUAIM 172.

Weissman, C. (1967) LISP 1.5 Primer, (Dickenson, Belmont, Ca.)

Whitehead, A. N. & Russell, B. (1925) Principia Mathematica, (Cambridge U.P.)

Wilkins, W. A. (1972) Conjoint Frequency, Category Size and Categorization Time, Journal of Verbal Learning and Verbal Behavior, 10, 338-385.

Wilks, Y. A. (1972a) Grammar, Meaning and the Machine Analysis of Language, (Routledge, London & Boston).

Wilks, Y. A. (1972b) Lakoff and Natural Logic, SUAIM 170.

Wilks, Y. A. (1973a) An Artificial Intelligence Approach to Machine Translation, in SAC.

Wilks, Y. A. (1973b) Preference Semantics, SUAIM 206 and in KEEN.

Wilks, Y. A. (1973c) Natural Language Inference, SUAIM 211.

Wilks, Y. A. (1974) Natural Language Understanding Systems within the AI Paradigm: A Survey and Comparisons, SUAIM 237.

Wilks, Y. A. (1975a) A Preferential Pattern-Seeking Semantics for Natural Language Inference, Artificial Intelligence, 6, 53-74.

Wilks, Y. A. (1975b) An Intelligent Analyzer and Understander of English, Comm. ACM, 18, 264-274.

Wilks, Y. A. (1975c) Seven Theses on Artificial Intelligence and Natural Language, ISSCO 17.

Winograd, T. (1971) Procedures as a Representation for Data in a Computer Program for Understanding Natural Language, (MIT Ph.D. Thesis).

Winograd, T. (1972) Understanding Natural Language, (Academic Press, New York).

Winograd, T. (1973) A Survey on Natural Language, (lecture given at IJCAI3)

Winston, P. H. (1970) Learning Structural Descriptions from Examples, MITAI TR-231.

Wittgenstein, L. (1922) Tractatus Logico-Philosophicus, (Routledge, London, 1961).

Wittgenstein, L. (1958) Philosophical Investigations, (Blackwell, Oxford).

Wittgenstein, L. (1975) Philosophical Remarks, (Blackwell, Oxford).

Woods, W. A., Kaplan, R. M. & Nash-Webber, B. (1972) The Lunar Sciences Natural Language Information System; Final Report, BBN Report 2378, (Bolt, Boranek & Newman, Cambridge, Mass.)

Woods, W. A. (1975) Some Methodological Issues in Natural Language Understanding Research, TINLAP.

INDEX